THE SCIENCE OF MODERN VIRTUE

The **SCIENCE** *of*
MODERN VIRTUE

On DESCARTES, DARWIN, *and* LOCKE

EDITED BY
Peter Augustine Lawler *and*
Marc D. Guerra

NIU Press
DeKalb, IL

© 2013 by Northern Illinois University Press
Published by the Northern Illinois University Press, DeKalb, Illinois 60115

Support for this volume was generously provided by the University of Chicago's A New Science of Virtues Project

Library of Congress Cataloging-in-Publication Data

The science of modern virtue : on Descartes, Darwin, and Locke / edited by Peter Augustine Lawler and Marc D. Guerra.
    pages cm
    Includes bibliographical references.
    ISBN 978-0-87580-475-0 (cloth : alk. paper) — ISBN 978-1-60909-097-5 (e-book)
    1. Descartes, René, 1596–1650—Influence. 2. Darwin, Charles, 1809–1882—Influence. 3. Locke, John, 1632–1704—Influence. 4. Virtue. I. Lawler, Peter Augustine, editor of compilation.
    B1875.S39 2013
    179'.9—dc23

2013024287

CONTENTS

PREFACE

MODERN SCIENCE ON WHO WE ARE
AS FREE AND/OR RELATIONAL BEINGS

THIS BOOK EXAMINES THE INFLUENCE the philosopher René Descartes, the political theorist John Locke, and the biologist Charles Darwin have had on our modern understanding of human beings and human virtue. Written by leading thinkers from a variety of fields, its thirteen chapters reflect on the complex relation between modern science and modern virtue, that is, between a kind of modern thought and a kind of modern action. The volume offers more than just a series of substantive introductions to Descartes', Locke's, and Darwin's respective accounts of who we are and the kind of virtue to which we can aspire, though it does do that. It ultimately invites the reader to think about the ways in which the writings of these three seminal thinkers shaped the democratic and technological world in which we modern human beings live.

The contributors to this volume cover a great deal of ground. Each author learnedly addresses subjects and questions drawn from the diverse disciplines of political science, philosophy, theology, biology, and metaphysics. But let the reader be warned: The authors of these essays are anything but consensual in their analysis. Set side by side and read as a whole, the chapters in this volume carry out an internal debate that mirrors theoretical modernity's ongoing debate about the true nature of human beings and the science of virtue. Authors like Larry Arnhart, Lauren Hall, and to a lesser degree, James Stoner, for example, argue powerfully that Locke's and Darwin's thought is, in principle, amenable to the claims made about human beings and human virtue by classical philosophers such as Aristotle and classical Christian theologians such as Thomas Aquinas. Others, such as Peter Lawler, Marc Guerra, Thomas Hibbs, and Paul Seaton make the opposite case, drawing attention to the ways in which Descartes, Locke, and Darwin knowingly and dialectically depart from central teachings of both classical philosophy and classical Christian theology. Readers can judge on their own which side of this argument they find most persuasive. Regardless of which side they fall on, however, I am sure they will walk away having learned something new and having seen a dimension of this debate they had not seen before.

Rather than walk the reader through short and sketchy treatments of the rich chapters that follow, I want to touch on some of the concrete ways in which theoretical or academic debates about the true relationship between science and virtue actually manifest themselves in American society today. After all, whatever differences they had, Descartes, Locke, and Darwin not only agreed (to use Richard Weaver's phrase) that "ideas have consequences," but each intended their ideas about human beings and human virtue to have real, world-changing consequences.

AMERICAN CARTESIANISM TODAY

One of the more curious features of America's contemporary political landscape is that the most resolute—if frequently unwitting—followers of the seventeenth-century French philosopher René Descartes tend to be libertarians. This is not a new phenomenon, however. Alexis de Tocqueville famously remarked that America is "the one country in the world where the precepts of Descartes are least studied and best followed." Contemporary Cartesian-libertarians are likely to be for gay rights and for property rights and against any claims that treat an individual as part of some greater whole. American Cartesians are typically "non-foundationalists." In their view, the individual's irreducible existence is the bottom line. Recourse to country or to nature or to God to defend the individual's existence only detracts from his singular existence. Worse still, such appeals might result in the individual being slaughtered in the name of some collective, ideological cause that is not his own.

American Cartesians frequently use academically trendy language like "deconstruct" (good) and "privilege" (bad). When analyzing American democracy, they are likely to deconstruct any theory that privileges one person's word over another. Such theorists assert that the democratic individual as democratic individual should resist being absorbed into any social or relational whole, from the family up to the nation. Democratic

Cartesianism liberates the individual from the authority of priests, poets, philosophers, preachers, politicians, (theoretical) physicists, parents, and the judgment of the Bible's personal God. It also, as the nineteenth-century democratic theorist Walt Whitman celebrated, inexorably marks the individual's unlimited, indefinite movement away from nature and toward self-creation.

Our Constitution is often read in this Cartesian light. That is not surprising. In many ways, the Constitution lends itself to such a reading. The Constitution treats human beings as wholly free or self-sufficient persons. It does not subsume the individual "I" into some pre-existing class or category—for example, as part of some religion or race or class or gender. Of course, as a political document the Constitution cannot help but recognize the distinction between citizen and non-citizen. But even this distinction is treated as an artificial construction, that is, not as reflecting some deep statement about who the citizen or non-citizen really is.

The Constitution of 1787 is remarkably silent about a remarkable number of things. It is silent about God, choosing not to employ theology politically. It is also silent about human beings' biological nature. The Constitution, for example, does not recognize the natural division of members of our species into men and women. As it presents them, Americans are free to consent to God's or nature's governance. Of course, by making all of these things subject to the individual's consent, the Constitution quietly saps the authority that earlier theologians and philosophers claimed belonged to God and nature. That sapping, however, is part and parcel with the claims of American Cartesianism. In fact, in some sense it is the very point of American Cartesianism.

The fabulously wealthy cofounder of PayPal, Peter Thiel, offers a good example of this kind of American Cartesianism. In his spirited 2009 essay, titled "The Education of a Libertarian," he writes, "I stand against confiscatory taxes, totalitarian collectives, and the ideology of the inevitability of the death of every individual." Simply put, he proclaims to stand against everything that works against the perpetuation of the authentic liberty of the irreducible "I" that is called Peter Thiel. Thiel is something of a rare bird: He is a Cartesian who may well have read Descartes. At Stanford, the French theorist René Girard taught him about "mimetic desire." From Girard, Thiel would have heard that people usually do not make choices about what they want from an individual perspective. Rather, our choices are usually mediated through and borrowed from other people. Traditionally, human beings have thoughtlessly lived in herds. As a result, they have tended to lack genuinely personal or liberated or Cartesian identities. Perhaps it was with these insights in mind that Thiel decided to invest in Facebook.

Thiel seems to think that freedom from the inevitability of death is a precondition for the pursuit of every other human good. Rejecting Socrates' claim that philosophy teaches us to die, Thiel criticizes intellectuals and philosophers who retreat "to tending their small gardens" instead of waging war on "the relentless indifference of the universe" to personal or individual being. For the Cartesian-libertarian, the escape from nature to freedom cannot be imaginary or merely intellectual. It must be real.

AMERICAN DARWINISM TODAY

Recent years have witnessed the emergence of a growing number of newfangled, Darwin-influenced theorists who publicly insist that their scientific research points in a moderately socially conservative direction. Darwin-friendly theorists ranging from Francis Fukuyama to Jonathan Haidt to the late James Q. Wilson have all argued that by serving his or her family, tribe, and species the social human animal provides a salutary, partial antidote to the self-absorbed and socially apathetic claims of today's dogmatic libertarianism. Their works remind us that our true significance lies in being somewhat self-sacrificing parts of wholes that are greater than ourselves. They also remind us that we human beings are naturally more like gregarious chimps than the solitary and emotionally challenged natural individuals described by Rousseau and mocked on *Seinfeld*.

Most evolutionary scientists, however, regard conservative social and political thought to be too religious or theological to be deserving of their reputable, scientific support. Yet academically fashionable postures can often be misleading. Take the father of the sociobiology movement, E. O. Wilson, for example. His magisterial *The Social Conquest of Earth* criticizes Pope Paul VI's encyclical banning the use of artificial contraception for being equal parts dogmatic and unscientific. But Wilson seems to go out of his way to criticize *Humanae vitae* in part in order to obscure the unfashionable ways in which he actually agrees with the encyclical. According to Wilson, the pope's argument reduces to the claim that God only intended sexual intercourse to be for the purpose of conceiving children. Wilson should have also pointed out that Paul VI thought that natural law was on his side as well. As embarrassing as Wilson and other sophisticated scientists like him may find it, Paul VI, from one point of view, also seems to be Darwinian here. After all, his argument is that members of the human species purposely pair, bond, reproduce, and raise their young and so human sex is deformed when it is artificially divorced from those naturally occurring social activities.

Wilson himself notes that natural selection points to a genetically present tension in each member of our species. On the one hand, natural selection produces cooperative social behaviors in human beings. On the other hand, it produces self-serving behaviors in human beings. In Wilson's words, that opposition "renders each of us part saint and part sinner." Religions, he explains, characteristically praise actions that are in accord with social instincts and behaviors and frown on actions that privilege the individual's private good over the good of the various groups of which he or she is a part. Neither Paul VI nor Wilson denies that members of our species have the biological capacity to choose to pursue their private good over the good of the group to which they belong. But Paul VI and Wilson both choose to call such choices sin because our natural flourishing to some degree depends on group selection, driven by social instinct, prevailing over individual selection. While they undoubtedly differ about many of the details, the effectual truth is that the pope and Wilson both think that each of us is fundamentally a social or relational being. For Wilson, organized religion has been pretty much "an expression of tribalism" and nothing more. For the pope, the Christian religion is much more. But he also thinks that the Christian religion, like every other legitimate religion, reflects and supports our social and relational duties as human beings.

Wilson further believes that the pope's encyclical overlooked yet another purpose for human sexual activity: Unlike females of other primate species, human females do not advertise estrus or "being in heat." As such, once bonded with a male, a human female can invite "continuous and frequent intercourse." The fertility-measuring method of Natural Family Planning that some Catholics practice, Wilson might have argued, can interfere with what nature intends for a husband and wife. In Wilson's mind, evolution adapted so that a woman could use sexual pleasure to entice the father of her children to stay around and help raise the children he has engendered. From an evolutionary point of view, it is clearly better for the parents of human children to stay bonded—sharing both parental responsibilities and sexual pleasure—until their offspring are fully raised. Reproduction and raising the young are equally indispensable functions of the social animal. Consequently, the social instinct of a woman, Wilson suggests, evolved so that she, unlike her male counterpart, would put her children first.

Sounding quite pro-family values, Wilson goes so far as to say that in the raising of children there is no reliable alternative to two "sexually and emotionally bonded mates." Even "in tightly-knit hunter-gather societies," human mothers cannot count on the broader community or tribe. From Wilson's evolutionary-informed point of view, the superiority of the two-parent heterosexual family with children is both natural and enduring. It may, as the saying goes, take a village to raise a child, but that village, Wilson adds, cannot take the place of the child's parents.

To use Wilson's word, women "sin" (and are unhappy) when they give and receive sexual pleasure as free individuals in the mistaken belief that they can remain "autonomous" and unguided by social instinct. The use of artificial contraception to rule out the possibility of having kids altogether, especially the casual use of artificial contraception outside of marriage, undermines the social or group cooperation that is, for Wilson, naturally responsible for the singular success of the most intelligent of the "eusocial" species. Ultimately, the pope and the professor agree that society, the family, and the human species all suffer when women are deceived by that mistaken judgment about who they naturally are. Catholics, with their appeal to natural law, find something of an ally in Wilson.

From a public-policy perspective, however, the big news is that Wilson's research shows social conservatism has more to do with what human beings can observe about themselves with their own eyes than it does with their blind adherence to some discredited, fundamentalist dogma. If Wilson were to think through the political implications of his scientific discoveries, his sociobiological concerns no doubt could move him to resist public policies that resolve the tension between the interests of the individual and the interests of the social community in a wholly individualistic direction.

TOWARD A TRUE SCIENCE OF VIRTUE

Today, post-modern—or non-Cartesian—conservative thinkers receive a good deal (if not plenty) of support from Darwinians in our effort to chasten the excesses of modern individualism. Playing a Lockean position off a Darwinian position does not capture the full truth about who we are as relational persons. But it is a start. I regularly make this point in my relatively countercultural blog, "Rightly Understood." One of that blog's purposes is to counter the libertarian excesses of the sophisticated techno-enthusiasts who post at its host site, *Big Think*. Responding to a post in which I used E. O. Wilson's book to show that a true Darwinian cannot be a libertarian true believer, Larry Arnhart, the author of a long and penetrating chapter in this volume, wondered out loud whether I had converted to his Darwinian or evolutionary faith. I conclude this introduction by responding to Dr. Arnhart's gracious, but mistaken, speculation, to show where, in my view, a true science of modern virtue needs to go from here.

I begin by calling attention to the thought of Jonathan Haidt, a professor of psychology at the University of Virginia. His *The Happiness Hypothesis* argues that we human beings are simultaneously brilliant like the chimps and ultra-social like some insects. Unlike chimpanzees, who seem to have "the brains" but just cannot seem to get along with each other, our reason has the eusocial tendency to foster our attachments to groups and each other. Our heads, as Jefferson says, serve our hearts—or our social instinct or moral sense. As a result, our lives have to be consciously balanced. That is why sensible social conservatism must be moderately moderated by enlightened individualism. Haidt and Arnhart more or less agree that the modern philosophers who make the most sense are empiricists associated with the Scottish Enlightenment, that is, David Hume, Adam Smith, and to an extent, Thomas Jefferson. They also prefer the scientific Aristotle to the rational idealist Plato. Neo-Darwinians like Haidt and Arnhart believe the most scientific and reasonable philosophers admit that we are animals whose reason most properly serves our social instincts.

I am periodically accused of being a Heideggerian existentialist. Heidegger might have been the greatest philosopher of the twentieth century. But he was also, for a brief time at least, a Nazi—something for which he never publicly apologized. Ironically, the existentialist or, in a way, resolutely individualist philosopher Heidegger justified an ideology that thought of people as nothing more than parts of wholes called "races" or the "Fatherland." Heidegger eventually criticized Hitler's "biologism," by which he meant Hitler's false identification of our biological features with what we are simply. Hitler, Heidegger protested, did not see that deep down we are truly free individuals. (I note in passing that this might be a problem with many strains of Darwinism too.)

Neo-Darwinians do not make it clear (because it would make them un-popular) that in their view anyone who does not believe that the science of biology can explain everything about who we are must be an existentialist. By this standard everyone from St. Paul to St. Augustine to St. Thomas Aquinas to contemporary American Evangelical Christians are Heideg-gerian existentialists. Descartes and Locke would also be Heideggerian existentialists, as would that rational defender of dignity and autonomy Immanuel Kant. Anyone who thinks we are in any way alienated or rest-less about who we are as purely biological beings would be a Heideggerian existentialist. My point is that, from this Darwinian view, Christians and Cartesians seem equally unscientific. They both introduce some alleged imaginary alien into the realm of biological nature and natural selection, the realm that houses members of every species, including our own.

St. Thomas Aquinas tried to reconcile Aristotelian naturalism with the Christian idea of the freely created, free, and irreducible human person. For someone with a Neo-Darwinian perspective, Aquinas displays both Darwinian and existentialist features—not surprisingly, when Dr. Arnhart chooses to invoke Thomas Aquinas he has to steer clear of all of Aquinas' references to our personal longing to know a personal God. For years now, I have argued that *the* great Thomist of (and for) the twentieth century was the American philosopher-novelist Walker Percy. Percy said that the scientific task of our time was to reconcile what is true about Anglo-Amer-ican empiricism with what is true about Continental existentialism.

It should not, then, come as a big surprise that I think some Darwinians—especially some Darwinian conservatives—are neither completely right nor completely wrong. I think the same thing about some Heideggerian existentialists, and some Cartesian and Lockean defenders of the free indi-vidual. Christians, Cartesians, Lockeans, and existentialists all defend the real existence of the free person who possesses a singular or "authentic" destiny. Still, a true science of modern virtue must recognize that, despite their enormous differences, Cartesian, Lockean, and Darwinian forms of science share certain basic features. One of these is their nominalism. Used as a way of defending the particular against the universal, nomi-nalism is not all bad. But it does tend to reduce words to weapons and nothing more.

The Lockean nominalist uses words to secure the flourishing of the individual; the Darwinian nominalist uses words to promote natural se-lection and species survival. A true science of modern virtue should be able to acknowledge what is true about Cartesian, Lockean, and Darwinian science even as it goes on to show why none of these sciences can begin to explain the joy we experience when we scientifically communicate the truth about our world or that none of these sciences can capture the truth about who we personal, relational, truth-sharing, and loving human beings really are.

Peter Augustine Lawler

THE SCIENCE OF MODERN VIRTUE

1

LOCKE, DARWIN, AND THE SCIENCE OF MODERN VIRTUE

Peter Augustine Lawler

S O I WANT AT LEAST TO COMPLICATE—or maybe even deconstruct—the narrative about our country that prevails among conservatives today. Here's the narrative: Our Founding was Lockean or according to a nature made by our Creator and therefore good. It's threatened by the Progressives who have a kind of Darwinian-Hegelian devotion to Historical evolution—meaning the growth of the paternalistic serfdom of Big Government. The Progressives are therefore bad. And the Progressives, conservatives believe, are on the move while the Lockeans are in retreat.

In my opinion, change in our country has typically been Lockean, and today the Lockean narrative of the liberation of the individual explains a lot more about what's going on these days than anything Progressives say. Lockeanism is on the move, and Progressivism is in retreat. Big Government is being defeated on two fronts. Our welfare state is eroding or even imploding, no matter what our Progressive president might want to do. And our courts—led, of course, by the Supreme Court—are continuing their war against the allegedly too big or too moralistic government of the states on behalf of individual liberty or autonomy.

Lockean change we can't simply call Progress, because it's both good and bad. It's change we can believe in only to some extent. Individual liberation is in many respects good, but it can be at the expense of indispensable social institutions. It can even be, our Darwinians tell us, at the expense of the happiness we can really enjoy as social animals by nature. Individual liberation makes particular lives more comfortable and secure in some respects, but more anxious, alienated, and lonely in others. In my view the right or prudent view of Lockean change is somewhere between the pessimism shared by Marxists and traditionalists (not to mention Marxist traditionalists such as Alasdair MacIntyre) and the techno-optimism of our libertarians (or Lockeans on steroids).

OUR CHARACTERISTICALLY LOCKEAN COUNTRY

Let me begin with a sketch of the key characteristics of our Lockean country. Most American arguments take place within the context set by our Founding's "revolutionary ideology"—which was, even at our country's beginning, much more about natural rights than classical republicanism. The individualistic, Lockean principles of the Declaration were understood to be opposed, from the very beginning, to legal distinctions based on religion, race, class, and gender. That is the "ideological" reason why even the Constitution of 1787 is strikingly silent on race, class, gender, and religion, and why Jefferson wrote so eloquently against the injustice of race-based slavery (even as he did so little actually to abolish it). So when we criticize "the practice" of Americans during the Founding generation and subsequently, we do it from the point of view of their "theory." It's the theory of our Founding that typically drives our practical reforms—reforms that have made our country today more of a meritocracy based on individual productivity than ever. Race, class, gender, and religion mean less than ever in our judgments about each other, which is not to say, of course, they don't mean anything at all. The perfection of our individualism remains a work in progress. A downside of this progress is that qualities disconnected from productivity—such as voluntary caregiving or the leisurely study of metaphysics and theology—are in some ways respected less than ever.

So our Progressives, when they imported alien theory into our political life from Hegel (namely, History, with a capital "H") or Darwin (organic evolution as antidote to the Constitution's allegedly Newtonian mechanism), never managed to come up with theoretical innovations that had "legs." That's why, for example, Roosevelt's new and allegedly improved list of rights in 1944 never caught on. It's also why our welfare state has been—comparatively speaking—minimalist and why our courts never bought into the idea of "welfare rights." It's also why our Supreme Court, when upholding affirmative action schemes, has consistently rejected quotas and insisted that every applicant be treated as a free and equal individual.

Our country's ambiguous and at this point seemingly temporary use of Big Government as a way of redistributing income and even eradicating poverty started to fade about 1966. Around that time, the Supreme Court began its war against Big Government understood as the police powers and moral regulations of the state. That war is being raised, of course, on behalf of liberty, understood as the expansion of individual autonomy over time. Our Court now thinks it's adhering to the Founders' view that the single word "liberty" in the Fourteenth Amendment's due process clause is a kind of Lockean weapon to be wielded on behalf of unprecedented individual liberation by people in every American generation. So it didn't have to rely on precedent to strike laws that interfere with the dignified, autonomous activity of homosexual individuals.

We've even, of course, Lockeanized marriage. It's gradually been turned into a kind of open-ended affirmation that's all rights and no duties—the purpose of which should be freely defined by any two or maybe more autonomous individuals. It makes a strange kind of sense, from this view, to say that same-sex marriage didn't used to be an individual right, but it's become one over time. Soon enough, it may well make a strange kind of sense to say that the entitlement of marriage itself is unjustified and oppressive; it arbitrarily privileges what married individuals do at the expense of the dignified autonomy of what single individuals choose to do.

OUR CHRISTIAN-LOCKEAN ALLIANCE

Although the Court's Lockean activism on abortion and soon on marriage seems directed mainly against our Christian religious believers, I don't want to create the impression that our individualistic progress is simply or even mainly anti-Christian. Scholars of various kinds characteristically neglect the place of biblical religion and particularly Calvinist Christianity in our Founding. There are two reasons, to begin with, why "classical republicanism"—with its subordination of the individual to the political community—never really caught on that much in America. The first is the individualism of Lockean natural rights: The free individual consents to government with his or her own interests or rights in mind. The other is Christianity, which teaches that the individual is not, deep down, a citizen; he or she is, as St. Augustine says, an alien or pilgrim in every earthly city.

Locke himself celebrates the breakthrough in egalitarian self-under-standing that came with the Christians, the understanding that comes with the discovering of personal inwardness or subjectivity. So, while I think Locke was no Christian, he did think of himself as providing arguments and evidence for the fundamental Christian insight into personal reality. Christianity established the principle of the limitation of government by personal identity. And Locke thought that, with his discovery of personal identity, he could prove individuals are both less and more than citizens. They consent to government to protect their interests as self-consciously needy and vulnerable beings with bodies, without surrendering their free-dom for conscientious self-determination in pursuit of happiness. For Locke, as for the Christians, both the individual and the church are au-tonomous—or free from political coercion—to determine the truth about the free being's duties to his or her personal Creator. Locke could defend this conclusion, let me emphasize, without believing that most of what any particular church taught is true. He was highly doubtful that there is a living and giving personal God on which free beings could rely for love and security, and he taught individuals not to trust primarily in God but, rather, in themselves as free and industrious beings caught in a hostile environment. But Locke wasn't so doubtful about personal freedom as, from a natural view, a mystery that left room for belief in a Creator. Locke seems to have thought that man made the biblical God in his image as a free or active and revealing person. His Deistic or Socinian innovation was to conceive of God as he conceived of us, as personal but not relational. That's why he denied the mystery of the Trinity, the mystery that reconciles monotheism with relational personality. From a Christian view, it's more mysterious still to conceive of a person—or individual—as having an iden-tity that's not deeply relational. But that's what Locke seems to have done.

Consider that our Christians and our Lockeans, inspired by the idea that the free individual or person, ally against the classical republicans—insofar as they think of people as basically citizens or part of a political community (or as city fodder). Our Christians and our Lockeans agree that Chesterton is right: America is a home for the homeless—a place for citizens who think of themselves as so equally unique and irreplaceable that they are far from merely citizens. In America, the homeless can be as at home as the homeless can be in any political community, precisely because that community does not compel them to deny what they really can know about themselves.

Christians, St. Augustine said, were often hated because they, on behalf of both the truth and their faith, had to dissent from the religious legislation of their political communities. They refused, like Socrates, either to believe in or to worship the gods of their cities. From the classical, political view, the Christians actually seemed like atheists. In our country, our Christians and our Lockeans have tended to ally against the classical republican idea of civil theology—or, as Lincoln once put it, political religion. The most noble Lockean interpretation of the silence on God in the Constitution of 1787 is that it's anti-civil theological. The Constitution can be criticized for not placing our country "under God," or for liberating political will from divine limits—for turning man into God. Or it can be praised for limiting the realm of political will, for freeing creatures and Creator from political domination for being who they truly are. Our Constitution, from the latter view, presupposes that the Christian view of the person and the God in whose image he or she is made is true. Our political leaders have always been free to express their faith in God, but not to turn it into legislation. For Christians, as John Courtney Murray says, American freedom is freedom for the church as an organized social entity with autonomous moral weight, and Locke, finally, wouldn't think of disagreeing.

God, for Locke, may well exist. Opinions about our duties to our Creator—as Madison, the most purely Lockean of our Founders, thought—are a personal or nonpolitical matter. God is not to be put to degrading political use, and so "civil theology" is not to direct or inhibit the natural, and inevitably social, human inclination toward theological concern. That's not to say that there haven't been various attempts to create a kind of Lockean American civil religion—a more than merely ceremonial creationist Deism. But they never achieve enduring success or real stability. That's not to say that Americans, both Lockean and Christian, don't readily unite against the coercive atheism—the Historical forms of civil theology—of the monstrous tyrants of the twentieth century.

Our Christians and our Lockeans ally against those Progressives who regard particular persons as basically History fodder, as expendable beings to be sacrificed for the perfect world of tomorrow. It's Christianity, as Tocqueville said, that was the source of the American view that not everything might be done in pursuit of the indefinite perfectibility pursued by reformist egalitarianism. They don't think, as the Marxists did, that human life as now experienced is miserably worthless, nor do they think that History could possibly deliver us from the miserable alienation we do experience. Our Christians and Lockeans agree in privileging the unique moral destiny of each of the lives of particular individuals, and in not sacrificing the rights of people today for those to come.

Our Christians and Lockeans united during the Cold War in defending what Leo Strauss called a "natural right" against "History," understanding, together, that it's the nature of each of us to be a free and dignified individual. It's our nature, in other words, not to be fundamentally either parts of History or parts of the impersonal nature. Both our Lockeans and our Christians share the ambiguity that it's our nature to be free from nature, and that ambiguity might be understood to be resolved by the discovery of History. But this resolution, our Lockeans and Christians agree, is at the expense of the strange and wonderful mystery of individuality or irreducibly personal reality. Human alienation, they agree, does not come to an end in this world, and our pursuit of happiness doesn't culminate in secure and stable happiness or contentment through our own efforts. The un-obsessive and unproductive lives Marx imagines under communism are both impossible and undesirable; they aren't the lives of free persons.

And our Christians and Lockeans ally against the various forms of the Darwinian view that we're nothing but species fodder. So they united against the various eugenics schemes promoted by both Progressives and fascists, those that tried to improve who we are as a species by eliminating the unfit or keeping them from reproducing. Those schemes have been completely discredited in our country. So, too, for that matter, is the eugenics scheme described in Plato's *Republic*, which also treats people as animals to be controlled for purposes not of their own choosing. In order to keep "Platonism" alive in our time, Leo Strauss had to convince us, against scholarly convention, that Socrates' eugenics scheme was ironic, a monstrosity constructed in speech for purely instructional purposes. Lockeans and Christians know, whatever some Darwinians say, that conscious and willful persons can't regard themselves as being born primarily to serve either their species or their country. So, from our view, Strauss, to maximize his influence, should have done more to discredit the Socratic "cave"—the image that presents people as totally dominated by the process of political socialization of their "regime." (This can be done, in my opinion: The image of the cave, in truth, is the ironic polar opposite of the ironic [or impossible and undesirable] imaginary perfection of the philosopher-king.)

PERSONAL FREEDOM TODAY

The progress of Lockeanism in our country also discredits the common secular faith (a kind of civil theology) favored by the rather communitarian and idealistic Progressives. Republicanism, not surprisingly, becomes more countercultural than even Christianity, and patriotism erodes. Sophisticated Americans today, and especially the young and sophisticated, aren't moved to action or even admiration by the noble Zeussianism of a John McCain. The manly novelist Tom Wolfe has shown how countercultural a real Stoic—a rational, noble man—such as Marcus Aurelius or George Washington or Robert E. Lee or even Atticus Finch would be these days. We can still admire portrayals of Stoics who know who they are as rational, relational, "classy" beings and so know what they're supposed to do in any or all circumstances. To state the obvious, we follow Locke in locating individuality in rights, not duties, and we regard the sacrifice of material being for rational principle or to display our magnanimity as being based on a misunderstanding of who we are. But we can't forget that the Lockean criticism of such pride—as really vanity—is also shared by the Christians.

Americans are seemingly less likely than ever to think of themselves as a devoted, self-sacrificing part of a political whole greater than themselves. The Special Forces—such as the Navy SEALs—that manage to defend us are more alien to most of our lives than ever. The fact that a Lockean citizen is, in principle, closer to an oxymoron than a Christian citizen explains a lot about the creeping and sometimes creepy libertarianism so characteristic of sophisticated Americans today. And our best citizens these days are the combination of Christian and southern (or the residually Stoic) man portrayed in country music, the man who stands up (and is ready to fight) when he hears that Lee Greenwood classic. That man, we can say, is more of, as Wolfe says, "a man in full" than the individual Locke describes.

We can also say that the "citizen soldier" celebrated in another recent country hit might be both more and less Christian than a pure Lockean. He's open to being more Christian because he's less narrowly self-absorbed and petty, but he hasn't, from a certain view, properly absorbed the Christian/Lockean criticism of both civic consciousness and martial virtue. Obviously, our citizen soldiers can't be called liberal fascists (a very unfriendly name conservatives give to our Progressives); they're fighting for home, freedom, country, and God and not for a glorious Historical future envisioned by some Leader. And our liberals, even insofar as they have Progressive tendencies, are repulsed by real fascist Historical warriors—by, in fact, the chauvinism of warriors in general. They may be for "humanitarian interventions" but not so much for those that involve the real risk of the lives of particular individuals.

PERSONAL THEORY VERSUS BOTH HISTORY AND DARWIN

Even the main philosophical inclination in our country, articulated by our liberal theorists, these days is much more Lockean than Progressive (or dutifully Stoic or Christian). Our alleged moral experts such as our Rawlsians think that only suckers think of themselves as wholes greater than themselves. The bottom line, they say, is the person—or the secure perpetuation of the being or the autonomy of all particular persons alive these days. No particular person should be subordinated to God, country, History, or even family or some other biological imperative. Even eugenics, as promoted, for example, by the transhumanists, has become intensely personal. The point of biotechnology is to keep ME (as opposed to the species or the citizenry) from being extinguished or replaced—a very Lockean point!

Our Lockeans and Rawlsians are, in principle, transhumanists. If we can inventively overcome or free ourselves from the limitations of our biological condition, we should. Any free and rational being, they say, would want to have his or her being more secure or less biologically limited, and they don't share the Christian belief that it's reasonable to hope our personal freedom becomes more than biologically contingent through God's grace. In this respect, the natural right of the Lockeans is not really living according to nature, and the faith in History (or political reform) is replaced by faith (supported so far by lots of works) in technology and biotechnology. We can say that "natural right" has defeated History if we mean the Lockean natural right to make ourselves more than merely natural, merely political, or merely Historical beings.

In this respect, our theorists, although they don't like to admit it, oppose themselves to the Darwinians. The best Darwinians (such as Larry

Arnhart) have become social conservatives. They remind us that, for most people, the desires that connect us to family, friends, and political community are the sources of happiness. People from large families, studies show, are usually happier than people from small ones, and men married with children are less pathological and suicidal than those who live alone. And we're usually wrong when, as autonomy freaks, we regard our social, biological desires as impediments to our effective pursuit of happiness, understood as genuine self-fulfillment. In the happiest cases, our social instincts are what guide our reason and our imagination in the direction of the natural ends given to members of our species. The Darwinians add that nature will inevitably defeat our efforts to escape from her guidance; individual freedom is largely a pretentious illusion. Even the longings for personal immortality or indefinite longevity are based on mistaken conceptions of who we are. The truth is that, so far, we haven't been successful in extending the duration of the longest human lives at all; our accomplishment has actually been the modest and, from a natural view, fairly insignificant one of getting a lot more lives closer to that natural limit.

The truth is also, Darwinian conservatives claim, that evolutionary nature's endlessly complex intention that each of us be replaced with the species' flourishing in mind will almost certainly thwart our misguided efforts to refocus existence on persons—as opposed to nature's own impersonal focus on species. We'll be happier to the extent that we can recapture the biologist Aristotle's idea of a complete life—one that achieves its wholeness on the basis of the satisfaction of our national desires through our fulfillment of our natural responsibilities. We can't, as the transhumanists imagine, make ourselves into robots or machines powered by the pure subjectivity—the "I" imagined by Descartes (and the Cartesian Locke). We'd be nothing without the guidance given to us by our bodies, the source of all erôs, our longings, our orientation toward completion, and even our openness to scientific truth.

Despite such reasonable scientific criticisms, we Lockeans still end up thinking that nature so understood remains our enemy. The assertion that we can't continue to produce unprecedented, inventive change we can believe in is a dogma. The theory of evolution as described by a pure Darwinian might have been completely true until the free individual emerged on the scene. Since then, impersonal evolution has been gradually displaced by conscious and volitional evolution—evolution with ME and YOU, particular persons with names (who, of course, can name) in mind. Despite the best efforts of some of our ecologists, we don't believe that it makes any sense for a person to take one for the species or rest content with being replaced. Being oriented by the requirements of the species is unconscious; the more conscious we are (the more we are oriented by a truthful sense of personal or individual identity), the more we resist that orientation. Contrary to Darwin's sentimental assertion that our social instincts or moral sense will evolve as our species' singular ability for conscious choice does, it's now clear that the latter form of evolution, at least to some extent, atrophies our social instincts.

Making our choices less instinctual and more calculated—or all about individual self-interest—has been the goal of Lockean theory. Even when our theorists attempt to soften that selfishness with observations about empathy (and sometimes even altruism), they really mean not forgetting the reasonableness of cooperation with others to achieve our personal goals or preferring long-term and less narrow interests over short-term, ill-considered inclinations. They don't mean, as Rousseau observes, actually devoting our lives to our families, friends, country, and the unfortunate (and a Darwinian would say we're hardwired for all of those), because then we'd have no time left for ourselves.

We are, in fact, more moral in the sense of being less violent, less animated by religious or political animosity, and even less likely to be moved by any consideration that would cause us to impinge upon the rights of others. So we commit fewer hate crimes, but we're also less moved by love or charity. Empathy, in fact, is a pitiful substitute for personal love. And as Tocqueville points out, for us individualists, indifference to the choices and fate of others has become a kind of virtue. The perfection of that virtue, in a way, is my affirmation of your choices as dignified just because they're personal or autonomous, an affirmation that usually costs me nothing.

Some critics such as James Ceaser say that our theorists today aren't Lockean, because they don't find a foundation in nature for our rights, but "non-foundational," because they think it's a mistake to even look for reasonable or natural evidence for their devotion to personal autonomy or "liberalism." In my view, non-foundationalism itself has emerged as a kind of Lockean theoretical weapon. The foundations of God and History led to all sorts of senseless killing and cruelty. Nature, meanwhile, is what's described by Darwin; it can't be investigated to find the source of or to defend our liberty. "Non-foundationalism" means, in a way, that personal freedom is self-evident and the bottom line; there's no need, and in fact it's counterproductive, to try to tether the individual's autonomy to any reality outside of itself. That liberty, as Locke says, is less by nature than an assertion against nature; it is sufficient, as our Court says, to think of it as the mysterious capability we have for self-definition and even indefinite self-expansion. The foundation, it follows, is securing as well as possible the lives and liberty of those persons alive right now; it is, to begin with, doing what we can't to remove all obstacles to our efforts to fend off personal extinction.

THE PERSON VERSUS BIG GOVERNMENT

Part of non-foundationalism is refusing to think of ourselves as bound by any biological limitation. The point of our Court's pro-choice opinion in *Planned Parenthood v. Casey* is that women are free to free themselves from being defined as women. The goal of keeping people around does point in the direction of transhumanism or trans-biological personal immortality, meaning that this goal is also hostile to Progressivism—which is about the Historical goal of sacrificing today for tomorrow. It's even hostile to Big Government in general; avoiding personal extinction is some combination of the unimpeded evolution of high technology and one's own discipline. Regulations that undermine one's own productivity in those areas for moralistic and redistributive reasons are increasingly discredited in our libertarian time. Our libertarians are better than ever at explaining that personal liberation depends on individuals' being more and more productive. The true Lockean, they explain, is what David Brooks called the bourgeois bohemian; liberty is for self-definition, one's autonomy will always depend on one's work, on the tough virtues connected with personal industriousness and inventiveness, on the unlimited and incessant development of technology (or measurable, powerful progress it makes sense to believe in). Marx—the first Progressive—was wrong to hold that natural scarcity could disappear in a way that would allow us to relax about acquisition and focus our attention only on the just distribution of resources and the cultivation of lifestyles. This means we know why LBJ's Great Society—the very ephemeral height of our Progressivism—was misguided and unsustainable.

If there is an expanding role for government, it's in the puritanical and prohibitionist mode of regulating for health and safety—laws that fend our unwitting exposure to secondhand smoke and trans-fatty foods, not to mention propaganda insisting that sexual morality be reduced to and enforced as safety (don't do anything to bring any person into the world or take one of those now existing out of it) and consent—and even this seems more Lockean than not. We consent to government for the good of our bodies, but (unlike the real Puritans or real Prohibitionists) we leave the soul (or personal identity) in the autonomous hands of the individual. Even the Progressives, in their sort of noble devotion to the cause of the national community, were more genuinely puritanical—or idealistically egalitarian—than the liberal political correctness of our time.

What about the main trend in economic regulation? you might say. Isn't our current president a Progressive? And isn't he making our Big Government bigger? Obama's Progressivism is going to turn out to be a blip on our political stage. Whatever he may want to do, Lockeanism is clearly on the move again on the economic front. Obamacare, our Lockeans say, violates natural rights, but more importantly, it just won't work. It will neither sustain our present employer-based health care system nor pave the way for the government to become directly responsible for being the single provider of our health care. Both the hopes and the fears surrounding this ill-considered mess of a reform are greatly exaggerated. The results of the 2010 election showed that our president had no Progressive mandate, and that people have lost confidence even more in the proposition that bigger and better government can cure what ails us.

The primary experience of ordinary Americans these days is the erosion—with the prospect of implosion—of the various safety nets characteristic of our relatively minimalist welfare state. The movement across the board has been and will continue to be from defined benefits to defined contributions. Private and even public pensions are toast. They have been and will continue to be replaced by 401(k)s. This kind of change will be true of health care, as employer-based plans become unsustainable. It will also soon be true of Medicare and probably Social Security—if not quite as soon as Paul Ryan thinks. The good news here (the new birth of freedom celebrated by the Tea Partiers) is more choice, a lot more choice, for individuals. The bad news is that risk is being transferred from the employer and the government to the individual. All of our entitlements—everyone really knows—are going to have to be transformed and trimmed in a Lockean or individualistic direction in what might well be futile efforts to save them.

Other, related change going on that Lockeans should believe in includes the fact that unions both public and private, despite our president's half-hearted efforts to prop them up, are also toast. Their reactionary efforts at protectionism have no place in a globalized and rigorously competitive meritocratic marketplace. The same can be said of the ideal of employer and employee loyalty. The various kinds of tenure won't last another generation. People are going to be able to be and will have to be a lot more entrepreneurial and self-employed or do a lot more switching and losing jobs. One reason among many that employer-based health care can't survive is that it depends upon an increasingly obsolete model—careerist and corporatist—of employment. The present health care system isn't so great for the self-employed, and this includes more and more of us. And fear of losing insurance shouldn't be a reason for passing up an entrepreneurial opportunity, and guilt about an employee's health care situation shouldn't be a reason for not firing superfluous or inadequately productive employees. It would be wrong to call these changes popular. The Tea Party has peaked, and it never got anywhere near a majority. People can't help but be conservative when it comes to preserving the entitlements on which they've come to depend.

THE ROAD TO SERFDOM NEVER GETS TO SERFDOM

We can still say Americans have lost that Progressive faith that Big Government could possibly be the cure for what ails them today. The good news for us Lockeans is that it's now clear, the road to serfdom will never get to serfdom. Alexis de Tocqueville worried that our "individualism"—meaning, for him, our apathetic emotional withdrawal—would turn us into easy prey for the schoolmarmish soft despotism of an omnicompetent bureaucracy. There's some truth to the observation that individualism so understood fueled the growth of our welfare state, just as there's some truth to the one that even our relatively minimalist welfare-state dependency has encouraged individualism, in the emotionally crippled sense of less reliance on our social attachments to other persons. The welfare state, it makes sense to say, both comes into existence with the atrophying of the "mediating" institutions—those that stand between the individual and the centralizing government—such as the family, local community, and church, and then it weakens them further by allowing individuals not to have to depend on them. The great social scientist Gunnar Myrdal predicted in 1940 that the welfare state would give people an incentive to stop having kids to support them in their old age, and it's obvious he was far from completely wrong. (But we also used to think that "welfare" [Aid to Families with Dependent Children] would give irresponsible people a perverse incentive to reproduce.) Families, economists tell us, have less incentive than ever to "invest" in children beyond love and the real happiness incompletely described by Darwinians. It turns out, our social instincts just aren't strong enough, by themselves, in our individualistic time.

From this view, welfare-state dependency opposes both Darwinian social instincts and Lockean industrious and inventive self-reliance. It deprives us of the happiness that comes from bonding with the persons we really know and love and doing our duty to the species by having and raising kids. It also deprives us of the restlessness that leads us to think and work hard to pursue happiness. Just as much as the Lockean, the true Darwinian—as opposed to the fake Darwinian or Progressive, who mistakenly equates natural evolution with the growth of Big Government— wants to limit government understood as bureaucratic dependence. The people Tocqueville imagines who have fallen below the level of humanity by surrendering control over the details of their lives and so any concern for their individual futures live both un-free and unnatural lives. They lack the autonomy of the Lockean individual and the gregarious sociality of the really smart primates who, according to the Darwinians (and for that matter the Aristotelians), we are by nature.

But those who blame the welfare state for who we are these days exaggerate how much its institutions really transformed our lives. Social Security and Medicare, by themselves, have never been enough to allow old people to live in security or anything approaching worry-free abundance. Surely nobody really believes that the history of our country over the last generation or two has been the story of people fecklessly surrendering any concern for their personal futures. The progress of our individualism hasn't been toward apathetic contentment (Tocquevillian individualism) but toward the intensification of personal self-obsession (Lockean individualism). People are more detached from others than ever, or less animated by personal love or moved by thinking of themselves as a part of a whole greater than themselves. This means that, in the Lockean sense, they're thinking more personally or individually; they connect their personal futures with the future of being, itself. Americans haven't been living some Progressive or Marxist dream of having freed themselves of all perceptions of scarcity for un-alienated self-fulfillment, and they know, better than ever, that such a dream can never become real in some post-productive age. They know their autonomy—their freedom from nature—is no entitlement from God, or History, or has any source beyond themselves. That's the key sense in which they are—following Locke himself—non-foundationalist about their personal identities.

OUR BIRTH DEARTH

Change over the last generation or two has largely been progress in Locke's sense. It has been in accordance with Locke's basic insight about who we are or might become, but sometimes in ways Locke himself didn't anticipate. It didn't occur to Locke, it seems, that so many free persons would become so self-absorbed (or that contraceptive technology would work so well) that so many individuals would choose to stop having enough children to replace themselves. The main reason for this "birth dearth" among our sophisticates is not some transfer of dependence from family to government but a kind of choice for radical autonomy over being species fodder. Nature may intend me to be replaced by my children, and even we self-conscious mortals can gain quasi-natural satisfaction by reflecting on the fact of successfully spreading our genes or living on through our kids. But we Lockeans are more concerned with living for ourselves—and so, among other things, thwarting nature's intention by staying around.

When Tocqueville described the pathologies of the emotional withdrawal of individualism, he was only concerned that individuals would lose the spirit of resistance characteristic of citizens. He thought that the natural limit to individualistic self-absorption would be the family. Free individuals would persist in thinking of themselves as parents and children too. He had a kind of "socio-biological" faith that a limit to individual liberation would be the natural, social inclinations that lead the species to perpetuate itself. Locke seemed to have that faith too: He thought people would continue to have kids, and their natural inclination supported by law would cause them to stay together long enough to raise them. But, in principle, Locke couldn't have rejected the conclusion of our Court in Planned Parenthood that women have an equal right to men to be free individuals or define for themselves their personal identities, and so the right to an abortion can be justified as what's required for women (when other contraceptive methods fail) to be liberated from the natural inclination to be moms in order to be equal participants in the nation's economic and political life. Individuals saddled with female bodies have the right not be species fodder or reproductive machines for the state. Tocqueville, we can say, was so afraid of this consequence unfolding that he talked up the American division of labor—which resulted, in fact, in pretty much locking up the wife and mom in the home—as what's required to sustain the family in democratic times. He praised the greatness of the American women for submitting to that injustice (from a Lockean view) out of love, while admitting that democracy causes people to be progressively less moved by love.

Until well into the legendary 1960s, the Republicans were the relatively Lockean or pro-business party. They were, for that reason, the party that pushed the Equal Rights Amendment. The Democrats were the more "paternalistic," union-enabling, welfare-state party that aimed for the family wage earned by husband-breadwinner, and so that presupposed the dignity of unproductive motherhood. The liberation of women to become wage slaves just like men that began in the 1960s with the Equal Rights Amendment became more Democratic than Republican only because the Democrats became the feminist party, the one more dedicated to liberating women to be free individuals. But neither party objected to women flooding the work force, which ended the dream of the family wage for most ordinary Americans, made it much more difficult for women to find dignity without earning money, and inevitably reduced the average size of the American family. Nobody denied for long that justice demanded equal opportunity for women as free individuals. Our two parties reached a kind of mainstream consensus that government would have little to do with the encouragement of virtue untethered to productivity, and the Democrats fairly quickly ended their flirtation with "welfare rights," with the right not to be productive. This consensus was not about letting people live as they please in some 1960s "do your own thing" sense; it was about perfecting our meritocracy based on productivity, the goal easily discovered through a very Lockean reading of the Constitution of 1787.

Insofar as our "neoconservatives" worried about the family and all that, it was what was required to fend off "dysfunctional" behavior that undermined individual liberty and economic prosperity. We can see that the liberation of women was more good than not, without denying the downside in terms of sustaining the safety nets that used to constitute the minimalist but real welfare state that found its heyday in the 1960s. One result of that liberation—and men being given more of a license to behave badly—is an explosion of the number of lonely single moms who sometimes desperately need the welfare state's safety nets to get by, but what they need, government is going to be less able to provide. And the routinization of divorce (far beyond Locke's or Tocqueville's expectations) with the individual's pursuit of happiness in mind has also produced lots of lonely men; the fastest-growing demographic category is men over 65 who aren't close to either a spouse or children. They too are going to need public help as they increasingly fade away from Alzheimers and other chronic forms of debilitation, but everyone knows we aren't going be able to afford what those individuals need either.

Our Lockeans are often criticized for reducing personal morality to health, safety, and consent, but they are very serious—very paranoid, puritanical, and prohibitionist—when it comes to that individualist trinity. So again: Our individualism is not about living as you please but getting the focus on doing what's required to secure one's own personal future. Our transhumanists give us an unprecedented incentive: With the right regimen of diet, exercise, and lots of supplements, young people around today can reasonably hope to stay around until the "singularity" hits and something like personal immortality becomes possible. St. Augustine was right that it's most important not to screw up with eternal life on the line, but what was, some of our Lockeans believe, in his case wish-fulfillment is now something we might do for ourselves. Certainly we're not told to relax and enjoy ourselves—or just give in to natural desires—when it comes to either eating or sex. In some ways, we're more preoccupied than ever with the bad things both of those natural processes can do to beings with bodies.

As Phillip J. Longman has ably chronicled, it's impossible to overplay the extent to which our entitlement programs were premised on "Baby Boom" demographics. As long as the population and the economy are both growing, then we can easily afford to sustain and even expand benefits for the elderly. Public policy deliberations in the late 1960s and early 1970s were also informed by deep concerns about overpopulation. So President Nixon's Commission on Population Growth and Economic Freedom actually endorsed the Equal Rights Amendment as a way of discouraging female fertility—of getting women to think of themselves less as mothers and more as free individuals. So "politically correct" experts were all about encouraging the detachment of sex from reproduction and undermining the demographic foundations of the welfare state. The funding of Social Security, as James Capretta explains, depends above all on the long-term fertility rate. If it were reasonable to hope we could soon be anywhere close to returning to Baby Boom birthrates, there would be no talk today of entitlement reform. It goes without saying that people would rather keep what they now have, and that our politicians would be relieved to let them have it. Tea Party constitutionalism would have, at best, a very marginalized constituency.

GETTING OLD AND OLDER IN A YOUNG PERSON'S WORLD

The Lockean might begin to attempt to solve this problem by saying that the old should just become more productive, and so we need to push the retirement age (and eligibility age) back, way back. If the elderly are healthy, they should keep working. We are doing a little of that, and all responsible experts say we're stuck with doing a lot more. But there are obvious limits to this remedy. A high-tech society is full of preferential options for the young; the old might be healthy, but they still often lack the mental agility required to keep up with all that techno-change. Even in my profession, college teaching, which isn't very hard and you don't have to be very smart to perform adequately in the classroom, there's plenty of complaining that the abolition of mandatory retirement is keeping the relatively ineffective and out-of-touch around at the expense of scholarly productivity and consumer (student) satisfaction. The aging, overpaid professorate is one of the most compelling arguments against tenure, one that will prevail soon enough in our techno-meritocracy. If the old keep working, we'll figure out soon enough, it'll have to be in less productive and (much) lower-paid—not to mention more insecure—positions. We, after all, value the wisdom connected with age (being chastened by experience and all that) less than ever, and we're getting more skeptical of the thought that being old means in many senses being entitled.

Locke himself rather coldly suggested that the only compelling tie parents will have on their grown children will be money. He wanted to free individuals up from the constraints of patriarchy; he didn't want parents to be able to rule—or order around—their grown children. And he didn't want people relying on love, except the love for little children (who are temporarily incapable of taking care of themselves). If you're going to get old, which Locke was all in favor of, you'd better get rich. And our libertarians aren't wrong to say we should do what we can to encourage people to save for their own futures. Now, the virtue that comes with that kind of self-reliance is coming back: Pensions and even Social Security have become unreliable (but so too have 401(k)s, which can no longer be counted on to produce returns that beat inflation).

The average person is less sure than ever that his money will last as long as he will, but he surely knows he'll be stuck, nonetheless, largely with depending on his own money to live well. The implosion of the welfare state, which is caused most of all by our aging society, doesn't look like a new birth of freedom for old persons. As we learn, say, from Socrates' musings in the *Republic*, there might be nothing tougher than being old and poor in a democracy, a "regime" or society that has no idea what old people are for. This is not to say that we're going to begin euthanizing them or even "rationing" them to early graves. We know they're persons, not nothing. And so we're committed to helping them stay around as long as possible.

So our demographic crisis—too many old and unproductive people and not enough young and productive ones—can be accounted for as a product, both good and bad, of Lockean individualism. And it's wrecked the progressive dream of an expanding social democracy humanely enveloping us all.

A COMPROMISE CONCLUSION

We can't conclude by saying that the one true progress these days is Lockean or "capitalist." Lockean theory will never define everything about who we are, and individual freedom or autonomy far from exhausts our longings. The Darwinians remain right that we're social animals, and so it's in many ways bad for us to experience the atrophying of our social institutions. The perversely individualistic behavior that's produced our birth dearth, however, probably can't be accounted for on Darwinian terms. The truth, as the great scientist E. O. Wilson (for one) acknowledged, is that impersonal natural evolution (where the individual, so to speak, is sacrificed for the species) is being displaced by conscious and volitional or personal evolution—evolution driven by the Lockean individual (and so, by nature), for the Lockean individual. It should be surprising that personal evolution—with its bias against being replaced for the good of the species—turns out to have negative consequences not only for the species' future but for each of our social and political futures.

Our Christians, remember, side with the Lockeans against the Darwinians by claiming that each particular person is unique or irreplaceable—or not, most fundamentally, a replaceable natural part. But they agree with the Darwinians that each person is also a social or relational being. So it's not surprising that our observant religious believers (not only Christians but those of other, personal religions—such as Jews and Mormons) seem to have best combined devotion to political freedom (meaning the person's freedom from political determination) with doing one's duty as a social animal by getting married, having kids, raising them well, and surrendering their biological existence without being too angry about it. Without saying that the personal Creator of the Bible actually exists, we can say that the relational criticism of Locke is true, and the personal criticism of Darwin is true. Lockean theory, thank God (and/or nature), will never express anywhere near the whole truth about who we are.

Reconciling the free pursuit of personal happiness with stable social institutions such as religion, the family, friendship, and local community that are indispensable for making the lives of social and moral beings worth living is a matter of prudence. The enemy of such statesmanlike prudence in America today is the tendency, reflected most of all in the imperial judiciary, to resolve every question, even modest questions that arise in local communities, according to high principle, according to the maximization of the liberty of the autonomous individual. The enemy of prudence is the judiciary and the experts directing centralized administration. The friend of prudence is the statesmanship required to elevate public discussion of moral and political differences and dilemmas and to compromise, as much as possible, in resolving the perhaps irreducibly different views of legislators.

The most obvious example is abortion. But Social Security, Medicare, and health care are good examples too. For many liberals, these entitlement programs have become inalienable rights; they think it immoral even to think about whether the country can actually afford these programs. For some libertarian conservatives, the whole welfare state is unconstitutional, and that is where the deliberation should begin and end. The truth is that most such programs are neither unconstitutional nor a government-guaranteed right; our deliberation should be about what is most sustainable economically and in terms of what is best for both individuals and families.

So government is going to have to be limited by our legislatures, but not with the thought that we can, in the name of liberty, dispense with the welfare state altogether. Americans, in truth, don't believe Big Government can cure what ails them these days, but this may be mainly because they see the various social and political safety nets collapsing around them. They know well enough that the so-called road to serfdom can't even get them to the schoolmarmish nanny state that Progressives affirm in their fantastic books. They want both personal liberty and some social and even moral security, and there's no high principle that can reconcile their conflicting demands.

Let me conclude with an affirmation of the Declaration of Independence as our political creed. Americans as a people are dedicated to the proposition that all men are created equal. As G. K. Chesterton noted, the "dogmatic lucidity" of our belief in the equal significance or equal liberty of every human person distinguishes "a nation with the soul of a church" and "a home for the homeless" everywhere. But maybe the time has come to acknowledge that the full achievement of the Declaration was made possible by a most prudent legislative compromise. The theoretical core of the Declaration—the part with the self-evident truths, the inalienable rights, and Nature's God—is pure Locke. If that were our whole civic faith, it would seem too lax or duty-free to Christians; it would have marginalized those who take their bearings from a personal God. If the Declaration were written by the New England Puritans, it might have been very dutifully egalitarian and full of social responsibilities, but also illiberally theocratic.

Jefferson's Lockean draft was amended by the more Christian members of Congress. References to a present-tense providential and judgmental God were added. In that way, the God of nature became the Creator of the Bible, and we can even say that the artful accommodation of both the secular Lockeans and Calvinist or residually Puritan members of Congress produced a result more truthful than the intentions of either of the parties to the compromise. Our devotion to personal equality was deepened, our view of who we are as natural beings became better and more purposeful in ways that preserved both political liberty and limited government.

I affirm these timeless truths. Yet I can't help but notice that their American articulation is not the absolute coherence of high principle but through legislative compromise. The compromise involves waffling on the Lockean versus the Thomistic understanding of nature. It also involves waffling on the Christian versus the Lockean understanding of who we are as free persons. It may well be the case, as John Courtney Murray wrote in *We Hold These Truths*, that our great founders built a better country as statesmen than they "knew" as theorists. Surely their deliberation should be a model for ours.

2

THE VIRTUE OF SCIENCE AND THE SCIENCE OF VIRTUE

DESCARTES' OVERCOMING OF SOCRATES

Thomas Hibbs

IN ONE OF HIS LETTERS TO PRINCESS ELIZABETH, Descartes writes:

> Beatitude seems to me to consist in a perfect contentment of spirit
> and an interior satisfaction. . . . It seems to me that each person is able
> to render himself content and without need of any others provided
> only that he observes three things, to which correspond the three
> rules of morality, which I have given in the *Discourse*.[1]

The passage does not resolve the famous debate about the relationship
between the "provisional morality" of the *Discourse* and what has come
to be called the final or definitive morality, but it does indicate that the
provisional morality contains important elements in Descartes' mature
understanding of the good life for human beings.[2] It also indicates that
beatitude is much more of a preoccupation of Descartes than has usually
been acknowledged. He speaks here, as elsewhere, of the sovereign good,

"the theme or the end to which our actions tend" (*le motif, ou la fin à laquelle tendent nos actions*).³ He explains, "to have a contentment that is solid, it is necessary to follow virtue, that is, to have a constant and firm will to execute everything that we judge to be better and to employ all the power of which we are capable to judge well" (*pour avoir un contentement qui soit solide, il est besoin de suivre la vertu, c'est-à-dire d'avoir une volonté ferme et constante d'exécuter tout ce que nous jugerons être le meilleur, et d'employer toute la force de notre entendement à en bien juger*).⁴

On the surface of his writings, Descartes apparently tables or ignores or suppresses the question of the good; he certainly addresses it in a manner that leaves its relationship to his overall project unclear. To discern the unity in his various projects, we not only need to display the connections between the different texts and parts of his philosophy, we also need to see the way the texts themselves operate as spiritual exercises, fields for the practice of the virtues constitutive of the sovereign good. As Matthew Jones convincingly argues in *The Good Life in the Scientific Revolution*, Descartes' most influential books such as the *Discourse* and the *Meditations* offer a "series of striking images and recondite reasoning intended to effect a moral and epistemic transformation of the attentive reader."⁵ In a manner that calls to mind Plato, even as it transforms the pedagogy of the Academy, Descartes' mathematical and natural-philosophical writings constitute "practices that can help one live the good life."⁶

Going beyond Jones, David Lachterman, in his groundbreaking *Ethics of Geometry*, argues that *The Geometry* is the key text in Descartes' corpus. The overcoming of the geometry of Euclid and Apollonius involves much more than a display of greater mathematical expertise. It demonstrates the success of the new method and reflects a very different conception of the relationship of intellect to nature, body, and human community. Lachterman speaks of the "disparate ways (*mores*) and styles in which the Euclidean and the Cartesian geometer do geometry, comport themselves as mathematicians both toward their students and toward the very nature of those learnable items (*ta mathemata*) from which their disciplined deeds take their name."⁷

As Amos Funkenstein has noted, in contrast to ancient, Aristotelian science, Cartesian science opts for linguistic univocity and methodological homogeneity.⁸ Cartesian logic drops discourse through middle terms in favor of sequential ordering. Reasoning in terms of proportions or relations was not novel; it was part of ancient geometry. What is new is the application of this mode of reasoning to the knowable as such, its elevation to the status of *universalis mathesis*.[9] Another noteworthy feature of the universal science is its accentuation of construction over demonstration and its introduction of motion into the very operation of geometrical proof. In Euclidean geometry, theorems or proofs predominate over problems or constructions; the elegant use of the perfect passive participle, for both problems (*Quod erat faciendum*) and theorems (*Quod erat demonstrandum*) indicates that the geometrical object and its properties have always already existed. By contrast, in Cartesian geometry, the focus is on problems rather than theorems and the constructions arise from temporal motion.

The transformations wrought within Cartesian geometry are crucial; in them can be found the roots and the promise of the fertility of a productive conception of human knowing.[10] Moreover, Descartes' geometry contains a sophisticated rethinking of the connections between geometrical objects and the natural world. In antiquity, geometry is often prized as the most rigorous form of reasoning. In the *Posterior Analytics*, Aristotle appeals to geometry as the paradigm of demonstrative reasoning. Even as it invites an ascent from the sensible to the intelligible, it remains anchored in the shared, pre-scientific understanding of nature and imagined shapes. Incorporating into geometry the techniques of algebra, with their indifference to the objects under consideration, Descartes largely frees geometry from the constraints of imagined shapes. Comparison is now possible across all genera of beings, whose qualitative differences recede from view.[11]

The readings of Descartes' scientific and mathematical writings by Jones and Lachterman suggest the possibility of a more intimate pedagogical and rhetorical connection between his more obviously stylized literary texts and his more technical writings. Descartes certainly stresses the virtues of his new science, but he also offers a new science of virtue, an account of the sovereign good and the means to its achievement. The topic of the good life, far from being unimportant or even secondary in Descartes, has a kind of primacy, if a veiled primacy. Recognizing this primacy helps us to relocate Descartes in the mainstream of classical philosophy, which takes its orientation from the great question of the good life for human beings. Yet, Descartes is not simply building upon the giants who preceded him. Indeed, except for Socrates (and his Plato), Descartes seems to envision the history of philosophy as populated by intellectual dwarfs. Nor does he pose the question of the good life in as direct or robust a fashion as his predecessors. His peremptory assertion toward the end of the *Discourse* that "health is unquestionably the first good and foundation of all other goods in this life" is instructive. It is as if Descartes wants to resolve a question without ever allowing the question itself to arise.

To see Descartes' complex and paradoxical stance toward inherited philosophy, we need to consider the role of Socrates in Descartes' project, a role that is more prominent than typically admitted. This neglect is at least partly attributable to another neglect, regarding the influence on Descartes of Montaigne, for whom Socrates is the exemplar of the learned ignorance of the philosopher. The significance of Descartes' engagement with Socrates is twofold. First, it serves (as it does in Montaigne) as the basis for a critique of the philosophy practiced in the schools, indeed in the entire history of philosophy since Plato. Second, it serves (as it does not in Montaigne) to establish a standard that must be overcome. For Montaigne, Socrates is the model of the philosophical life, a life devoted to unending inquiry, a life characterized by learned ignorance. For Montaigne, such a life constitutes the sovereign good for human beings. Descartes' attitude toward Socrates is quite different. Just as he presents his physics and his geometry as advancing beyond the ancients in its solution of problems the ancients deemed insoluble, so too Descartes' philosophy itself will now resolve the key questions, precisely the ones Socrates and Montaigne deem intractable. The question of the best way of life and the related question of the genres of writing suitable to introducing potential students to that life prompt the further question as to whether Descartes, like Socrates and Plato, deploys an ironic mode of speech.

RECOVERING AND OVERCOMING SOCRATES

In the preface to the French edition of the *Principles*, in the course of defining philosophy and explaining its benefits, Descartes describes the ultimate goal of philosophy as a

> search for the first causes and the true principle which enable us to deduce the reasons for everything we are capable of knowing, both for the conduct of life and for the preservation of health and the discovery of all manner of skills.

> (*une parfaite connoissance de lo toutes les choses que l'homme peut sçauoir, tant pour la conduite de sa vie, que pour la conseruation de sa*

santé & l'inuention de tous les arts; & qu'afin que cette connoissance soit
telle, il est nécessaire qu'elle soit déduite des premières causes, en forte
que, pour estudier à l'acquérir, ce qui se nomme proprement philoso-
pher, il faut commencer par la recherche de ces premières causes, c'eft à
dire des Principes).[12]

It is difficult to imagine a more comprehensive philosophical vision, encompassing the traditional division into theoretical and practical—and, within the practical, the orders of doing and making. As Richard Kennington observes, "Mastery is neutral between thinking and making, between philosophy and technē." Even as it calls to mind it subverts ancient distinctions. Indeed, seen from the vantage point of medieval thought, Descartes' philosophy looks more like theology than philosophy.[13] Thomas Aquinas, we should recall, claimed that sacred doctrine, unlike speculative philosophy, was both theoretical and practical (*Summa Theologiae* I.1.4). Moreover, the famous marks of the new science—certitude and utility—are, for Thomas, signs of the superiority of the believer's pursuit of wisdom over that of the philosopher (*Summa contra Gentiles* I.2).

Descartes goes on to provide a brief genealogy of philosophy, particularly of its roots in Plato and Aristotle. The former, following Socrates, "Ingenuously confessed that he had never yet been able to discover anything certain" (*a ingenuëment confessé qu'il n'auoit encore rien pu trouuer de certain*).[14] By contrast, Aristotle was "less candid" and put forth a new method and proposed principles as "true and certain, although it seems most unlikely that he in fact considered them to be so" (*les a proposez comme vrays & assurez, quoy qu'il n'y ait aucune apparence qu'il les ait jamais estimé tels*).[15]

As was true for the ancients, so too for Descartes, unlearning is often the first step in learning. The common practice of philosophy in the centuries separating Descartes from Socrates has only exacerbated the problem, inculcating bad habits and spreading erroneous opinion. The habit of passive reading and the substitution of commentary for the active engagement with vital questions have made true philosophy nearly non-existent. Here we detect a consonance between Descartes, on one hand, and Montaigne, who crafts a new genre of philosophical writing as a way of circumventing the desiccated commentary tradition.[16]

In the *Principles*, what stands in the way of progress in philosophy is the authority of the texts of Aristotle: "the majority of those aspiring to be philosophers in the last few centuries have blindly followed Aristotle" (*la pluspart de ceux de ces derniers siècles qui ont voulu estre Philosophes, ont fuiuy aveuglement Aristote*).[17] Descartes grants that much of the confusion has to do with poor readers who import claims into Aristotle's works that he would never recognize; the influence of Aristotle is so pervasive that even those who have not followed him are nonetheless "saturated with his opinions in their youth (since these are the only opinions taught in the Schools)" (*n'ont pas laissé d'auoir esté imbus de ses opinions en leur jeunesse [pource que ce sont les seules qu'on enseigne dans les escholes]*).[18] Aristotle's influence must be extirpated because his starting points are insecure and misleading. The situation is so grave that "among those who have studied whatever has been called philosophy up till now, those who have learnt least are the most capable of learning true philosophy" (*D'où il faut conclure que ceux qui ont le moins apris de tout ce qui a elle nommé jusques icy Philosophie, sont les plus capables d'apprendre la vraye*).[19]

Socratic unknowing, in opposition to Aristotelian dogmatism, is thus the path to reawakening the possibility of true philosophy. But this suggests for Descartes a new type of reading and writing. As potentially positive sources of knowledge, Descartes includes only those books "capable of instructing us well; for in such cases we hold a kind of conversation with the authors" (*mais particulièrement de ceux qui ont esté écrits par des personnes capables de nous donner de bonnes instructions, car c'est une espèce de conuersation que nous auons avec leurs autheurs*).[20] The quest to discern a manner of composition that would provoke rather than enervate thought aligns Descartes with Plato, among the ancients, and with Montaigne, among his contemporaries.

Like Plato and unlike Socrates, Descartes writes books. Like Plato, he writes a book to disabuse readers of the influence of books, both certain types of books and certain conventional ways of reading books. In one of the more perplexing statements in all of his writings, he describes his *Discourse on Method*, whose goal is to portray his "life as if in a picture," as a "history or, if you prefer, a fable in which, among certain examples worthy of imitation, you will perhaps also find many others that it would be right not to follow" (*une histoire, ou, si vous l'aymez mieux, que' comme une fable, en laquelle, parmi quelques exemples qu'on peut imiter, on en trouiiera peutestre aussy plusieurs autres qu'on aura raison de ne pas fuiure*).[21] Although Descartes is not typically given to poetic discourse, the genre to which he assigns his *Discourse* is closer to what Aristotle calls poetry than it is to what he calls history. In the *Poetics*, Aristotle says that poetry is more philosophical than history because the former has to do with the universal rather than the particular (9.1451b.6–7). Descartes is writing about matters whose significance and pedagogical implications transcend the particular conditions of his own life. That is perhaps the point of the added reference to the genre of the fable, whose latent meaning must be deciphered by the reader. As he puts it in the course of reviewing his own education, "fables awaken the mind." But well-crafted fables need not make their lessons obvious. As is clear from Descartes' repeated claims that not everyone should follow his example, he needs to write so that his true meaning is grasped by his intended audience and so that the remaining readers will not do harm to themselves or others.

The proximate source of this mode of writing is not Plato but Montaigne. As Jonathan Ree notes in "Descartes's Comedy," *The Discourse* is a kind of autobiography, a "first-person narrative about a protagonist who the narrator used to be."[22] Complicating matters is that Descartes offers a critique of fables in the very work that he presents as a fable. If Montaigne's strategy is to reduce philosophy to autobiography as a means of dissolving philosophical systems into anecdote, Descartes puts Montaigne's technique to an opposite use: "building anecdote into philosophy."[23] The difference between the narrators of Montaigne and Descartes is reflected in their divergent attitude toward temporality. In Montaigne, temporality dissolves into a flux that the narrator cannot reduce to order; the best he can do is to record its passing and remind himself and us in the present of its very passing. Temporality signifies "restless indeterminacy" and gives rise to an "unbridled irony" that undermines even the narrator. Temporality is also prominent in *The Discourse* and *Meditations*, but there is a striking difference between time as experienced prior to the discovery of the method and time as experienced after the mind has subjected itself to liberating spiritual exercises. Descartes thus tempers irony and directs it only toward those unaware of the method or toward the former self of the narrator. It is, as Ree puts it, the "irony of a confidently anticipated retrospect."[24]

From his youth, Descartes observes, he was "nourished upon letters" (*I'ay esté nourri aux lettres dés mon ensance*).[25] He supposed that by means of such training he could acquire a "clear and certain knowledge of all that is useful in life." But the promise was not realized. "I found myself beset by so many doubts and errors that I came to think I had gained nothing from my attempts to become educated by increasing recognition of my ignorance" (*Car ie me trouuois embarassé de tant de doutes & d'erreurs, qu'il me sembloit n'auoir fait autre profit, en taschant de m'instruire, sinon que i'auois découuert de plus en plus mon ignorance*).[26] This is precisely the Socratic moment in education, the moment in which one comes to know that one does not know. The reference to Socrates is instructive not just because it reinforces the notion that Socrates' insight is superior to that of Descartes' teachers but also because Descartes moves past it so quickly. The key insight of Socrates' entire life, the awareness that made him wiser than others, provides for Descartes merely an occasion to underscore the defects of his own education. Descartes obliquely indicates his own superiority both to the tradition of philosophy since Plato and to his contemporary teachers, who are unaware of their own ignorance.

There are other telling Socratic allusions in Descartes' writings, particularly in the *Discourse*. His reduction of extant philosophy to a rhetorical art of speaking reflects Socrates' denigration of the Sophists, who are able to give impressive speeches before large crowds but are incapable of responding in private to the perspicuous questions of a serious interlocutor. Later in that work he will speak of his own method as allowing light to flow into a cellar—an image that both calls to mind the Allegory of the Cave and promises to deliver enlightenment of the most important human affairs. But Descartes is interested in much more than illumination; he is committed to transformation. Whereas Plato provided images and wrote ironically about the reordering of society by reference to philosophical knowledge, Descartes rejects metaphors or, rather, uses metaphors as a first stage in a philosophical pedagogy that will ultimately transcend metaphor. Descartes goes directly to what one might call, following Machiavelli, the "effectual truth of things." Moreover, in his reference to "ancient moral teachings as proud and magnificent palaces built only on sand and mud" (*les escris des anciens payens, qui traitent des meurs, a des palais fort superbes & fort magnifiques, qui nestoient battis que sur du fable & sur de la boue*), he echoes Machiavelli's critique of the "imagined republics" of the ancients.[27] Even in this passing reference we can detect Descartes' standard practice with respect to Socratic philosophy: cite its aspirations in order to demonstrate the path toward their fulfillment or overcoming—in this case by a jarring fusion of Plato and Machiavelli.

To transcend both Plato and Aristotle, Descartes introduces both a novel accent upon and an interpretation of utility, which rest upon the intimate connection between knowledge and the activity of production.

Indeed, one of Descartes' principal objections to Aristotle rests upon the latter's failure to supply true knowledge of causes, a failure evident from the poverty of Aristotle's productive sciences. If he had known the causes, as Bacon would put it, he would have produced the effects. As Descartes puts it in the Preface to the French edition of the *Principles*, "the best way of proving the falsity of Aristotle's principles is to point out that they have not enabled any progress to be made in all the many centuries in which they have been followed" (*on ne sçauroit mieux prouuer la fausseté de ceux d'Aristote, qu'en disant qu'on n'a sceu faire aucun progrez par leur moyen depuis plusieurs siècles qu'on les a fuiuis*).[28]

There is much more operative here than a simple objection to stagnant technological progress. Basing his argument on a careful reading of the *Geometry* and the works on physics, Lachterman argues that Descartes shifts the balance from contemplative knowing to productive knowing, a model of knowing that discloses a more intimate connection between certitude and utility than might initially be apparent. This has far-reaching metaphysical implications: "Method, in Descartes, not only codifies rules of procedure; it constrains those 'objects' to which it is applied to such an extent that their very intelligibility becomes identical with their suscepti-bility to methodical treatment."[29] Objects owe their intelligibility to their mode of genesis; this means that the distinction between the natural and the artificial nearly vanishes. Descartes invites the "reader to regard the natural as a result of the artificial."[30] Consequently, the "*topos* of wonder," characteristic of the life of the philosopher, "now has a new home"—"the artistry of the technician."[31]

Like Socrates, Descartes adopts a skeptical stance toward received opin-ion. His insistence upon doubting every opinion that admits in any way of being doubted can be seen as an exaggeration of Socrates' practice of questioning the deeply held beliefs of his fellow citizens. The need to go beyond Socrates is counseled by philosophy itself, which seeks knowledge and wisdom. On Descartes' view, the zetetic conception of philosophy (what Montaigne would call Socratic philosophy, that is to say, philosophy simply) subverts, not just conventional opinion, but philosophy itself. A promising protreptic, the ancient genre of speech that aimed to persuade potential philosophers to take up the life of wisdom, ends up as a reduc-tio ad absurdum of the philosophical life. The pondering of variant and contradictory philosophical positions confirms only the futility of the at-tempts of the greatest intellects to give an account of nature and human nature. If Descartes had not discovered his method, he might well have concluded, with Pascal, that the philosophers "weary those who search."[32]

Careful readers can pick up hints of Descartes' reservations about Socrates in odd places. Consider, for example, the discussion in *The Passions of the Soul* of the passion of wonder, first of all the passions, a sudden surprise of the soul provoked by objects that seem "unusual and extraordinary." The use of wonder is to "make us learn and retain in our memory things of which we were previously ignorant" (*qu'elle est utile en ce qu'elle fait que nous apprenons & retenons en nostre mémoire les choses que nous avons auparavant ignorés*).[33] It can also "dispose us to acquire scientific knowledge" (*nous dispose à l'acquisition des sciences*).[34] But Descartes seems most concerned with castigating excessive wonder, what he calls "astonishment," a kind of rapture of the soul in which the "whole body remains as immobile as a statue" (*ce qui fait que tout le corps demeure immobile comme une statue*).[35] The problem with this state, to which those who have a low estimation of their abilities are most inclined, is that it precludes careful analysis of the subject matter in question. One cannot help but read in these passages an admonition against the classical understanding of philosophy as both arising from and issuing in wonder. Even more pointedly, the passage directly targets Socrates, whom Plato depicts in the *Symposium* as immobilized by thought.

DESCARTES' NEW SCIENCE OF VIRTUE

In a variety of contexts, Descartes refers to the life of virtue as the sovereign good, a life that breeds in the soul tranquility and harmony. Commentators have noted the resemblance between Descartes' account of virtue and the third rule in the provisional moral code in the discourse:

> Try always to master myself rather than fortune, and change my desires rather than the order of the world. In general I would become accustomed to believing that nothing lies entirely within our power except our thoughts, so that after doing our best in dealing with matters external to us, whatever we fail to achieve is absolutely impossible so far as we are concerned.
>
> (*Ma troisiesme maxime estoit de tascher tousiours plutost à me vaincre que la fortune, & à changer mes desirs que l'ordre du monde;*

*et généralement, de m'accoustumer à croire qu'il n'y a rien qui foit
entièrement en nostre pouuoir, que nos pensées, en forte qu'après
que nous auons fait nostre mieux, touchant les choses qui nous sont
extérieures, tout ce qui manque de nous réussir est, au regard de nous,
absolument impossible.*[36]

The task of self-mastery with its attendant attitude of indifference
toward what escapes our control calls to mind classical Stoic conceptions
of the good life. What is novel in Descartes is his expansive, but not limit-
less, view of what lies within our control. Toward the end of the *Discourse*,
he speaks of the fruits of his method. And, before making the famous
announcement of a new philosophy that would "replace the speculative
philosophy taught in the Schools" (*qu'au lieu de cete Philosophie spécula-
tiue, qu'on enseigne dans les escholes*),[37] he describes the method as assist-
ing both in resolving "certain difficulties in the speculative sciences" and
in "governing his own conduct." The method will have decidedly public
benefits as well. Descartes proposes that it will contribute to the "general
welfare of mankind." He amplifies:

> Through this philosophy, we could know the power and action of fire,
> water, air, the stars, the heavens, and all the other bodies in our envi-
> ronment, as distinctly as we know the crafts of our artisans; and we
> could use this knowledge—as the artisans use theirs—for all the pur-
> poses for which it is appropriate and thus make ourselves, as it were,
> the masters and possessors of Nature.
>
> (*par laquelle connoissant la force & les actions du feu, de l'eau, de l'air,
> des aftres, des cieux, & de tous les autres cors qui nous enuironnent,
> aussy distinctement que nous connoissons les diuers mestiers de nos
> artisans, nous les pourrions employer en mesme façon à tous les usages
> ausquels ils font propres, & ainsi nous rendre comme maistres & posses-
> seurs de la Nature*).[38]

This calls to mind the original title for the *Discourse*: "The Project of a
Universal Science Which Can Elevate Our Nature to Its Highest Degree
of Perfection."[39] Having counseled conformity in external matters to conventional laws and customs and indifference to the order of the world, he
now engages in what he elsewhere calls "boldness," redefined against the

tradition as a form of courage, rather than a vice, that "disposes the soul to carry out the most dangerous tasks" (*qui dispose l'âme à l'exécution des choses qui sont les plus dangereuses*).[40] The audacity of the goal is made feasible by a new conception of the relationships among the intellect, the body, and the external world: a new *ethos*, as Lachterman puts it, in the human inquirer's way of being in and toward other beings.

While not absolute or immediate, control over the external world is indeed possible. For example, the world to which we return in the final section of the *Meditations* is the world as understood by mathematical physics; the only features of things that are clearly and distinctly known are those susceptible to a quantitative description. There is, then, an important connection between the final meditation and Descartes' *Geometry*, which aims to provide "rules for the measurement of all bodies."[41] Some see Descartes' emphasis on mathematics as reprising a Platonic or Augustinian theme. In this tradition, mathematics occupies an intermediate and subordinate stage in the ascent to the Good; a partial overlap with that tradition is operative in the *Meditations*, where, for example, the second proof for the existence of God contains as one of its crucial steps an analogy to geometrical necessity. With the bracketing of the moral or practical and the exclusive focus on the theoretical operations of the mind, Descartes decisively reshapes ancient philosophical pedagogy. God is not encountered as the one who calls, the one who beckons alluringly, arousing and satisfying our erotic longing for beauty and love. Whereas in the Platonic tradition, the notion of God as geometer is but a likely story, in need of supplementation by other likely stories or myths, Descartes takes this notion literally. Thus, the meditation ends, not with a hierarchical reflection on the likenesses between image and exemplar, but with the announcement of the infinite and linear project of mapping nature in mathematical terms. Descartes' method and its success in a variety of fields testify to the existence of resources at our disposal for the mastery of the external world.

The peculiar intelligibility that the world manifests when seen under the purview of mathematical physics might be said to constitute a new way of being in the world for rational beings. Some, such as Lachterman, have seen in Descartes' description of the new philosophy a thoroughgoing constructivist conception of knowledge. Yet, Lachterman may go too far here. Despite Descartes' penchant for aligning knowledge to the model of the artisan, he also insists upon the indispensable role of the natural light, the claim that all knowledge must repose upon an indubitable foundation, a basis acknowledged but not constructed by human knowledge or will. Stanley Rosen thus speaks of a central ambiguity in Descartes. Descartes aims at two goals, which may not be fully compatible with one another. The first is to identify the structure of nature, and so all of rational order, with mathematical properties of extension; the second is to give man mastery over this order, thanks to the new technique of mathematics. If order is to provide man with certitude and security, it must be eternal, regular, and independent of, although accessible to, subjective mental activity. Unfortunately, if man is to be master of this order, it must be subject to his will.[42]

The common picture of the Cartesian understanding of the relationship of the mind to its body and to the external world has given rise to the notion of Cartesian angelism, the abstraction of the mind from the world of matter. Yet, in other works (perhaps most importantly in the *Passions*), Descartes tempers the tendencies toward angelism. The key, to turn from physics to the cultivation of the virtues constitutive of the good life, is proper self-knowledge, ignorance of which is the gravest source of vice. We need, as Descartes tells us in the *Passions*, to distinguish clearly what is in our power from what is not.

Descartes is clearly aware of the problem; its negotiation is both a theoretical and an ethical task. The theoretical point echoes Bacon's claim that if we wish nature to master nature, we must first obey her. Without a clear sense of nature, the investigator of her powers is likely to suppose that she can do more or less than she actually can. But it is also ethical. Given the tension between aspiration and resistance, how can the soul dwell in the tranquility that Descartes prizes as the sovereign good of human life? The answer to this question has to do with the practice of virtue, especially the virtue of generosity.

In the course of his comments on generosity, a virtue rooted in proper self-esteem, Descartes observes that "no virtue is so dependent on good birth as the virtue which causes us to esteem ourselves in accordance with our true value, and it is easy to believe that the souls which God puts into our bodies are not all equally noble and strong" (*Ainsi encore qu'il n'y ait point de vertu, à laquelle il semble que la bonne naissance contribue tant, qu'à celle qui fait qu'on ne s'estime que selon sa juste valeur; & qu'il foit aysé à croyre, que toutes les âmes que Dieu met en nos corps, ne font pas également nobles &. Fortes*).[43] Despite the disparities of nature, "a good upbringing is a great help in correcting defects of birth." Through training, "we may arouse the passion of generosity in ourselves and then acquire the virtue"

(*on peut exciter en soy la Passion, & ensuite acquérir la vertu de Générosité*).[44]
Generosity, which "causes a person's self-esteem to be as great as it may
legitimately be" (*qui fait qu'un homme s'estime au plus haut point qu'il se
peut légitimement estimer*), has two parts.[45] The first is an awareness that
nothing truly belongs to us but the freedom to dispose our volitions. Following upon that knowledge, second, is a "firm and constant resolution to
use it well—that is, never to lack the will to undertake and carry out whatever he judges to be best (*partie en ce qu'il sent en foy mesme une ferme
& constante résolution d'en bien user, c'est à dire de ne manquer jamais de
volonté, pour entreprendre & exécuter toutes les choses qu'il jugera estre les
meilleures*).[46] Descartes concludes: "To do that is to pursue virtue in a perfect manner" (*Ce qui est suivre parfaitement la vertu*).[47]

Irresolution, a kind of anxiety, results from "too great a desire to do well
and from weakness of the intellect" (*d'un trop grand désir de bien faire, &
d'une foiblesse de l'entendement*).[48] The remedy for this is "to believe that
we always do our duty when we do what we judge to be best, even though
our judgment may perhaps be a very bad one" (*à croire qu'on s'acquite
tousjours de son devoir, lors qu'on fait ce qu'on juge estre le meilleur, encore
que peut estre on juge tres-mal*).[49] The practice of generosity would seem
to involve the same sort of elimination of regret and repentance that we
find in Montaigne's account of human flourishing.[50] It would also alleviate
anxiety in the soul over the incomplete mastery of nature.

Generosity is a self-regarding virtue, but it has salutary social and political consequences. For Descartes, pride is not a vice, as it was for his Christian predecessors; instead, it is "a kind of joy based on the love we have for
ourselves and resulting from the belief or hope we have of being praised by
certain other persons" (*une espèce de love, fondée sur Amour qu'on a pour
foy mesme, & qui vient de l'opinion ou de l'espérance qu'on a d'estre loué par
quelques autres*).[51] Yet, as much as Descartes may concede that, perhaps in
contrast to common sense, generosity is not evenly distributed, it has for
him a decidedly egalitarian character. It engenders in its possessor the recognition that, unlike wealth, honor, or intelligence, generosity is "capable
of being present in every other person" (*ou du moins pouvoir estre, en chacun des autres homes*).[52] Generosity also uproots the vices regarding others, such as jealousy and envy, "because everything they think sufficiently
valuable to be worth pursuing is such that its acquisition depends solely on
themselves" (*à cause qu'il n'y a aucune chose dont l'acquisition ne dépende
pas d'eux, qu'ils pensent valoir affez pour mériter d'estre beaucoup souhaitée;*

& de la Haine envers les hommes, à cause qu'ils les estiment tous).[53] Generosity thus serves the ends of both theory and practice; it has a direct impact upon our conduct in the pursuit of knowledge and in our comportment toward fellow human beings. Generosity calls to mind, on the one hand, some of the central virtues in pagan accounts of the good life, virtues such as magnanimity, without its offensive aristocratic elements, and justice, without its degree of difficulty or seeming other-orientation. On the other hand, generosity seems to do much of the work of Christian charity without its sacrificial character or its dependence on divine grace for its very existence.

Descartes treats virtues—indeed, the passions themselves—as thoughts or perceptions or cognitive dispositions. The accent on cognitive awareness does not diminish the role of the will, which remains prominent because virtue is a firm resolve. It does diminish the older sense of the passion as a suffering or passive recipient of what comes from outside. That is not eliminated entirely; indeed, receptivity of passion is precisely the reason for its need of governance. But the accent is on the susceptibility of passion to rational control, or rather, upon the discovery of a master passion that can regulate the rest.[54] What is also diminished, particularly from the Aristotelian perspective, is action itself. Descartes here sets things up in such a way that what is internal to the soul is the principal source of virtue and happiness. Resolute action is the natural result of the virtue of generosity while what recedes from view is the significance of the division of acts into diverse types, particularly the difference between the moral and the productive acts.[55] If, in the classical understanding, tragedy results from a mysterious mixture of internal character traits and external circumstance, then Descartes can be seen as limiting the prospect, coming from outside, of tragedy. His very conception of virtue renders the individual less susceptible to tragedy and more capable of responding to it, if it should occur.

Despite his emphasis on mastery and rational control, Descartes does not exalt human nature entirely above the natural or bodily order. For example, he does not follow the Cynics in deeming the passions to be evil. On the contrary, he insists that the passions are "all by nature good" (*Car nous voyons qu'elles font toutes bonnes de leur nature).*[56] Only their "misuse or excess" is bad, and for this Descartes' study of the passions provides a variety of remedies, chiefly the "foresight and diligence" that will enable us to "correct our natural faults by striving to separate within ourselves the movements of the blood and spirits from the thoughts to which they are usually joined" (*Mais pource que j'ay mis entre ces remèdes la préméditation, l'industrie par laquelle on peut corriger les défauts de son naturel, en s'exerçant à séparer en foy les mouvemens du sang & des esprits, d'avec les pensées ausquelles ils ont coustume d'estre joins*).[57] We can limit the destructive influence of the passions and cultivate habits that will help us to experience ills in a tranquil way. In quite a different way from its original, Descartes incorporates Montaigne's strategy of accommodation to our condition.[58] In this, there is an unstated response to the accusation of angelism.

THEOLOGY, THE SOVEREIGN GOOD, AND IRONIC PHILOSOPHY

The original title for the *Discourse*: "The Project of a Universal Science Which Can Elevate Our Nature to Its Highest Degree of Perfection" raises an interesting theological puzzle.[59] How can a believer propose to raise our nature to its highest degree of perfection and exclude theology, revelation, and grace from that process? Descartes is always careful both to avoid direct contravention of religious doctrine and to rank the divine above the human. Descartes here seems to deploy the same strategy as Montaigne with respect to theology: exaltation and separation. This allows him the freedom to investigate the most important human questions as if theology shed no significant light on them. In the *Discourse* itself, he mentions theology only to set it aside as merely practical, as teaching "how to get to heaven." The reduction of theology to a merely practical discipline that has no direct bearing on the intellectual life here and now is telling.

Thoughtful readers cannot help but pose pressing questions. What are we to make of the status and content of revelation in relation to the method and claims proposed in Descartes' philosophy? Is it possible that moral and theological matters could remain unaffected by this standard of human perfection?

One might suppose that faith and reason, theology and philosophy, could simply co-exist, that they could constitute two separate but non-conflicting spheres. With the demise of ancient and medieval conceptions of hierarchy, a new arrangement of the relationship between faith and reason seems both possible and required. But this is the point at which Descartes' focus on the question of the best way of life puts such an arrangement in jeopardy. If a way of life not only has to do with the intellectual assent to a set of principles but also involves a set of practices, authoritative texts, and standards of what is best, then the both/and approach cannot be sustained. While a Christian can certainly engage in philosophical argument, a Christian cannot accept the claim that philosophy is the best way of life available to human persons, a way of life constitutive of human happiness and wisdom. The question of human excellence, of the sovereign good, arises here in an especially dramatic way. Leo Strauss's formulation is pertinent:

> Man cannot live without light, guidance, knowledge; only through knowledge of the good can he find the good that he needs. The fundamental question, therefore, is whether men can acquire that knowledge of the good without which they cannot guide their lives individually or collectively by the unaided efforts of their natural powers, or whether they are dependent for that knowledge on Divine Revelation. No alternative is more fundamental than this: human guidance or divine guidance.[60]

One begins to wonder whether Descartes' philosophical project is not essentially a defense of the autonomy and self-sufficiency of the philosophical life against an unstated theological challenge. This is to suggest that Montaigne and Descartes treat theology ironically, that they dissimulate on this matter, and that their writing reflects the gap between what they seem to hold and what they actually hold.

The strategy with respect to theological discourse resembles, as we have noted, that of Montaigne. But the strategy for defending the philosophical life is distinct because the two philosophers construe that life quite differently. Montaigne defends philosophy by reviving a proper understanding of Socrates and his way of life. Descartes defends it by accepting the standard set by Socrates and transcending it, by turning philosophy from a dubious pursuit of wisdom into a possession of wisdom.

Wisdom remains for Descartes the telos of philosophy. Not just its recognition and pursuit but its achievement is the decisive matter. The *Meditations* are crucial to the foundations of a new physical science and to the articulation and realization of the best way of life. The last point has been unduly neglected in the reading of Descartes. As was true for Plato, so for Descartes philosophical texts are themselves spiritual exercises, fields for the recognition and exercise of the very virtues propounded, often only indirectly, in them.[61] Like Plato, Descartes sought a way of writing that would foster the practice of reading as dramatic reenactment. The new account of nature renders it more susceptible to the probing and manipulation of human intelligence and will, even as it suits a novel articulation of the sovereign good. Before Descartes, Montaigne had downplayed the role of teleology, the ordination of nature to a transcendent cause, a final cause that draws all things to itself by appealing to the erotic inclination to the good built into the very structure of natural things. The ancients sought sufficiency, but for them certitude and control—in a phrase, modern autonomy—were less important than the longing or erôs for the good and the beautiful. Aristotle, and after him Aquinas, urge that, where there is a conflict between the nobility of the object known and certitude, we should prefer a dim and partial apprehension of the more noble object to an exhaustive and sure knowledge of a less noble object.[62]

Montaigne's repudiation of teleology puts him at odds with Socrates. Montaigne's understanding of the complacency of the philosopher in the face of his own ignorance is void of the erotic longing for the whole that characterizes Socrates—what Montaigne dismisses as flights of transcendent fantasy, his "ecstasies and daemonizings."[63] Descartes goes much further and supplies a comprehensive rival account of nature, an account that not only supplants Aristotle but also renders otiose the dialogue between philosophy and theology, reason and faith. In this way, Descartes' overcoming of Socrates, his new science of virtue, is simultaneously a strategy for bypassing the debate between Athens and Jerusalem.

Descartes' new science would prove unpersuasive to another Frenchman whose obsession with Montaigne exceeds that of Descartes. Pascal counters the new science and its ironic stance toward Christianity by a twofold reversal. First, he argues that mature reflection on nature and the human condition does not minimize but in fact exacerbates wonder. The proper response is precisely what Descartes identifies as the vice of amazement.[64] Second, he counters the philosopher's ironic stance toward theology with an account of divine irony, which he articulates in terms of a proportion: as the philosopher stands in relation to the ordinary run of mankind, so does the believer stand in relation to the philosopher.[65] That irony exceeds in power the virtues of the new science event as it exceeds in wisdom the new science of virtue.[66] Pascal's account of the sovereign good differs from that of Montaigne and Descartes and provides another distinctively modern perspective. Yet, here again Socrates is prominent. However much these early modern French philosophers might want to move beyond antiquity, they remain haunted by the founding figure of philosophy.

NOTES

I would like to thank my colleague Rob Miner, my graduate assistant John Spano, and especially my assigned commentator, Dan Maher, for their comments on previous versions of this chapter.

1. *La béatitude consiste, ce me semble, en un parfait contentement d'esprit et une satisfaction intérieure . . . il me semble qu'on chacun se peut rendre content de soi-même et sans rien attendre d'ailleurs, pourvu seulement qu'il observe trois choses, auxquelles se rapportent les trois règles de morale, que j'ai mises dans le discours de la Méthode* (translation mine). René Descartes, *Oeuvres de Descartes*, trans. Charles Adam, Paul Tannery, and Louis-Charles d'Albert Luynes (Paris: L. Cerf, 1910), p. 1193.

2. On this debate, see Gary Steiner, *Descartes as a Moral Thinker: Christianity, Technology, Nihilism* (Amherst, NY: Humanity Books, 2004), pp. 15–49. Also see Etienne Gilson, *Discours de la Méthode: Texte et commentaire*, 5th ed. (Paris: Vrin, 1976); Michèle le Doeuff, *The Philosophical Imaginary*, trans. Colin Gordon (Stanford, CA: Stanford University Press, 1989), p. 62; Martial Gueroult, *Descartes' Philosophy Interpreted according to the Order of Reasons*, trans. Roger Ariew, 2 vols. (Minneapolis: University of Minnesota Press, 1984–1985), 2:192; M. H. Lefebvre, "De la morale provisioné à la générosité," in *Descartes*, Cahiers de Royamount, Philosophie no. 2 (Paris: Les Editions de Minuit, 1957); and T. Keefe, "Descartes's 'Morale Definitive' and the Autonomy of Ethics," *Romantic Review* 64 (1973).

3. *Descartes: Oeuvres et lettres*, ed. André Bridoux (Paris: Gallimard, 1953), p. 1199.

4. *Oeuvres et lettres*, ed. Bridoux, p. 1200. In the "Dedicatory Letter" to the *Principles of Philosophy*, he offers a unified account of the "pure and genuine virtues, which proceed solely from knowledge of what is right," which have "one and the same nature," and which "are included under the single term 'wisdom'" (*fed illæ puræ & sinceræ, quæ ex folâ | recti cognitione profluunt, unam & eandem omnes habent naturam, & sub uno sapientiæ nomine continentur*). *Oeuvres de Descartes* VIIIA.2.23–25; Dedicatory Letter to the *Principles of Philosophy*, p. 191.

5. Matthew Jones, *The Good Life in the Scientific Revolution: Descartes, Pascal, Leibniz, and the Cultivation of Virtue* (Chicago: University of Chicago Press, 2006), p. 79. See also Matthew Jones, "Descartes's Geometry as Spiritual Exercise," *Critical Inquiry* 28.1 (Autumn 2001): 40–71.

6. Jones, *The Good Life in the Scientific Revolution*, p. 3. On philosophy and spiritual exercises, see Pierre Hadot, *Philosophy as a Way of Life: Spiritual Exercises from Socrates to Foucault* (Hoboken, NJ: Blackwell, 1995).

7. David Lachterman, *The Ethics of Geometry: A Genealogy of Modernity* (New York: Routledge, 1989), p. xi. The simplest way to put the contrast between the ancient (Greek) and the modern (Cartesian) conception of mathematics and science is to say that, while the ancients had a hypothetical awareness of *mathesis universalis*, they resisted its blandishments, for ontological, epistemological, and ethical reasons. Descartes stakes his entire method on the establishment of just such a universal science of learning, with important repercussions for metaphysics, epistemology, and ethics.

8. Amos Funkenstein, *Theology and the Scientific Imagination from the Middle Ages to the Seventeenth Century* (Princeton, NJ: Princeton University Press, 1986), pp. 72–76.

9. On the antecedent, Greek discussions of *mathesis universalis*, see Lachterman, *Ethics of Geometry*, pp. 177–78.

10. Descartes indicates the significance of geometry at the end of the *Meditations* when he repeatedly speaks of considering physical objects as "objects of pure mathematics" (Meditation, 6).

11. The most important philosophical study of the history of these transformations remains Edmund Husserl's *The Crisis of European Sciences and Transcendental Phenomenology: An Introduction to Phenomenological Philosophy* (Chicago: Northwestern University Press, 1970).

12. *Oeuvres de Descartes* IXB.2.10-16; Preface to the *Principles of Philosophy*, in *The Philosophical Writings of Descartes*, vol. 1, trans. John Cottingham, Robert Stoothoff, and Dugald Murdoch (Cambridge: Cambridge University Press, 1985), p. 179.

13. Richard Kennington, "René Descartes," in *History of Political Philosophy*, 2nd edition, ed. Leo Strauss and Joseph Cropsey (Chicago: University of Chicago Press, 1981), pp. 395-415. Kennington's essay is especially helpful on the political setting and implications of the *Discourse* (pp. 401, 408).

14. *Oeuvres de Descartes* IXB.5-6; Preface to the *Principles of Philosophy*, p. 181.

15. *Oeuvres de Descartes* IXB.6.9-10; Preface to the *Principles of Philosophy*, p. 181.

16. On Descartes and Montaigne, see Carol Collier, "The Self in Montaigne and Descartes: From Portraiture to Indigence," *De Philosophia* 13.2 (1997): 249-58; E. M. Curley, *Descartes against the Skeptics* (Cambridge: Harvard University Press, 1978); John Lyons, "Descartes and Modern Imagination," *Philosophy and Literature* 23.2 (1999): 302-12; Hassan Melehy, *Writing Cogito: Montaigne, Descartes, and the Institution of the Modern Subject* (Albany: SUNY Press, 1998); Leon Brunschvicg, *Descartes et Pascal lecteurs de Montaigne* (1942).

17. *Oeuvres de Descartes* IX.7.19; Preface to the *Principles of Philosophy*, p. 182.

18. *Oeuvres de Descartes* IX.7.25-27; Preface to the *Principles of Philosophy*, p. 182.

19. *Oeuvres de Descartes* IX.9.10-12; Preface to the *Principles of Philosophy*, p. 183.

20. *Oeuvres de Descartes* IXB.5.9-11; Preface to the *Principles of Philosophy*, p. 181.

21. *Oeuvres de Descarte* VI.4.14-16; *Discourse on Method*, part 1, p. 112, in *The Philosophical Writings of Descartes*.

22. Jonathan Ree, "Descartes's Comedy," *Philosophy and Literature* 8.2 (1984): 153.

23. Ibid., p. 154.

24. Ibid., p. 162.

25. *Oeuvres de Descartes* VI.4.21; *Discourse on Method*, part 1, p. 113.

26. *Oeuvres de Descartes* VI.4.27-29; *Discourse on Method*.

27. *Oeuvres de Descartes* VI.7-8; *Discourse on Method*, p. 114.

28. *Oeuvres de Descartes* IXB.18-19; Preface to the *Principles of Philosophy*, p. 189.

29. Lachterman, *Ethics of Geometry*, p. 175.

30. Ibid., p. 172.

31. Ibid., p. 151.

32. In an early fragment, entitled "Letter to induce men to seek God," Pascal comments, "Then make them look for him among the philosophers, skeptics, and dogmatists, who will worry the man who seeks" (*Et puis le faire chercher chez les philosophes, pyrrhoniens et dogmatistes, qui travaillent celui qui les recherche*). *Lettre pour porter à rechercher Dieu*, in Blaise Pascal, *Pensées*, trans. A. J. Krailsheimer (New York: Penguin Classics, 1995), no. 4, B.184.

33. *Oeuvres de Descartes* XI.384.4-5, *Des Passions* II.75; *On the Passions*, pp. 353-54.

34. *Oeuvres de Descartes* XI.384.10, *Des Passions* II.76; *On the Passions*, p. 353.

35. *Oeuvres de Descartes* XI.383.7, *Des Passions* II.73; *On the Passions*, p. 354.

36. *Oeuvres de Descartes* VI.25.20–27; *Discourse on Method*, p. 123.

37. *Oeuvres de Descartes* VI.61.30–31; *Discourse on Method*.

38. *Oeuvres de Descartes* VI.62.1–8; *Discourse on Method*, p. 142.

39. See Lachterman, *Ethics of Geometry*, p. 129.

40. *Oeuvres de Descartes* XI.460.19, *Des Passions* III.171; *On the Passions*, p. 391.

41. René Descartes, *Geometry* (New York: Dover Books, 1925), p. 43.

42. Stanley Rosen, "A Central Ambiguity in Descartes," in *Ancients and Moderns: Rethinking Modernity* (New Haven: Yale University Press, 1989), pp. 22–36.

43. *Oeuvres de Descartes* XI.453.17–22, *Des Passions* III.161; *The Passions of the Soul*, in *The Philosophical Writings of Descartes*, vol. 1, p. 388.

44. *Oeuvres de Descartes* XI.454, *Des Passions* III.161; *The Passions*, p. 388.

45. *Oeuvres de Descartes* XI.445–46, *Des Passions* III.153; *The Passions*, p. 384.

46. *Oeuvres de Descartes* XI.446.5–8, *Des Passions* III.153; *The Passions*, p. 384.

47. *Oeuvres de Descartes* XI.446.10, *Des Passions* III.153; *The Passions*, p. 384.

48. *Oeuvres de Descartes* XI.460.5, *Des Passions* III.170; *The Passions*, pp. 390–91.

49. *Oeuvres de Descartes* XI.460.13–14, *Des Passions* III.170; *The Passions*, p. 391.

50. For an interesting study of the departure of both Montaigne and Descartes from Augustinian models of autobiography and of repentance, see Patrick Riley, *Character and Conversion in Autobiography: Augustine, Montaigne, Descartes, Rousseau, and Sartre* (Charlottesville: University of Virginia Press, 2004), pp. 60–87.

51. *Oeuvres de Descartes* XI.482.1–5, *Des Passions* III.204; *The Passions*. p. 401.

52. *Oeuvres de Descartes* XI.447.5, *Des Passions* III.154; *The Passions*, p. 384.

53. *Oeuvres de Descartes* XI.448.6–9, *Des Passions* III.156; *The Passions*, p. 385.

54. On this and on the relationship of other virtues to generosity, see Kennington, "René Descartes," pp. 398, 407.

55. The indifference to particular acts might well signal another parallel between the ethical and the geometrical. In both cases, the exaltation of artistic creativity counsels flexibility in starting points and material conditions. What is most important is the resolve to bring to completion whatever is deemed most desirable.

56. *Oeuvres de Descartes* XI.485.24, *Des Passions* III.211; *The Passions*, p. 403fd.

57. *Oeuvres de Descartes* XI.486.5–8, *Des Passions* III.211; *The Passions*, p. 403.

58. For Montaigne, see especially the concluding paragraphs of Michel de Montaigne, "On Experience," in *The Complete Essays*, trans. M. A. Screech (New York: Penguin Classics, 2003).

59. See Lachterman, *Ethics of Geometry*, p. 129.

60. Leo Strauss, *Natural Right and History* (Chicago: University of Chicago Press, 1965), p. 74.

61. The role of text as spiritual exercise is nowhere more prominent than in Descartes' most influential book, *The Meditations on First Philosophy*. Numerous features of the *Meditations* call to mind the *Spiritual Exercises* of St. Ignatius of Loyola. The famous text from the founder of the Jesuits is designed to lead a Christian, over a series of four weeks, to discern his or her calling and elect a way of life. Meditation on scripture, the primary vehicle of spiritual exercise, begins with what Ignatius calls a "composition of place," an attempt to imagine all the sensible details of the scriptural scene and thus to insert oneself into the living setting of Christ encountered in the flesh. At each stage in the course of the retreat, one comes to a deeper self-knowledge and a greater awareness of God. The retreat

ends by returning the individual to the world, and to the taking up of his or her calling. The regime of the exercises involves a series of daily meditations, regular reviews of one's progress, and volitional acts of repentance and reaffirmations of amendment. Void of scriptural elements, Descartes' *Meditations* nonetheless echoes the *Exercises* in a number of ways.

62. Aristotle, *De Anima* I.1.402a1–20; Aquinas, *Ethics* X.7.1177b26–78a5.

63. Montaigne, "On Experience," p. 1268.

64. For example, in the famous meditation on the twin infinities of large and small, Pascal thinks we should "tremble at these marvels" (*il tremblera dans la vue de ces merveilles*). *Pensées*, no. 199, B.72.

65. "Philosophers: they surprise the ordinary run of men. Christians: they surprise the philosophers" (*Les philosophes. Ils étonnent le commun des hommes. Les chrétiens, ils étonnent les philosophes*). Pascal, *Pensées*, B.443. The Socratic preference for the study of man to the inquiry into the exact sciences—an affirmation of the primacy of the intuitive over the mathematical mind—underscores Pascal's greater proximity to Montaigne than to Descartes. Jean-Luc Marion, who takes Descartes rather than Montaigne as Pascal's chief interlocutor, speaks of Pascal's overcoming of metaphysics and philosophy. Because Marion takes Descartes to be an exemplar of philosophy, he overstates Pascal's victory over philosophy. On the level of direct polemic, it is much easier for Pascal to combat Descartes' claims on behalf of the sufficiency of reason. But Descartes' is neither the only nor the most cogent defense of the philosophical life. See the final chapter of Jean-Luc Marion, *On Descartes' Metaphysical Prism* (Chicago: University of Chicago Press, 1999) and, for a more detailed reading of Pascal on both Descartes and Montaigne that develops Marion's thesis, Vincent Carraud, *Pascal et la philosophie* (Presses universitaires de France, 1992).

66. This type of irony is also indebted to Socrates, in ways that I do not have the space to articulate here. For an examination of a use of irony compatible with that in Pascal, see Anthony Esolen, *Ironies of Faith* (Wilmington, DE: ISI Books, 2007).

3

NOTES ON "THE VIRTUE OF SCIENCE AND THE SCIENCE OF VIRTUE"

Daniel P. Maher

BENE VIXIT, BENE QUI LATUIT. Descartes chose this line from Ovid's *Tristia* (III.4.25) as a personal motto, which I translate as "He lived well who hid well."[1] It seems, then, that Descartes' art of living involves hiding and, according to the portrait of Descartes that Thomas Hibbs presents in this volume, Descartes' art of writing hides his preoccupation with the art of living. If we overlook the primacy of the question of the good life for Descartes, we risk obscuring "the unity in his various projects" (*25).[2] By discovering or restoring the centrality of this question, Hibbs finds the key to unraveling how Descartes combines his well-known antipathy toward the philosophical and theological tradition with his unduly neglected Socratism, which ties him irrevocably to that tradition. And because that tradition includes Christianity, Descartes' focus on the good life necessarily implicates him in theological matters, at which point his view of the good life slips out of focus or, better, at which point Descartes blurs our access to that view in its relation to Christian faith. Thus, we come to see the reason that the precise character of Descartes' understanding of the good life could be both central to his thought and yet neglected in contemporary scholarship.

Descartes exercised greater diligence in obscuring any tension or conflict with the Catholic Church than he did in concealing his attack on Aristotle, which he seemed eager to veil only insofar as he suspected it might offend those churchmen whose support he wanted.[3] Hibbs explores these themes with an impressive command of Descartes' published and unpublished writings, and although his portrait is not finished in every respect (e.g., he refrains from weighing in on the relation between the provisional and the final morality), he invites us to think anew about Descartes in relation to the fundamental issues of classical philosophy. I find it a most agreeable task to comment on his chapter—a task I see as requiring me neither to dissect Hibbs' portrait nor to provide an alternative. Instead, with these remarks I intend to probe the three focal points of Hibbs' chapter and to encourage further consideration along the same path he has cleared.

Hibbs divides his essay into three parts: "Recovering and Overcoming Socrates," "Descartes' New Science of Virtue," and "Theology, the Sovereign Good, and Ironic Philosophy." The three parts converge, and he integrates the central theme of each in a single sentence near the end: "In this way, Descartes' overcoming of Socrates, his new science of virtue, is simultaneously a strategy for bypassing the debate between Athens and Jerusalem" (*41). This formulation encapsulates the parts of the essay as neatly as one could hope. With the convergence of these three themes clearly in mind, let us proceed to a consideration of the main theme of each part of the essay.

THE NATURE OF CARTESIAN IRONY

It seems most appropriate to begin at the end and focus especially on the theme of irony. According to the argument, Descartes' "focus on the question of the best way of life" puts him irreconcilably at odds with the tradition of Christian faith (*39). Descartes habitually confines theology to dealing with mysteries that exceed our understanding and with the practical question of how to get to heaven. Thus neutered, theologians should have nothing to say about the proper concerns of the various arts and sciences, including philosophy, and are at best useful to Descartes for the approbation he hopes to win from them, inasmuch as ecclesiastical authority influences those not governed by reason. Hibbs leads us to see, nevertheless, that co-existence without conflict between Christian theology and Cartesian philosophy proves impossible because Descartes conceives the best way of life as to be achieved not through grace but by Descartes' own efforts. Philosophy as a way of life has become not just a pursuit but a possession, especially in the new science of nature (*40). In this Descartes distinguishes himself from Montaigne, whose more skeptical complacency does not present the same challenge. According to Hibbs, the *Meditations on First Philosophy* not only contains the principles of the new science of nature[4] but also advances "the articulation and realization of the best way of life" (*40). Descartes' confidence in his grasp of the human good enables him to avoid open engagement with theology. There is no gap in his philosophy that theology might fill, he has no taste for open confrontation, and therefore he limits himself to treating theology only ironically (*40–41).

The most difficult elements here concern the relation between the new science of nature and Descartes' science of virtue (a topic to which I return below). The first theme that demands attention is Descartes' irony, by which he keeps the Sorbonne theologians and others at bay. Whereas Socrates seems always to have been known for his irony, Descartes has avoided this reputation—or at least today Descartes is not so widely associated with irony. And this suggests his irony deserves closer attention. As Hibbs notes, Descartes praises Socrates for *candor* in confessing his ignorance and criticizes Aristotle for disingenuous pretensions to knowledge. In the third part of the *Discourse on Method*, likening himself inexplicitly but unmistakably to Socrates, Descartes describes the desire to combat his own reputation for wisdom, which he supposes may have arisen due to his "confessing more frankly" than is customary what he does not know and to his not "boasting of any doctrine."[5] In the same breath, he eschews irony and assures us that, "being proud" (*ayant le coeur assez bon*), he wishes not to be taken for something other than he is. On the same note, in the first part of the *Discourse*, he mentioned that he hoped everyone would be grateful for his frankness.[6] Descartes' irony occurs side by side with a celebration of sincerity that enables him to insinuate the lack of any need for irony, because everyone can—by means of the method—know the truth, or so it appears.[7]

This movement in Descartes' thought toward general enlightenment stands in some tension with the irony he directs at least toward the theologically minded. In what seems to be another striking allusion to Socrates (or Plato) in the sixth part of the *Discourse*, Descartes expresses his unwillingness to be completely forthcoming with the principles of the science of nature he has discovered. He complains about certain contemporaries who take Aristotle as their authority and attempt to use him to solve difficulties he never addressed. They are like ivy that not only can ascend no higher than the trees on which it depends but also tends not to remain at that height but often turns and descends. Perhaps Descartes has in mind theologians for whom Aristotle serves as the principal philosophical authority. Whoever they may be, Descartes says one can convince these people of nothing because "the obscurity of the distinctions and principles they use enables them to speak of all things as boldly as if they knew them, and to defend whatever they say."[8] They are like blind men, and to converse with them one would need to abandon the superiority afforded by sight and descend "to the bottom of some extremely dark cave" (*dans le fond de quelque cave fort obscure*).[9] Descartes' own principles are so clear and so evident that, were he to publish them, it would be like opening windows and letting daylight into the cellar. Descartes' enlightenment would be *sunlight* in the cave.

Three elements especially deserve attention here. First, the cave or cellar is not conceived as the natural or inescapable home of all educated people. It is the place to which a clear-sighted person must descend in order to compensate for the disadvantages afflicting these Aristotelians with "only mediocre minds."[10] Second, even when the daylight enters, these interlocutors will still see nothing, because their blindness does not result merely from the darkness of their location. Some people are blinded from within, and Descartes seems uninterested in reaching at least some of them. As he indicates in *Meditations*, Descartes demands a reader who has abandoned attachment to the senses and prior opinions; he does employ a kind of protreptic argument to lead his readers to methodical doubt, but even then he does not engage ordinary opinions so much as he undermines or incinerates them.[11] Third, Cartesian principles do at least provide the light of day for any mind free of all prejudices, which thus promises enlightenment to all who are willing to conduct their reason rightly. The *cave* may not be Plato's cave, but perhaps there is a cellar at the foundation of the edifice of the sciences as Descartes reconstructs them. If so, Descartes seems willing to let in the daylight rather than be in the position of needing to compel someone who has seen the sun to return to a darkened cellar. Metaphors aside, Descartes appears to prefer enlightenment to Platonic acquiescence concerning the limited openness of political life to knowledge.

To bring these remarks on irony to a point, I note that the light shed by Descartes' principles seems to be both for and not for everyone's benefit. After all, he did not publish *Le Monde* (the treatise containing these principles), although he advertises its existence in the sixth part of the *Discourse* as he explains his decision to reverse his prior resolution to publish it (a practical decision, incidentally, in flagrant violation of the second maxim of morality). Ultimately, he published the *Discourse* instead, which he presents as a story or a fable, the whole of which therefore participates in "the necessary indirection of storytelling."[12] In the *Discourse*, Descartes speaks ironically to the learned and at least affects frankness with his popular audience. By simulating (in some passages) the equality of all minds and dissimulating his own superiority, Descartes makes the extent of his irony much more difficult to discover; he seems to invite the reader to see through his irony much less than does Plato or Socrates. It seems less protreptic, and indeed in Hibbs' reading Descartes' refusal to take received opinion seriously implies a rejection of the genre of protreptic writing (*32). Even so, Hibbs emphasizes in the first part of his essay that Descartes is concerned to write in a manner conducive to provoking rather than enervating thought (*29). If Descartes does intend to do this, we could benefit from a more precise taxonomy of Cartesian readers. How many kinds of readers does Descartes envision, and what are his aims with each?

A few further observations may help clarify this question. It seems to me that Descartes has neither a strategy for nor any interest in enlivening the minds of the blind Aristotelians shuffling around in his cellar. This seems to be the force of Hibbs' appropriate emphasis on the use of irony to keep theology away from direct contact with philosophy, but the complexity and the range of Cartesian irony requires further consideration. At the least we should note that his irony pleases much more than does the Socratic variety. As Richard Kennington has observed, everybody enjoys the first sentence of the *Discourse*, whether he sees the irony or he does not.[13] If Locke is correct, pain moves us to change our condition but pleasure inclines us to stay as we are. Does Descartes exercise irony principally for our benefit or his own? Finally, in an intriguing passage in the first part of his paper, Hibbs connects irony to temporality and to method and claims that Descartes directs irony "only toward those unaware of the method or toward the former self of the narrator" (*30). Further elaboration of this claim would lead to interesting and helpful reflection on the particularity of Descartes' narrative and the universality of his intention (cf. *30).

THE SCIENCE OF NATURE AS EXTENSION

A second theme, which surfaces most clearly at the juncture of the first and second parts of Hibbs' essay, is the certainty of the new science of nature. Hibbs presents Descartes as dissatisfied with the zetetic conception of philosophy that appears to be embraced by Socrates or by Montaigne. "The key insight of Socrates' entire life, the awareness that made him wiser than others, provides for Descartes merely an occasion to underscore the defects of his own education" (*31). Hibbs shows beautifully how Descartes likens his own opponents to the sophists with whom Socrates contended (*31). My concern lies with the character of his surpassing Socrates. Hibbs quotes David Lachterman, who says that Cartesian method constrains its objects such that "their very intelligibility becomes identical with their susceptibility to methodical treatment."[14] One could find a great deal of support for the claim that Descartes thinks the essence of material beings is identical with their mathematically knowable features.

But perhaps this is part of his irony. Perhaps Descartes constrained the human *erôs* for knowledge of the whole to something more pedestrian and achievable (a suggestion that seems to be entertained but underdeveloped near the end of the essay). A steady will in the face of "the distracting effect of wonder"[15] may enable us to concentrate our energies on what we *can* know. We can satisfy the mind's desire to know at the same time that we satisfy the needs of the body, principally health, provided that we rigorously follow the method and do not get lost in search of first causes, those noble but to us barely knowable principles (*41). One can see the appearance of a version of this line of thinking in Locke's *Essay concerning Human Understanding*. Much as Locke does not think that natural science is genuinely demonstrable (and Locke knew of "the incomparable Mr. Newton"),[16] so Descartes might conceive his physics as a science that does not apprehend the real essence of material things. It might be instead a science constricted to that part of nature that is conformable to the human mind and subject to mastery, although that part (quantity) is understood *not* to be ultimate in things.

Francis Bacon seems to be the inspiration for this line of thinking. He criticized the ancients for flying too swiftly from consideration of a few particulars to first principles. He substituted a slow and steady ascent in the direction of the *summa lex* in all of nature, even if one had to admit that the first and most universal principle(s) remained beyond our grasp.

For his part, Descartes speaks similarly in the *Rules for the Direction of the Mind*. Rule Eight announces the need to limit investigation to those things that can be intuited by our intellect. Knowledge of the limits of achievable inquiry "is just as much knowledge as that which reveals the nature of the thing," and it so "abundantly" satisfies curiosity that it would be irrational to inquire further.[17] The proto-critique of pure reason that Descartes sketches in this rule is accompanied by this assertion: "We should then turn to the things themselves; and we should deal with these only in so far as they are within the reach of the intellect."[18] In this manner Descartes sketches the combination of a limited science of nature with the abundant satisfaction of the human desire to know.

It is difficult to draw definitive conclusions from Descartes' early, incomplete, and unpublished *Rules*,[19] but we are compelled to wonder about the extent to which Descartes regarded his science of nature as the fulfillment of the classical *erôs* to know the first principles of nature. In one reading, Descartes gives himself a knowable object that enables him to pass beyond the skepticism of Socrates and Montaigne, and he *wittingly* ignores and invites the rest of us to ignore any desire to know the whole. We find satisfaction in achieving a human science in place of the frustrations accompanying the apparently vain pursuit of the divine science Aristotle described—wisdom through knowledge of the first and most universal causes. In this interpretation, the Cartesian life of the mind consists in the carrying out of the project described in the *Discourse*, and in view of the image of philosophy as a tree, Descartes himself would miss out on the principal benefit of philosophy.[20]

In another reading, this is all part of Descartes' irony. He distracts most of those who are attracted to knowing with this intoxicating tale of the ability to comprehend all of nature, while he hides from them the fact that he offers comprehension only of an abstraction—quantity. This enables him to guarantee some success in the pursuit—namely, success for those whose desire to know is satisfied by the knowledge of laws of nature, which serve as rules of operation for the expansion of power, without insight into the nature of things. To the extent that the new science of nature becomes the source of untold humanitarian benefits, Descartes is in a position to give philosophy the reputation of being beneficial to ordinary people and thereby to reorder the relation between philosophy and non-philosophers (society or the political community).[21] In this reading, we are forced to take very seriously the distinction in the sixth part of the

Discourse that Descartes makes between himself and any followers who adopt and execute his method. Descartes, the inventor of the method that others merely follow, withdraws behind yet another mask to live a life he declines to reveal. In either of these readings, we are more likely to overlook philosophy entirely.[22] The philosophical life, as classically conceived, is discredited by comparison to the new human possibility: the scientific life, which emerges as the successful-because-humanitarian offspring of philosophy. Philosophy as search for wisdom recedes from view. In Descartes' understanding of his own life, does *scientific* wisdom in this sense displace philosophical pursuit of wisdom in the classical sense?

THE CHARACTER OF DESCARTES' PHILOSOPHICAL LIFE

The new science of nature is intimately connected to the new science of virtue, as Hibbs has argued persuasively, and for this reason my remarks in the last section have already begun to bleed over into this one. The precise character of the connection between natural science and virtue remains somewhat elusive. Descartes speaks again and again in the *Discourse* of the contentment, tranquility, and happiness that characterizes his life, which either is the life of an inquirer after the truth (that is, a philosopher in the traditional sense, as the fourth maxim of the provisional morality tends to suggest)[23] or is, as Hibbs has presented it, the life of a man who possesses wisdom (*40). If it is the latter, could a philosopher be satisfied or content with a life contemplating the simple necessities that matter must obey—matter understood as extension and as excluding goods or ends, which is how Descartes characterizes the principles of his physics?[24] As much as Descartes promises that his new science of nature will lead (in the future) to technical devices for the mastery of nature, he also stresses his own current satisfaction even in the absence of those practical benefits. He does not mourn his inability to enter the technological Promised Land. Is Descartes genuinely contemplative of nature as constrained by method? Is he genuinely tranquil or just tranquilized?

Alternatively, is the object of his contemplation something more traditional and more Socratic than might first meet the eye? I have in mind here the Baconian precedent. Bacon admits that the new method or the *New Organon* does not generate itself and does not justify its own goodness. His new method is the only adequate method for dealing with nature, but "the logic now in use" is very properly applied to civil matters.[25] That is,

Bacon's argument with his predecessors as to the goodness of the new approach to nature is an argument that cannot be had scientifically but must be had by appeal to traditional political and moral categories. Descartes' *Discourse* has essentially the same nature: a civil or popular argument in defense of the goodness of a new method.

Perhaps, then, Descartes turns out to be rather like his philosophical predecessors after all. The argument of the *Discourse* (most emphatically its sixth part) does not take its shape from the new method or from the provisional morality (except possibly from the fourth maxim); it is instead a prudential, dialogical, even classical bit of reasoning. In order to engage in it, Descartes must take seriously, at least provisionally, the opinions of the non-Cartesians among whom he lives. The sixth part of the *Discourse* addresses the reasons that have made him write,[26] and so this text concerns his end as a philosophical author. To put all of this in the form of a question, are the good life and the new science of virtue devoted to contemplation, technical benefits, hedonism in the Lockean sense, or what? What is the end animating Descartes?[27]

NOTES

1. See Descartes' Letter to Mersenne, April 1634, in *The Philosophical Writings of Descartes*, vol. III, trans. John Cottingham, Robert Stoothoff, Dugald Murdoch, and Anthony Kenny (Cambridge: Cambridge University Press, 1991), 43 (hereinafter cited as CSM-K, with page numbers; the first two volumes of this work are cited as CSM, with volume and page numbers). See also *Oeuvres de Descartes*, vol. I, ed. Charles Adam and Paul Tannery (Paris: J. Vrin, 1996), 286.2–3. (Subsequent references to Descartes' works in this edition will identify volume, page, and line numbers.) Descartes' motto reflects a sentiment famously expressed in *Cogitationes privatae: -sic ego, hoc mundi theatrum conscensurus, in quo hactenus spectator exstiti, larvatus prodeo* (thus, about to set out on this theater of the world, in which hitherto I have been a spectator, I go forth masked) (*Oeuvres de Descartes* X.213.5–7).

2. Page numbers cited parenthetically in the body of this paper indicate a reference to Hibbs' contribution to this volume, "The Virtue of Science and the Science of Virtue."

3. For example, see the famous Letter to Mersenne, 28 January 1641 (CSM-K, 173; *Oeuvres de Descartes* III.297.31–298.7). Compare Descartes, Letter to Mersenne, 11 November 1640 (CSM-K, 157; *Oeuvres de Descartes* III.233.15–26).

4. See the letters cited in previous note.

5. René Descartes, *Discourse on Method*, trans. Richard Kennington, ed. Pamela Kraus and Frank Hunt (Newburyport, MA: Focus Publishing, 2007), 31–32; *Oeuvres de Descartes* VI.30.21–28.

6. *Discourse*, 17; *Oeuvres de Descartes* VI.4.18–20.

7. "In this I perhaps will not appear too vain, if you consider that since there is only one truth concerning each thing, whoever finds it knows as much as can be known about it,

and that a child, for example, instructed in arithmetic, having made an addition according to the rules, can be assured of having found, regarding the sum, all that the human mind can find" (*Discourse*, 26–27; *Oeuvres de Descartes* VI.21.6–13). Hibbs also notes the egalitarian dimensions of Descartes' virtue of generosity (*37).

8. *Discourse*, 53; *Oeuvres de Descartes* VI.70.28–71.1.

9. *Discourse*, 54; *Oeuvres de Descartes* VI.71.5. Kennington is not the only translator to render the French *cave* as "cave," thereby suggesting Plato's cave. French translations of the *Republic* typically use *caverne* because *cave* means not "cave" but "cellar," as Hibbs has it (*31). Still, the connection with Plato's image does not depend upon the word *cave* but on the character of our sight and our blindness. In fact, Descartes' substitution of *cave* for *caverne* suggests that the darkness at issue is not natural but somehow man-made. Much as ivy climbs no higher than the top of the tree and often descends after having reached the top, Descartes' contemporary Aristotelians end in obscurities that derive from their own misuse of Aristotle. The differences between Plato's image and Descartes' image help reveal Cartesian irony more clearly.

10. *Discourse*, 53; *Oeuvres de Descartes* VI.70.28.

11. In the Letter to the Sorbonne Theology Faculty, attached to the *Meditations*, Descartes says that his arguments "require a mind which is completely free from preconceived opinions and which can easily detach itself from involvement with the senses" (*requirunt mentem a præjudiciis plane liberam, & quae se ipsam a sensuum consortio facile subducat*). CSM 2:5; *Oeuvres de Descartes* VII.4.28–30. In the sixth meditation Descartes does engage ordinary opinion under the label "the teaching of nature," but he has by this point eviscerated it as a source of knowledge for human beings; rather, certain knowledge begins from the light of nature (see the third meditation, ninth paragraph). The teaching of nature remains relevant as an uncertain guide for practical affairs.

12. Glenn Arbery, d'Alzon Visiting Professor at Assumption College, used this phrase in a lecture on Tolstoy's *The Death of Ivan Ilych* to emphasize the fact that even this novel, which seems overtly didactic, remains a novel in which the author speaks only through the narrative. The clarity with which Descartes expresses parts of his message should not induce us to lose sight of his pervasive indirection. (For his comments on histories and fables, see fifth, seventh, and eighth paragraphs of *Discourse*, part 1.)

13. Richard Kennington, "Descartes's *Discourse on Method*," in *Discourse*, 61.

14. David Lachterman, *The Ethics of Geometry: A Genealogy of Modernity* (New York: Routledge, 1989), p. 175. Hibbs quotes this passage on page *32.

15. Richard Velkley, "Masks of Mastery: Richard Kennington on Modern Origins," *Political Science Reviewer* 31 (2002): 21. I am greatly indebted to Velkley's essay for the central idea discussed in the rest of this paragraph and for his interpretation of Kennington's published and unpublished work.

16. John Locke, *An Essay concerning Human Understanding*, ed. Peter Nidditch (Oxford: Oxford University Press, 1975), p. 10.

17. CSM 1:28, 30; *Oeuvres de Descartes* X.392.10–13, X.393.13–21, X.396.21–25.

18. CSM 1:32; *Oeuvres de Descartes* X.399.6–7.

19. "Between the *Regulae* and the composition of the *Discours* in 1636 Descartes all but completed the physical treatise, *Le Monde*. . . . It is in this pre-*Discours* and post-*Regulae* interval that he most probably turned to the writings of Bacon in which he found the stress on utility, the arts as model of beneficence, and mastery of nature, all of which are absent in the *Regulae* and *Le Monde*, and thematic in the conception of philosophy in

his first publication, the *Discours*. The structure of the Cartesian philosophy is best understood as the attempt to unite two originally diverse lines of thinking, the mathematical science of nature of the *Regulae* and *Le Monde* and the utility-mastery theme of Baconian origin." Richard Kennington, "Descartes and Mastery of Nature," in *Organism, Medicine, and Metaphysics*, ed. Stuart F. Spicker (Dordrecht: D. Reidel, 1978), 210.

20. Preface to the French edition of *Principles of Philosophy* (CSM 1:186; *Oeuvres de Descartes* IX.14.23–15.5).

21. See Kennington, "Descartes and Mastery of Nature," 201–23; Richard Kennington, "René Descartes," in *On Modern Origins*, ed. Pamela Kraus and Frank Hunt (Lanham, MD: Lexington Books, 2004), 187–204.

22. See Velkley, "Masks of Mastery," 9.

23. Descartes speaks of "three or four" maxims. The first three maxims guide action rather directly, but the fourth stands on a different plane insofar as it involves the choice of a life devoted to the pursuit of truth. That life of inquiry is presented as if it were identical to the resolute attachment to the method (mentioned several times in the first two parts of the *Discourse*). It is this attachment that leads him to embrace the first three maxims. As Kennington was known to say, Descartes' provisional morality incorporates a non-provisional conception of the good. For another estimation of the non-provisional dimensions of the morality, see Robert Spaemann, "La morale provisoire de Descartes," *Archives de Philosophie* 35 (1972): 353–67.

24. See *Discourse*, part 5, and the sixth meditation.

25. See the end of the long first paragraph in *The Great Instauration*. In various writings, including the *Distributio Operis* (or "Plan of the Work," published with *The New Organon*), Bacon asserts the necessity for an argument on the nature of the arts and sciences in order to win faith in his new method. *The Advancement of Learning*, in its two versions, is as close as Bacon came to providing the missing argument.

26. *Discourse*, 15; *Oeuvres de Descartes* VI.1.16.

27. See Letter to Princess Elizabeth, 18 August 1645 (CSM-K, 261; *Oeuvres de Descartes* IV.275.1–13). In that letter Descartes says our final end may be either the supreme good at which we aim or the contentment that results from possessing it.

4

MORE CARTESIAN THAN DESCARTES

REFLECTIONS ON SPINOZA IN THE SPIRIT OF TOCQUEVILLE

Samuel Goldman

I N THE OPENING CHAPTERS OF THE SECOND VOLUME of *Democracy in America*, Alexis de Tocqueville identifies two ways of thinking that hold special appeal in a democratic age. Both methods of thinking have roots in the radical Enlightenment of the seventeenth century, but each has a different national constituency and different political implications. The first position that Tocqueville discusses is Cartesianism, which he finds to be particularly strong among Americans. The second is pantheism, which thrives on the Continent, especially in France.

Although he describes each tendency as a philosophy, Tocqueville is less interested in technical arguments than in the unarticulated background assumptions we would today describe as culture. The Americans, he observes, do not read Descartes and may not even know the great man's name. Despite or because of this ignorance, however, "America is one of the countries in the world . . . where the precepts of Descartes are best followed."[1] The French, on the other hand, do read philosophy. But Tocqueville attributes the influence of pantheism mostly to popular literature.[2]

A number of scholars have examined Tocqueville's analysis of Cartesianism and pantheism as features of modern democratic culture.[3] Much less attention has been paid to their common point of departure in seventeenth-century philosophy, which I intend to address in this essay. In what follows, I argue that the ideas Tocqueville describes as "pantheism" have their origin in Spinoza's attempt to apply the "precepts of Descartes" more rigorously and widely than Descartes himself was willing to do. Following Tocqueville, I also suggest that this effort has dangerous implications for democracy—among them, an erosion of the principles of personal freedom and responsibility on which a free society depends.

PANTHEISM AND THE PRECEPTS OF DESCARTES

Tocqueville's conception of Cartesianism has little to do with doctrines about the relation between thought and extension, optics, or geometry that historians of philosophy group under the name. Instead, Tocqueville identifies Cartesianism as a set of normative "precepts"—or directions for conducting the mind—that Descartes articulated most dramatically in the *Meditations on First Philosophy*. The theme of these precepts is doubt. By doubting every claim to truth that he could not verify, Tocqueville observes, Descartes' achievement was "in philosophy properly so-called, [to] abolish the received formulas, destroy the empire of traditions, and overturn every authority."[4]

Tocqueville acknowledges that Americans are not interested in "philosophy properly so-called." They apply the Cartesian approach without being aware of it, because they find it "in themselves" rather than in books.[5] Under their untutored but powerful "philosophic method," the Americans strive "to escape from the spirit of system; from the yoke of habits, from family maxims, from class opinions, and up to a certain point, from national prejudices; to take tradition only as information, and current facts only as a useful study for doing otherwise and better; to seek the reason for things by themselves and in themselves alone, to strive for a result without letting themselves be chained to the means, and to see through the form to the foundation."[6] The result is a kind of cognitive autarky that leads to a highly individualistic conception of virtue: "Each then undertakes to be self-sufficient and find his glory in making for himself beliefs that are his own about all things."[7]

Despite their extraordinary freedom from tradition and prejudice, however, Tocqueville suggests that the Americans operate under certain checks that prevent them from applying their philosophic method to every sphere of life. The most important is religion, which both inspires and limits the precepts of Descartes.

Although Descartes professed to be a faithful Roman Catholic, Tocqueville notes that his doubt of authority is consistent with the Protestant Reformation. In his view, Luther and Descartes "made use of the same method."[8] But Luther and Descartes did not apply their doubt universally. Instead, they limited it to particular issues. The Protestant theologian Luther called into question the religious authorities but not the philosophical or political ones. The Catholic philosopher Descartes called into question the philosophical authorities but not the religious or political ones. The Americans seem to offer a third possibility and call into question social and political hierarchies while they leave intact the authority of religion. Tocqueville suggests that universal respect for religion prevents Americans' general anti-authoritarianism from turning into subversive anti-nomianism.

The religious check on doubt does not obtain among the French. In fact, "this same method [of doubt] is followed more rigorously and applied more often by the French than by the Americans." Tocqueville means that the French do not doubt only religion (like Luther), only philosophy (like Descartes), or only political and social authorities (like the Americans). Rather, they doubt all of these at the same time, challenging every source of authority. As Tocqueville vividly puts it, the Americans are led by the "precepts of Descartes" to "see through the form to the foundation" but are inclined leave that foundation intact. The French, on the other hand, try to change or abolish the foundation itself. Rather than discarding only useless prejudices or burdensome authorities, they use their philosophic method to "attack *all* ancient things and open the way to *all* new ones." This is why the French are an essentially revolutionary people, while the American Revolution was basically aberrant—at least in Tocqueville's view.[9]

Despite the rigor and consistency of their doubt, however, Tocqueville declines to describe the French as Cartesians. A few chapters later, he suggests that their ethos is best understood as "pantheism." What is the connection between these approaches?

Tocqueville's main discussion of pantheism occurs in volume 2, chapter 7, of *Democracy in America*. "It cannot be denied," Tocqueville claims, "that pantheism has made great progress in our day. The writings of a portion of Europe visibly bear its imprint. The Germans introduce it into philosophy, the French into literature." Tocqueville does not name any of the German philosophers or French literary men who are responsible for pantheism's "great progress." It is most likely that he had in mind the Young Hegelians in Germany, as well as French writers on philosophy and politics such as Alphonse de Lamartine and Edgar Quinet.[10] Tocqueville would have been familiar with these contemporary writers. But behind them lurks Spinoza, whose name was virtually synonymous with pantheism, and with democracy—at least up to the French Revolution.[11]

It is unlikely that Tocqueville had intimate knowledge of Spinoza's philosophy, but this by no means discredits his observations about the influence of pantheism. Like Cartesianism, pantheism as discussed in *Democracy in America* is not primarily a learned doctrine. Rather, it is a worldview available to every normally constituted man and woman. Yet the defining feature of the pantheist attitude is not doubt, as in Cartesianism. Instead, it is a longing for metaphysical unity that is encouraged by the equality of social and economic conditions that characterizes democracy. As Tocqueville puts it:

> As conditions become more equal and each man in particular becomes more like all the others, weaker and smaller, one gets used to no longer viewing citizens so as to consider only the people; one forgets individuals so as to think only of the species. [¶] In these times, the human mind loves to embrace a host of diverse objects at once; it constantly aspires to be able to link a multitude of consequences to a single cause. [¶] The idea of unity obsesses [the mind]; it seeks on all sides, and when it believes it has found it, it willingly wraps it in its bosom and rests with it. Not only does it come to discover only one creation and one Creator in the world; this first division of things still bothers it, and it willingly seeks to enlarge and simplify its thought by enclosing God and the universe within a single whole.[12]

This passage brilliantly connects social context to philosophical and ultimately theological conclusions. According to Tocqueville, the tendency of democracy to level distinctions of rank, fortune, and talent makes people ever more alike. Due to their similarity, individuals decline in importance. They are replaced as objects of political reflection by the people, or by the whole human race. This aggregating tendency carries over to consideration of the causes of human action. Personal goals and limited causes become less visible. In their places rise national or even universal aims, and the most general causes.

According to Tocqueville, democrats tend to reason that a world dedicated to a single purpose must have a single Creator and governor. Thus democracy encourages theology or discourse about God. Theology, however, is a complicated matter. Citizens of democracy, therefore, are inclined to seek a simplified version that suits both their relatively low intellectual level and their taste for general ideas. In Tocqueville's view, this search is resolved in the concept of a God that is at the same time cause and effect, Creator and creation. In short, the democratic mind tends toward "pantheism"—the doctrine that God and the world are the same thing.

Although there are earlier precedents, the term "pantheism" was popularized by the eighteenth-century English rationalist John Toland to designate a philosophical sect ostensibly inspired by Spinoza. Toland claimed that, like Spinoza, the pantheists reject the biblical doctrine of a transcendent, personal deity in favor of a single immanent substance. They conclude from this that all things are in some sense one.[13] Again, without acknowledging the historical background, Tocqueville expresses the basic thought remarkably well. Pantheism is a "philosophic system according to which all things material and immaterial, visible and invisible that the world includes are considered as no more than diverse parts of an immense being that alone remains eternal in the midst of the continual change and incessant transformation of all that composes it."[14] This "immense being" is the God of the democratic age.

For Toland and Spinoza, pantheism was what might be called an esoteric doctrine. This was not only because it was theologically heterodox and therefore likely to attract unfavorable attention or even violent persecution. They reserved pantheism to a minority also and more profoundly because they believed it was accessible only to the most advanced minds. According to Spinoza, the majority of human beings were unable to understand his philosophy. For this majority, he acknowledges, the untruths of revealed religion may have some utility as an encouragement to moral behavior.

Tocqueville, by contrast, suggests that the limitation of pantheism to an intellectual elite depended on intellectual and educational inequalities that were characteristic of an aristocratic age. Since the seventeenth century, he observes, what were once esoteric teachings have steadily entered the public sphere. At first, this vulgarization was a movement within philosophy itself, as writers like Voltaire strove to reach a broader audience than their predecessors had done. By Tocqueville's own day, the trend had gone even farther: the people of France, or at least the middle class, got their philosophy from novels rather than from learned treatises.[15] Extrapolating from Tocqueville, I argue below that Spinoza's failure to anticipate this transformation is among the major limitations of his political thought. To preview, he does not see the challenge that pantheism poses to political freedom because he presumes that its appeal is restricted to a small minority.

If pantheism were really so limited, Tocqueville suggests, it wouldn't be a matter of concern. The problem is that it has become both available and appealing to many. Discouraged by the equality of conditions, democratic citizens take solace in the doctrine of causal unity. Rather than blaming themselves for their failure to achieve personal distinction, they are eager to believe that all results are determined by immutable, impersonal causes. For this reason, Tocqueville concludes, "such a system, although it destroys human individuality, or rather because it destroys it, will have secret charms for men who live in democracy: all their intellectual habits prepare them to conceive it and set them on the way to adopt it. It naturally attracts their imagination and fixes it; it nourishes the haughtiness and flatters the laziness of their minds."[16]

The association with homogeneity and laziness distinguishes pantheism from Americans' Cartesianism. Because of their emphasis on doubt, the precepts of Descartes encourage their holders to think of themselves as free subjects responsible for the truth—or at least the efficacy—of beliefs that they develop for themselves. Indeed, this "glory" is available to every individual, however lowly his social position. Pantheism, by contrast, denies the individual the glory of finding and confirming his own beliefs. Rather than fostering responsible agents, it leads people to see themselves as embedded within impersonal nature and subject to the same causal laws as mere things.

So the precepts of Descartes turn out to be compatible with the energetic, associative individuality of the Americans. This seems to be the reason that Tocqueville describes America as the country where those precepts are applied "best," if not most rigorously. The French, by contrast, are led by their pantheistic beliefs to renounce civic action in favor of merely private gratification. This makes them susceptible to the condition of infantilizing dependence that Tocqueville describes as "soft despotism." Later on in volume 2, Tocqueville describes the tutelary state characteristic of soft despotism as an "immense being." The term is the same that he used for the God of the pantheists.[17]

In addition to its ethical and political differences, then, pantheism is distinct from "Cartesianism" in its relation to religion. Although it includes the Greek word for "god" (*theos*), pantheism does not hesitate to criticize theistic principles that Americans' unwitting appropriation of Descartes left untouched. In America, as Tocqueville documents at length, practical Cartesianism is compatible with a fragmented but still recognizably Christian religious landscape. In Europe, on the other hand, the writers he seems to have in mind were publicly associated with experiments in non-revealed, anti-clerical forms of spirituality.

Moreover, pantheism seems incompatible with the precepts of Descartes on the level of epistemology. In principle, the Cartesian believes nothing that he can't prove to his own satisfaction. This may leave him with relatively few beliefs, but those that survive the test of doubt will be secure and intimately connected with his own perceptions and judgments. The pantheist, on the other hand, believes something that necessarily exceeds his own experience. Pantheism, in Tocqueville's account, involves a kind of metaphysical credulity that parallels citizens' excessive trust in the state.

For all these reasons, Cartesianism and pantheism look like very different forms of "philosophy." Yet Tocqueville indicates that they are intellectually connected. The French are especially susceptible to pantheism. The reason, however, is not that they rejected the precepts of Descartes but, rather, that they applied those precepts more widely and less well than the Americans. Even if he was unaware of it, the connection that Tocqueville draws between too-rigorous Cartesianism and pantheism mirrors the historical relationship between Descartes and Spinoza. In the next section, therefore, I turn to these master thinkers of the seventeenth century.[18]

DESCARTES ON DOUBT

The classic document of Descartes' method is the *Meditations on First Philosophy*, which Descartes published in 1641. Although the doctrines of formal Cartesianism are more fully elaborated elsewhere, it is in the *Meditations* that we find Descartes' precepts applied most radically and vividly.

The *Meditations* tell the story of a certain "I"—the stylized narrator who resembles but should not be identified with the real Descartes—concerned about the possibility of knowing anything. Reflecting the ways in which error creeps into our minds, the narrator determines that "once in my life all things are fundamentally to be demolished and that I have to begin again from the first foundations if I were to desire ever to stabilize something firm and lasting in the sciences."[19] This demolition is be achieved by the application of doubt. More precisely, the narrator proposes to reject "all my opinions if I shall have found any reason for doubting in each one," leaving only those propositions that are absolutely certain.[20]

The narrator quickly discovers that tradition and even his own senses give ample reason for doubt. All beliefs founded upon them are therefore to be rejected (at least provisionally). Yet it appears that "arithmetic, geometry and others of this kind—which treat only of the simplest and maximally general things and which care little about whether these would be in the nature of things or not—contain something certain and indubitable. For whether I would be awake or sleeping, two and three added together are five, and a square has no more than four sides."[21]

But it turns out that even the truths that obtain in dreams are not immune to doubt. For it is possible that our cognitive faculties are so flawed that we only *think* 2+3=5, when in fact 2+3=4. This possibility seems absurd. Yet the narrator adverts to the "old opinion that there is a God who can do all things, and by whom I, as such as I exist, have been created."[22] If an omnipotent God created him, the narrator reasons, it is possible that he made him in such a way as to be radically susceptible to error. In that case, even the principles of logic and mathematics would be dubitable.

The narrator goes on to acknowledge that the prospect of a deceiver God is incompatible with another "old opinion" about God—that God is good. He therefore proposes an alternative possibility: "that not the optimal God— the font of truth—, but rather some malign genius—and the same one most highly powerful and most highly cunning—, has put all his industriousness therein that he might deceive me."[23] This hypothesis—the so-called evil genius scenario—is among the most dramatic moves in the history of modern philosophy. For it allows Descartes to apply the radical doubt implied by God's omnipotence *without* directly questioning God's goodness.

For some readers, these passages show that Descartes' method was a kind of revolution against the doctrine of divine omnipotence. If Descartes could overcome even this form of doubt, the argument goes, he would have proved that human reason has no need of transcendent guidance. The basis of this overcoming turns out to be the so-called cogito. By showing that even a malicious Creator could not make one doubt one's own existence in the activity of thinking, Descartes is said to have identified a new, purely secular ground of knowledge—and thus, as the first lines of the *Meditations* indicate, for the sciences.[24]

The problem with this interpretation is that Descartes explicitly rejects it. In the fifth meditation, the narrator makes the famous argument that we cannot be deceived concerning the most fundamental things only if we are the creations of a perfect God. These fundamental things include one's own existence as a thinking being, that is, the cogito. In a way, then, theology proves to be the ground of all other knowledge.

The dispute between scholars who read Descartes as a pioneering secularist and those who see his thought as continuous in important ways with scholasticism is too intricate to engage here. The important thing, for the present purpose, is the mutual dependence in Descartes' *official* doctrine between God and the human subject. According to that doctrine, my individuality is guaranteed by the necessity of the I engaged in the act of thinking. But the reality of the cogito is guaranteed by the omnipotence and goodness of God. For without this guarantee, the principle of noncontradiction need not apply. In this case, indeed, I might think without existing—as unthinkable as that is. One might say, on Descartes' argument, that the proposition "I am" is thus tenable only as an expression of religious commitment. At the same time that it gives me an epistemological first principle, then, this religious commitment gives me an irreducible significance within a normatively inflected scheme of Creation.

So Tocqueville was onto something when he stressed the compatibility between the precepts of Descartes, appropriately limited in matters theological, and the personal initiative to which nineteenth-century Americans devoted themselves. The Americans, Tocqueville suggests, are able to pursue their "self-interest well-understood" because they follow Descartes by looking inside themselves—by which means they discover souls in immediate connection with God. This connection endows them with the conviction that they are free in their thoughts and actions, but it also implies a responsibility to think and act rightly in the eyes of their maker. This balance of freedom and responsibility allows the Americans to doubt without becoming revolutionary. Put differently, it leaves intact a religious foundation for civil society.

Yet there is a well-known epistemological problem with this theologico-political synthesis: the existence and perfection of God are not known to us immediately. On the contrary, they are conclusions we must reach by using our reason. But reason itself is suspect, in Descartes' argument. For even the principles that seem clearest and most distinct—those of mathematics—can be called into doubt by the evil genius scenario. We are relieved from this doubt by knowledge of our divine origin. We cannot be certain of this origin, however, until we know that God exists and is perfect. And we cannot know that God exists and is perfect unless we have confidence in our reason. In short, we appear to be caught in a vicious circle.

One way out of the circle is to admit that God is an object of faith rather than knowledge. The trouble with this admission is that it contradicts Descartes' central precept: doubt of uncertain beliefs irrespective of their source. As an admirer of Descartes' project, Spinoza thought that he had a better solution. This was to redirect doubt from what seems clear and distinct (the principles of logic and mathematics) to the sources of doubt of itself. If we reject the old opinion that God is the omnipotent Creator, Spinoza reasoned, we don't have to worry about being misbegotten creatures. And if we don't worry about being misbegotten creatures, we needn't be concerned about the certainty of our reason. By applying Descartes' "precepts" to religious matters that Descartes himself avoided, in other words, Spinoza proposed to liberate himself from doubt. In the process, he liberated himself from the nexus of transcendent theism and human individuality that Tocqueville would identify as crucial to political freedom.[25]

DOUBTING DOUBT

The starting point for this argument is the *Principles of Cartesian Philosophy* (*PCP*), which was completed in 1663 and became the only book that Spinoza published in his own name. Although it is ostensibly an exposition *more geometrico* of Descartes' *Principles of Philosophy*, Spinoza's *PCP* is actually a wide-ranging interpretation and critique of the master. The discussion begins in a way that seems closer to *Meditations* than to the *Principles*: "Why Descartes doubted everything, the way in which he laid the solid foundations of the sciences, and finally, the means by which he freed himself from all doubt." According to Spinoza, the reasons that Descartes doubted everything were four: (1) to put aside all prejudice, (2) to discover the foundations on which everything should be built, (3) to uncover the cause of error, and (4) to understand everything clearly and distinctly.[26] Although it is unlikely that Tocqueville ever read it, this is as clear an account of the "precepts" of Descartes as anyone has ever given.

But there is something odd, Spinoza believes, about the way Descartes brought God into this process. On the one hand, he agrees with Descartes that we cannot be certain of anything until we have a clear and distinct idea of God. On the other hand, Descartes' doubt seems to trap him in a vicious circle. We need God to guarantee the accuracy of clear and distinct ideas. But we can't do this unless we first have a clear and distinct idea of the divine nature. On Spinoza's interpretation, Descartes called everything into doubt "not indeed like a Sceptic [*sic*] whose sole aim is to doubt, but to free his mind from all prejudice so that he might finally discover the firm and unshakable foundations of the sciences."[27] In order to reach the goal, therefore, a rigorous Cartesian would need to subject ideas about God to a degree of scrutiny that Descartes himself resisted.

Spinoza pursues his goal by ignoring the possibility that man was created with such a nature that it is difficult or impossible for him to recognize clear and distinct ideas. The omission is unannounced and unexplained— and for this reason provides a crucial clue about the intention of the work. The *PCP* is not simply a reconstruction of what Descartes actually said. Rather, it seems to be an argument for what he should or would have said if he were not so impressed by old opinions about God.[28]

In place of doubt rooted in traditional beliefs about Creation, Spinoza presents two possible views of the relation between our knowledge and God. On the first argument, we are unable to doubt clear and distinct ideas as such. Instead, we are able to doubt only our memory of the way in which they were deduced. It seems that Spinoza has in mind something like the ability to repeat one of Euclid's theorems without understanding its proof. So long as we don't have the deduction before us, we need God to guarantee the correspondence of our memories to the truth. When we actually confront the proof, however, we have no need of God: our innate ability to recognize clarity and distinctness kicks in. In this view, the evil genius might be a problem for lazy schoolboys—or humanists who've forgotten whatever they once knew of geometry and mathematics. But it is not a problem for a serious philosopher.[29]

Spinoza admits that "some" do not find this argument acceptable. Without saying who these doubters might be, he goes on to admit that certainty is impossible so long as we acknowledge the slightest possibility that God is our arbitrary and omnipotent Creator. So we don't just need to secure the veracity of clear and distinct ideas as such. In a second argument, he suggests that we also need a specific clear and distinct idea:

> Such a conception of God as so disposes us that it is not as easy for us to think that God is a deceiver as that he is not a deceiver, a conception that compels us to affirm that he is supremely truthful. When we have formed such an idea, the reason for doubting mathematical truths will be removed. For in whatever direction we now turn the mind's eye with purpose of doubting one of these truths, we shall not find anything that itself does not make us conclude that this truth is most certain, just as was the case with regard to our existence.[30]

Spinoza does not explain in detail in the *PCP* what is involved in such a conception of God. That may be because his answer is so disturbing: such a God is not an intentional Creator. For Spinoza, the nature of God is to be strictly deduced from certain principles of mathematics and logic. As a result, he is deprived of the will and understanding implied by Descartes, and which (from Spinoza's point of view) made doubt inescapable.[31] This redirection of doubt from science to religion is what I mean by describing Spinoza as more Cartesian than Descartes.

Before we consider the pantheistic replacement that Spinoza proposed for Descartes' relatively traditional monotheism, it's worth considering an objection: What made Spinoza so confident that his principles of reasoning were applicable to all matters, including God? As the historian of early modern philosophy Richard Popkin has pointed out, there is little need to speculate about what Spinoza might have said.[32] We have a rather direct answer in Spinoza's response to Albert Burgh, a former student of his who had a personal crisis and converted to Roman Catholicism. In September 1675, Burgh wrote to his old teacher demanding that Spinoza justify his heterodoxy. Given the testimony of so many saints and martyrs, wasn't religion worth approaching with some humility?[33]

Certainly not, Spinoza responds. For he knows what is true, in just the same way as he knows that the three angles of a triangle are equal to 180 degrees. No one could possibly doubt this unless they dream of "unclean spirits who inspire us with false ideas as if they were true." But the only reason to take such dreams seriously, Spinoza suggests, is that they are encouraged by the church Burgh had joined—and to which Descartes professed allegiance. Official Cartesianism can never escape uncertainty and error because it exempts the central teaching of that church (that is, that God is an omnipotent Creator) from scrutiny and even takes that central teaching seriously as a philosophical hypothesis. He, Spinoza, had been able to reach Descartes' goal because he dismissed those teachings as the nonsense that they were.[34]

For Spinoza, then, Descartes was right to say that "arithmetic, geometry and other subjects of this kind . . . contain something certain and indubitable."[35] In keeping with Descartes' foundationalism, he proposed to develop, on their basis, an idea of God that could be embraced with equal certainty, and that would therefore ground all other knowledge. But this idea of God is very different from the relatively conventional God endorsed by Descartes. It is one of the most extravagant and provocative metaphysics teachings ever proposed.

SPINOZA'S GOD

Book 1 of Spinoza's *Ethics* does no less than deduce from first principles a clear and distinct idea of God. In the course of just a few pages, Spinoza provides us with what he regards as irrefutable arguments that God exists and that he is omnipotent, eternal, and the origin of all finite creatures. It is not only, as Spinoza argued in the *PCP*, that nothing can be *known* without understanding God. Without God, nothing could possibly exist: "What is, is in God, and nothing can be or be conceived without God."[36] This proposition is the starting point for Toland's later description of Spinoza's thought as pantheism.[37]

The key feature of Spinoza's God is monism—which is the view that there is only one Being or "substance." According to Spinoza, this "substance" is identical to God. Spinoza does not deny that there appear to be many different kinds of beings. He argues, however, that these are merely "modifications" of the one substance and have no reality independent from it.[38]

It follows from this claim that, as Spinoza puts it, "What is, is in God." It seems to be entailed that God is also "in" every one of his modifications. Spinoza scholars dispute whether Spinoza's position is better understood as pantheism in the strict sense (the latter view) or panentheism (the former view). Either way, there is no ontological difference between the divine and finite reality. In Spinoza's doctrine, God is not hovering over us, untouchable by thought or sense, in the heavens. Instead, he is *immanent* or present in all that we do and think.[39]

The unity and immanence of substance, Spinoza argues, makes absurd any distinction between God and Nature. Because there is, in fact, only one thing, these are simply convenient names for the whole of Being. Later in the *Ethics*, Spinoza expresses this thought with the famous phrase *Deus sive Natura*—God or Nature. The precise meaning of the phrase continues to be disputed. In my view, Spinoza's neologism is intended to make a point about language rather than to express an additional metaphysical claim. What Spinoza is suggesting, I think, is that the words "God" and "Nature" must be interchangeable, *salva veritate*, in any true sentence.[40]

Spinoza's naturalism has important theological consequences. Perhaps the most serious consequence is that it excludes divine personality. According to Spinoza, God has neither will nor understanding in the conventional sense. Instead, God's "will" is nothing more than the fixed laws of nature according to which all things occur. Divine "understanding" is merely a clumsy way of expressing the fact that these laws are conceived as necessary—or, in other words, that they are *true*. The consequence is that God has or had no freedom to make things otherwise than they are. For Spinoza, the origin of the world is not intentional creation but rather a kind of cosmic self-determination.[41]

These are some key features of what Spinoza called for in the *PCP*: a conception of God that makes it impossible to think of God as a deceiver. More accurately, it is a conception that makes it impossible to think of God as either a deceiver or a non-deceiver, at least to the extent that these ideas refer to an intentional being. Rather than an agent with will and understanding, Spinoza's God simply *is*. And this conception, Spinoza insists, is the *only* foundation for the sciences.

One of the sciences that Spinoza has in mind is what we might call the science of man. Indeed, the *Ethics*, after book 1, is largely an attempt to answer the question "what is man?" in light of the preceding response to the question "what is God?" Spinoza's answer is that a human being is a body whose corresponding "idea" is a mind. Each of these qualities exists under a different attribute of substance—extension and thought, respectively. To this extent, the human being may be said to exist "in" God.[42]

This pantheistic conclusion is provocative enough. But what Spinoza says about freedom is even more disturbing. According to Spinoza, there is no interaction between beings conceived under the different attributes of

God. As such, each belongs to an independent causal system. Everything that happens to the body is caused by interactions with bodies. Everything that happens in the mind, on the other hand, is caused by the consequences of ideas. Since these causal chains are completely distinct, there is no possibility of an idea causing a physical result. For Spinoza, man has no power to act intentionally—that is, to initiate a series of effects on the basis of his thoughts. In fact, freedom of the will is an illusion that results from our ignorance of the natural necessity by which our bodies are moved.[43]

It is sometimes argued that Spinoza was trying to enhance the freedom we actually possess by contrasting it to matters that are beyond our control. Sober reflection on what is necessary, Spinoza suggests, allows us to better understand what is possible. In other words, his philosophy allows us to distinguish those things that are under our control from those that are not. By acquiring this knowledge, we relieve ourselves from unreasonable hopes and fears—especially those associated with revealed religion, which links divine rewards and punishments to deeds and intentions.[44]

The obstacle to this essentially humane conclusion is that very little is under our control. In the *Ethics*, our freedom turns out to consist solely in the freedom to philosophize properly. And this means little more than the freedom to form the correct idea about God—the very idea that undermines any conventional understanding of freedom.[45] By contemplating this idea, Spinoza argues in book 5, we do gain a kind of immortality that is not tainted by superstition about pleasing God. Yet this is only an impersonal immortality, in which our minds are in some way fused with the immense being that simply *is*.[46]

So Spinoza's arguments for the epistemic, ontological, and ultimately anthropological significance of God are no victories for *religion*. Quite the contrary, they imply that almost all the central doctrines of biblical religion are not merely dubitable, but demonstrably false. Because Spinoza was absolutely certain of his philosophy, as he explained to Burgh, he was not satisfied to pass over these implications in silence—although he was unwilling to speak in his own name. Making them explicit is the task of the *Tractatus Theologico-Politicus* (*TTP*), which Spinoza published anonymously in late 1669 or early 1670, about ten years after he began work on the *Ethics*.

PANTHEISM, SCRIPTURE, DEMOCRACY

The essential document of Spinoza's being "more Cartesian than Descartes" is the *Tractatus Theologico-Politicus*. In it, Spinoza does precisely what Descartes hesitated to do: apply the method of doubt to revealed religion. He was enabled to do this, paradoxically, by the fact that he did not doubt at all. Spinoza was absolutely certain that his science was true, at least in its foundations, and he therefore had no need for humility when confronted with ancient opinions about God. The source of this certainty was the denial of any sort of divine transcendence. With clear and distinct knowledge of God or Nature, Spinoza was free to reject traditional theology as patent nonsense.

Spinoza believed that this rejection contributed in two ways to the establishment of the regime that he described as "democracy."[47] The first may be described as the negative contribution, that is, the removal of religious influence from thought and politics. Working systematically through Scripture, Spinoza shows how his philosophy exposes revelation, miracles, and the concept of divine law as the products of either ignorance or overheated imagination. With these elements removed, the only content of Scripture is a vague moral teaching. Spinoza describes this teaching, in a phrase that can be properly understood only in the context of the *Ethics*, as the "natural divine law."[48]

The natural divine law is accessible to all human beings by means of their own reason. Therefore, they have no need of priests, prophets, or historical narratives. However, Spinoza acknowledges, many people are not sufficiently perspicacious in the use of reason to recognize natural divine law on their own. They may, therefore, have to be motivated by certain stories about God, which, while untrue in themselves, encourage precisely the same behaviors that are demanded by a rational appreciation for our place in the universe. This motivation, Spinoza argues, is the *sole* legitimate activity of "theology." Any questions pertaining to the nature of God are matters of philosophy—whose results I have briefly sketched.[49]

If religious guidance is unnecessary in thought, it is actively pernicious in politics. Priests, prophets, and independent churches, according to Spinoza, are the main cause of civil disorder, because they preach that men are condemned to eternal torment for violating God's arbitrary commands. Because this is evidently worse than any temporal punishment, clerics acquire a hold over simple souls, a hold that is much stronger than that of the civil ruler. In the preface to the *TTP*, Spinoza blames this fear for the fact that "doctrinal conflicts are fought out in Church and Court with intense passion and generate the most bitter antipathies and struggles, which quickly bring men to sedition."[50]

In philosophy, then, Spinoza hoped to expose fear of a capricious God as groundless in order to clear the road to knowledge. In politics, he aimed to elevate the rational calculation of worldly interests over theological dispute. The negative contribution of "pantheism," in other words, is to open a space for peaceful politics by clearing away the prejudices and terrors encouraged by traditional religion.

The bulk of the *TTP* is devoted to this negative argument. But Spinoza also thought that pantheism could make a positive contribution to the common good by providing a theoretical justification for democracy. Such, at least, is the argument of *TTP* chapter 14. There, Spinoza argues that the inherence of all things in God or nature affords each a "natural right" to persist in its own being. To quote the well-known passage in full:

> By the right and order of nature I merely mean the rules determining the nature of each individual thing by which we conceive it is determined naturally to exist and behave in a certain way. For example, fish are determined by nature to swim and big fish to eat little ones, and therefore it is by sovereign natural right that fish have possession of the water and that big fish eat small ones. For it is certain that nature, considered wholly in itself, has a sovereign right to do everything that it can do, i.e. the right of nature extends as far as its power extends. For the power of nature is the very power of God who has supreme right to all things. However, since the universal power of the whole of nature is nothing but the power of all individual things together, it follows the individual thing has the sovereign right to do everything that it can do, or the right of each thing extends so far as its determined power extends. And since it is the supreme law of nature that each thing strives to persist in its own state so far as it can, taking no account of another's circumstances, but only of its own, it follows that each individual thing has a sovereign right to do this, i.e. (as I said) to exist and behave as it is naturally determined to behave.[51]

The argument that each thing has the "sovereign right" to do everything that it can seems like an unpromising foundation for democracy. It amounts to an assertion that might makes right. By this standard, the big fish have the right to devour the small. The human analogue is an anarchic condition in which unattached individuals assert their natural right in a struggle to survive.

Up to this point, Spinoza's argument resembles Thomas Hobbes' description of the state of war in *Leviathan*. Like Hobbes, Spinoza argues that the establishment of security requires a social contract in which individuals agree to observe the rules established by a common authority or sovereign. The difference between them is rooted in Spinoza's insistence that greatest right is *always* possessed by the stronger. Since many are always stronger than a few, Spinoza argues that a sovereign constituted by the active agreement of a majority of citizens has the highest right of all. Hobbes, on the other hand, defended the alienation of sovereignty to a monarch.[52] For Spinoza, then, the most stable alternative to the state of war is a democratic commonwealth in which laws are made with the consent of the majority— who can then be counted upon to observe and enforce them. According to Spinoza, "Democracy . . . is properly defined as a united gathering of people which collectively has the sovereign right to do all that it has the power to do. It follows [in this case] that sovereign power is bound by no law and everyone is obliged to obey it in all things."[53]

It might be thought that Spinoza's position culminates in what Tocqueville would famously call the tyranny of the majority, namely, a condition in which not only actions but also thoughts are subject to public opinion. That is not so, he argues in chapter 20 of the *TTP*, which describes the "free state" that results from democracy. What is "free" about a regime characterized by unlimited sovereignty? A great part of the answer is that the sovereign, however strong, is literally incapable of controlling men's thoughts. Therefore, the state has no "right" to impose restrictions on rational discourse, including the doubt that sound reason will lead men to direct against revealed religion.[54]

The freedom to seek truth about God thus turns out to be the cornerstone of democratic liberty. This freedom is, above all, the liberty to philosophize, which Spinoza insists must be legally protected from interference by adherents of traditional theism. It is notable that Spinoza's conception of a "free state" does not seem to include parallel protections for the practice of religion. Although he admits that the conventionally pious cannot be forcibly diverted from their madness, he suggests limits on religious preaching or practice that encourages disobedience to the sovereign.[55]

I suggested above that Spinoza considered pantheism in certain respects an esoteric doctrine. This description requires some qualification. In principle, Spinoza argues, all the conclusions of reason are available to all normally constituted human beings. This, after all, was the bottom line of his critique or correction of Cartesian doubt. But Spinoza acknowledges in the *TTP* that not everyone is inclined to reason with the rigor and consistency that philosophy requires:

> Often though, a long chain of linked inferences is required, to come to firm conclusions from basic ideas alone. Furthermore, this requires great caution and perspicacity and supreme mental discipline, qualities only seldom met with among human beings. People prefer to be taught by experience than to deduce all their ideas from a few premises and connect these together. Consequently, where someone wants to teach a whole nation, not to speak of the entire human race, and wants to be understood by everybody, he must substantiate his points by experience alone and thoroughly adapt his arguments and the definitions of his teaching to the capacity of the common people (the majority of mankind), and not make a chain of inferences or advance definitions linking his arguments together. Otherwise he will be writing only for the learned, that is, he will be intelligible only to what is, in comparison with the rest of mankind, a very small handful of people.[56]

For Spinoza, then, the human race can be divided into two basic groups, each of which has a distinctive theologico-political orientation. On the one hand, more or less rational people are supposed to endorse what would come to be called pantheism. According to Spinoza, this should lead to their embrace of democracy on proper philosophical grounds. Although Spinoza does not tell us how large this class of readers is likely to be, there is reason to think it would be relatively small. This, at least, would seem to be why he wrote the *TTP* in Latin instead of the vernacular.[57] On the other hand, the great mass of society is incapable of acquiring this knowledge and is unlikely to read philosophy anyway. Their obedience is to be secured by the adoption of "true religion" as a civil cult, in which God is presented in anthropomorphic terms as the commander of an arbitrary divine law, and rulers are regarded as God's regents on earth.[58]

The stability of Spinoza's free state thus seems to depend on a certain degree of self-censorship. Although they have very different views about God and freedom, the rational few must be careful not to undermine the civil cult that supports democracy by encouraging the loyalty of the many. For all the radicalism of his philosophy, Spinoza seems to have taken this responsibility seriously. The *TTP* actually begins and ends with the submission of its contents to the judgment of the duly constituted authorities.[59]

But the distinction between the rational few and the ignorant many threatens to undermine Spinoza's commitment to democracy. His argument culminates, despite its majoritarian account of sovereignty, in a sort of "epistocracy." This interpretation raises serious questions about the applicability of Spinoza's ideas under the more equal conditions characteristic of later modernity. Despite his lack of interest in metaphysics and probable ignorance of the historical background, Tocqueville puts these questions in a remarkably direct fashion.

REFLECTIONS ON SPINOZA IN THE SPIRIT OF TOCQUEVILLE

The first problem with Spinoza's position, Tocqueville's arguments suggest, was that even though he was a democrat in politics, his epistemology belonged to an aristocratic age. In other words, Spinoza assumed a fundamental gap between the few philosophers or potential philosophers and the ignorant many. This assumption was reasonable in the seventeenth century, when literacy—let alone the wherewithal to buy books—was far from universal. It had become unreasonable by the nineteenth century, when cheap printing and improvements in education had created a vast reading public. Put differently, Spinoza was wrong to assume that the pantheistic elements of philosophy would remain esoteric. In a democratic age, it was inevitable that they would enter the public sphere.

Spinoza might object that any vulgarization of his thought would be a bastardization—and therefore not his responsibility. In fact, he makes precisely this disclaimer in the Preface to the *TTP*.[60] But philosophers cannot count on their ideas remaining outside the life of democracy, nor can they ensure that their ideas are received in the right way. The tendency of philosophical arguments to enter the public sphere could be taken as a justification for more rigorous practices of concealment. I think they imply rather the opposite: Tocqueville's account suggests that esotericism, whether as a manner of thought or writing, simply does not work under modern democratic conditions.

Once conceived, then, pantheism was almost destined to become accessible. What was wrong with that? Tocqueville suggests a plausible answer. Democratic citizens are basically disinclined to take responsibility for public affairs. Under the equality of conditions, they regard themselves as too insignificant to influence the great forces by which they are governed. Pantheism, especially in its "vulgar" form, provides a theoretical justification for this renunciation. By encouraging citizens to believe that everything that occurs must happen (and that they themselves are immersed in a universal being), it undermines the habits and assumptions necessary to an engaged citizenry. Simply put, Tocqueville thinks that the spread of pantheism encourages an attitude of fatalism that is easily manipulated by the ambitious few who promise to relieve citizens of the burdens of self-government.

This disagreement underlies Spinoza's and Tocqueville's different evaluations of religion in democracy. Spinoza saw religion primarily as a source of moral norms. In other words, he thought that people rely on religion to help them distinguish right from wrong, just from unjust. In his view, this function made religion a tool of despotism. By appealing to hopes and fears of divine reward and punishment, unscrupulous priests and prophets could easily convince the people to accept their rule. This is why Spinoza saw the critique of revealed religion as a necessary condition of the establishment of democracy. Only by exposing the truth about God—that he is identical to Nature or Being itself—could the political theologians be deprived of their authority.

Tocqueville suggests that traditional religion makes a different contribution to civil society. Its role, he suggests, is to preserve the conception of agency that underlies civic association; the belief of personal responsibility that leads us to curb our own appetites; the expectation of immortality or metaphysical worth that gives dignity even to the lowly. Without these ideas, Tocqueville leads us to think, there is no reason *not* to accept the comfortable subjugation of soft despotism. On the contrary, if we are naturally determined and essentially corporeal beings, we have every reason to take the easy course.

I suspect that Spinoza would have been horrified by this outcome. An admirer of the civic virtue that characterized the Roman republic, Spinoza's every statement on politics encourages citizens to take responsibility for the fate of the commonwealth. Nevertheless, the "pantheism" that he developed in his formal philosophy contributes little to this end. By attacking old ideas about God that Descartes left relatively untouched, it risks removing beliefs in individual agency, responsibility, and dignity that have turned out to be politically salutary, however theoretically dubious. Spinoza defended pantheism in an effort to rescue philosophy from the epistemic despotism of transcendence, and political society from the horror of sectarian war, and he contributed much to our liberation from these dangers. But the immense being of the tutelary state, which Tocqueville identified as the characteristic danger of modern democracy, was undreamt of in his philosophy.

NOTES

I am grateful to the panelists at the Stuck with Virtue conference, Berry College, for insightful comments on an earlier version of this chapter. Subsequent drafts were read and improved by David Grewal, Matthew Landauer, and members of the Religion and Critical Thought Workshop, Princeton University. I particularly thank Jeffrey Stout for encouraging me to consider the possibility of a pantheism that might be salutary for democracy—a subject that will have to await a future essay.

1. Alexis de Tocqueville, *Democracy in America*, trans. Harvey C. Mansfield and Delba Winthrop (Chicago: University of Chicago Press, 2000), 403.

2. Ibid., 425.

3. For example, Sheldon Wolin, *Tocqueville between Two Worlds* (Princeton, NJ: Princeton University Press, 2001), 314–15.

4. Tocqueville, *Democracy in America*, 404.

5. Ibid.

6. Ibid., 403.

7. Ibid., 406.

8. Ibid., 405.

9. Ibid.; emphasis added.

10. Ibid., 425, translators' note.

11. Jonathan Israel traces Spinoza's broad influence on the eighteenth century in *Democratic Enlightenment* (Oxford: Oxford University Press, 2011).

12. Tocqueville, *Democracy in America*, 426.

13. Stephen H. Daniel, *John Toland: His Method, Manners, and Mind* (Montreal: McGill-Queen's University Press, 1984), 212.

14. Tocqueville, *Democracy in America*, 426.

15. Ibid., 405.

16. Ibid., 426.

17. The phrase "*être immense*" may be derived from Rousseau's *Emile*. Although I don't pursue it in this chapter, it's worth noting that this text also shows strong traces of Spinozism.

18. Leibniz makes a similar point when he suggests that Spinozism is "exaggerated Cartesianism." See §393 of Gottfried Wilhelm Leibniz, *Theodicy* (New York: Cosimo Classics, 2010), 359.

19. René Descartes, *Meditations on First Philosophy*, ed. George Heffernan (Notre Dame, IN: University of Notre Dame Press, 1990), 87. This edition is based on the Latin text of the *Meditations*.

20. Ibid., 89.

21. Ibid.

22. Ibid., 93.

23. Ibid., 97.

24. For a powerful statement of this view, see Michael Gillespie, *Nihilism before Nie-tzsche* (Chicago: University of Chicago Press, 1996), ch. 2.

25. No one can write about these issues without acknowledging the contribution of the late Richard Popkin. My interpretation of Spinoza in this section relies on Richard Popkin, *The History of Scepticism* (Oxford: Oxford University Press, 2003), ch. 15.

26. Baruch Spinoza, *Principles of Cartesian Philosophy*, trans. Samuel Shirley (Indianapolis: Hackett, 1998), 7.

27. Ibid.

28. In this respect, Spinoza synthesizes the two interpretations of Descartes sketched above. In his view, Descartes needed to overcome the Creator God in order to complete his foundational project. But Spinoza does not seem to think that Descartes succeeded in doing so.

29. Spinoza, *Principles of Cartesian Philosophy*, 12.

30. Ibid., 13.

31. On Descartes' view of God's will and understanding, see Robert Ariew and Marjorie Grene, *Descartes and His Contemporaries: Meditations, Objections, and Replies* (Chicago: University of Chicago Press, 1995), 152.

32. Popkin, *History of Scepticism*, 251–52.

33. Steven Nadler, *Spinoza: A Life* (Cambridge: Cambridge University Press, 2001), 336–40.

34. Spinoza, Letter 76 in *The Letters*, trans. Samuel Shirley (Indianapolis: Hackett, 1995), 340.

35. Descartes, *Meditations*, 89.

36. Baruch Spinoza, *Ethics in A Spinoza Reader*, trans. Edwin Curley (Princeton, NJ: Princeton University Press, 1994), I.15.

37. Rather than working through the argument according to Spinoza's order of presentation, I only highlight a few major themes of the ostensibly rational alternative that Spinoza opposed to the old opinions about God. The selection of these themes follows Michael P. Levine, *Pantheism* (New York: Routledge, 1994), 25–40.

38. What this means and how it is related to pantheism is hotly contested. For an overview of debates concerning Spinoza's monism, see Richard Mason, *The God of Spinoza* (Cambridge: Cambridge University Press, 1997), 31–32.

39. On Spinoza's conception of immanence, see Yirmiyahu Yovel, *The Adventures of Immanence* (Princeton, NJ: Princeton University Press, 1989), vol. 1, ch. 2.

40. For a different perspective on this issue, see Jonathan Israel, *Radical Enlightenment: Philosophy and the Making of Modernity* (Oxford: Oxford University Press, 2001), 345–46.

41. This theme is explored in Stephen Nadler, "Baruch Spinoza and the Naturalization of Judaism," in *The Cambridge Companion to Modern Jewish Philosophy*, ed. Michael L. Morgan and Peter Eli Gordon (Cambridge: Cambridge University Press, 2007).

42. An accessible explanation of this point can be found in Steven Nadler, "Baruch Spinoza," in the *Stanford Encyclopedia of Philosophy*, spring 2011 edition, ed. Edward N. Zalta, at http://plato.stanford.edu/archives/spr2011/entries/spinoza/.

43. Spinoza, *Ethics*, I.app.

44. Steven B. Smith presents a version of this argument in *Spinoza's Book of Life* (New Haven: Yale University Press, 2003).

45. Spinoza, *Ethics* IV.67.

46. Ibid., V.39.

47. Baruch Spinoza, *Theological-Political Treatise*, ed. Jonathan Israel (Cambridge, UK: Cambridge University Press, 2008), 200–202.

48. Ibid., 61.

49. Ibid., ch. 15.

50. Ibid., 8.

51. Ibid., 195–96.

52. The best brief study of this issue is Edwin Curley, "Kissinger, Spinoza, and Genghis Khan," in *The Cambridge Companion to Spinoza*, ed. Don Garrett (Cambridge: Cambridge University Press, 1996), 315–42.

53. Spinoza, *Theologico-Political Treatise*, 200.

54. Ibid., 250.

55. Ibid., 252–53.

56. Ibid., 76.

57. Straussian readers generally argue that Spinoza limits knowledge of the truth about God and nature to a tiny minority of philosophers. Etienne Balibar, by contrast, suggests that Spinoza's teachings are meant to be more broadly available, perhaps to all reasonably well-educated people. See *Spinoza and Politics*, trans. Peter Snowdon (New York: Verso, 1998), 1–5.

58. Spinoza, *Theologico-Political Treatise*, ch. 19.

59. See J. Thomas Cook, "Did Spinoza Lie to His Landlady?" in *Piety, Peace, and the Freedom to Philosophize*, ed. Paul J. Bagley (Dordrecht: Kluwer, 1999).

60. Spinoza, *Theologico-Political Treatise*, 12.

5

LOCKE'S EXPLANATION OF HOW THE SCIENCE OF CIVIL SOCIETY CORRECTS THE NATURAL AUTHORITY OF VIRTUE

James R. Stoner, Jr.

H AVING BEEN ASSIGNED THE QUESTION of how the British Enlightenment philosopher John Locke contributes to the science of
virtue, I want first to raise the question of the relation of the classical and
modern accounts of virtue, society, and politics, and to begin with the classical question of the relation of the order of the city and the order of the
soul. For being "stuck with virtue" means at least this: "being stuck" with
paying attention to the human soul, or at least to what Friedrich Nietzsche
called (for those whose scientific conscience cannot quite abide the notion
that the soul is a real entity) the "soul hypothesis."[1] Whatever virtue is (in
the precise sense), every virtue is an excellence of soul, and the crisis of
virtue in the modern world is derivative, I think, from the collapse of the
idea of the soul.

Now, classical political philosophy—most famously in its first great
text, Plato's *Republic*—was founded on the analogy between the city and

the human soul. As Socrates there explains, the classes of the city mirror the parts of the soul: The lower "money-making" classes resemble the appetites, the military or auxiliary class corresponds to spiritedness, and the philosopher-kings exemplify intelligence.[2] Socrates and his interlocutors discover justice in the city when each class minds its own business, or in other words, when the spirited class follows the precepts of reason and masters the appetites. Justice is not the whole of virtue—the dialogue finds prudence as the virtue of the calculating part, courage as the virtue of the spirited part, and moderation in harmony among the parts—but in every case virtue in the soul and virtue in the city reflect one another. The political good is congruent with the human good, the analogy would have us suppose, and the happiness of the city is congruent with the happiness of man.

I will address in a moment some of the problems with the analogy that its author probably meant for us to notice, but I want to start by discussing its advantages. Within the dialogue, Socrates proposes looking at the city rather than the soul, because justice will be seen more clearly there than in a single soul, which is after all invisible, even or especially to itself. This seems to me to be a good and true argument, and therefore fundamental to any science of virtue: Throughout nature one learns about invisible causes from visible effects, and it hardly seems to be a stretch to consider the city to be a creature of human soulfulness. Moreover, we learn about ourselves by seeing ourselves or our likenesses in others. Left alone any soul might experience terror or hubris, but among others, souls naturally find their place, learn to strive, gain comfort, and even find love. You may or may not agree with the way Plato's Socrates describes the soul, much less the way he and his companions design their city, but there is nothing foolish about the plan to seek to find the good of the individual in the way we understand the common good.

If the analogy holds, then the science of virtue and the science of politics are the same, or at any rate as congruent as the soul and the city. Political science, then, would grow naturally out of ethics, or ethics would complete political science: The good city would be a city of good men and would encourage men to be good, while an association of good men built upon their goodness would be a good city. Aristotle does not stress the analogy as Plato does, but these very consequences are the principles of his *Politics* and *Ethics*: The city exists by nature, its end is to promote virtue and thereby secure happiness, and the best city is the city of best men.[3]

Aristotle does not restrict himself to the best in his analysis of politics: Even lesser cities are built upon human virtues, though lesser ones, as fortune or necessity allows, indeed on virtues of the body not only the soul. So widespread—or again, so natural—is the strength of the analogy of the city and man that it endures long after the demise of the polis. The medieval monarchy personified the polity in the king and the medieval church claimed to be the body of Christ. Even today, not only does the Catholic Church insist on this in her theology, but sovereign states in the international system, whether or not they have a monarchical head, are typically spoken of as though they had attributes of character, capacities of action, and moral responsibilities analogous to those of a single human being. And as the famous frontispiece of Thomas Hobbes' *Leviathan* and its author's introduction make plain, the analogy of the city and man continues to be employed by those whose political philosophy bears little other resemblance to that of Plato or Aristotle.[4]

Now, there is not a little about the analogy of the city and the soul that is problematic, most especially to modern ears. Plato's account of human nature, and so Socrates' city, is aristocratic; it supposes so radical an inequality among men that its fundamental myth describes the different classes as different substances—gold, silver, iron, or bronze[5]—and it assigns them radically different roles in the city's activity. Moreover, there is a paradox in comparing the city to the soul. Although every soul has all three parts (the calculating, the spirited, and the desiring), in the city each class allows two of them to atrophy, for the rulers do all its thinking, the auxiliaries do its fighting, and the money-making class gets all its ordinary pleasures— well almost all: At one point it seems as though the rulers get the most sex, but it is not clear that they are allowed to enjoy it.[6] Pushing the analogy of city and soul seems perverse if not unjust: Can the money-makers really not think? Should fighters not be allowed to enjoy the gentler pleasures? Don't the rulers have to fight? But I suppose Plato's reply might be to remind us of the insight embodied in the division of labor: Everybody thrives if those do most what they do best. That the happiness of the city and that of its members are not identical—that is, that some seem to be made miserable for the sake of the whole—is a point made by several of Socrates' interlocutors, and the real-life drama of Socrates' demise at the hands of Athens lies behind the dialogue and indeed behind everything Plato wrote.[7] In the end, Socrates acknowledges that the city in speech is a pattern for a man to imitate in the ordering of his own soul rather than a plan for any actual city. The city in the *Laws*, designed to be more practical, abandons the conceit, and Aristotle acknowledges the city to be an aggregate of incommensurable parts.[8] Still, even Aristotle acknowledges that it is one of the tasks of every science, perhaps its noblest task, to account for the best.[9] And what among the human things is better than the soul?

The modern science that Locke exemplifies takes a very different approach to the question of virtue, the question of the soul, and the question of science. To the theorists of the Enlightenment, society is not to be anthropomorphized but operates according to its own laws, some traditionally acknowledged and classically explained, others newly discovered and surprising in what they reveal. Their new science of society requires some insight into human motivation and a basic acceptance of human rationality, but the soul itself is not the model for society, nor is virtue the key political cause or end. In the modern account, the place of virtue is taken by the concept of freedom, and to emphasize freedom is to make an end of the capacity to choose other ends; as many have noted, not happiness but the pursuit of happiness is stressed, and the new science will maximize the occasions for free choice, not the deeds of right reason, in order to maximize the rewards of diligent activity. Society can be structured, in other words, in such a way as to summon from men their effort and engage their creativity for the sake of human success. Virtue, too, might contribute to the success of society, but this relationship would have to be shown empirically now; it can no longer be seen as inherent. As Adam Smith, the great heir to the Lockean tradition, makes clear, it is an invisible hand that ensures the selfish actions of innumerable individuals lead to the general wealth of society.[10] What's virtue got to do with it? Even a moralist like Kant could say of the political or constitutional question that it can be solved in principle even for a nation of devils, provided they be smart.[11]

John Locke is part of this movement, indeed perhaps its most important author, but he is hardly so radical in his dismissal of reliance upon virtue. Indeed, in contrast to later Enlightenment figures, Locke makes quite extensive use of virtue in his writings. But it is always good counsel to be suspicious (or at least a little suspicious) of Locke, and reading Locke's discussion of virtue suspiciously brings out three things worth noting. First, Locke redefines virtue away from the classical, not to mention the Christian account—more specifically, diminishing the importance of courage and charity while raising the importance of the social virtues or the virtues of civility, virtues included in Aristotle's catalogue, to be sure (remember friendliness, truth telling, and wittiness),[12] but mostly in a secondary role. Second, Locke is very clear that liberty rather than virtue is the defining end of man, or the characteristic whose exercise makes people happy. Third, since government has as its end the protection of liberty, through the protection of property, it is not only largely indifferent to virtue in the people as anything besides an occasional instrument for liberty but even distrusts virtue as politically dangerous. Let me try to elaborate through a glance at four of Locke's texts.

The first is his famous *Letter concerning Toleration*, perhaps his most widely read text in our time. In making his case for religious toleration, Locke distinguishes sharply the civil interests of man (he lists these as life, liberty, health, indolency of body, and possession of outward things) from care for the salvation of men's souls.[13] Socrates in his *Apology* refutes his accuser Meletus by showing that he, Socrates, really cares for souls and their virtue, while Meletus actually does not care, but Locke insists that government adopt toward souls that very indifference.[14] Locke would leave care for salvation to each individual soul, and to such voluntary associations as men form to help themselves to their end (namely, churches), which, he says, are "absolutely separate and distinct from the Commonwealth."[15] Each man cares for his soul as he cares for his health and his property, but government, charged with protecting these, concerns itself with religion only to suppress religious doctrines that upset the civil peace. Every denomination that tolerates others—that tolerates them equally—should itself be tolerated, unless it engages in practices that violate the civil law, and since Locke prefers to limit the exercise of legislative power even over indifferent things, civil society ought to allow religious groups sufficient space to live as they want. Locke does not openly teach *tolerance* as a new virtue, as our modern liberals typically do, but in the opening remarks of his *Letter*, made to Christians in the name of Christianity, he subtly turns charity into toleration. A robust charity is what makes traditional Christianity apostolic, not to say proselytizing, or at least Christians who confidently hold their faith as truth describe as an act of charity their insistence that others acknowledge that truth and learn to see its truthfulness; after all, isn't it easier and so uncharitable to retreat into our own self-certitude and let others persist in their erroneous ways?[16] But Locke would make charity tolerant, merely: Resisting one's own uneasiness with difference and allowing faith to be a private thing, and then perhaps requiring it to be a private thing. I had said of Plato's *Republic* that it deputes one to think for all; Locke, by contrast, forbids anyone to think for anyone else, even with that person's consent, since "if I be not thoroughly persuaded [of the soundness of religion] in my own mind, there will be no safety for me in following it."[17]

The second text of Locke's I want to address is *Some Thoughts concerning Education*.[18] Thomas Hobbes, who despised Aristotle, nevertheless was very fond of Aristotle's *Rhetoric* and in fact translated it into English.[19] Likewise, even the critic of Locke might be indulged a secret soft spot for *Some Thoughts*, at least if he is a father: Locke (albeit a tutor, not a father) explains how to get your sons to obey you without having to beat them (too much), offers lots of sensible advice about how children come to learn to reason and respect reason, and concludes with a discussion of how learning to dance is critical to manliness. Nevertheless, when Locke summarizes the education of a young gentleman, the subjects are virtue, wisdom, breeding, and learning, and several of these are surprisingly defined.[20] Not wisdom: by this he seems to mean prudence in a more or less classical sense, explicitly distinguishing it (as did Aristotle) from cunning. And the discussion of learning is fascinating, beginning with a proto-Sesame Street account of teaching children to play games with letters; recommending Aesop, in a book with pictures; developing a book of Bible stories for children; and so on through Latin, French, geography, arithmetic, history, and eventually natural philosophy; and finally, a manual trade as a hobby.

For our purposes, though, it is the other two—virtue and breeding—I want to comment upon. All he says about virtue is that "there ought very early to be imprinted on the mind a true notion of God, as the independent Supreme Being, Author and Maker of all things, from whom we receive all our good, who loves us, and gives us all things. . . . This is enough to begin with," lest heads "be either filled with false or perplexed with unintelligible notions of him . . . without being too curious in their notions about a Being, which all must acknowledge incomprehensible."[21] This sounds as innocuous as toleration, until one realizes that there is no place for the story of original sin, the Incarnation, the Passion—not to mention the Resurrection or the Second Coming. Knowing only this deist God, who would think there might be virtues that emerge through enduring suffering, through self-emptying, through the unconditional gift of self? Nor can there be anything like classical courage, for it is essential to keep children from believing in ghosts or spirits or any "bugbear thoughts" lest they grow up afraid.[22] Instead of any list of virtues, Locke gives us the elements of good breeding or civility: no natural roughness, no showing contempt, no censoriousness, no captiousness, that is, "tendency to find fault or raise petty objections."[23] Social virtues (Locke's term) replace the sturdier virtues, classical or Christian, and while the social virtues are truly virtues, something changes when they are the only virtues, or rather, the only virtues that can be taught or formed. They are the virtues that contribute to success in this world, in society, the way men build their reputations or, at least, preserve them. Harder virtues come later—chiefly, industriousness—and that is something new.

An Essay concerning Human Understanding is my third text, and it is much too long to discuss thoroughly in the confines of a chapter. It begins, famously, with the denial that human beings have innate ideas (importantly, for our topic, no innate idea of virtue, or of the soul itself), but I want to say something about chapter 21, "Of Power," where Locke undertakes to explain—or is it, to explain away?—free will and introduces the phrase so famous to Americans, "pursuit of happiness."[24] Men are free, wrote Locke, simply because they can delay acting upon their desires so that thought or understanding can intervene between the desire and action upon the desire—based on a calculation of consequences, respect for rules, or simple caution. Desire itself is defined indirectly, not as attraction to the good, but as *uneasiness*, an undifferentiated awareness of a lack. The word "uneasiness"—translated by the French Enlightenment as *inquiétude* (later Tocqueville's word, sometimes translated as "restlessness" or "restiveness"), and maybe translated by Locke from Frenchmen such as Montaigne, Descartes, and Pascal[25]—parses the meaning of the "pursuit of happiness." For Locke implies that happiness is found in the removal of uneasiness and that its *pursuit* is by *self-restraint*, holding back from gratification in order to give thought to the matter.[26] The psychology, here, explains how virtues are replaced with *interests*—calculated goods, recognized by the intervention of the understanding upon desire. Human happiness does not involve the proper ordering of a natural being, the soul, but the regulation of a mental process. The title of the chapter is "Of Power" because power, I think, is what really replaces virtue as an end, in Locke, though it is rational power, experienced as liberty and prosecuted as interest.

The last text I wanted to mention is the *Second Treatise*, "Of Civil Government." Here I want to highlight two main points. First I want to draw attention to Locke's justly famous chapter 5, "Of Property," where he explains in embryo the modern or capitalist idea of economic growth.[27] Because men own themselves (that is, their bodies), they own their labor and so the products of their labor. It is a little more complicated: They need material to work upon, and this comes from nature, and to claim ownership of that there has to be more than enough for everyone, like air, or dead leaves on a wooded campus in November, or water in the ocean or flowing from a plentiful spring, and the like. Or maybe not. As Locke unfolds the argument, so little of the value of things comes from nature and so much from labor that one has the right to withdraw a little even of scarce goods like land if one makes it more productive than it was by nature—something that happens by a factor of ten, writes Locke, which he revises to one hundred, then to one thousand, and by implication to much more.[28] Think of the modern computer industry developed in Silicon Valley—the source of silicon is sand. As I wrote above, this is not yet Adam Smith, but it does suggest that the laws of social order are grounded in human energy and inventiveness rather than in some model of human nature; the laws themselves may be dynamic, and society itself certainly is. The virtue, if it could be called that, indicated by Locke's account of property appears in his famous phrase contrasting the "industrious and rational" with the "quarrelsome and contentious."[29] Hitherto existing societies fought over the distribution of a fixed inheritance, which grew only little by little over time. Locke imagines economic growth without limits, at once improving the lot of the least advantaged and allowing the most successful many more times the lowest estate than, for example, the factor of four permitted in the established unequal class society of Plato's *Laws*.[30] Industriousness and rationality, still, are virtues—but they point to many different ways of life. And Locke intends this. In the *Essay concerning Human Understanding*, he had explained it was foolish to seek a *summum bonum*, for men's minds were different and relished different goods; and in *Thoughts on Education* he had praised free play for children, on the grounds that it allows the parent or the tutor to discern what the child relishes, his or her *interests*, again, now in the sense of likes and dislikes.[31]

Does politics depend upon virtue? People naturally think so, and I drew the title for my essay—the reference to the natural authority of virtue—from *Second Treatise*, chapter 7, §94, where Locke explores the actual, probable origin of society in men's deference to someone they naturally recognize as superior in virtue, in human excellence—a phenomenon Aristotle also describes.[32] But Locke argues against it or, at the very least, argues that natural authority is primitive and ought to be replaced by the model of the social contract and the institutions of constitutional government. Yes, virtue might be needed in a crisis—doing good without a rule, "prerogative" he calls it, acting without the law or even against it.[33] But as Locke states, the reigns of the best kings have been dangerous to the liberties of the people. Constitutionalism is an inheritance, and like all property, it draws only a little from nature. Even when it returns to natural authority (in the use of prerogative or the judgment to make an "appeal to heaven" or revolution), Locke would have men refer to a standard—"preservation of property"—that makes only the most indirect nod toward virtue but concentrates instead upon results.[34]

Where does this leave us? In our political institutions, "stuck with Locke"—respectful of freedom of conscience, and so, religious toleration; attentive to the virtues of civility; accepting of the different relishes of different minds, and so the varieties of pursuits of happiness; and most of all, committed to the practices of constitutionalism, government by consent, and the rule of law. This is not Plato's *Republic*, for society here does not correspond to the soul, even if the traces of soulfulness inform each of these ways. Locke, however, though he rejected the analogy, was not the first or only political philosopher to do so. It should suffice to mention Thomas More's *Utopia*, imitative in so many ways of Plato's *Republic*, but I believe completely free of the analogy of the city and the soul. The civil society Locke describes—and maybe even more, the civil society protected and summoned by the American Founders, who lacked his passive-aggressive hostility to traditional Christianity—is porous enough to allow and even require human virtue, even traditional virtue, in the various institutions of civil society, from the family and the church, to the university and the theater, from the army and the sports team to a business firm or a hospital, or even the press. What this constitutionalism denies is that virtue can be coerced without corruption and therefore that its establishment is the business of the state. It is not that the formation of virtue does not require discipline but, rather, that free men (and women) can only truly show their virtue if they are free also to fail. Let the discipline come from civil society, not the state; there is no reason that their action should be considered "private" rather than public, any more than the "public schools" in England did not deserve their name because they were not state creatures. The authors of *The Federalist* praise virtues they expect to summon among the officers in the different branches of government, even though they do not make such virtues a qualification for office, nor do they even discuss the schools where virtue can be formed.[35] The classical republics subjected officers to the scrutiny when their terms were over, punishing them when their virtue was judged to fall short. Modern republics, by contrast, are willing to allow their parties to alternate in office, bringing forward their alternate virtues, and they find the punishment of predecessors usually vindictive and small-minded—or in other words, vicious, not just.

Are the less political, more workmanlike virtues that Locke praises able to sustain a liberal republic? Perhaps Locke would not expect them to, and the American Founders almost certainly did not. But civil society leaves men free to cultivate virtue in its many kinds, and its sometimes harsh world of social, economic, and political competition provides an incentive against softness, mobilizing the energies of the people and focusing their attention. To be "stuck with Locke" in one's political institutions is to be stuck with a need for virtue beyond what the institutions themselves ensure. In a world where the will is recognized as free, is there another path to virtue?

NOTES

1. Friedrich Nietzsche, *Beyond Good and Evil*, trans. Walter Kaufmann (New York: Vintage, 1966), sect. 12, p. 20.

2. Allan Bloom, trans., *The Republic of Plato* (New York: Basic Books, 1968). The analogy is introduced in book 2, at 368e; it is apparently completed and its virtues explained in book 4, at 428a–44a.

3. See Aristotle, *Politics*, books 1, 3, 7, and *Nicomachean Ethics*, book 8.

4. Thomas Hobbes, *Leviathan*, ed. Richard Tuck (Cambridge: Cambridge University Press, 1991), pp. 9–10; the frontispiece is reproduced at p. lxxiv.

5. *Republic*, book 3, at 414c.

6. Ibid., book 5, at 458d–61e.

7. See, for example, *Republic*, book 4, at 419a; cf. translator Bloom's "Interpretive Essay," pp. 307–11.

8. *Republic*, book 9, at 592b; Thomas L. Pangle, trans., *The Laws of Plato* (New York: Basic Books, 1980), esp. book 5, 739a–40a; Aristotle, *Politics*, book 2, at 1261a18; book 3, at 1283a4.

9. Aristotle, *Politics*, book 4, at 1288b22.

10. Smith famously uses this phrase once in his work of moral philosophy and once in his foundational work of economics: *The Theory of Moral Sentiments*, ed. D. D. Raphael and A. L. Macfie, vol. 1 of *The Glasgow Edition of the Works of Adam Smith* (Oxford: Oxford University Press, 1976), 4.1.10, p. 184; *An Inquiry into the Nature and Causes of the Wealth of Nations*, ed. R. H. Campbell and A. S. Skinner, vol. 2 of *Glasgow Edition*, 4.ii.11, p. 456.

11. Immanuel Kant, "Perpetual Peace," First Supplement, in *Political Writings*, ed. Hans Reiss (Cambridge: Cambridge University Press, 1970), p. 112.

12. *Nicomachean Ethics*, book 4, at 1126b11–28b9.

13. John Locke, *A Letter concerning Toleration*, ed. James H. Tully (Indianapolis: Hackett, 1983), p. 26.

14. Plato, *Apology of Socrates*, 25c.

15. Locke, *Letter concerning Toleration*, p. 33.

16. See, for example, Thomas Aquinas, *Summa Theologica*, IIa–IIae, Q.33, A.1: "Whether Fraternal Correction Is an Act of Charity?" a question answered in the affirmative.

17. Locke, *Letter concerning Toleration*, p. 38.

18. John Locke, *Some Thoughts concerning Education*, in Peter Gay, ed., *John Locke on Education* (New York: Teachers College Press, 1964).

19. John T. Harwood, ed., *The Rhetorics of Thomas Hobbes and Bernard Lamy* (Carbondale: Southern Illinois University Press, 1988).

20. Locke, *Some Thoughts concerning Education*, sect. 134.

21. Ibid., sect. 136.

22. Ibid., sect. 138.

23. Ibid., sect. 143.

24. John Locke, *An Essay concerning Human Understanding*, ed. Peter Nidditch (Oxford: Clarendon Press, 1975). The phrase "pursuit of happiness" is in ch. 21, sect. 43, p. 260.

25. See Thomas Hibbs, "The Virtue of Science and the Science of Virtue: Descartes' Overcoming of Socrates."

26. Locke, *An Essay concerning Human Understanding*, ch. 21, sect. 29–53, pp. 249–68.

27. John Locke, *Two Treatises of Government*, ed. Peter Laslett (Cambridge: Cambridge University Press, 1988), 2.5.25–61 (citations refer to treatise, chapter, and section numbers, respectively).

28. Ibid., 2.5.37, 40, 43.

29. Ibid., 2.5.34.

30. *The Laws of Plato*, 744e–45a, where the largest allotment is only four times the smallest, and if anyone should acquire excess wealth, "let him dedicate the surplus to the city and to the gods who possess the city." See also ibid., 742a: "no one is allowed to possess any gold or silver in any private capacity . . . they should possess a kind of coin that carries value among themselves but is valueless among other human beings."

31. Locke, *An Essay concerning Human Understanding*, ch. 21, sect. 55, p. 269; Locke, *Some Thoughts concerning Education*, sect. 108.

32. Locke, *Two Treatises*, 2.7.94, p. 329; cf. Aristotle, *Politics* book 3, at 1286b10.

33. Locke, *Two Treatises*, 2.14.160, p. 375.

34. Ibid., 2.19.221–22.

35. See Harvey C. Mansfield, Jr., *America's Constitutional Soul* (Baltimore: Johns Hopkins University Press, 1991).

6

THE PROBLEM OF HUMAN EQUALITY IN LOCKE'S POLITICAL PHILOSOPHY

Sara M. Henary

Near the beginning of the *Second Treatise*, John Locke offers a recapitulation of the *First Treatise*'s political teaching and its primary implication: pace Sir Robert Filmer, God did not "manifest[ly]" "appoin[t]" a ruler over men, who must accordingly institute government for themselves.[1] The *Second Treatise* proceeds to elaborate the "premise"[2] of this position: a state of nature, or the "state all men are naturally in"—a premise that also serves as the point of departure for Locke's alternative account of the "rise of government," the "origin of political power," and the means "of designing and knowing the persons that have it."[3] Locke describes the state of nature as a condition of "*perfect freedom*" and equality, with "no one having more [power and jurisdiction] than another."[4]

Apparently more confident of the fact of natural freedom than that of natural equality, Locke twice asserts the "eviden[ce]" of the latter.[5] At one point he invokes the authority of the "Judicious [Richard] *Hooker*," according to whom natural equality cannot but be acknowledged.[6] Nevertheless, Locke's actual defense of equality is quite robust and depends on men's belonging to the same "species" and occupying the same "rank":

There being nothing more evident, than that creatures of the same species and rank, promiscuously born to all the same advantages of nature, and the use of the same faculties, should also be equal one amongst another without subordination or subjection, unless the lord and master of them all should, by any manifest declaration of his will, set one above another, and confer on him, by an evident and clear appointment, an undoubted right to dominion and sovereignty.[7]

Although Locke does not explicitly elaborate these relations, it would seem that men's possessing the "same faculties" places them in the same species, and their relative equality in using those faculties means that each stands in a roughly similar position with respect to Nature.[8] Absent a "manifest declaration of [God's] will" to the contrary, men so equipped and situated should be considered equal vis-à-vis one another.

This talk of species and rank should sound somewhat curious to the reader of Locke's *An Essay concerning Human Understanding*, which engages in an unrelenting assault on the existence of natural species. Locke argues that we develop ideas about species of things, including the species "man," for convenience's sake, but he insists that such ideas are not grounded in the nature of things.[9] From the perspective of the *Essay*, one might argue that nothing appears less "evident" than the notion of a species of beings that are, by Nature, equal.

In this chapter I consider what I designate the problem of human equality in Locke's thought, or the tension between the *Second Treatise*'s reliance on something like a notion of "shared species-membership"[10] to ground the idea of equality and the *Essay*'s pronounced anti-essentialism concerning natural species. Among Locke scholars who recognize the problem of equality as such,[11] the responses to this interpretive issue are, generally speaking, two. First, one could argue that the religious dimension of Locke's thought figures prominently in overcoming this tension. The most compelling instance of such argument is Jeremy Waldron's recent book, *God, Locke, and Equality: Christian Foundations in Locke's Political Thought*. Waldron argues that Locke's theoretical commitment to human equality cannot be understood apart from his Christian belief that the human person is God's special creature. More specifically, Waldron's argument attempts to demonstrate that the "God stuff" is integrated into Locke's broader philosophical framework in a way that reduces, if it does not altogether eliminate, the nettlesome problem of Locke's species skepticism.[12]

Second, some scholars have argued that Locke offers a freestanding argument for equality that depends neither on the notion of species nor on the existence of a Creator God. Associated with the interpretation of Leo Strauss, the primary version of this thesis maintains that the common desire for "self-preservation" constitutes the ground of human equality.[13] In this chapter, however, I will focus on Michael Zuckert's variant of the thesis, in part because Zuckert's interpretation points out important problems with Strauss's version.

Responding to Waldron and Zuckert, I suggest that each scholar is partly right and partly wrong. Zuckert correctly grasps Locke's ambivalence about religion but fails to see that one of religion's important functions in Locke's thought is to ground the idea of equality. Waldron accounts for religion's importance in grounding equality but does not appreciate that such a move is political on Locke's part. Inasmuch as equality is inextricably bound up with Christianity in Locke's thought, Locke's commitment to equality is political in nature.

The analysis of this chapter proceeds in five stages. First, I provide an account of the *Essay*'s critique of natural species. Second, I sketch Waldron's interpretation of Locke, which highlights the importance of Locke's theism for his account of human equality. Third, I then consider the chief weakness of Waldron's interpretation, which stems from its relatively uncritical acceptance of Locke's recourse to religious argumentation and premises. Fourth, I present Zuckert's interpretation of the ground of equality in Locke. Zuckert accepts, with some qualification, the political status of God in Locke's thought but goes on to argue that Locke successfully articulates a secular argument for equality. Fifth, I assess Zuckert's argument. Zuckert admits to being somewhat free with his interpretation of Locke, so I generally focus on the weaknesses of his theoretical argument regarding equality.[14]

LOCKE'S CRITIQUE OF NATURAL SPECIES

In the *Essay*, Locke rejects the "usual supposition" concerning natural species, that is, that there exist "certain precise *Essences* or *Forms* of Things, whereby all the Individuals existing, are, by Nature, distinguished into *Species*."[15] According to the "usual" or "Scholastic-Aristotelian" view, Nature possesses an orderly, intelligible structure that is generally accessible to man through the deployment of his reasoning powers.[16] In the realm of natural phenomena, this order manifests itself in the form of distinct "species" that are modeled on pre-existing "forms" or "essences."[17] These species are taken to be natural "classes or kinds with distinct, non-arbitrary boundaries."[18] Just as Nature demarcates a group of beings we identify as "men," it produces numerous other kinds, sorts, or "species" of things—all natural categories existing prior to and independently of human discovery, such as horses, gold, and iron.[19] Locke's scrutiny and ultimate rejection of this kind of "essentialist" thinking has two theoretical bases: a secondary, epistemological one and a primary, ontological one.[20]

The first prong of Locke's critique of natural species is epistemological, as it involves an analysis of the mental processes whereby men come to have ideas about species.[21] According to Locke, the ideas that men have about natural species, or "particular sort[s] of corporeal Substances,"[22] originate in the following way: After noticing that a number of "simple *Ideas*[23] go constantly together," the mind "presume[s]" them "to belong to one thing" and applies to this collection of simple ideas "one name" for purposes of "quick dispatch."[24] The mind "presume[s]" that a collection of simple ideas "belongs" to a "unitary subject" because we cannot "imagin[e] how the simple *Ideas* can subsist by themselves."[25] Thus, we "accustom our selves to suppose some *Substratum*, wherein they do subsist, and from which they do result, which therefore we call *Substance*."[26] Following the original moment of presumption, habit and custom reinforce our sense that substance ideas are "unitary," rather than composite.[27] As a result, "by inadvertency we are apt afterward to talk of and consider as one simple *Idea*, which indeed is a complication of many *Ideas* together."[28]

As Michael Ayers has observed, Locke's description of this mental process recalls Aristotle's account of conception formation and "theory of definition." For Aristotle, observing repeated instances of what they presume to be the same thing, men formulate a "universal notion of the same species present on all these perceptual occasions." From this general concept, men can then construct a "scientific definition" that specifies what is distinctive about a particular phenomenon.[29] Aristotle maintains that this process enables us to pick out real distinctions in Nature. In contrast to Aristotle, Locke argues that the inference of a "unitary" "subject"[30] from repeated observations of apparently similar phenomena is an unwarranted presumption. That we make inferences concerning the existence of "*substantial Forms*"[31] speaks to the weakness of our intellectual faculties and perhaps to our desire for order in Nature, but it does not prove the reality of natural kinds. Ayers aptly captures both the nature and the audacity of

Locke's departure from Aristotle and the Peripatetics: "Locke . . . rewrite[s] the Aristotelian account of the apprehension of natural principles as the psychological explanation of a vain delusion."[32]

On its own, Locke's "epistemological critique" of species is far from decisive.[33] While it suggests that the "Scholastic-Aristotelians" were presumptuous in concluding that our ideas about species provided evidence of their reality, it does not actually refute the existence of natural species. To accomplish this, Locke's epistemological argument—which only sows doubt—must be accompanied by an ontological argument.

The real basis on which Locke rejects the commonsense notion of what Leo Strauss would call the "noetic [or essential] heterogeneity"[34] of Nature, which would imply the existence of natural kinds or classes, lies in his assumption that Nature fundamentally consists of elementary particles or corpuscles.[35] The combining and separating of these corpuscles gives Nature what form it has—a form that, unguided by underlying essences, is fundamentally subject to change with the movement of these particles. As Locke says:

> All Things, that exist, besides their Author, are all liable to Change; especially those Things we are acquainted with, and have ranked into Bands, under distinct Names or Ensigns. Thus that, which was Grass to Day is to Morrow the Flesh of a Sheep; and within few days after, becomes part of a Man.[36]

It is this theoretical orientation that acts as a solvent for the world of ordinary experience that bows to the perception of phenomenal similitude and difference.

With this theoretical assumption of Locke's in view, let us consider the specifics of his attack on species. When we "la[y] aside" our preconceived notions of species and essences and seriously examine the beings that exist in the world, Locke argues, we will find only "particular Beings," or individual entities:

> All such Patterns and Standards [of "essences" or "species"], being quite laid aside, particular Beings, considered barely in themselves, will be found to have all their Qualities equally *essential*; and every thing, in each Individual, will be *essential* to it, or which is more true, nothing at all.[37]

Each of these "particular Beings" is a unique, individual phenomenon. In the passage above, Locke indicates that in one sense all of the attributes of a "being" or "thing" must be "essential" to it or necessarily present in order for it to be *this* particular "being" or "thing." Were such not the case, the "being" or "thing" would not be identical with itself—a logical "absurdity."[38] On Locke's use of "essential" here, the "essence" of a thing consists solely in the properties or qualities that happen to be united in a certain material arrangement at a particular moment in time; "essence" is thus synonymous with chance occurrence or accident. In other words, individual entities possess "essential" qualities only in a trivial sense. Fundamentally, or from an elongated temporal perspective, they lack "essential" characteristics, for one cannot distinguish between properties that are "accidentally" joined to an entity and properties that are "essentially" joined to it.[39]

The material composition of these particular beings is fluid, thus the boundaries between beings will also be in flux. Contrary to the theory of "*substantial Forms*," one observes in "the visible corporeal World" "no Chasms, or Gaps" whereby one thing can be readily distinguished from another. Rather, Nature consists of a "continued series of Things . . . that differ very little one from the other."[40] Locke supplies the following portrait of the being of corporeal reality:

> There are Fishes that have Wings, and are not Strangers to the airy Region: and there are some Birds, that are Inhabitants of the Water. . . . There are some Brutes, that seem to have as much Knowledge and Reason, as some that are called Men: and the Animal and Vegetable Kingdoms, are so nearly join'd, that if you will take the lowest of one, and the highest of the other, there will scarce be perceived any great difference between them; and so on till we come to the lowest and the most inorganical parts of Matter, we shall find every-where, that the several Species are linked together, and differ but in almost insensible degrees.[41]

With this unorthodox and ironic rendering of the "great chain of being,"[42] Locke suggests that Nature does not spontaneously differentiate among phenomena, thereby affording an ontological basis for grouping things together into distinct species according to the particular essence of each kind.

Our actual use of "species" language obscures the truth about Nature.[43] Contrary to the "usual supposition" that Nature contains "*substantial Forms*" corresponding to our use of general "species" terminology, our classification of beings as human or non-human, simple or complex, low or high, derives not from Nature but from a pragmatic need to impose order on the aforementioned "continued series" of particular beings that closely resemble one another.

> But the sorting of Things by us, or the making of determinate Species, being in order to naming and comprehending them under general terms, I cannot see how it can be properly said, that Nature sets the Boundaries of the Species of Things: Or if it be so, our Boundaries of Species, are not exactly conformable to those in Nature . . . but we our selves divide them, by certain obvious appearances, into Species, that we may the easier, under general names, communicate our thoughts about them.[44]

Grouping beings into classes according to "certain obvious appearances" enables us to talk about them with greater facility.

Since Nature produces only "particular Things," it seems that to be fully true to Nature, one would have to consider each entity in all its particularity, as given by Nature. However, Locke insists on the utter impracticality of such an alternative—which would make the "[Mind's] Progress . . . very slow, and its Work endless."[45] He observes that the mind already possesses a faculty—"abstraction"—with which it confronts and organizes the infinite diversity of particular phenomena:

> If every particular Idea that we take in, should have a distinct Name, Names must be endless. To prevent this, the Mind makes the particular Ideas, received from particular Objects, to become general; which is done by considering them as they are in the Mind such Appearances, separate from all other Existences, and the circumstances of real Existence, as Time, Place, or any other concomitant Ideas. This is called ABSTRACTION, whereby Ideas taken from particular Beings, become general Representatives of all of the same kind; and their Names general Names, applicable to whatever exists conformable to such abstract Ideas.[46]

Put another way, abstraction is the process whereby the mind fashions general ideas by selecting features or aspects of particular phenomena to which it will then apply a general name. Abstraction "bind[s] [things] into Bundles, and rank[s] them so into sorts," "collect[ing] Things under comprehensive *Ideas*, with Names annexed to them into *Genera* and *Species*; *i.e.* into kinds, and sorts."[47]

"Abstraction" is merely the name Locke confers on the process of sorting things by their "obvious appearances" and "sensible Qualities," and he insists that the general ideas about "genera" and "species" produced by this mental operation are but conventional categories, or "Fictions and Contrivances of the Mind."[48] Abstract ideas about supposed "essences" and their linguistic correlates—general words—convey "no Knowledge of real Existence at all" but only knowledge of nominal essences, or conventional denominations of the world based on "obvious appearances."[49] Man wrongly supposes that his abstract ideas mediate between words and things, serving to conceptualize accurately the content of the latter in order to create a word symbol that properly communicates the essence of the material referent. By insisting on this "*double Conformity*," man forgets the man-made character of abstract ideas, instead positing a kind of natural correspondence among particular objects, abstract general ideas, and language.[50] Again, the faculty of abstraction aids man in coping with the abundance of sensory experience and particular phenomena. To suppose that the abstract ideas that issue from this process have anything to do with the nature of things is simply a mistake.[51]

As "man's" inclusion in the "great chain of being" implies, Locke does not hesitate to apply this general analysis of natural species to the species "man."[52] Because Nature does not demarcate a group of human beings from all other beings, we must establish a definition of "man" that regulates which beings do and do not fall into that category. Only after one has determined the content of an "abstract *Idea*" of "man" can one proceed to determine who or what counts as a "man."[53] Locke illustrates this point by considering the classical definition of man as "*Animal Rationale.*" However, in opposition to the substance of the classical view—that reason somehow fundamentally differentiates man from other animals—Locke argues that reason can be understood as "essential" to man only if rationality is stipulated as part of the verbal definition of "man":

> So that if it be asked, whether it be essential to me, or any other corporeal Being to have Reason? I say no; no more than it is essential to this white thing I write on, to have words in it. But if that particular Being, be to be [sic] counted of the sort man, and to have the name

Man given to it, then Reason is essential to it, supposing Reason to be a part of the complex Idea the name Man stands for.[54]

The "essence" of "man" or the human "species" rises not from Nature, but from the conferral or "annex[ation]" of "the name Man" to a certain set of properties, often "voluntary Motion, with Sense and Reason, join'd to a Body of a certain shape."[55]

On the level of theory, Locke says little to disturb his conclusion that our definition of man is ultimately arbitrary. Rather, hints of species skepticism—regarding man, in particular—appear throughout the *Essay*, often in discussions formally devoted to other topics. For example, as evidence for his claim that all ideas derive from sensation and reflection, Locke considers the condition of a "new born Child" who has not had occasion to experience much in the way of sensation and therefore has few or no ideas "to think on."[56] The person "who considers" the condition of such a being might be led to make the following speculation: "He . . . , will, perhaps, find Reason to imagine, *That a Foetus in the Mother's Womb, differs not much from the State of a Vegetable*."[57] Locke offers no commentary that would blunt the force of the fetus-vegetable analogy. Also, when discussing the "danger" of mistaking propositional maxims regarding complex ideas for the "manifest Truth," Locke "prob[es]" the "Instance" of "man" by examining three definitions of this complex substance idea. The definitions respectively render color, reason, and shape central to the essence of man.[58] In the first example, Locke describes how an English child could arrive at an understanding of man in which the color white was an essential part of the definition:

First, a Child having framed the Idea of a Man, it is probable, that his Idea is just like that Picture, which the Painter makes of the visible Appearances joined together; and such a Complication of Ideas together in his Understanding, makes up the single complex Idea which he calls Man, whereof White or Flesh-colour in England being one, the Child can demonstrate to you, that a Negro is not a Man, because White-colour was one of the constant simple Ideas of the complex Idea he calls Man.[59]

To be sure, Locke's point in this section is that one must be extremely cautious in making inferences about the natures of things on the basis of their nominal essences. Nevertheless, Eugene F. Miller observes without surprise that the *Essay's* "teaching" regarding substances has led to Locke's "com[ing] under attack as a progenitor of modern racism." Miller states, "I can find no basis in Locke's account of substances for criticizing someone who chooses to define the essence of man in such a way as to exclude Negroes or any other racial group."[60]

The *Essay's* explicit attack on the "usual supposition" concerning "species" sounds of anti-essentialism: "'Tis evident [essences] *are made by the Mind*, and not by Nature: For were they Nature's Workmanship, they could not be so various and different in several Men, as experience tells us they are."[61] However, Locke also acknowledges that the "Mind, in making its complex *Ideas* of Substances, only follows Nature," which, "in the constant production of particular Beings, makes them not always new and various ideas."[62] Admissions of this sort raise the question as to whether Locke concedes, somewhat in spite of himself and in tension with the main thrust of the *Essay's* argumentation, the existence of a Nature that classifies.[63]

Locke does suggest that there exist resemblances among particular beings in Nature. Moreover, he avers that such resemblances are likely grounded in more fundamental similarities of "internal frame and Constitution."[64] This admission does not, however, undermine his point concerning the absence of a natural classification scheme. I would submit that the hypothesis that phenomena with apparently similar properties likely resemble one another with respect to "internal frame and Constitution" is a rather mundane point, not a concession to essentialism. Similar arrangements of atoms (or "corpuscles") will tend to generate apparently similar structures at the level of human observation. Something like this internal structural arrangement is what Locke means by "internal frame and Constitution," which is not a synonym for "essence" in the classical sense. It is important to note that these resemblances at the micro and phenomenal levels do not translate into the functional equivalent of species concepts based on "essential" natural differences. To extend an earlier point, it is impossible to distinguish between "essential" and "accidental" properties because no two natural things are constituted in *exactly* the same manner. On Uzgalis' interpretation of Locke, the fact that there exists "a continuous distribution of different properties" means that, even at the level of "real essence," "it is impossible to find non-arbitrary boundaries of the species."[65] Locke's analogy between the internal workings of different men and those of different timepieces illustrates the point that a detailed knowledge of "internal Constitution[s]" does not reveal a natural classification scheme. Even if man could, as is possible with different sorts of timepieces, obtain full knowledge of the inner workings of different human beings, he would realize that in men, as in watches, "each of these hath a real difference from the rest: But whether it be an essential, a specifick difference or no, relates only to the complex *Idea*, to which the name *Watch* is given."[66] Thus man's inability to classify beings in Nature in accordance with their "internal Constitution[s]" does not result from the weakness of his faculties, or otherwise from his inability to gain "epistemic access" to preexisting natural categories.[67]

On this understanding of natural resemblances, we can make more or less useful classifications of phenomena. As Waldron observes in his excellent discussion of this topic, however, any resemblances between entities in Nature will be resemblances that are deemed relevant to *our* particular purposes in classifying. For Locke, says Waldron, "The pragmatic idea of an improvement in our nominal classifications is entirely relative to our purposes in making such classifications."[68] In the following section, I discuss Waldron's response to what appears to be a fairly strong defense of ontological nominalism.

WALDRON'S ARGUMENT: MAKING LOCKE CONSISTENT

In the *Second Treatise*, Locke suggests that God ordered the situation of original human equality which he describes. "For Men being all the Workmanship of one Omnipotent, and infinitely wise Maker," they are to have dominion over the "inferior ranks" of Creation while partaking equally in the advantages of Nature afforded members of the highest species— the only species made in the image of God.[69] As creatures equally free yet equally subject to the strictures of "God's moral order,"[70] human beings, as agents "about his business," have a right to a certain level of consideration from others and a duty to attend seriously to the rights of similar beings.[71] Although Locke appeals primarily to reason when describing the formation and maintenance of human societies,[72] he invokes Scripture both implicitly and explicitly (in the language of Dunn), "when we come upon the normative creaturely equality of all men in virtue of their shared species-membership."[73]

Given the apparent straightforwardness of Locke's meaning in the early pages of the treatise, it is unsurprising that the probable connection in his thought between the ideas of God and human equality has been noted. Nevertheless, Waldron reflects anew on this connection in light of Locke's species skepticism. He acknowledges that the *Essay*'s "pretty thorough-going anti-realism" concerning the "natural kind" notion of species has the potential to undermine the *Second Treatise*'s robust defense of human equality.[74] In the final analysis, Waldron argues, understanding the position of God within the broader context of Locke's philosophical project is essential for grasping his defense of equality. Locke's commitment to a theologically motivated conception of what it means to be a human being ultimately directs and tempers the conclusions he draws from an otherwise skeptical philosophical position.

Waldron's interpretation commences with a charitable presumption in favor of the "unity of Locke's thought": "In order to *make* Locke's account of equality in the *Two Treatises* consistent with his discussion [of species] in Book III of the *Essay*," Waldron states, a "species" or "natural kind" concept cannot supply the foundation for equality.[75] Locke's opposition to the notion of natural species in the *Essay* is simply too unequivocal. Having conceded Locke's denial of a natural human species, Waldron proposes to "focus instead on what Locke is prepared to concede [in the *Essay*]— namely, real resemblances between particulars."[76]

For a "real resemblance" among beings to do the heavy lifting required of Locke's equality principle, Waldron argues, "it must be an interesting or relevant similarity for the purposes of the weight that is going to be placed on it."[77] In this view, equality cannot be established by reference to a trivial feature that all men share, such as their constitution by molecular particles. Locke must meet the challenge of locating a resemblance that is both common to all men *and* unique to mankind.[78] Furthermore, he must demonstrate that this single point or cluster of resemblances, this "threshold" that one must meet to earn the designation "human," operates by classifying individuals in a "non-scalar" rather than a hierarchical manner. That someone attains the minimum criterion or criteria for "humanness" should matter much more than further distinctions within the category "human."[79] This is Locke's project, according to Waldron.

Locke's use of marginal examples (e.g., "monsters," the irrational) illustrates in dramatic fashion that there exist virtually no resemblances shared by all members of the human species, however defined.[80] A common resemblance among men is difficult enough to locate, yet any resemblance that grounds human equality must also elevate and distinguish man from beasts and other natural things. To revisit a previous argument, however, Nature supplies only a continuum of beings and things. The chain of being "ascend[s] upward" and downward from man by "gentle degrees," and the differences—between, for instance, vegetables and human fetuses—are "almost insensible."[81] Locke's account of the chain of being permits the simultaneity of what are, for the proponent of human equality, two inimical outcomes: the equation of man and beast or any other natural thing as well as the acknowledgment of radical differences between and among men.

According to Waldron, it is at this moment that Locke's religious commitments come into play. To buttress the presentation of "man" proffered in the *Two Treatises*, theology must participate in what often appears to be a skeptical philosophical project. Building on Locke's discussion of a feature that most humans have and that all "brutes" lack, the power to abstract or "the capacity to reason on the basis of general ideas,"[82] Waldron argues that this "real resemblance" among men, when paired with Locke's attempt to demonstrate God's existence, assigns humans a "special status" as a "class" of creatures set apart by Nature as capable of experiencing a "special *moral* relation[ship]" with God:[83]

> To motivate and explicate the power of abstraction as the relevant equality-threshold, we must consider the moral and theological pragmatics which lie at the back of Locke's account of the human intellect . . . each [standard-model human] has intellect enough for some fundamental purpose [i.e., "to lead them to the Knowledge of their Maker"].84
>
> Anyone with the capacity for abstraction can reason to the existence of God, and he can relate the idea of God to there being a law that applies to him both in his conduct in this world and as to his prospects in the next. The content of that law may not be available to everyone's reason, but anyone above the threshold has the power to relate the idea of such law to what is known by faith and revelation about God's commandments.[85]

As men have "[l]ight enough to lead them to the Knowledge of their Maker, and the sight of their own Duties," they enjoy a special moral status as a result of this "corporeal rationality."[86] While all humans, especially those possessing dim cognitive capacities, may not understand Locke's rational demonstration of God's existence, most have *intellect enough* to consider themselves as persons and to follow the light of revelation to knowledge of their status as subject to an omnipotent Deity.[87] If one can abstract or "reason on the basis of general ideas," one merits inclusion as part of the "species" on display in the *Second Treatise*.[88] Again, Waldron's idea is that humans who possess "corporeal rationality" and can abstract functions, in most circumstances, to distinguish man from beast yet ensures that extreme dissimilarities among men are of minimal import.

According to Waldron's interpretation of Locke, ordinary men can, through reason or revelation, find their way to the existence of God. The idea of a Creator God brings into existence a class of beings that is both more internally homogenous (when compared to the majesty of the Creator) and more special than is evident from an empirical point of view. "Corporeal rationality" alone cannot create a "class" of human beings; the distribution of human intelligence is simply too uneven. However, the potential for human beings to utilize their "corporeal rationality" in a particular way—in contemplation of God's existence whether through reason or revelation—separates them as a group from the rest of natural things. Waldron describes the egalitarian attitude that flows from this conceptualization of the "human." Despite vast differences in the intellectual abilities of humans,

> the fact that one is dealing with an animal that has the capacity to approach the task [of considering himself in relation to God] in one way or another is all-important, and it makes a huge difference to how such a being may be treated in comparison to animals whose capacities are such that this whole business of knowing God and figuring out his commandments is simply out of the question. . . . When I catch a rabbit, I know that I am not dealing with a creature that has the capacity to abstract, and so I know that there is no question of this being one of God's special servants, sent into the world about his business. But if I catch a human in full possession of his faculties, I know I should be careful how I deal with him.[89]

It is critical to note that introducing these theological considerations does not eliminate all of the problems associated with drawing a boundary around the human species; marginal cases will continue to arise. Nevertheless, the recognition that God created a certain kind of being capable of relating to Him in a special way ideally engenders an attitude or spirit of openness toward and acceptance of all those who might possibly be "one of God's special servants."

In Waldron's view, to dispense with the "God stuff" in Locke's thought is to dispense with the reference point that he employs to "give shape" to the "shapelessness" of an otherwise unintelligible and incoherent mass of individual beings. Given Locke's skepticism about species, without the existence of a Creator God one cannot argue that there are certain "facts about humanity" that merit special consideration as features toward "which we might take up egalitarian attitudes (for any reason)." "[A] certain cluster of characteristics" associated with human equality "might seem arbitrary, shapeless, even insignificant apart from [Locke's] religious context."[90]

RESPONSE TO WALDRON

I am inclined to agree with Waldron that criteria-based arguments for equality are, on their own, doomed to fail. Any argument for equality will have to make reference to certain features and capacities—for purposes both of capturing the anthropological fact of embodiment and of elucidating, shall we say, something like the "specific difference" that establishes a human category. Nevertheless, by failing to identify an appropriate cocktail of similitude and difference among beings, these kinds of arguments generally falter because of their inability to establish a common humanity that is sufficiently dignified. The notion of a Creator God has the potential to solve this intractable empirical problem by generating a very specific type of relationship-based orientation toward God (hierarchical) and the "other" (horizontal).[91] Additionally, given Locke's attentiveness to the problem of natural species (and of categorization more generally), Waldron appears to be on firm ground when arguing that the only possible source of human equality in Locke's thought is the idea of a Creator God.

Without denying that the "God stuff" functions for Locke in much the way Waldron describes, I think that Waldron mistakes the manner in which Locke incorporates religious argumentation into his philosophical enterprise. On Waldron's interpretation, religion is integrated into the very structure of the Lockean philosophical apparatus in several ways, the most important regarding his conception of the "*corporeal rational Being*,"[92] a concept whose potency depends on the demonstrable existence of the God with whom this being can have a certain kind of relationship. Upon closer inspection, Waldron seems to have it backward. Even when Locke's religious arguments appear "foundational" to a certain aspect of his political thought, he seems to have reached for them when all other possibilities have been exhausted.[93] Religion comes along *after the fact*, and its incorporation is typically due to the failure of philosophy to supply sufficient moral or political guidance. Before considering explicitly the status of God in Locke's thought, I will examine the related issue of Waldron's reliance on a "real resemblance" in order to ground equality.

THE PROBLEM WITH "REAL RESEMBLANCES"

As Waldron himself acknowledges, Locke's philosophy does not allow "real resemblances" to function as proxies for species concepts. As discussed above, Locke is keen to delegitimize our habit of generalizing based on the perceived existence of recurrent similarities—"real resemblances"—between beings. Waldron's initial analysis of "real resemblances" in the natural world parallels his pronouncement on the status of "species" in the *Essay*. Before determining that, in lieu of a species concept, certain "real resemblances between particulars" are "doing the crucial work in Locke's account of equality," Waldron admits that categorizations grounded in such similarities are based on "nothing in nature" but, rather, derive from the human "propensity" to use "general words." Distinctions rooted in "resemblances and differences," like species concepts, amount to little more than "nominal essences" or "projections onto [the] nature of our own linguistic habits."[94] Constant refinement of these nominal classifications might facilitate social interaction, prevent misunderstandings, and so on, but again, "improvement in our nominal classifications is entirely relative to our purposes in making such classifications." How *well* human beings collect, divide, or relate the phenomena of existence is not a question to which there is an "objective[ly]" correct response. Provided the honing of species or other categories is simply "pragmatic," having no correspondence with divisions that inhere in Nature, our evaluative judgments concerning better and worse orderings of the natural world are also simply "pragmatic."[95] This analysis would seem to disallow Waldron's subsequent reversion to "real resemblances" as a relatively firm basis on which to ground Lockean equality.

Waldron justifies this unexpected move to consider "characteristics" and "resemblances" rather than "species or ranks of species" by pointing to a passage in Locke where he makes (claims Waldron) a "philosophical" distinction "between species and real resemblance":[96]

> Substances, when concerned in moral Discourses, their divers Natures are not so much enquir'd into, as supposed; v.g. when we say that Man is subject to Law: We mean nothing by Man, but a corporeal rational Creature: What the real Essence or other Qualities of that Creature are in this Case, is no way [sic] considered. And therefore, whether a Child or Changeling be a Man in a physical Sense, may amongst the Naturalists be disputed as it will, it concerns not at all the moral Man, as I may call him, which is this immoveable unchangeable Idea, a corporeal rational Being.[97]

Rather than speculating about the natures of species, one must adopt the aforementioned notion of "*moral Man,*" who is a "*corporeal rational Being.*" The nature or essence of the species man is to be "supposed" in order to avoid "Obscurity" in "moral Discourses."[98]

Absent Waldron's assumptions about Locke's "strategy" for locating a "similarity among faculties that would be robust enough to sustain the sort of equality thesis [he] wants," there does not seem to be anything in this passage that would suggest a philosophical distinction "between species and real resemblance."[99] There is, in Locke's view, a practical imperative to "suppose" that man has a nature in order to avoid analyses of "Substances" "when concerned with moral Discourses." Such a move might be considered philosophical, but only if it refers to philosophy's self-awareness regarding its own inability to answer certain questions that are raised in everyday life: for example, "What is a man?" Moreover, Locke makes it abundantly clear that philosophers ought, especially when moral discourses are concerned, to work with the common "signification[s]" of words as they appear in everyday discourse.[100] This would seem to be the primary explanation for Locke's introducing the notion of *a corporeal rational Being* in this passage. It might just so happen that "our way" of talking about man also has an aspect to it that posits something like human equality—Locke does not say so here. In any event, the entire context of Locke's treatment of substances indicates that the definition of man as "*a corporeal rational Being*" should be understood to enjoy a privileged status practically or politically, not ontologically.

To serve as the "host property" for human equality, the "real resemblance" of "corporeal rationality" must be (at least potentially) exercised in a particular way.[101] Additionally, the relevant exercise of our "corporeal rationality"—abstraction—involves an infusion of "religious content."[102] Insufficient on its own, this "real resemblance" must be ennobled. Waldron suggests that this enlivening occurs *within* the parameters of Locke's philosophical apparatus. An analysis of what Locke actually says about the faculty of abstraction and the "God stuff" will suggest that it does not.

ABSTRACTION AND AN ABSTRACT IDEA OF GOD

Again, the following claim is crucial to the success of Waldron's argument: "Anyone with the capacity for abstraction can reason to the existence of God."[103] The rational demonstration of God's existence provided by Locke in the *Essay* is, on this view, generally accessible: "Locke believed the argument for God's existence was . . . something which required no particularly abstruse reasoning and might be arrived at by the intellect of the meanest person."[104] "If showing [that God exists] had required an irrational *leap* of faith," Waldron states, "then morality would not in principle be capable of demonstration." The result would be, as Locke argues in the *Essays on the Law of Nature*, that men could be bound by nothing but the will of the strongest.[105]

The rational demonstration of God's existence occurs in book 4, chapter 10, of the *Essay*, where Locke sets out to "shew . . . that we are capable of *knowing, i.e. being certain that there is a GOD.*"[106] Waldron follows other commentators in acknowledging the weaknesses of this demonstration, as well as Locke's awareness of them.[107] He does not, however, seriously attend to the rather odd situation of a demonstration of God's existence within the context of an empiricist epistemology. Bluhm, Wintfeld, and Teger investigate some "difficulties internal to the proof" itself, contending that it amounts to a vacillation on Locke's part between the "inconceivability" of creation ex nihilo and its necessary "supposition," a "circularity" necessitated by the logical impossibility of all such demonstrations.[108] However, Bluhm et al. are more persuasive when they point to evidence from Locke's epistemology that problematizes his claim that the demonstration produces *knowledge* of God's existence.[109] Though inspired by their analysis as well as by that of James Tully, my own analysis is stated in somewhat different terms.[110]

First, assigning the faculty and process of abstraction such a prominent role in saving equality for Locke presents problems that Waldron does not explore. As discussed above, Locke relates the faculty of abstraction to man's need to impose order on a world of particulars; only conventional categories issue from this process of forming general ideas. Waldron's discussion of species in Locke indicates that he is keenly aware that the products of abstraction have such a status. However, he does not investigate the implications of this acknowledgment for Locke's view that our concept of God is an abstract idea.

We form our idea of God, argues Locke, by abstracting from existence all of its positive aspects and joining them with the idea of infinity. His account of the formation of this idea is worth quoting at length:

> For if we examine the Idea we have of the incomprehensible supreme Being, we shall find, that we come by it the same way; and that the complex Ideas we have both of God, and separate Spirits, are made up of the simple Ideas we receive from Reflection; v.g. having from what we experiment in our selves, got the Idea of Existence and Duration; of Knowledge and Power; of Pleasure and Happiness; and of several other Qualities and Powers, which it is better to have, than to be without; when we would frame an Idea the most suitable we can to the supreme Being, we enlarge every one of these with our Idea of Infinity; and so putting them together, make our complex Idea of God. . . . For it is Infinity, which, joined to our Ideas of Existence, Power, Knowledge, etc. makes that complex Idea, whereby we represent to our selves the best we can, the supreme Being. For though in his own Essence, (which certainly we do not know, not knowing the real Essence of a Peble, or a Fly, or of our own selves,) God be simple and uncompounded; yet, I think, I may say we have no other Idea of him, but a complex one of Existence, Knowledge, Power, Happiness, etc. infinite and eternal.[111]

As Bluhm et al. observe, this is not "a description of a universal psychological process."[112] In other words, the process of abstraction is not a mechanism through which God ensures that all people have access to knowledge of Him. Indeed, Locke speaks of whole societies that have not developed an idea of God at all.[113]

According to Locke's classification scheme, the abstract idea of God is a substance idea.[114] Just as the formation of our ideas about particular substances such as man and gold stems from the desire for intelligibility and coherence in the material world, the formation of our idea of God is motivated by the psychological desire for what Bluhm et al. call "existential coherence."[115] As is the case with our ideas of particular substances, we suppose that our ideas about God "cannot subsist" independently of "something to support them," even if that something is unknown.[116] With the idea of "man" we suppose a "substratum" that underpins a natural kind; with the idea of God we suppose a Being that underpins all things. However, Locke insists that abstract ideas—of which God is one—are but "Fictions and Contrivances of the Mind," regardless of one's belief about their content.[117] Locke's epistemology thus supports our having the notion of God, yet this is rather different from arriving at *knowledge* of His existence.

Second, despite his claim that God's existence has been demonstrated, Locke suggests that it is not possible to arrive at such knowledge by means of a verbal demonstration. Rather, he claims that verbal demonstrations add nothing to our knowledge of existence, including our knowledge of substances.[118] Given Locke's view that our "knowledge" of substance concepts is purely definitional, this conclusion should not be surprising. Our knowledge of substances is "trifling," and to the extent that knowledge of substances is "instructive," Locke claims that it is necessarily "uncertain." Generally speaking, however, the business of making propositions about substances and engaging in demonstrations on the basis of such propositions tells us only what we already know, i.e., the content of the nominal definitions of these substances:

> For 'tis plain, that Names of substantial Beings, as well as others, as far as they have relative Significations affixed to them, may, with great Truth, be joined negatively and affirmatively in Propositions, as their relative Definitions make them fit to be so joined; and Propositions consisting of such Terms may, with the same clearness, be deduced one from another, as those that convey the most real Truths; and all this without any knowledge of the Nature or reality of Things existing without us. By this method, one may make Demonstrations and undoubted Propositions in Words, and yet thereby advance not one jot in the Knowledge of the Truth of Things; v.g. he that having learnt these following Words, with their ordinary mutually relative Acceptations annexed to them; v.g. Substance, Man, Animal, Form, Soul, Vegetative, Sensitive, Rational, may make several undoubted Propositions about the Soul, without showing at all what the Soul really is;

and of this sort, a Man may find an infinite number of Propositions, Reasonings, and Conclusions, in Books of Metaphysicks, School-Divinity, and some sort of natural Philosophy; and after all know as little of GOD, Spirits, or Bodies, as he did before he set out.[119]

Because most of our propositions about substances are "trifling," they carry with them only a "*verbal Certainty*" associated with our definitions of nominal essences; they do not communicate "*real Knowledge*."[120] Seemingly learned verbal demonstrations do nothing to alter this conclusion.

Locke does express the view that our ideas about God are exceptions to the general rule that having ideas about things in no way implies anything concerning their "real existence":

> For there being no necessary connexion of *real Existence*, with any *Idea* a Man hath in his memory, nor of any other Existence but that of GOD, with the Existence of any particular Man. . . . For the having the *Idea* of any thing in our Mind, no more proves the Existence of that Thing, than the picture of a Man evidences his being in the World, or the Visions of a Dream make thereby a true History.[121]

> The having the *Ideas* of Spirits does not make us know, that any such Things do exist without us, or *that there are any finite Spirits*, or any other spiritual Beings, but the Eternal GOD. . . . No existence of any thing without us, but only of GOD, can certainly be known farther than our Senses inform us.[122]

These passages do, however, have a rather hollow ring.

LOCKE'S POLITICAL DEFENSE OF CHRISTIANITY

Finally, Waldron fails to appreciate an important aspect of Locke's discussion of the superiority of Christianity (belief) to ancient philosophy (reason alone) in the *Reasonableness of Christianity*. For Waldron, this discussion speaks primarily to Locke's vindication of the ordinary intellect over and against the pretentions of philosophy to moral knowledge.[123] While this is true, as far as it goes, Locke's primary intention in the passages that Waldron cites is to supply a *political* defense of Christianity.

In the *Reasonableness*, Locke cites the failure of ancient philosophy to supply a clear, rational foundation for moral conduct. Prior to the advent of Christianity, mankind did not have recourse to a "sure Standard" of morality that had "the force of a Law" and "could with certainty [be] depend[ed] on."[124] At its worst, the unassisted reason of philosophy raised too many questions left unanswered; at its best, it could only point to the "excellency of Virtue" and recommend the "exalting of human Nature."[125] In short, not only did it prove "too hard a task for unassisted Reason, to establish Morality in all its parts upon its true foundations," but philosophy could not attract many "Followers" to the loftiness of a life lived according to virtue, which was difficult and "not often accompan[ied]" by prosperity.[126] The great advantage of Christianity in this regard is its provision of a relatively straightforward body of morals and ethics the authority of which is supported by divine revelation, which also admonishes men to comply with the promise of eternal rewards and threat of eternal punishments.[127] Christianity's self-proclaimed universality implies that the application of its "sure Standard" is at least potentially universal.

These last two sets of considerations suggest that Waldron is insufficiently probing in his analysis of the status of religious argumentation in Locke's thought. Because religion has important work to do in political society, religious argumentation will have important work to do in Locke's political thought. It helps to get things off the ground, so to speak, in a way that human reason alone cannot. In addition to its other political advantages, Christianity furnishes Locke with a particular conception of human *being* that allows him to advance political arguments in a particular time and place. While Waldron elaborates nicely the work accomplished by these premises, he does not explore the ways in which the logic of Locke's other forms of argumentation (e.g., epistemological) jeopardizes the fundamental status of these premises. If these premises are political, as I have suggested, *and* the ultimate ground of Locke's defense of equality, such would imply that the latter is ultimately political as well. Granting that Locke's religious premises are political, in the following section I explore a possible alternative to this conclusion.

ZUCKERT'S ARGUMENT: THE EQUALITY OF LOCKEAN "SELVES"

Primarily in *Natural Rights and the New Republicanism* but also in other works, Michael Zuckert puts forward an account of human equality that is ostensibly derived from the political philosophy of John Locke.[128] His interpretation of Locke has two important components. First, conceding the force of Locke's critique of natural species, Zuckert argues that one can find in Locke resources for an account of human equality that does not ultimately depend upon the existence of a natural human kind or species.[129] Zuckert argues that this conception, which is grounded in an analysis of the Lockean self, distinguishes human beings as a class from the rest of Nature in a way that approximates the function of a species concept. Second, by following a variant of Leo Strauss's interpretation of the status of God in Locke's writings, Zuckert effectively denies himself the luxury (enjoyed by Waldron, as we saw above) of appealing to the Creator God as the real grounding of equality in Locke.[130] I will address the two elements of Zuckert's argument in reverse order.

In Strauss's reading of Locke, not only is the latter's invocation of theology and Scripture in the *Two Treatises* and elsewhere purely rhetorical, but it is also motivated by the malevolent intention of introducing the unsuspecting reader to the materialist, hedonistic precepts of Thomas Hobbes.[131] Zuckert acknowledges that much of Locke's religious argumentation is mere rhetoric conceived in order not to offend the religious sensibilities of certain contemporaries, but he insists, contra Strauss, that the deployment of such rhetoric (a) reveals Locke's "reservations" about—rather than his rejection of—theism and (b) signals benevolent, as opposed to malevolent, intention on the part of Locke. According to Zuckert, Locke's doubts about the strength of his religiously based arguments (e.g., his purported demonstration of God's existence in the *Essay*) led him to offer parallel structures of argumentation—one religious, one rationalist or secular—for his doctrine of equal natural rights.[132] Furthermore, the implications of the two structures of argumentation, Zuckert holds, largely converge.[133]

If some perceive duplicity in this two-pronged approach to the justification of political principles, Zuckert sees the assumption of political and social responsibility. Despite personal doubts, Locke recognized that religion must continue to perform its traditional function of supplying the political community with moral and theoretical foundations.[134] While many might find Locke's divine "workmanship" argument compelling, Zuckert maintains that Locke seems hesitant to ground important political concepts such as equality solely on so tenuous a premise as the existence of a Creator God who legislates the good and the right for human beings.[135] Locke the empiricist would prefer that equality be grounded on something *real*, something in this world. Such is the logic that led him to offer, in addition to the argument from Creation, a freestanding argument for human equality.

Finally, Zuckert is openly critical of Strauss's claim that the idea of self-preservation can serve as an adequate secular basis for human equality and, therefore, modern natural right, or the equal right of everyone to self-preservation and non-domination.[136] This is a position that Strauss attributes to both Hobbes and Locke. Zuckert argues, however, that Hobbesian equality premised on the desire for self-preservation—a desire shared by men and beasts—cannot be *real* equality, for it does not adequately distinguish man from the rest of Nature. For this reason, "Hobbes's right of nature" cannot serve as the ground of human equality or, by extension, modern natural right.[137] By contrast, Zuckert claims, Lockean philosophy offers more promising resources for constructing a secular argument for equality.[138]

Zuckert's argument draws upon both the *Essay*'s account of the "self" and the *Second Treatise*'s discussion of "self-ownership," and its success depends upon the crucial claim that the Lockean "self" is sufficiently structured to act in certain ways. For our purposes, it is enough to note the claim that this "self" is "structur[ally]" bound to recognize both the existence and the equality of other selves.[139] According to Zuckert, Locke's secular argument for equality unfolds in roughly two stages. First, the notion of "self-ownership" enables Zuckert's Locke to distinguish man from the rest of the natural world. Second, the all-too-human process whereby men are distinguished from Nature effectively generates a class of equal human beings in a way that does not rely on the dubious notion of "species."

For Zuckert's Locke, what serves to differentiate men from animals and other natural beings and things is their ability to generate and hold property, including "property in [their] own person[s],"[140] or "selves." For Locke, property issues exclusively from the efforts of human labor—the sole means whereby, through "appropriation" and "transformation," one can confer value on the "almost worthless raw material" of the "given world." For example, when I invest my labor in cultivating a parcel of land, the activities of plowing, sowing, and reaping justify my appropriating the fruits of my labor. Labor divides, classifies, and distinguishes; through it, man actively and "self-consciously" confronts the world, establishing his "purposes as the end for the sake of which the rest of nature is to be transformed."[141] Animals might "also interact with the world and must seize and digest other beings in order to survive," but they do not generate claims of property, or of that which is wholly and exclusively *mine*. Similarly, through the exercise of the higher mental faculties, man comes to acquire property in himself; "self . . . comes to consciousness" of itself and becomes the owner of its own actions and activities. One of these faculties—abstraction—plays an especially important role in separating man from Nature. On Locke's view, Zuckert states, abstraction "frees the mind of the givenness with which ideas first are received. Abstraction lifts the mind out of the given flow of sensation and allows it to stand in semisovereign sway over its own contents."[142] In the same way that human labor gives rise to property "outside" us, the active deployment of our mental faculties and the self-consciousness with which humans—as opposed to animals—raise claims of right makes men owners of themselves. When coupled with their power to generate property by laboring both on the external world and on themselves, the subsequent claims of right made by human beings about both phenomena suggest a way in which human beings differ profoundly from the rest of Nature—and this without recourse to problematic notions of "species" and human "essences."[143]

On Zuckert's interpretation, "self-ownership," a comportment peculiar to human beings, helps Locke to construct from Hobbesian (materialist) premises what materialism seemed not to permit: a relatively clear distinction between man and the rest of Nature. However, Zuckert continues, certain features of Locke's "self-ownership" argument also enable him to effect this distinction in a way that secures all persons *equal* access to the privileges and responsibilities of "self-ownership." All (able-bodied and able-minded) humans are equally "self-owners." By examining the "phenomenology . . . of human-rights claiming," which is peculiar to human property owners, Zuckert's Locke advances the following position:

> The claim of right is thus more than and different from Hobbes's claim of liberty. So far as I raise a claim to property, in myself or my belongings, I raise *by definition* a claim with implications of exclusivity. On that basis I expect of right that others ought to respect my claim and forbear from my property.[144]

In other words, "[m]y claim of my right to my life as a matter of observed fact includes a claim of exclusivity" and implies that unprovoked external interference on your part with my claims of right is therefore wrong, or unjust. While others might choose not to forbear, the structure of my articulation of a "right" to either my*self* or the efforts of my labor as property implies the injustice of another's interference with such. "This is,"

Zuckert says, "an analytic truth, implicit in the very notion of property I am deploying."[145] It follows, he continues, that

> [t]he logic of my own claim for myself leads me beyond the claim I raise for myself to recognize like claims of others. If my being owner of myself gives me a rightful expectation that others will not gratuitously harm me, I am led to see that their claim to be owners of themselves gives them the same rightful expectation that I and others will not gratuitously harm them.[146]

Although he does not say so explicitly, Zuckert seems to be arguing that asserting one's own rights claims without recognizing another self's right to do the same involves one in a "performative contradiction," or a speech act in which "the propositional content of what the speaker says contradicts the conditions of the asserted proposition itself."[147] Based on my own experience as a self-owner and proprietor I must, by logical necessity, recognize that similar utterances made by other beings must be made by beings that are like me. These beings' statements imply the same right of exclusivity and forbearance on the part of the aggressor as do mine. To do other than recognize such claims would involve one in a performative inconsistency.

To recapitulate, starting from non-theistic premises, Zuckert's Locke makes the following argument for equality. The idea of humans as "proprietors" and "self-owners" functions in lieu of a suspect "species" category to differentiate human beings from the rest of Nature. Only humans have the capacity to attempt mastery of both Nature and themselves. To deny any minimally rational person the right to make property claims by refraining to forbear entangles one in a "performative contradiction." While no circumstance compels an individual to assent to the proposition that all are equally rights claimants and thus owed a certain duty of forbearance, the logic of argumentation itself accuses the one who refuses to do so of performative inconsistency. Thus inherently linked to the notion of the "self" as a "self-owner" is the obligation to recognize one's fellow human selves.

The implications of this argument for human equality are fairly straightforward. Although the duties imposed on the human will appear slight and are essentially negative (i.e., not to inflict "gratuitou[s] harm" on another), if the argument of Zuckert's Locke works, it would appear to rescue the idea of human equality from the corrosiveness of anti-essentialism without resorting to theism. While it cannot be said to engender in most an active, attentive concern for the other, the argument professes to group human beings together as equal members of a class—if only in speech that reveals something true about the character of the human "self."

RESPONSE TO ZUCKERT

There is much to say about Zuckert's account, but I will examine in particular two claims: (a) that the ability of humans to generate property, especially property in their persons, adequately distinguishes man from the rest of the natural world; and (b) that the very structure of rights-based claims that rises from the phenomenon of human property ownership presupposes the speaker's (rights claimant's) implicit recognition of the equality of other persons (or selves) who make similar claims.

Zuckert's observation that humans differentiate themselves from the rest of Nature through the use of physical and mental labor seems correct as far as it goes. Unlike animals, which are directed by instinct alone, man must make use of his reason if he is to survive, much less thrive. In the case of human beings, Nature furnishes man with a general desire for self-preservation but little in the way of positive direction (via inclination or instinct) regarding how he might go about preserving himself. Rather, Nature's gift to man is the faculty of reason, that versatile tool with which he confronts and, if necessary, subdues Nature in the course of pursuing his ends. Most humans soon discover that some form of property is useful in helping them overcome the difficulties posed by Nature's unwillingness to produce spontaneously for all their needs. Locke observes, "And the Condition of Humane Life, which requires Labour and Materials to work on, necessarily introduces *private Possessions*."[148]

Additionally, Zuckert places the bar for who counts as a property owner and what counts as the assertion of a property claim quite within reach of most of those the good liberal would seek to include in a definition of humanity. To utter the word "I" (i.e., assert property in one's person) or to give some indication that this or that is *mine* seems sufficient to constitute a declaration of property ownership. Again, this standard is generous enough to encompass most people.

While the idea of human proprietorship conveys important information about how most beings traditionally defined as "human" interact with the world in contradistinction to most animals, it does not justify a clear distinction between "man" and "Nature" on the order that Zuckert suggests.

Especially since Zuckert acknowledges Locke's anti-essentialism concerning species, the most one should be able to say about his description of (most) men as "self-owners" is that such might be an interesting and useful way to think about the "human species" for purposes of nominal classification. "Self-ownership" captures the unique ability of most human beings to interact with the world in a meaningful way ("To be a self is to be owner of self, proprietor of one's actions, and actor in terms of one's happiness, that is, one's pleasures and pains")[149] but does not draw the necessary line. In short, "self-ownership" will generally be subject to the same kinds of problems that plagued other pretenders to the title of "specific difference," such as rationality.

What about the claim that the logical necessity of mutual recognition follows from the self's assertion of its own rights? Do statements that explicitly assert or implicitly assume self-ownership require one—if he is to avoid involvement in a performative contradiction—to recognize the rights of other "self-owners"? I do not think that any formulation of a "self-ownership" claim requires that one acknowledge the legitimacy of similar claims made by others. The denial of such claims does not, therefore, entangle one in a performative contradiction. Again, a performative contradiction is a speech act in which "the propositional content of what the speaker says contradicts the conditions of the asserted proposition itself."[150] Borrowing Descartes' famous example, to doubt one's own existence would involve one in a performative contradiction:

> In the next place, I attentively examined what I was, and as I observed that I could suppose that I had no body, and that there was no world nor any place in which I might be; but that I could not therefore suppose that I was not; and that, on the contrary, from the very circumstance that I thought to doubt of the truth of other things, it most clearly and certainly followed that I was.[151]

In uttering the phrase "I do not exist," the phrase's "propositional content"—a denial of my own existence—contradicts an assumption necessarily made in my articulation of the statement: the fact that "I am." It follows from this assumption that I cannot reasonably doubt my own existence upon making this statement. By contrast, in Zuckert's case, nothing about how I ought to treat another self-declared "self-owner" seems to follow from an act or statement that implies or declares my awareness of my own status as a "self-owner." The possibility that one might reach the conclusion that my self-concern indicates something about how other "self-owners" ought to be treated does not follow from the logic of "self-ownership" but would seem to require a theory of the "self" that is not, as Zuckert's is, "self-constituting."

Divorced from any concept that might give one some sense of the value of other selves (e.g., divine "workmanship"), the notion of "self-ownership" is purely self-referential. It cannot establish the equality of other selves, thereby placing them in a relationship of mutual regard (or even indifference) with me. On the contrary, by drawing attention to my own capacities and powers without imposing corresponding limits on my will, it risks calling forth an assertive, blatant disregard for beings and things that might present themselves as obstacles to the execution of my projects.

CONCLUSION

In this chapter, I have explored the problem of human equality in Locke's thought. The weaknesses apparent in the two dominant solutions to this problem point, I have argued, to a third, more plausible answer to this interpretive dilemma. While Zuckert is right to call attention to the somewhat disingenuous *political* character of Locke's religious argumentation, he is wrong to insist that Locke's incorporation of such argumentation does not limit and shape the political vision he is able to articulate. The implications of Locke's strictly secular arguments do not point in the same direction as the religious premises he adopts, at least with regard to the matter of human equality. Waldron's argument suggests this much, though he is overly sanguine concerning the ultimate status of Locke's religious argumentation. In the end, the idea of equality in Locke's thought rises and falls with his willingness to argue publicly from specifically Christian premises, however minimalist or unorthodox.

NOTES

I thank Colin Bird, James W. Ceaser, Joshua Foa Dienstag, Nadim Basem Khoury, George Klosko, Allan Megill, Jeremy Mhire, David Novitsky, Justin Rose, Sami-Juhani Savonius-Wroth, A. John Simmons, Greta Snyder, Will Umphres, Rachel Verbois, and Stephen K. White for their comments on earlier versions or portions of this essay. Audiences at the Midwest Political Science Association and the University of Virginia also provided helpful feedback.

1. John Locke, *Two Treatises of Government*, ed. Peter Laslett (Cambridge: Cambridge University Press, 1960), §4, p. 269; for the full recapitulation, see §1, pp. 267–68. Citations to this work refer to section and page number(s), respectively.

2. Harvey C. Mansfield, "On the Political Character of Property in Locke," in *Powers, Possessions and Freedom: Essays in Honour of C. B. Macpherson*, ed. Alkis Kontos (Toronto: University of Toronto Press, 1979), p. 32. Mansfield notes that the state of nature receives only one mention in the *First Treatise*, in §90.

3. Locke, *Second Treatise*, §1, p. 268. Two of the key questions concerning Locke's State of Nature are (1) whether the state of nature is a "moral fiction, historical fact, a combination of both, or something else" (Goldwin, p. 126); and (2) whether Locke's State of Nature is Hobbesian. For discussion of these and many other questions concerning Locke's State of Nature, see Richard Ashcraft, "Locke's State of Nature: Historical Fact or Moral Fiction?" *American Political Science Review* 62.3 (1968): 898–915; Robert A. Goldwin, "Locke's State of Nature in Political Society," *Western Political Quarterly* 29.1 (March 1976): 126–35; A. John Simmons, "Locke's State of Nature," *Political Theory* 17.3 (August 1989): 449–70.

4. Locke, *Second Treatise*, §4, p. 269.

5. Ibid., §4–§5, pp. 269–70.

6. Ibid., §5, p. 270.

7. Ibid., §4, p. 269.

8. Note: I will retain Locke's convention of capitalizing the term "Nature" when he uses it to mean something like "Being."

9. John Locke, *An Essay concerning Human Understanding*, ed. Peter H. Nidditch (Oxford: Clarendon Press, 1975), II.xxiii, pp. 295–317, and III.vi, pp. 438–71. Citations to this work refer to book, chapter, section, and page numbers, respectively.

10. John Dunn, *The Political Thought of John Locke: An Historical Account of the Argument of the "Two Treatises of Government"* (Cambridge: Cambridge University Press, 1969), p. 99.

11. I do not discuss here the Cambridge School's interpretation of Locke, which may be briefly characterized as follows: Two Cambridge scholars, historian Peter Laslett and political theorist John Dunn, argue that Locke's *Essay* and his *Two Treatises* are simply incompatible. The disjuncture between the two works may be explained by acknowledging that Locke's historical context was one of competing intellectual and historical forces. In the end, the "conjunction" of political, religious, and philosophical controversies "which set [Locke's] mind at work" on the great issues of his time serves as both cause of and explanation for the disjointed relationship between the *Essay* and the *Two Treatises*. J. G. A. Pocock, *Politics, Language, and Time* (New York: Atheneum, 1971), p. 204, quoted in Michael Zuckert, *Launching Liberalism: On Lockean Political Philosophy* (Lawrence: University of Kansas Press, 2004), p. 44. With such a view of the relationship between Locke's works, the issue of equality does not emerge as a problem requiring a particularly sophisticated explanation. Those such as Zuckert and Waldron who are inclined to view Locke as a relatively consistent thinker are more likely to seek out internal solutions to problems of interpretation. For firsthand accounts of the Cambridge view, see Peter Laslett, "Introduction," in Locke, *Two Treatises of Government*, esp. pp. 79–92; Dunn, *Political Thought of John Locke*, esp. pp. 203–41. More recently, Dunn has moved to distance himself somewhat from his earlier, stronger claims about Locke's inconsistencies and general irrelevance for "contemporary political theory." John Dunn, "What Is Living and What Is Dead in the Political Theory of John Locke?" in *Interpreting Political Responsibility: Essays, 1981–1989* (Oxford: Polity Press, 1990), pp. 13–15.

12. Jeremy Waldron, *God, Locke, and Equality: Christian Foundations in Locke's Political Thought* (Cambridge: Cambridge University Press, 2002), p. 81.

13. Leo Strauss, *Natural Right and History* (Chicago: University of Chicago Press, 1953), esp. pp. 180–90.

14. See Michael Zuckert, "Human Dignity and the Basis of Justice: Freedom, Rights, and the Self," *Hedgehog Review* 9.3 (2007): 43, where he says that his account of human dignity will be of a "loosely Lockean sort."

15. Locke, *Essay*, III.vi.14, p. 448.

16. W. L. Uzgalis, "The Anti-Essential Locke and Natural Kinds," *Philosophical Quarterly* 38.152 (1988): 330.

17. Cf. Aristotle, *The Metaphysics*, trans. Hugh Lawson-Tancred (London: Penguin Books, 1998), Z.4.

18. Uzgalis, "Anti-Essential Locke," p. 330.

19. Locke, *Essay*, II.xxiii.6, p. 298.

20. My own analysis of these points is much indebted to that of Myers and Waldron. See Peter C. Myers, *Our Only Star and Compass: Locke and the Struggle for Political Rationality* (Boston: Rowman and Littlefield, 1998), pp. 68–101; Waldron, *God, Locke, and Equality*, ch. 3.

21. Michael Ayers, "The Foundations of Knowledge and the Logic of Substance: The Structure of Locke's General Philosophy," in Vere Chappell, ed., *Locke* (Oxford: Oxford University Press, 1998), p. 36.

22. Locke, *Essay*, II.xxiii.4, p. 297.

23. See ibid., II.ii, pp. 119–21, for Locke's initial discussion of simple ideas, the most basic or fundamental kinds of ideas.

24. Ibid., II.xxiii.i, p. 295. I lift this language from Locke's general discussion of the formation of (all) substance ideas. For his discussion of the formation of corporeal substance ideas in particular, see II.xxiii.3, pp. 296–97.

25. I borrow the term "unitary" from Ayers, "Foundations of Knowledge," p. 37.

26. Locke, *Essay*, II.xxiii.i, p. 295.

27. Ayers, "Foundations of Knowledge," p. 37.

28. Locke, *Essay*, II.xxiii.i, p. 295.

29. Ayers, "Foundations of Knowledge," p. 37.

30. Locke, *Essay*, II.xxiii.i, p. 295.

31. Ibid., III.vi.10, p. 445.

32. Ayers, "Foundations of Knowledge," p. 38.

33. I borrow the term "epistemological critique" from Myers, *Our Only Star*, p. 68.

34. Leo Strauss, "The Problem of Socrates," in *The Rebirth of Classical Political Rationalism: An Introduction to the Thought of Leo Strauss*, ed. Thomas L. Pangle (Chicago: University of Chicago Press, 1989), p. 142.

35. Locke, *Essay*, IV.iii.16, p. 547.

36. Ibid., III.iii.19, p. 419.

37. Ibid., III.vi.5, pp. 441–42.

38. Ibid., II.xxvii.1, p. 328; III.vi.5, p. 441.

39. Ibid., III.vi.4, p. 440.

40. Ibid., III.vi.10, p. 445; III.vi.12, pp. 446–47.

41. Ibid., III.vi.12, p. 447.

42. Uzgalis observes that Arthur O. Lovejoy wrongly attributes to Locke a more

orthodox understanding of the "great chain of being" in which Nature produces non-arbitrary classes of things. Uzgalis, "Anti-Essential Locke," p. 330; Arthur O. Lovejoy, *The Great Chain of Being: The Study of the History of an Idea* (Cambridge: Harvard University Press, 1970), pp. 228–29.

43. Locke, *Essay*, III.vi.12, p. 446.

44. Ibid., III.vi.30, p. 458.

45. Ibid., II.xxxii.6, p. 385.

46. Ibid., II.xi.9, p. 159.

47. Ibid., II.xxxii.6, p. 386.

48. Ibid., III.vi.25–26, p. 452; IV.vii.9, p. 596.

49. Ibid., III.vi.26, p. 453.

50. Ibid., II.xxxii.8, p. 386.

51. For discussion of the problems connected with Locke's notion of abstraction, see Donald L. M. Baxter, "Abstraction, Inseparability, and Identity," *Philosophy and Phenomenological Research* 57. 2 (1997): 307–30; Jonathan Bennett, *Locke, Berkeley, Hume: Central Themes* (Oxford: Clarendon Press, 1971), pp. 21–25; J. L. Mackie, *Problems from Locke* (Oxford: Clarendon Press, 1976), ch. 4.

52. Locke, *Essay*, III.vi.4, p. 440.

53. Ibid., III.vi.4, p. 441.

54. Ibid.; see also III.vi.29, p. 456.

55. Ibid., III.vi.3, pp. 439–40.

56. Ibid., II.i.20–21, p. 116.

57. Ibid., II.i.21, p. 117. The fetus "passes the greatest part of its time without Perception or Thought, doing very little, but sleep in a Place, where it needs not seek for Food, and is surrounded with Liquor, always equally soft, and near of the same Temper; where the Eyes have no Light, and the Ears, so shut up, are not very susceptible of Sounds; and where there is little or no variety, or change of Objects, to move the Senses."

58. Ibid., IV.vii.15–16, p. 606.

59. Ibid., IV.vii.16, pp. 606–7.

60. Eugene F. Miller, "Locke on the Meaning of Political Language," *Political Science Reviewer* 9 (Fall 1979):178, n. 6.

61. Locke, *Essay*, III.vi.26, p. 453.

62. Ibid., III.vi.28, p. 455; III.vi.37, p. 462.

63. Cf. Mackie, *Problems from Locke*, pp. 88, 138.

64. Locke, *Essay*, III.vi.36, p. 462.

65. Uzgalis, "Anti-Essential Locke," p. 336.

66. Here is the parallel passage addressing "Man," specifically: "No body will doubt, that the Wheels, or Springs (if I may say so) within, are different in a *rational Man*, and a *Changeling*, no more than that there is a difference in the frame between a *Drill* and a *Changeling*. But whether one, or both these differences be essential or specifical is only to be known to us, by their agreement, or disagreement with the complex *Idea* that the name *Man* stands for: For by that alone can it be determined, whether one, or both, or neither of those be a Man, or no." Locke, *Essay*, III.vi.39, pp. 463–64.

67. Waldron, *God, Locke, and Equality*, p. 58.

68. Ibid., pp. 54–59 (56–57).

69. Locke, *Second Treatise*, §4, §6, pp. 269, 271.

70. Stephen K. White, "Uncertain Constellations: Dignity, Equality, Respect and . . .,"

in *The New Pluralism: William Connolly and the Contemporary Global Condition*, ed. David Campbell and Morton Schoolman (Durham, NC: Duke University Press, 2008), p. 144.

71. Locke, *Second Treatise*, §6, p. 271.

72. Cf. Joshua Foa Dienstag, *Dancing in Chains: Narrative and Memory in Political Theory* (Stanford: Stanford University Press, 1997), pp. 48–74 (esp. pp. 48–52).

73. Dunn, *Political Thought of John Locke*, p. 99. Also, Dunn rightly criticizes the "Western parochialism" lurking behind Peter Laslett's contention that human equality is a "matter" of "common sense." Laslett, Introduction, *Two Treatises*, p. 93.

74. Waldron, *God, Locke, and Equality*, p. 59.

75. Ibid., pp. 52, 66; emphasis mine.

76. Ibid., p. 66.

77. Ibid., p. 76.

78. "Now among the very grossest differences in mental capacity, Locke is evidently not committed to any thesis of equality. That is, he is not committed to following our nominal conception of humanity where it leads, and to drawing a rationality-line that will include all whom we pre-theoretically describe as human." Ibid., p. 73.

79. Ibid., pp. 76–77.

80. See Locke, *Essay*, III.vi.26, pp. 453–54. For commentary on the problem of the "monstrous birth" in early modern philosophy, see Hannah Dawson, *Locke, Language, and Early Modern Philosophy* (Cambridge: Cambridge University Press, 2007), pp. 97, 116, 119, 128, 204, 222.

81. Locke, *Essay*, III.vi.12, p. 447.

82. Waldron, *God, Locke, and Equality*, p. 75.

83. Ibid., pp. 49, 80.

84. Ibid., pp. 78–79.

85. Ibid., pp. 79–80.

86. Ibid., pp. 75, 79, quoting Locke, *Essay*, I.i.5, p. 45.

87. Waldron, *God, Locke, and Equality*, pp. 71, 79.

88. Ibid., pp. 75, 80–81.

89. Ibid., p. 80.

90. Ibid., p. 48. Waldron borrows the term "shapeless" from Simon Blackburn. See ibid., p. 48, n. 11.

91. John E. Coons and Patrick M. Brennan, *By Nature Equal: The Anatomy of a Western Insight* (Princeton, NJ: Princeton University Press, 1999), pp. 8–9, 56–58, 61–63.

92. Locke, *Essay*, III.xi.16, p. 516.

93. Ashcraft notices that Locke routinely has recourse to the "Holy Scriptures" as a final source of authority when he is forced to consider—by the logic of his own argumentation or at the behest of certain philosophically informed interlocutors—the more radical implications of his empiricism: "At those crucial points in Locke's thought, when knowledge, reason, philosophy, and history disclose the ignorance and failings of men, and one is led to the brink of the abyss, it is faith that is [in Locke's own words] 'allowed to supply the defect', providing a bridge to the immanent order and the wisdom of God." Richard Ashcraft, "Faith and Knowledge in Locke's Political Philosophy," in *John Locke: Problems and Perspectives*, ed. John W. Yolton (Cambridge: Cambridge University Press, 1969), p. 223. In Ashcraft's view, this kind of move is evidence of Locke's foundational commitment to Christian principles.

94. Waldron, *God, Locke, and Equality*, pp. 56, 66.

95. Ibid., pp. 56–57.

96. Ibid., p. 68.

97. Locke, *Essay*, III.xi.16, p. 516.

98. Ibid., III.xi.16, pp. 516–17.

99. Waldron, *God, Locke, and Equality*, pp. 67, 82, 68.

100. Locke, *Essay*, III.xi.11, pp. 514–15.

101. I borrow the term "host property" from Coons and Brennan, *By Nature Equal*, ch. 2.

102. Waldron, *God, Locke, and Equality*, p. 95.

103. Ibid., pp. 79–80.

104. Ibid., p. 234.

105. Ibid., p. 96; Locke, *Essays on the Law of Nature*, in *Locke: Political Essays*, ed. Mark Goldie (Cambridge: Cambridge University Press, 1997), p. 120.

106. Locke, *Essay*, IV.x.1, p. 619.

107. Waldron, *God, Locke, and Equality*, p. 234. See also Michael Ayers, *Locke*, vol. 2, *Ontology* (London: Routledge, 1991), p. 182; Ashcraft, "Faith and Knowledge," p. 205. Strauss, *Natural Right and History*, p. 207, cites Locke's "Letter to the Bishop of Worcester," in which Locke admits to Stillingfleet that he deliberately concealed the weakness of his purported demonstration of God's existence. *The Works of John Locke in Nine Volumes*, 12th ed. (London: Rivington, 1824), vol. 3, pp. 353–54.

108. William T. Bluhm, Neil Wintfeld, and Stuart H. Teger, "Locke's Idea of God: Rational Truth or Political Myth," *Journal of Politics* 42.2 (1980): pp. 419–23. For the crucial passage in Locke, see *Essay*, IV.x.18, p. 629. Of such attempted demonstrations in general Eric Voegelin observes, "scholastic proofs for God, including the Cartesian, do not have the aim of assuring the thinker who employs this proof of the existence of God. The existence of God for the Christian thinkers from Anselm of Canterbury to Descartes is known from other sources. The proof is, however, the stylistic form of scholastic thinking, and the demonstratio in this style is extended to problems that are not susceptible of a demonstratio, and in no way need one. Certainly all the proofs of God are logically untenable." "Letter from Voegelin to Alfred Schutz on Edmund Husserl," September 17, 1943, in *Faith and Political Philosophy: The Correspondence between Leo Strauss and Eric Voegelin, 1934–1964*, ed. and trans. Barry Cooper and Peter Emberley (University Park: Pennsylvania State University Press, 1993), pp. 32–33.

109. Bluhm et al., "Locke's Idea of God," p. 423.

110. James Tully, *An Approach to Political Philosophy: Locke in Contexts* (Cambridge: Cambridge University Press, 1993), pp. 225–31.

111. Locke, *Essay*, II.xxiii.33–34, pp. 314–15.

112. Bluhm et al., "Locke's Idea of God," p. 425.

113. Ibid. See Locke, *Essay*, I.iv.19–20, pp. 96–98.

114. Bluhm et al., "Locke's Idea of God," p. 423; Locke, *Essay*, III.xxiii.33–35, pp. 314–15.

115. Bluhm et al., "Locke's Idea of God," p. 424.

116. Locke, *Essay*, II.xxiii.2, p. 296.

117. Ibid., IV.vii.9, p. 596.

118. Bluhm et al., "Locke's Idea of God," p. 425.

119. Locke, *Essay*, IV.viii.9, p. 615.

120. Ibid., IV.viii.8, p. 614.

121. Ibid., IV.xi.1, p. 630.

122. Ibid., IV.xi.12, p. 637; IV.xi.13, p. 638.

123. Waldron, *God, Locke, and Equality*, pp. 99–107.

124. John Locke, *The Reasonableness of Christianity, As Delivered in the Scriptures*, ed. John C. Higgins-Biddle (Oxford: Clarendon Press, 1999), pp. 152–53.

125. Ibid., p. 161.

126. Ibid., pp. 148, 161.

127. Ibid., pp. 134–35. See Thomas L. Pangle's discussion of "The Lockean Critique of Ancient Rationalism," in *The Spirit of Modern Republicanism: The Moral Vision of the American Founders and the Philosophy of Locke* (Chicago: University of Chicago Press, 1988), pp. 209–15.

128. Zuckert, "Human Dignity"; Zuckert, *Launching Liberalism*.

129. Cf. Michael Zuckert, *Natural Rights and the New Republicanism* (Princeton, NJ: Princeton University Press, 1994), p. 265.

130. Zuckert, *Launching Liberalism*, pp. 4–5, 15; Strauss, *Natural Right and History*, see esp. pp. 202–21; Leo Strauss, "Locke's Doctrine of Natural Law," in *What Is Political Philosophy? and Other Studies* (Chicago: University of Chicago Press, 1988), p. 215.

131. Strauss, *Natural Right and History*, pp. 201–21.

132. Zuckert, *Launching Liberalism*, pp. 4–5, 15.

133. Ibid., p. 4.

134. Zuckert states that Locke purveyed ideas that "undermine the possibility of the religious attitude and thus of civil religion." Michael Zuckert, "John Locke and the Problem of Civil Religion," in *The Moral Foundations of the American Republic*, ed. Robert H. Horowitz, 3rd ed. (Charlottesville: University of Virginia Press, 1986), p. 202. For a similar argument, see Steven Forde, "Natural Law, Theology, and Morality in Locke," *American Journal of Political Science* 45.2 (2001): pp. 396–409.

135. Zuckert, *Launching Liberalism*, p. 5.

136. See Strauss, *Natural Right and History*, esp. pp. 180–90.

137. Zuckert, *Natural Rights and the New Republicanism*, p. 276.

138. In support of his argument, Zuckert might also have cited Hobbes' own reservations about the strength of his argument for human equality. In his initial discussion of human equality in *Leviathan*, Hobbes declares men to be (a) roughly equal with respect to natural physical and mental endowments and, more important, (b) equally vulnerable to the fear of violent death at the hands of another in the state of nature. Hobbes, *Leviathan* (Indianapolis: Hackett Publishing, 1994), pp. 74–76. Two chapters later, however, Hobbes displays less confidence than he had before in the probability that men would actually prove more alike than different "when all is reckoned together" (p. 74): Whether men are equal by nature or no, men who consider themselves equal must be treated accordingly out of political expediency: "If nature therefore have made men equal, that equality is to be acknowledged, or if nature have made men unequal; yet because men that think themselves equal, will not enter into conditions of peace, but upon equal terms, such equality must be admitted" (p. 97).

139. Zuckert, *Natural Rights and the New Republicanism*, p. 287.

140. Locke, *Second Treatise*, §27, p. 287.

141. Zuckert, *Natural Rights and the New Republicanism*, p. 265.

142. Ibid., p. 283.

143. Ibid., p. 265.

144. Ibid., p. 276; emphasis mine.

145. Ibid.

146. Ibid., p. 277.

147. Martin Morris, "On the Logic of the Performative Contradiction: Habermas and the Radical Critique of Reason," *Review of Politics* 58.4 (Autumn 1996): 740; see also Jürgen Habermas, "Discourse Ethics," in *Moral Consciousness and Communicative Action*, trans. Christian Lenhardt and Shierry Weber Nicholsen (Boston: MIT Press, 1990), pp. 81–82.

148. Locke, *Second Treatise*, §35, p. 292.

149. Zuckert, *Natural Rights and the New Republicanism*, p. 285.

150. Morris, "Logic of the Performative Contradiction," p. 740.

151. René Descartes, *Discourse on Method and Meditations on the First Philosophy*, trans. John Veitch (New York: Barnes and Noble, 2004), p. 30.

7

LOCKE, DARWIN, AND THE SOCIAL INDIVIDUALISM OF VIRTUE

Lauren K. Hall

THE STUDIES OF HUMAN NATURE and political systems have always been inextricably linked. From Plato's tripartite soul to Hobbes' solitary man (with a life poor, nasty, brutish, and short), all political systems start with an account of the nature of the creature for whom we construct political institutions. Oddly, contemporary scholars often forget this fact, instead requiring that we recognize the so-called fact-value distinction or the naturalistic fallacy, both of which argue that what we are as natural human creatures should not or cannot tell us anything about how we should live in organized groups. Obviously, such a view is shortsighted and ultimately worthy of rejection.

A more important source of confusion, however, is gaining agreement on what constitutes human nature in the first place. Those who believe that human nature is fundamentally inflexible and self-interested (like Hobbes, Locke, and the Federalists after them) will support much different political systems than those who believe that human nature is flexible or even fluid over history (like Hegel and Marx, among others). So the question then arises: How do we know what human nature actually *is?*

The advent of Darwinian theory offered the first truly scientific study of what traits constitute human nature, as well as what traits might predictably differ across time, place, and culture. The science of human nature began to explain more about where humans came from and what their permanent, shared characteristics might be. Sadly, some used this new theory badly, making an argument that governmental control over evolution was necessary to prevent the pollution of the species with degenerate genes. The specter of eugenics has hung over us for the past hundred years, and it is important that we not forget those experiences.

Social Darwinism used a faulty understanding of evolution to support massive government interference in individual lives, culminating in the mass sterilization and institutionalization of those suffering from what were actually complex social ills such as alcoholism and poverty. Assigning complex traits purely genetic causes meant that social planners no longer had to concern themselves with difficult political questions regarding justice, equity, and freedom. Instead, preventing the unfit from reproducing became a quick and easy way to create a utopian society.

In the end, eugenical policies failed for both scientific and social reasons. The eugenicists' understanding of Darwinian thought was flawed because it rested on a profound genetic determinism that failed to take into account environmental and social influences and the various ways genes interact with the environment and each other. Genetically improving the population ended up being as complex and difficult a task as effecting social and political change. Perhaps more importantly, the eugenics movement violated the moral sense of many people; this moral sense became stronger over time as the abuses of the eugenics movement became more apparent, and we now have a healthy—if not perhaps overly strong— suspicion of biological explanations of political phenomena.

While the suspicion of government-run eugenics programs is well deserved, we must also recognize that Darwinian explanations are no less powerful because they have been used poorly before. In fact, Darwinian explanations of human behavior actually support the rejection of those early eugenical policies. The early eugenicists' understanding of both evolution and human nature was facile and incomplete. A true Darwinian science of politics will take cues from the Aristotelian approach as well as from thinkers such as Smith and Montesquieu. It will not be the mere study of institutions but instead the complex study of biological, moral, and political explanations for social behavior. None of these explanations can operate without the others.

Obviously, I cannot in this chapter lay out such a comprehensive framework in any detail. I will, then, start with my conclusion and hope that the rest of the details will be filled in over time. Very simply, I believe Darwinian theory supports a Lockean limited government that protects individual rights. Unlike the simplistic Darwinians of the eugenics era, who took the principle of survival of the fittest and applied it to all social and political activity, Darwinian theory follows Locke by supporting a complex balancing of individual needs and community claims. Darwinian theory supports a limited Lockean government, structured by nature and habit, and founded on a special kind of virtue that requires reasonable, prudent balancing of the needs of individuals simply and the needs of those individuals in society.

DARWIN AND LOCKE: AN INTRODUCTION TO THE ARGUMENT

Both Darwin and Locke are criticized for being rooted in selfish individualism. Darwin's focus on the survival of the fittest and Locke's focus on individual rights rather than duties make both thinkers susceptible to arguments that their theories create dangerously low "floors," which reduce human societies to mere individual self-interest and eradicate the duties required for virtue. Both authors' view of nature is criticized for minimizing human rationality and reducing us to our passionate or biological foundations.

Both authors have faced rejection from both sides of the political aisle. Social conservatives view Darwin's teaching as anathema to religious teachings about the sanctity of human life, while they are also suspicious of Locke's use of religion and his eschewing of duties in favor of rights. The Left, on the other hand, is suspicious of Darwin because they fear his teachings justify human inequality. At the same time, they often reject Locke for his teachings on commercialism and property rights. What both Locke and Darwin have in common ultimately is that they are both criticized for reducing human behavior and human social life to selfish individualism, thus moving virtue from the center of human life to the fringes. Many believe that Darwinian science and Lockean interest are thus incompatible with older understandings of virtue.

I argue that Darwin and Locke do indeed share much in common, but what is shared is not simply the devotion to individual survival as is so often assumed. As opposed to a political system where survival of the fittest is the guiding principle, Darwinian theory leads us to a limited Lockean government with natural laws to guide it, free markets based on self-interest and reciprocation, and finally, a vibrant private sphere that supports education in virtue, both civic and individual. More foundationally, both authors share a conviction that the goal of political life is the balancing of the claims of the individual and the community and that such a balancing act requires prudence and attention to specific circumstances.

Briefly, my argument is as follows. First, I argue for the shared foundation of individual liberty in Locke and Darwin, supported by natural laws that limit the powers of government and support a prudent balancing of individual and community claims. Second, I briefly explore the interaction between freedom and virtue in Locke and Darwin, arguing that Locke's view of limited government is supported by Darwin's understanding of the moral sense and that both support a balance between the individual and the community. Last (and perhaps most relevant for this volume), I argue that the relationship between Darwinian science, Lockean theory, and virtue is one of the emergence of values from the complex interplay between our social, individualistic, and rational selves.

DARWIN, LOCKE, AND THE STATE OF NATURE

At first glance, both Locke and Darwin have similar understandings of nature, in their simplest forms. Locke argues in his *Second Treatise of Government* that man has fundamental rights to life, liberty, and property, and that the end of society is to protect those rights. The foundation of Darwinian theory is survival and reproduction, and evolution occurs primarily through a process of natural selection, or "survival of the fittest." Both authors begin with the basic desire for self-preservation that seems to place the individual above society and poses problems for those who believe nature must support virtue. The nature of Locke and Darwin, at first glance, seems almost amoral. But only at first glance.

Upon further investigation, the thought of both becomes more complex and more social, as the laws of nature modify and moderate our selfish desires for simple self-preservation. Locke ends up moderating our individualism to preserve the community. Darwin's theory modifies the state of nature still further by underscoring the natural sociality of human life, starting with the centrality of family roles and ending with the complex interactions of unknown individuals based on reciprocity and the moral sense.

Those familiar with Darwin's thought will notice that one primary difference between Locke and Darwin is that Locke seems to downplay our natural sociability. Locke argues "God . . . put [man] under strong obligations of necessity, convenience, and inclination, to drive him into society, as well as fitted him with understanding and language to continue and enjoy it."[1] Man must be driven into society for Locke, rather than being born into it. The state of nature for Locke, while ostensibly ruled by the law of nature (Reason), quickly devolves into a state of war, since men's passions and interests lead them to be biased judges. Even the family for Locke seems to be based on self-interest; families stay together only as long as is necessary for the children to survive.

For Darwin, everything about humanity, from our speech, our reason, our innate sense of justice, our love of kin, fits us to our destiny as social creatures. Our moral sense comes from our sociality and the close affectionate bonds we have to family and friends. We start out social because we need others to survive. The double-edged sword of evolution requires both survival and reproduction. Both require close alliances and tightly bonded communities based on kinship and reciprocity.

On this level at least, Locke and Darwin seem at odds with one another. Darwin's sociality seems at odds with Locke's individualism. Ultimately, though, the issue is one of emphasis rather than real disagreement. Darwin's man is naturally social; Locke's man is ultimately social, and Locke's focus on the individual may be more rhetorical than anything else. Locke's goal is to make the argument for the primacy of the individual in order to limit the power of government. Darwin's goal is to demonstrate how an individualistic principle like survival of the fittest can create creatures specially fitted for social life. Although they have different goals, both end up with a creature who balances individualistic desires with strong social needs and desires.

DARWIN, LOCKE, AND NATURAL LAWS

The relationship between the state of nature in Locke and the survival of the fittest in Darwin is strengthened and deepened by the existence in both of natural moral laws that exist prior to, and thus control, govern-

ment. These natural laws also represent the complex balance between individual and community needs.

The state of nature, rather than being an anarchic state, has laws, argues
Locke. We know that "reason, which is that law, teaches all mankind, who
will but consult it, that being all equal and independent, no one ought to
harm another in his life, health, liberty, or possessions."[2] Locke attributes
this natural law to the existence of a divine creator, but if we eliminate God
from the picture (à la Jefferson), Locke and Darwin look very similar. The
content of the laws of nature for Locke and Darwin are roughly the same,
however different their origins might be.

The law of nature and the state of nature represent an uneasy balance between individual and community. The law of nature prevents the harming
of others, but the state of nature (as Locke later admits) is the essence of
individual freedom. The individual is both executor and judge of the law of
nature. As Locke points out, there are inconveniences to this state: "it is unreasonable for Men to be Judges in their own Cases. . . . Self-love will make
Men partial to themselves and their Friends. And on the other side, that ill
Nature, Passion and Revenge will carry them too far in punishing others."[3]
We move out of the state of nature and into civil society in order to better
preserve our freedoms by handing some of them over to the community.

This balancing act between individual and community claims continues once in civil society. All individuals must consent to leave the state of
nature, but once in civil society, only the majority is required to set up government. The same sacrifice of individual consent occurs when government violates rights. Locke argues, "Where the Body of the People, or any
single Man, is deprived of their Right and have no Appeal on Earth, there
they have a liberty to appeal to Heaven."[4] Yet later in the same paragraph
he argues that the appeal to heaven "operates not, till the Inconvenience is
so great, that the Majority feel it, and are weary of it, and find a necessity
to have it amended."[5] This apparent contradiction may be adequately explained by the practical difficulties attending the preservation of individual rights alongside stable communities. The community needs power to
enforce the law, which may at times require the loss of individual freedom.
Similarly, when individuals enter civil society and decide to set up government, nothing but a majority would do, since requiring consensus would
leave you back in the state of nature, with ill-protected rights for everyone.

Locke does as well as he can to protect individuals while also preserving
the community, but he recognizes that the specific decisions in particular

circumstances will have to be made by prudent men who carefully weigh and balance individual good and community preservation. The community, necessary as it is for the preservation of each individual, often triumphs: *"the first and fundamental natural Law*, which is to govern even the Legislative itself, is *the preservation of the Society*, and (as far as will consist with the publick good) of every person in it."[6] The state of nature leans toward the individual, but the individual cannot be preserved adequately without the presence of government. Once the individual enters civil society, his importance wanes in light of the need to preserve a multitude of individuals and the civil society that supports them all.

This same balancing of individual and community is present in Darwin's thought. Accusations against Darwin that his theory is overly reductionistic or individualistic are usually leveled by those unfamiliar with his work. Darwin had a complex understanding of humanity, and reading works like *The Descent of Man* introduces us to a thinker who was very much aware of human complexity, reason, and man's natural sociality. Those who criticize Darwinian thought for being selfish usually refer to more recent thinkers like Richard Dawkins or they reduce Darwin's teaching to the principle of survival of the fittest, ignoring his deep and intricate appreciation for human complexity.

Darwin believed man was naturally social, so much so that natural selection had fitted us especially for social life with social instincts, a moral sense, and the ability to communicate moral ideas. Darwin's moral sense is similar to Locke's Law of Nature: "It is obvious that every one may with an easy conscience gratify his own desires, if they do not interfere with his social instincts, that is with the good of others; but in order to be quite free from self-reproach, or at least of anxiety, it is almost necessary for him to avoid the disapprobation, whether reasonable or not, of his fellow men."[7] While not identical with Locke's Law of Nature, both Locke and Darwin argue for individual liberty so long as it does not interfere with the peaceful existence of the social group. Darwin's account relies on empirical observations regarding regret, conscience, and disapprobation of one's fellow man. Locke's account comes (at least ostensibly) as an a priori investigation of man. Because there is no original state of nature for Darwin, his man is naturally social and naturally changes his behavior to align himself with the group. Locke's man does this only after entering civil society. In both cases, however, the importance of preserving the individual is balanced against the needs of the group supporting him.

Darwin believes, moreover, that our natural moral sense is in some sense inevitable. He argues in *The Descent of Man* that he believes it probable that "any animal whatever, endowed with well marked social instincts, the parental and filial affections being here included, would inevitably acquire a moral sense or conscience, as soon as its intellectual powers had become as well, or nearly as well, developed as in man."[8] The combination of our sociality and our rationality leads us to develop morality. However, because our sociality is limited to small groups, our morality is limited as well. Our sociality is the sociality of close-knit, inter-related groups. Thus, our natural moral sense will be linked to specific communities; nothing in natural selection supports universal benevolence. The virtues in primitive tribes "are practiced almost exclusively in relation to men of the same tribe; and their opposites are not regarded as crimes in relation to men of other tribes."[9] Darwin is making an empirical claim, not a normative one. He would prefer that acts like infanticide, human sacrifice, and slavery did not exist, but he does note that in "rude ages" these kinds of activities were common and were generally directed at outsiders.

In rude societies, the self-regarding virtues are ranked low. While Darwin does not lay out his argument clearly, the thought must be that, because the individual is so intricately bound up with the survival of his society in primitive societies, the individual's needs are secondary to the survival of the group. An individual without a group in a nomadic tribe would soon fall prey to starvation, predators, or members of other tribes. Thus, his identity as a member of a group becomes all.

The situation shifts in civilized societies. Darwin notes that the self-regarding virtues are "now highly appreciated by civilized nations."[10] These self-regarding virtues are those that benefit the individual without obvious benefits for the group as a whole. Darwin attributes the shift in civilized societies to important institutions that are lacking in "rude societies." First, morality in rude societies is restricted to members of the same tribe. Second, in these societies, the "powers of reasoning [are] insufficient to recognize" that these self-regarding virtues benefit the tribe. Finally, "a weak power of self-command" in these societies is unstrengthened by "habit, instruction, and religion."[11] The importance of individual virtues becomes obvious only over time, and these virtues must also be nurtured over time, over both the history of a group and the life of an individual.

In an important sense, then, Darwin's and Locke's "states of nature" are flipped. In Locke's view, the individual has unlimited rights in the state of nature but eventually sacrifices those rights for the safety of civil society. In Darwin's view, we start out with very limited powers as individuals because our survival is so intertwined with that of the group. Civilized countries, while preserving a greater moral control over their members due to religion and education, nevertheless allow for more freedom since the individual is no longer inextricably bound to one society. Darwin does not make this argument explicit, but the shifting balance between individual and society is at the root of his understanding of savage versus civilized morality. Darwin's State of Nature is communitarian and non-individualistic. Individual freedom becomes possible only in civilization.

NATURAL LAWS AND LIMITED GOVERNMENT

These natural laws of morality in both Locke's and Darwin's theories structure the political and social laws that create complex systems of government. The systems of government that arise from these natural laws are complex and limited because the natural laws laid out by Locke and Darwin require the careful balancing of the needs of the individual and society, which can only be attained through a complex, limited government with a vibrant private sphere that includes education in virtue (a point I will make later).

In Locke, the need for limited government comes most directly from his understanding of the natural rights of individuals. Self-preservation is the "low but solid" foundation of Lockean philosophy, and all else rests on this universal assumption. Individuals are important because they all have the foundational desire to survive. Thus, society becomes a way of ensuring the survival of all, an end that is not consistent with the wild freedom of the state of nature.

More than mere preservation, the desire to survive, when combined with our rational faculties (given us by God), creates robust and inalienable natural rights that form the basis for limited government. In fact, our natural rights are so foundational that we cannot consent to absolute, arbitrary power even if we wanted to: "This freedom from absolute, arbitrary power, is so necessary to, and closely joined with a man's preservation, that he cannot part with it, but by what forfeits his preservation and life together: for a man, not having the power of his own life, cannot, by compact, or his own consent, enslave himself to any one, nor put himself under the absolute, arbitrary power of another, to take away his life, when he pleases."[12] While the argument for natural rights in Locke may seem to rest on God, he offers an alternate understanding of these rights, grounded in reason, particularly in the assumption that no rational person would consent to give away those rights. Since what differentiates us from beasts is our rationality, the argument goes, no human can consent to absolute government while claiming his humanity.

Thus humanity for Locke is twofold: rational individuals with rights and a society based on natural law. These natural laws are twofold as well—both a requirement to protect other individuals when possible and the requirement to preserve oneself. Government itself represents the sum of this complex balancing act; preserving individual rights as far as is possible alongside the rights of the community. Any government attempting this balancing act will be both limited and complex, since no simple or absolute government will be able adequately to balance individual rights (indeed, it is unclear whether any absolute government can secure rights at all) with the needs of the community.

Darwin's view of limited government is more indirect, since Darwin does not lay out any kind of consistent political doctrine in his works. He does, however, provide a view of man that closely follows Locke's, a view that requires limited government because it recognizes that man is limited, fallible, and self-interested. While Darwin recognizes the natural sociality of man, he does not believe that man cares for all members of society equally. Man's natural sociality comes with an important proviso; man cares the most for those closest to him and cares very little for those he does not know. This limited virtue is connected to a problem of limited knowledge. Just as man cares little for those he does not know, his ability to make good decisions for those outside his direct knowledge is limited because his knowledge is limited to his own specific circumstances. Moreover, man may desire power to help himself and his family and close friends and may be willing to sacrifice the lives of those he does not know in order to do it. Thus, limited care (or nepotism) and limited knowledge lead to potentially devastating situations when man is put in charge of other men absolutely. The tendency of man to love those closest to him more than others can be mitigated somewhat by habit (see the discussion on virtue below), but we will always be limited by our natural desires for kin and community.

From a Darwinian perspective, limited government is required because all men, even leaders, are fallible, limited, and characterized by limited virtue. The desires of humans to survive and reproduce can only be universally supported within a system of limited authority where individuals have expansive control over their own lives and those of their families, friends, and communities, with less control over the fates of those they do not know (leading to a kind of federalism).

Finally, and perhaps most importantly, limited government is required because both Locke and Darwin recognize the importance of the individual while recognizing the importance of the community for individual survival and flourishing. The goal of government for both Locke and Darwin should be to balance the needs of individuals against the needs of individuals in communities. Such a balancing act requires individual freedom within a rule of law. Individual freedom allows individuals to make the majority of decisions regarding survival, reproduction, and other human needs independently, while the rule of law prevents any one individual from harming the rights of another.

NATURAL LAWS AND VIRTUE

The problem with the above analysis (at least from some perspectives) is that both limited government and science are both seen as incompatible with virtue. Thus, a science of limited government would seem to be the exact opposite of a regime based on thoughtful prudent statesmanship that supports human virtue in its robust sense. In the section that follows, I will argue that a properly constructed Lockean or Darwinian limited government will support virtue by creating a robust and vibrant private sphere that helps educate individuals in civic and individual virtue. Central to this argument is the idea that virtue consists of controlling the immediate passions through the use of reason and balancing individual interests with the interests of the group. Locke's argument for education focuses more on the former, while Darwin's focuses more on the latter, but both ultimately argue that virtue consists partially of the sacrificing of an individual's short-term desires for long-term well-being, which makes life in any society possible.

Locke focuses most clearly on the development of the virtues in his work on education. According to Locke, education supports and develops the natural rationality of man that would otherwise be subsumed over time by desires. Locke argues that "the great principle and foundation of all virtue and worth is placed in this, that a man is able to deny himself his own desires, cross his own inclinations, and purely follow what reason directs as best though the appetite lean the other way."[13] Good education should be directed toward the proper relationship between reason and desire—or in "denying ourselves the satisfaction of our own desires where reason does not authorize them."[14] This denial may consist in denying one's immediate desires for the sake of a greater good, including membership in a community. Locke's education prepares one, in part, for citizenship in a limited government by inculcating a kind of virtue that supports the balancing of the needs of the individual and the community, insofar as a reasonable person is more likely to understand this balance than one ruled by the passions.[15]

Locke's political treatise rests on precisely this kind of education. The rationality Locke argues we possess in the state of nature turns out to be nothing more than a potentiality. Our misuse of reason (or failure to consult it, as the case may be) leads us to judge ourselves partially. A Lockean education, focusing as it does on "a good mind, well principled, tempered to virtue and usefulness, and adorned with civility and good breeding," is the ideal education for a citizen in a limited government, who must partake himself of the difficult balancing act between his own needs and those of the community.[16] Locke's education does not teach the self-denial of the Spartans. Instead, it teaches the individual to discover, rationally, his own worth and how that worth can be made compatible with community claims. Lockean virtue is certainly not the high virtue of the ancients, but this does not make it worth dismissing out of hand. It is a kind of virtue worth protecting in part because it protects the individual against the harsh claims of the community so prevalent in ancient society.

Darwin also recognizes the importance of cultivating virtue. For Darwin, our nature is not merely given by genetics but is a potential that must be nurtured by caring parents, involved communities, and close friendships. Darwin even goes so far as to argue that habit is the last required stage of the development of rational and social creatures. Habit reinforces our social instincts and, in conjunction with our rational capacities and language, will help develop virtuous individuals. Darwin's theory is hardly the biological determinism so often ascribed to him. He believes that biology and culture play interconnected roles, and that culture, instruction, and habit can all support our biologically evolved social and moral instincts.

Darwin expands on this point in his analysis of the evolution of cultures. The difference between rude societies and civilized societies is partly that rude societies lack sufficient education and habituation to allow their members to control their immediate desires. They are led by necessity to sacrifice themselves for the good of the group, but the development of self-regarding virtues like modesty, temperance, and prudence are not required and thus are neglected.

Darwin believes that man evolves morally in some sense like he evolves physically (though not through the same mechanisms): "As man advances in civilization, and small tribes are united into larger communities, the simplest reason would tell each individual that he ought to extend his social instincts and sympathies to all the members of the same nation, though personally unknown to him."[17] Virtue consists in part in the development of the sympathy one feels toward one's family and friends to all humanity. This does not happen on its own. The extension of sympathy toward unrelated individuals requires, first, heroic individuals to set the example and, then, "experience, instruction, and habit" to help solidify the concern one has for others.[18]

As the social virtues grow in civilized societies so do the self-regarding virtues, which are only to be found in civilized societies. The assumption here, though never laid out explicitly, is that self-sacrifice to the community is absolutely necessary in primitive societies, but these societies are defined narrowly—usually closely related groups of extended families. Thus, the self-sacrifice required can be justified on the basis of kin selection. As man becomes more civilized, his social instincts expand to incorporate larger groupings; at the same time, his self-regarding virtues are given freer rein since the individual actually gains in importance as he is freed from the necessities of day-to-day survival. Thus, civilization at its height represents the highest development of both our social and our self-regarding virtues. In essence, civilization is "complete" when the balance between individual and social virtues has been achieved.

For Darwin and Locke, the virtues are the result of nature or instinct, reason or intellect, and habit or education. Both end up with some version of the Golden Rule, quoted by Darwin as "As ye would that men should do to you, do ye to them likewise."[19] The Golden Rule, like Locke's admonition to preserve all mankind as much as possible, balances the good of the community with the good of the individual, reminding the individual that his existence is both necessary for and dependent on a stable community. Both Locke and Darwin believe that virtue is "contrary to unguided nature" but that it is natural, in that it unfolds out of our natural rational and social capacities.[20] Thus, while virtue does not emerge directly from nature, it can properly be understood as the fulfillment of our nature.

SCIENCE, VIRTUE, AND LIMITED GOVERNMENT

Lockean liberalism is supported by our Darwinian history, and both support an understanding of virtue that balances individual and social virtues. While there are important differences between Locke's account of human nature and morality and Darwin's account (which I conveniently gloss over in this short chapter), both tend to support limited government, natural instincts, and habit or education in society. Locke provides the individualism that Darwin's account may underestimate, and Darwin provides the robust sociality that Locke's account underemphasizes. Both, however, recognize the mixed nature of man, both social and individualistic, altruistic and selfish.

It is true that we cannot extract virtue directly from science. Simply knowing what we are as animals does not tell us what to do in specific situations. The fact-value distinction holds in this very narrow sense. But those who believe our nature tells us nothing about virtue are mistaken. Virtue emerges from our nature, and we can discover many fundamental moral rules from simply knowing what our species needs in order to survive and how we have evolved. Nature is both a floor and a ceiling in this sense; it provides us with the basic necessities for human life while at the same time allowing a complex virtue of excellence to emerge over time.

This emergence is not random or relativistic. It comes from the constant balancing of our individual selves and the communities that nurture and support our individualism. Both Locke and Darwin struggled with this balance, and it is ultimately in a limited government—where people are free to experiment with different ways of life, receive approbation and blame from their fellow man, and balance on the unstable equilibrium of the individual's relationship with the community—that true virtue emerges. Both Locke and Darwin teach us that the virtuous man is the product not of nature, society, or government alone but of the complex interplay of all three. Virtue thus is both an art and a science or, rather, demonstrates the interconnected nature of the two.

NOTES

1. John Locke, *Second Treatise of Government* (1690; Cambridge: Cambridge University Press, 1988), 318–19.

2. Ibid., 271.

3. Ibid., 275.

4. Ibid., 379.

5. Ibid., 380.

6. Ibid., 356.

7. Charles Darwin, *The Descent of Man* (1871; New York: Barnes and Noble Books, 2004), p. 96.

8. Ibid., 81.

9. Ibid., 97.

10. Ibid., 98.

11. Ibid., 99.

12. Locke, *Second Treatise*, 284.

13. John Locke, *Some Thoughts concerning Education* (Indianapolis: Hackett Publishing, 1996), p. 25.

14. Ibid., 29.

15. This argument is much more complex than laid out here. I am merely trying to show a similarity between Locke's and Darwin's thoughts when it comes to the importance of education in preparing a person for participation in society.

16. Locke, *Education*, p. 63.

17. Darwin, *Descent of Man*, p. 102.

18. Ibid., 104.

19. Ibid., 105.

20. Locke, *Education*, 32.

8

DESCARTES, LOCKE, AND THE VIRTUE OF THE INDIVIDUAL

Marc D. Guerra

RENÉ DESCARTES IS ROUTINELY CREDITED with being the "founder" of modern philosophy. That noteworthy title is laden with ambiguity. For while it identifies Descartes as the architect of "modern philosophy," the exact meaning of that ponderous term remains anything but "clear and distinct." Is the type of philosophy that Descartes is credited with founding one specific thing? Or does it include several types of philosophy that all fall under one common genus? Does the "modern" in modern philosophy mean "current"? Or does it simply mean "new"? If it is the latter, does this mean that modern philosophy is a wholly new kind of philosophy? Or is it only a new way of philosophizing, a practical innovation in the traditional pursuit of wisdom?

Modern philosophy initially—and in some sense, most discernibly—comes to sight as something radically different from the *kind* of philosophy that came before it. The "modern" in modern philosophy does not so much designate a specific period or time in the history of philosophy as it specifies a new understanding of the nature and scope of philosophic inquiry. One can agree with this general claim and still debate what exactly constitutes the decisive shift in this understanding. For example, the twentieth-century political philosopher Leo Strauss routinely emphasized the essential difference between classical political philosophy, by which he meant primarily the kind of theoretical reflections undertaken by Plato and Aristotle, and modern political philosophy, by which he primarily meant the kind of "realistic" approach taken by Niccolò Machiavelli. By contrast, the twentieth-century intellectual historian Etienne Gilson stressed the essential difference between the kind of speculative theological and philosophical reflection that marked twelfth-, thirteenth-, and fourteenth-century Scholasticism and the kind of anthropocentric and worldly thought that animated the philosophical treatises of the sixteenth century.

Unlike the classical philosophy of Plato and Aristotle and the Scholasticism of Bonaventure and Aquinas, the kind of rationalism Descartes publicly advocated fused together, in a new and unprecedented way, philosophy and natural science. Under this new configuration, natural science became a constitutive, and to some degree central, element of philosophical inquiry. Illustrative of this fact is that modern philosophy, as the title of Descartes' *Discourse* reminds us, proudly possessed and championed a method. Over and against the purportedly nebulous and imprecise speculations of pre-modern philosophy, Cartesian rationalism methodologically deployed scientific "rules." These rigorous and precise procedures, Descartes reports, allowed their practitioner to unravel age-old questions that vexed earlier philosophers. Where the philosophic tradition that began with Socrates proceeded dialectically, examining commonsense opinions and ordinary experiences in the hope of unearthing the principles undergirding them, Descartes' new, quasi-mathematical method ostensibly guaranteed certainty and genuine knowledge. Dogmatically and systematically doubting all inherited opinions, this method ushered in a philosophical science that no longer had the character of ascent. Cartesian rationalism proclaimed that method, not speculative metaphysics, provided the real grounds or foundations of knowledge. Under its new configuration, epistemology would replace metaphysics as the science of sciences. It would become the new first philosophy.

But Descartes' turn to method signaled more than a mere change in philosophic approach or orientation. At its core, it reflected a new understanding of the nature of things as well as a new understanding of the nature of human beings. Despite their real and irreducible differences, most notably over the divinely created nature of nature and the reality (and therewith the effects) of original sin, classical philosophy and Christian theology both affirmed the existence of an ordered cosmos or whole that human beings, to greater and lesser degrees, could reasonably come to know. As Descartes presents it, however, the turn to method is largely necessary because the human mind is not equipped to know the whole. In fact, the human mind is not really equipped to know any kind of whole, let alone "the whole." This claim is enshrined in the second rule of Descartes' new method: resolve "to divide each of the difficulties . . . into as many parts as possible and as may be required to resolve them better."[1] Aristotle had famously noted that human beings possess a natural desire to know. That desire ultimately culminated in their longing to know the cosmos or the whole. But according Descartes, the reach of the being Aristotle movingly describes finally exceeds its grasp. The gap between the nature of things and the human mind's natural ability to know is, and will always be, too great. In the end, human beings' natural desire to know the whole is rebuffed by nature itself.

Method is thus meant to be Descartes' scientific and self-asserting response to this rebuffing. It allows human beings to conceptualize and, hence, to organize nature along lines the human mind can actively grasp and consequently actively control. In Descartes' hands, method becomes an instrument through which human beings can theoretically describe the inner workings of the universe *and* harness the energies operative in the laws of nature, "which are the same as the laws of mechanics," and press them into human beings' service.

For Descartes, nature does more than thwart human beings' deepest and loftiest intellectual desires. While frustrating, this obstacle in all likelihood would prove painful to a relatively small number of human beings. On a much larger and more palpable level, nature seems indifferent, perhaps even hostile, to the concrete bodily and physical needs of individual human beings. Far from being unquestionably benevolent and supportive of human beings' aspirations and well-being, Descartes reminds us, nature visibly and universally sanctions human disease, death, and decay. By nature, each and every human being finds himself or herself not in the tranquil garden of Genesis or Lucretius but, rather, in a world that subjects each individual to constant bodily afflictions and the ever-encroaching "infirmity of old age."[2]

Taking his cue from Francis Bacon, Descartes responds to nature's perceived stinginess by outwardly infusing philosophy—and with it, all "useful" forms of knowledge—with an undeniably earthy goal. Under the Cartesian dispensation, knowledge ceases to be something pursued for its own sake; likewise, the contemplation of truth (at least as it is popularly presented by Descartes) ceases to be seen as an end in itself. Instead, knowledge is said to be desirable only if it is useful—that is, only if it helps fulfill human beings' visible, and seemingly endless, bodily desires and physical needs. Punctuating this point, Descartes announces at the end of his *Discourse* (the full title of which is *Discourse on the Method of Rightly Conducting One's Reason and Seeking the Truth in the Sciences*) that he long ago vowed to direct his intellectual energies toward "gaining knowledge which would be very useful in life, and of discovering a practical philosophy which might replace the speculative philosophy taught in the schools."[3] As Daniel Maher points out in his contribution to this volume, to the extent that Descartes successfully depicts "the new science of nature" as the source of "untold humanitarian benefits, [he] is in a position to give philosophy the reputation of being beneficial to ordinary people and thereby to reorder the relation between philosophy and non-philosophers (society or the political community)."

Descartes' artful attempt to portray the utility of his new philosophy and natural science is vividly put on display in the preface to the French edition of his *Principles*, where he likens "the whole of philosophy" to a tree, "the roots of which are metaphysics . . . the trunk is physics, and the branches emerging from the trunk are all the other sciences, which may be reduced to three principle ones, namely, medicine, mechanics, and morals." Descartes concludes his visual with a reference to "the highest and most perfect moral system, which presupposes a complete knowledge of the other sciences and is the ultimate level of wisdom." It is important to note that Descartes' tree is not so much a tree of knowledge of good and evil as it is a tree of knowledge of the useful and the moral. His image reverses the claims of *both* Aristotelian philosophy and Christian theology: metaphysical truths—no matter how difficult to grasp or how ambiguous their precise formulations may be—are not presented as the heights of human knowledge. They occupy the lowest point on the tree. As is often noted, Descartes never published an account of this "most perfect moral system." Less often noted is the fact that this perfect moral system is said to rest on metaphysical foundations that, by Descartes' own account, his new scientific and mathematical method does not need. Perhaps this is why he likens metaphysics to the roots of a tree. Like the roots of a tree, metaphysical knowledge, as Descartes presents it at least, remains hidden underground, out of the human eye's natural field of vision.[4]

Indeed, the naïve and misguided belief that moral science or a science of virtue must be wedded to some metaphysic, according to Descartes, was classical philosophy's fatal flaw. Echoing chapter fifteen of Machiavelli's *Prince*, Descartes compares the moral writings of the classical philosophers to "very proud and magnificent palaces built only on sand and mud." Like the other sciences before his time, classical moral philosophy too had "shaky foundations." As a result, what it routinely called virtue was "nothing but a case of callousness, or vanity, or desperation, or parricide." When all is said and done, classical philosophy could not "adequately explain how to recognize a virtue."[5]

What, then, is virtue for Descartes? Or, to put it another way, what constitutes a virtuous action for Descartes? The answers to these questions obviously lie well beyond what can reasonably be achieved in this chapter. In their place, let me offer three brief preliminary observations. Each observation sheds some light on Descartes' complicated and somewhat hidden understanding of virtue. And each sheds some light on how his depiction of human beings' place in the world relates to the corresponding views of human beings, human freedom, and human virtue that would later be advanced by early modern political philosophers such as Thomas Hobbes and John Locke.

Contrary to Charles Taylor's provocative claim, Descartes' cogitating self does represent something new under the sun. Taylor alleged to find early intimations of the Cartesian "I" in the first-person discourse that runs through St. Augustine's *Confessions*.[6] To be sure, Descartes' *Discourse* and his *Meditations*, like St. Augustine's *Confessions*, are written from the perspective of the first person. But in truth this is where the similarities end. Where the self-conscious and unique person on display in the *Confessions* memorably declares that God is more intimate (and real) to him than he is to himself, the one—and perhaps only—thing the "I" at the center of Descartes' famous cogito knows for certain is himself. But what exactly does the Cartesian "I" know other than that he doubts and, hence, that he thinks and, hence, that he exists? As Descartes elsewhere makes clear, the cogitating "I" knows he has passions. In *The Passions of the Soul*, Descartes locates six essential passions in human beings: wonder, love, hatred, desire, joy, and sadness. Originating in material, biological changes in the body, these passions "dispose our soul to want the things which nature deems useful for us, and to persist in this volition."[7] Lacking any natural order, the human soul, as Descartes describes it, is a cauldron of passions. Whatever order the passions take in the soul therefore needs to be imposed. In a perhaps unexpected way, the famed rationalist Descartes here readily describes reason as playing a subordinate role to the passions in the moral life of most human beings. As he notes in the conclusion of his work on the passions, for most human beings "it is on the passions alone that all the good and evil of this life depends."[8]

Yet human beings are not simply cogitating, passionate beings. They are also, as Descartes emphasizes in a myriad of ways, volitional beings. The volitional power that we human beings possess "renders us in a certain way like God by making us masters of ourselves."[9] Descartes, however, wants human beings to realize that their volitional powers extend well beyond the boundaries of self-mastery; at their core, they hold out the promise that, aided by the new philosophy and new natural science, human beings can at long last become god-like "masters and possessors of nature." Because his scientific method cannot affirm a natural order in the human soul, self-mastery for Descartes takes on a very different meaning than it had in either classical philosophy or Christian theology. Self-mastery comes to look more and more like willful, individual self-direction. If mechanistic, non-teleological nature fails to give us a goal and our souls do not point, even dimly, to any pre-established, external end, the self-conscious, cogitating individual must appoint an end or ends for himself.

The need to rely upon willful resolution and willful self-determination finds multiple expressions in Descartes' writings. For example, though clearly not his final word on the matter, Descartes' *self-imposed* provisional moral code required him "to be as firm and decisive in [his] actions as [he] could, and to follow even the most doubtful opinions."[10] What is more, moral truths, Descartes admits, are rarely "clearly perceived." In fact, in moral matters all too often we find that we do not even have "probable truths" at our disposal. For this reason, when it comes to matters of morality and virtue, "it is . . . not necessary that our reason . . . be free from error." As Descartes informs Princess Elizabeth of Bohemia in their long correspondence, in the realm of moral action "all that is needed is for a conscience to testify that we never lacked resolution and virtue to carry out whatever we have judged the best course."[11]

Yet what precisely does a morally virtuous person seek to do? What if anything does Descartes, unlike the "ancient pagans," present as a "recognizable" moral or political virtue? The answer to this question is the Cartesian virtue of generosity, which, as Descartes presents it, is not an acquired virtue—lacking any naturally established order or end, the human soul is not fitted to acquire virtues for which it has any natural potential. Rather, generosity is rooted in a humor or a disposition with which one is born. The generous human being knows "in what manner and for what reason anyone ought to have esteem or contempt for himself."[12] Conceptually, Cartesian generosity, perhaps not surprisingly, can be broken down into two parts: "the first consists in knowing that nothing truly belongs to [the generous person] but this freedom to dispose his volitions, and that he ought to be praised or blamed for no other reason than his using this freedom well or badly"; the second "consists in [the generous person's] feeling within himself a firm and constant resolution to use it well—that is, never to lack the will to undertake and carry out whatever he judges to be best."[13]

In his *Ethics*, Aristotle described magnanimity not by giving speeches about the virtue as a mean between extremes but by painting a nuanced, complex picture of the great-souled man.[14] One cannot help but get the impression that Descartes deliberately sought to go Aristotle one better. He does not offer a nameless, faceless picture of his outstanding virtuous type. Quite the contrary, the *Discourse* presents Descartes himself as a model of generosity. In this work, Descartes informs his reader that he was forced to publish his findings in accord with the "law which obliges all who desire the general well-being of mankind."[15] While all human beings presumably are obliged to follow this law, not all can follow it in the same way. And not all (indeed apparently no one else) can follow it in the way Descartes does. After all, by his telling, he was the first person to discover the utility and certainty of the new method. He was the one who discovered a new science that is (or claims to be) both *theoretical* and *practical* at one and the same time. Plato and Aristotle spoke of no such science. Admittedly, Catholic Christianity speaks of such a science, namely, the science of theology or sacred doctrine. But that science, by Catholicism's own admission, possesses this unique ability due to the unique nature of its object, the triune God who cannot be known unless He is loved. By contrast, Descartes' science possesses this ability because he reportedly uncovered the true complexity and true nature of nature. Studying in isolation, Descartes discovered that nature cannot be truly and certainly known unless it is acted upon, that is, unless it is methodically subjected to a series of experiments. (The deliberate aping of Catholic theology's claim to be theoretical and practical, we take it, is part of what Thomas Hibbs has in mind when he speaks of Descartes' "strategy for bypassing the debate between Athens and Jerusalem"). "Communicating faithfully to the public," his discovery is thus a great act of generosity on Descartes' part. By doing this—and *seemingly* undoing the overall thrust of the "single architect" argument he had initially used to lend legitimacy to his new method, Descartes claims he hopes to combine "the lives and labors of many . . . working together" for mankind's general welfare. United in this project, Descartes proposes humanity "might make much greater progress . . . than anyone could make on his own."[16]

Descartes' act of generosity issues in an outward call for future generations to rally around a new and unprecedented scientific, humanitarian project. The allure of this project unites human beings on the level of the passions. But the unity it achieves, on closer inspection, is more apparent than real. Descartes' rhetoric masks the fact that this scientific, humanitarian project turns on the recognition not of a common moral, social, and political good that human beings substantially share but on the self-identified and self-recognized good of the Cartesian individual, that is, the ego that methodologically thinks of itself as separate from, and jeopardized by, the world around it. Within such a framework, philosophy's new purported goal, mastery of nature, appeals to *all*—philosophers, scientists, technicians, and ordinary human beings—alike, because it appeals to *each* individually. The cogitating individual, along with other cogitating individuals, wills Nature's mastery in the hope that such control will bring about his or her future health, security, comfort, and tranquility.

Recognition of (and aversion to) "innumerable diseases, both of the body and of the mind, and . . . the infirmity of old age . . . and the brevity of life" is the touchstone Descartes uses to solidify his rhetorical appeal to the individual's particular concerns with self-interest. Self-interest thus understood is the true basis and standard of moral and political virtue in the Cartesian humanitarian project, whether that standard is viewed on a small or on a grand scale. It links the particular concerns for health and longevity of particular individuals with the particular desires for health and longevity of every other individual. Yet the appeal of this notion of self-interest studiously gains force from describing both the self-conscious individual and "mankind" or "humanity" abstractly. It is only when viewed abstractly that disease, decay, and death appear to be particular, embodied—hence, related—human being's primary and most palpable experience of

Nature. It is only when viewed abstractly that disease, decay, and death appear to be what human beings collectively and communally most hold in common.

The great paradox is that the method that lies at the heart of Descartes' new science and new philosophy cannot rationally account for the moral reason that Descartes should exercise generosity on behalf of other human beings in the first place. His passionate appeal for others to enlist the new science he discovered in a humanitarian project to transform the natural world feeds off moral capital for which his new method cannot account. But the paradox is more complicated than this. Descartes' new method erodes the theoretical credibility of this kind of moral capital, at least inasmuch as it portrays such moral capital as having no scientific basis in the method. Here, we encounter a feature of Descartes' thought that today has become conventional—hence unquestioned—wisdom, namely, the familiar scientific distinction between "facts and values." Descartes' new scientific method renders facts, not values. Yet this means it cannot scientifically validate itself as morally good. Descartes' appeal to take up the new science of mastery is meant to evoke a moral response in individuals even as the new science methodologically insists that such appeals are unscientific.

In the final analysis, the moral science behind the project of mastery turns out to be, in this crucial respect, remarkably similar to the older moral science it was meant to replace: each form of science rests on presuppositions that the strict requirements of Cartesian rationalism—indeed, any kind of strict rationalism, whether it be ancient, medieval, or modern—cannot reasonably prove. One important difference between the two sciences is that the moral science advanced by the "ancient pagans" quietly, but openly, admitted it was not a presupposition-less science. Descartes, unlike many of his exuberant and all too uncritical followers, no doubt knew of this similarity. He intimates as much in his work *Le Monde*, a volume he chose not to publish after witnessing Galileo's condemnation by the Roman Inquisition. As he does in the *Discourse*, Descartes there sets forth "rules" that would seem to allow future generations of human beings to pursue the project of producing a "new world."[17] But he also informs us that his reader should look upon this project and the promise it holds forth "as if" it were "a fable."[18]

In writing a fable, an author necessarily has to paint a picture that uses both "shadow as well as bright colors."[19] The juxtaposition of shadows and bright colors allows the artist to paint stark contrasts. Yet stark contrasts often make objects appear far more defined and far more vivid than they really and naturally are. The Cartesian individual is one such object. Descartes makes his account of the cogitating "I" *and* his account of the freedom and power wielded by this "I" *and* his account of nature's indifference and hostility to particular human beings seem more real and more natural than they are.

The moral and political utility of this exaggeration was not lost on Descartes' most serious politically minded student, John Locke. There are important differences between the two men's thought, to be sure. Most obviously, in his writings Locke pays far more attention to politics and civil affairs than Descartes does in his. The *First* or *Second Treatise* or *A Letter concerning Toleration* finds no exact parallel in Descartes' corpus. Less obvious are the philosophic differences between the two. For example, Locke, in contrast to Descartes, explicitly argues against the claim that human beings possess innate knowledge. Locke, in fact, seems to suggest that Descartes' famous cogito incorrectly depends on a doctrine of innate ideas.[20] Still, such differences do not obscure the fact that Locke takes up key aspects of Descartes' account of the individual, nature, and morality, even as he enlists these accounts in his own moral and political project.

Locke develops his idea of the autonomous individual amid a description of life in the state of nature. This description is not primarily meant to provide a historical account of human origins and beginnings, though it does purport to do just that. It is meant to bring to light the fundamental social relation that one human being naturally has to another. The state of nature does not refer to a bygone human era; it remains the de facto natural state of human existence. As Locke describes it, the state of nature exists where human beings exist. Illustrative of this is his claim that "all Princes and Rulers of Independent Governments all through the World are in a State of Nature." Indeed, the "World never was, nor ever will be, without Numbers of Men in that State."[21]

Locke describes life in the state of nature as a "state of perfect freedom."[22] He goes so far as to say that "*in the State of Nature, every one has the Executive Power* of the Law of Nature."[23] Bound only by those bonds to which they freely give their consent, individuals in the state of nature are unfettered by the bonds and the demands of blood, friends, and society.[24] The state of perfect freedom is simultaneously a state of perfect isolation and autonomy. Locke is quick to add, however, that while born into perfect freedom individuals in the state of nature live under "a Law of Nature . . . which obliges every one. . . . Reason, which is that Law, teaches all mankind who will but consult it that, being all equal and independent, no one ought to harm another in his life, health, liberty, or possession."[25] This Law is "plain and intelligible to all rational Creatures."[26] The "Law of Nature" or "Reason," as Locke describes it, actually underscores the solitary and autonomous life that individuals lead in the state of nature and governs human beings in the state of nature as individuals. More specifically, it reminds them that their foremost concern must necessarily be for their own self-preservation: "wrought into the very principles of their nature," self-preservation is the "first and strongest desire God planted in men."[27] To be a rational being, Locke intimates, is to think of oneself as an individual seeking self-preservation.

The desire for self-preservation is "a foundation of a right to the Creatures."[28] As such, it can "never" be neglected.[29] This holds true, for Locke, even after human beings consent to live in civil society: "no Man, or Society of Men, having a Power to deliver up their *Preservation*, or consequently the means of it . . . whenever any one shall go about bringing them into such a Slavish Condition, they will always have a right to preserve what they have not a power to part with; and to rid themselves of those who invade this Fundamental, Sacred, and unalterable law of *Self-Preservation*."[30] The law of nature and the right to self-preservation it is based upon powerfully reaffirm the individual and self-referential nature of human existence. Both remind human beings that "Man [is never allowed] to abandon himself, as to neglect his own preservation."[31]

The "unalterable" demands of self-preservation explain Locke's initially perplexing claim that "Princes and Rulers of Independent Governments" exist in a state of nature. Their relation remains outside the consensual agreements that construct civil society. Absent a consented-upon authority to rule over them, the relation between sovereigns of different political communities reverts back to the relation of human beings in the state of nature. The example Locke uses to illustrate the reality of the state of nature indirectly illuminates the ambiguous existence human beings currently enjoy. As Locke describes it, human life is the product of a curious and delicate combination of nature and historical construction. Abdicating some of their natural freedom, human beings consent to live within the confines of civil society. And yet even after doing this, on some level, they retain possession of the liberty they naturally possess as human beings. Human life as it is experienced is, to use Locke's terminology, a mixed mode. It blends together natural freedom and unnatural, because acquired, restraint. The individual Locke describes—and to whom his work is addressed—accordingly is also something of a construction. As Sara Henary aptly shows in her contribution to this volume, the "I" who is the Lockean individual is the joint product of the complex (and partially mysterious) comingling of nature and history.

Locke recognizes that his claim about the executive power wielded by individuals in the state of nature is extraordinary. He repeatedly calls it a "strange Doctrine."[32] Though strange, this claim is not absurd; after all, the demands of the law of nature are explicitly identified with the demands of Reason. The claim's strangeness stems from the fact that it is so seldom followed. The problem is not general ignorance. All human beings know they have an overriding right to self-preservation. The problem stems from knowing the proper relation of the universal to the particular. For surprisingly few human beings truly—that is, rationally—know what the demands of self-preservation actually call for at any particular time or in any particular situation. Locke traces this failure back to the individual's prejudices and passions as well as to his lack of study.[33] Each of these obstacles prevents individual human beings from rationally applying the universal demand of the law of nature "to their particular cases."[34]

The full measure of the awe-inspiring freedom individuals are said to possess comes to sight in Locke's treatment of property. Locke's account of property, like Descartes' account of the new science, ultimately requires human beings to think of themselves as remarkably separate from, and in many ways jeopardized by, the world around them. According to Locke, in the state of nature no one had "a private dominion exclusive to the rest of mankind."[35] Because private property did not originally exist in the state of nature, the fruit of the trees and the beasts of the land could be enjoyed by any individual at any time. Despite the uninhibited access individuals had to the flora and fauna, life in the state of nature was characterized by penury and neediness. For when left untouched, the bounty that nature naturally produces jeopardizes the individual's survival: "Land that is left wholly to Nature, that hath no improvement of Pasturage, Tillage, or Planting, is called, as indeed it is, *waste*."[36] Whereas Hobbes had said that violence at the hands of another is the chief threat to human life in the state of nature, Locke suggests that hunger, something less outwardly alarming but occurring more regularly and therefore more menacing, is the individual's true enemy.

There is one great and decisive exception to the lack of ownership that characterizes life in the state of nature. Locke asserts that "every Man has a Property in his own Person. This nobody has any right to but himself."[37] Self-ownership, a claim to absolute autonomy that is inconceivable to anyone who does not think of themselves as a self-subsisting individual, provides a basis for overcoming nature's indifference to the lived life of individual human beings. To the extent that a human being is the rightful possessor of himself he is the rightful possessor of what he produces with his own hands. Locke's argument is as follows: because each individual owns himself, and because each laborer is a self-owning individual, each laborer owns the products or property he produces.[38] Every possession a human being can rightfully make claim to, whether in the state of nature or in civil society, ultimately rests on the individual's primordial and most essential natural possession, namely, himself. Self-ownership and productive, self-interested freedom, Locke argues, come together to rescue individuals from the hunger and likely starvation that nature blithely sanctions as their birthright.

The connection between Descartes' idea of mastery of nature and Locke's theory of ownership and labor is clear. From the Lockean individual's point of view nature on its own provides little of vital human importance and value. If it were simply up to nature, the individual human being would most likely perish. Fortunately, through his labor an individual can "improve" on nature.[39] Such improvement, Locke states, necessarily requires the transformation of nature. As a result of his labor, the individual "add[s] something . . . [to] Nature."[40] This added something "alter[s] the intrinsick value of things" for the better, at least from the self-identified and self-referential perspective of the individual.[41] Having "subdued" and "changed" nature, the individual introduces goods of genuine "value" and meaning into the human world. Again and again in his treatment of property, Locke states that the transformative effect of labor "*puts the difference of value* on everything."[42] In fact, chapter 5 of the *Second Treatise* strongly suggests the individual is the only natural thing that possesses inherent value. Everything else that comes from the hand of nature is "almost worthless." Taken together, the discussions of the state of nature, labor, and property in the *Second Treatise* indicate that "value," for all practical purposes, is a construction of the autonomous individual's making.

The extent to which Locke extends the idea that "value" is a human construct is drawn out and put on partial display in his *Essay concerning*

Human Understanding. The *Essay* seeks to identify the precise source and discernible limits of human knowledge. Although unmistakably theoretical in tone as well as content, the work is replete with moral import. Locke actually makes some of his most jarring, yet revealing, claims about the rational status of moral knowledge and moral virtue in this seemingly purely epistemological and scientific work.

In book 1 of the *Essay*, Locke cites human beings' common and reoccurring desire to have the reason behind this or that moral rule explained to them as evidence of the lack of innate ideas and principles in the human mind. Expanding on this claim, he notes that if asked a "Christian," a "Hobbist," and an "old heathen" philosopher would give different explanations as to why a particular moral rule should be obeyed. Locke's comparative remark has the calculated, direct effect of shifting attention away from the question of what the human mind objectively knows about a specific moral principle to a consideration of the internal psychic reason that a Christian or a Hobbist or a classical philosopher does what he does. Christians perform moral acts not because they seek the beatitude and happiness that come from being in communion with God but because "God, who has the power of eternal life and death, requires it of us."[43] The morality of the Christian, Locke states, has little to do with the perfection of his being. It is predicated on a calculated cost/benefit analysis of the comparative desirability of eternal life and eternal perdition. A similar calculus is made by the Hobbist. The Hobbist acts morally out of fear; he seeks to avoid the wrath that awaits law-breakers in the Leviathan state. Apparently, only the classical philosopher refuses to act out of a moral calculus. When asked why he acts morally, the philosopher would respond "because it was dishonest, below the dignity of man, and opposite to virtue, the highest perfection of human nature."[44]

However, the philosopher's response does not accurately reflect the truth of the matter, as Locke states later in the *Essay*. Because it is built on a faulty epistemology, the classical philosopher's understanding of virtue falsely invests specific moral claims with an objective weight and solidity that cannot be scientifically supported. In the second book of the *Essay*, Locke speaks of the "*Philosophical law.*" This law is said to be "*the measure of virtue and vice.*" Yet Locke quickly qualifies this claim; he associates the philosophical law, the measure of virtue and vice, with "the *law of opinion or reputation.*"[45] Virtue and vice are simply "names," words that are "pretended, and supposed everywhere to stand for actions in their own *nature* right and wrong."[46] Like the property and goods individuals value, virtue also finds little or no support in nature. In making this claim, Locke does more than reduce, say, Aristotle's arguments about the moral or ethical virtues to mere opinions—though he undoubtedly does do that. Locke effectively reconfigures the entire "scientific" discussion of morality and moral virtue along nominalist lines. What is called a virtue or a vice, he argues, does not, in the final analysis, correspond to any objective, rationally knowable reality. What goes by the name of courage or moderation or justice is simply a name that "stands for" a quality that has been invested with "reputation or discredit" in a specific "country and society."[47] The term "virtue" merely names a concept; it does not correspond to a reality that the word "virtue" captures and signifies. This is what the old heathen philosopher failed to recognize when he mistakenly said that a particular moral act did or did not comport with "the dignity of man" and the "perfection of human nature."

Locke's theoretical nominalism allows him to recast virtue as a man-made value or construct. Under this configuration, virtue ceases to be understood as a fixed, objective excellence that perfects a human being because he is a human being. At best, specific qualities or characteristics can only be understood as virtues of this or that particular human being. From this conceptually narrowed but carefully focused perspective, the difference between one proposed moral end and another is seen to have the same scientific status as the difference between an individual preference for a relish made out of "apples, plumbs, or nuts."[48] This is the understanding of virtue that someone who looks upon Nature as personally indifferent and wasteful must have. In other words, this is the virtue of the Individual, abstractly and systematically conceived.

To a great degree, the proponents of modern political philosophy and the liberal, democratic regime it helped bring into existence deliberately took the idea of the abstract individual as their point of departure. Descartes and Locke played key (though by no means exclusive and exhaustive) roles in shaping our understanding of the modern individual. Descartes and Locke managed to do this by providing calibrated and rhetorically powerful alternative accounts to the descriptions in both classical philosophy and Christian theology of human beings and their unique and privileged place in the world. And yet, as we have seen, these alternative accounts achieved their clarity by engaging in extreme exaggerations—whether it was exaggerating the indifference or the stinginess of nature and the natural order, or exaggerating the freedom enjoyed by individual human beings, or exaggerating the independence one individual human being has from another.

The individuals depicted by Descartes and Locke do not really exist by nature. They are the products, to use Descartes' word, of a "fable." But they are the products of fables that have some real and recognizable moorings in reality: truthfully, the natural order does seem to be noticeably indifferent to many of the personal desires and aspirations of embodied human being, and human life really does seem to be marked by both our dependence on and independence from other self-conscious, free human beings. Cartesian science and Lockean science, each in its own way, give us partial truths, partial truths that present themselves as whole or all-explanatory truths. As the essays in this volume demonstrate, one of our challenges is to think seriously about what these partial truths can and cannot tell us about ourselves and our world. Put another way, one of the challenges facing *post*-modern human beings is to think seriously about the real relation that the virtue of the Individual *and* the virtuous human individual have to each other.

NOTES

1. René Descartes, *Discourse on the Method of Rightly Conducting One's Reason and of Seeking the Truth in the Sciences*, trans. John Cottingham, Robert Stoothoff, and Dugald Murdoch, in *The Philosophical Writings of Descartes*, vol. 1 (Cambridge: Cambridge University Press, 1985), 120.

2. Ibid., 143.

3. Ibid., 142.

4. All quotations in this paragraph are taken from Descartes' *Principles of Philosophy*, trans. John Cottingham, Robert Stoothoff, and Dugald Murdoch, in *The Philosophical Writings of Descartes*, vol. 1 (Cambridge: Cambridge University Press, 1985), 186.

5. Descartes, *Discourse on the Method*, 114.

6. Charles Taylor, *Sources of the Self: The Making of the Modern Identity* (Cambridge: Harvard University Press, 1989), 127.

7. René Descartes, *The Passions of the Soul*, trans. John Cottingham, Robert Stoothoff, and Dugald Murdoch, in *The Philosophical Writings of Descartes*, vol. 1 (Cambridge: Cambridge University Press, 1985), 349.

8. Ibid., 404.

9. Ibid., 384.

10. Descartes, *Discourse on the Method*, 123.

11. René Descartes, *Letter to Princess Elizabeth of Bohemia*, written on August 8, 1645. René Descartes, trans. John Cottingham, Robert Stoothoff, Dugald Murdoch, and Anthony Kenny in *The Philosophical Writings of Descartes*, vol. 3 (Cambridge: Cambridge University Press, 1991), 258.

12. Descartes, *The Passions of the Soul*, 152.

13. Ibid., 153.

14. See Aristotle, *Nicomachean Ethics*, 1123a35–25a35.

15. Descartes, *Discourse on the Method*, 144.

16. Ibid., 143.

17. René Descartes, *The World*, trans. John Cottingham, Robert Stoothoff, and Dugald Murdoch, in *The Philosophical Writings of Descartes*, vol. 1 (Cambridge: Cambridge University Press, 1985), 97.

18. Ibid., 98.

19. Ibid., 97.

20. See John Locke, *An Essay concerning Human Understanding*, II.1.9.

21. John Locke, *The Second Treatise of Government: An Essay concerning the True Original, Extent, and End of Civil Government*, ed. Peter Laslett (Cambridge: Cambridge University Press, 1988), §14. Citations to this work refer to paragraph numbers.

22. Ibid., §4.

23. Ibid., §13.

24. Ibid., §119.

25. Ibid., §6.

26. Ibid., §124.

27. John Locke, *The First Treatise*, ed. Peter Laslett (Cambridge: Cambridge University Press, 1988), §88.

28. Ibid.

29. Locke, *The Second Treatise*, §168.

30. Ibid., §149.

31. Ibid., §168.

32. See, for example, ibid., §9 and §13.

33. Ibid., §124.

34. Ibid.

35. Ibid., §26.

36. Ibid., §42.

37. Ibid.

38. Ibid., §27.

39. Ibid., §32.

40. Ibid., §28.

41. Ibid., §37.

42. Ibid., §40. See also ibid., §41 and §42.

43. John Locke, *An Essay concerning Human Understanding*, ed. Peter H. Nidditch, The Clarendon Edition of the Works of John Locke (Oxford: Oxford University Press, 1975), I.3.5. Citations to this work refer to book, chapter, and section numbers respectively.

44. Ibid.

45. Ibid., II.28.10.

46. Ibid.; italics added.

47. Ibid.

48. Ibid., II.21.55.

9

SCIENCE, VIRTUE, AND THE BIRTH OF MODERNITY

OR, ON THE TECHNO-THEO-LOGIC OF MODERN NEUROSCIENCE

Jeffrey P. Bishop

I T SHOULD NOT BE SURPRISING TO US THAT the figures of the early modern period that shaped the new science were also the figures that shaped our political philosophies. Both the rationalists and the empiricists shaped this early modern philosophy of both our political and scientific practices. Politics and science seem always to have gone together. In analyzing René Descartes' political philosophy and epistemology, Catherine Pickstock notes that the second part of the *Discourse on Method* begins with the metaphor of the city. Descartes appeals to analogies "of architecture, city-planning, and governmental structure to describe his method for the composition and organization of knowledge."[1] Pickstock goes on to describe the way in which the ordering of knowledge mimics a city that is defended from chaos. This citadel of one person, alone, ordering knowledge is the paradigm of knowing for Descartes. Formal consistency is more important than embodied and communal goods. Moreover, by appeal to the work of several Cartesians scholars, Thomas Hibbs has drawn our attention to the univocity of language and homogeneity of method used by Cartesian science.[2] The universal *mathesis* allows one not only to know geometry but also to order all knowledge according to the same measure, including political and moral goods.

Thomas Hobbes attempts to deploy the univocal geometry of Descartes to build the new city. Hobbes, a geometrician and friend of Descartes, was also secretary to the Lord Chancellor, Francis Bacon. According to Hobbes, the geometer king would make the space of the city to cohere in a manner similar to the axioms of geometry. Within the geometric mathesis of the city, a person might withstand the violence of the state of nature, where life "is solitary, poor, nasty, brutish, and short."[3] It seems to me that it was Hobbes' motif of survival against the state of nature that would take a more Victorian and romantic turn in Darwin's natural selection, such that Hobbesian political philosophy helped to shape Darwinian biology.

John Locke, a physician, thought of himself as a natural philosopher (that is to say, a scientist), yet we think of him as a political philosopher. For instance as a scientist, we find him speaking of primary qualities in *An Essay concerning Human Understanding*, which are properties or powers inherent in objects. Reason and liberty are powers, properties, of human being.[4] And in the *Second Treatise of Government*, he states that men band together in society "for the mutual Preservation of their Lives, Liberties and Estates," which he calls "by the general Name, Property."[5] In both his natural philosophy and his political philosophy, much hangs on the ideas of properties and powers. Properties adhere closely to the essence of things, including humankind. As he notes, "man . . . hath by Nature a Power . . . to preserve his Property, that is, his Life, Liberty and Estate."[6] Life is a property of human being; liberty is a property of human being.

Still, for me, the one figure we have not dealt with is someone who predates all of these figures—namely, Francis Bacon, the father of modern empiricism. Bacon was also a political operative his entire life.[7] I want to draw our attention to Bacon not because he gives us a new inductive science, a new empirical science, though surely this is true. I shall argue that the stance he takes to nature transforms early modern philosophy into techno-science even before robust technological innovation had begun. In other words, rather than his being the father of the new, inductive method for the acquisition of new knowledge, it was instead the stance that he took to nature that transformed science. This form of techno-science— knowledge that can do things—comes to shape the recent research into things like moral formation, all with an eye to controlling human virtue and vice. In short, I shall conclude with Heidegger that modern science is really techno-science, knowledge that does technological work. It seems that human beings become the raw material for a better, more moral polis.

BACON ON KNOWLEDGE OF PHYSICS AND METAPHYSICS

Before getting to Francis Bacon, I need, with the assistance of Simon Oliver, to provide some background. In a thoroughgoing historical and conceptual analysis of the philosophy of motion, Oliver examines how understandings of motion shifted after the publication of the *Principia Mathematica*.[8] Oliver describes how that shift in understandings of motion had begun centuries prior to Isaac Newton. He traces the philosophy of motion from Plato through Aristotle, Avicenna, Robert Grosseteste, Roger Bacon, and Thomas Aquinas. A brief explication of Oliver's admirable work is warranted, as it will assist in my thesis.

Today, we think of motion as movement through space, that is, locomotion. With Aristotle motion is not limited strictly to the realm of physics and local movement through space. Motion, for Aristotle, is the passage from "potency to act."[9] Where today we think of "act" or "action" as a kind of doing of something, Aristotle thought of act as more a state of being, where being itself is in motion. A rock, as rock, can be said to be in the act of being rock. Thus, Aristotle's understanding of motion had metaphysical import; to move from potency to act is to move from potential through becoming to being actualized. "Such motion," Oliver claims, "is explained not in terms of mechanistic chance and necessity, but rather in terms of teleology and the order of formal and final causes which render the cosmos intelligible."[10] For Aristotle, then, there is a hierarchy of the sciences, and motion is relevant at every level. "The sciences are productive, practical or theoretical according to whether their goal consists in the making of artifacts, the human performance of actions or the attainment of principles."[11] Thus, Aristotle could speak of motion at the level of physics, at the level of the poetical and rhetorical sciences, at the level of politics and ethics, and finally at the level of the theoretical sciences (natural philosophy, mathematics, and metaphysics).[12]

However, Oliver notes, as early as the great Persian philosopher Ibn Sina (Avicenna), we begin to see a kind of dualistic separation between physics and metaphysics.[13] This dualism trickles down through history to shape the thinking of Roger Bacon and finds its most robust articulation in the work of Isaac Newton. Oliver notes that, in Newton's account, motion

becomes movement through efficient causation, solely. Thus, with Newton, we see a decisive break with the Aristotelian understanding of motion
as something relevant to many spheres of being and doing, along with a
break with Aristotelian metaphysics. Newtonian physics is concerned not
with motion per se but with the forces that cause a body to move or to
resist movement.[14] That is to say, the study of motion became the study
of forces and the study of prior efficient causes in the immanent series
of causes and effects. There is not space here to describe it, but with
the work of the great physiologist Claude Bernard we see that physiology, following a Newtonian physics, would become concerned primarily
with efficient causation.

With this explanation, we can return to Francis Bacon, who was clearly
already influenced by the shift in metaphysics after Ibn Sina, Robert Grosseteste, and Roger Bacon. For Francis Bacon, the relationship of knowledge
to power is of great interest, because power, the use of force, is how one
controls the world and knowledge of power is how one knows what to do
in order to cause new things to come into being efficiently. Bacon states:

> Finally, we want all and everyone to be advised to reflect on the true
> ends of knowledge (*scientia*): not to seek it for amusement or for dis-
> pute, or to look down on others, or for profit or for face or for power
> or any such inferior ends, but for the uses and benefits of life, and to
> improve and conduct it in charity. For the angels fell because of an ap-
> petite for power; and men fell because of an appetite for knowledge.[15]

Bacon continues, just two sentences later, by noting that his *New
Organon*—the new work—should be seen not as an opinion but as a *work*
and not for the laying down of dogma "but for human progress, and empowerment."[16] So, on the one hand, knowledge is not to be sought for power,
but it is nonetheless sought for empowerment. Knowledge is power; but
it ought to be a power to bring effects into the world for good, and not for
self-aggrandizement.

Thus, the end of power over nature, at the level of human action, is
human progress. We seek knowledge for empowerment, but still, power
must be exercised over nature if we are to get nature to reveal her secrets.
In opposing his inductive method to the deductive method, Bacon states:
"They [the deductive reasoners] defeat and conquer their adversary by
disputation; we conquer nature by work."[17] Inductive science is work done

to nature. Inductive science is born in the "bowels of nature" and not in the minds of men.[18]

Knowledge—science—is work. Bacon claims that knowledge is obtained by the inductive method in two ways; he calls the two ways the two parts of knowledge. The first part of knowledge is description of nature as it freely follows the laws to which it has been set. But Bacon goes further than mere observation and description. Much more can be learned when nature is "confined and harassed, when it is forced from its own condition by art and human agency, and pressured and molded."

Bacon continues, "Moreover (to be plain) we put much more effort and many more resources into this [second] part than into the other, and pay no attention to men's disgust or what they find attractive, since nature reveals herself more through the harassment of art than in her own proper freedom."[19] The work of the new scientists requires the harassment of nature; she must be coerced so that her secrets can be extracted from her. Bacon is an advocate of experimental science.[20]

This brings us to the second feature of Bacon's contribution to the new science, namely, his understanding of knowledge as it relates to causes. He notes:

> The sorry state of current human knowledge is clear even from common expressions. It is right to lie down: "to know truly is to know by causes." It is also not bad to distinguish four causes: Material, Formal, Efficient, and Final. But of these the Final is a long way from being useful; in fact it actually distorts the sciences except in the case of human actions. Discovery of Form is almost hopeless. And the Efficient and Material causes (as commonly sought and accepted, i.e. in themselves and apart from the latent process which leads to the Form) are perfunctory, superficial things, of almost no value for true, active knowledge.[21]

Bacon is afraid that the simplistic reading of cause and effect—that is to say, efficient causes—will mislead. Efficient and material causes at the level of the latent structure and processes will get us closer to true knowledge. By latent process and latent structure, Bacon means something akin to the hidden mechanism and hidden structure. Bacon continues by showing that we creep along by investigating material and efficient causes, with hopes of constructing perfect knowledge, which is knowledge of the laws of nature—which he takes to be the forms of nature, that is to say, the formal causes. "[H]e who knows forms comprehends the unity of nature," and so he can "bring forth things which have never been achieved."[22]

Here, Bacon shifts the emphasis of the four Aristotelian causes, balancing them differently than would Aristotle. Final causes are not part of knowledge or science; formal causes are truly laws of nature, but they can be known only through a deep understanding of efficient and material causes. By studying material and efficient causes, along with the latent process and the latent structure, one can come close to having full knowledge of the laws of nature, the forms.[23] So, in his division of the sciences, metaphysics is "inquiry after forms."[24] Physics is the examination of material and efficient causes, along with the latent process and latent structure. Emerging from these sciences, there are two practical arts, one subsidiary to physics and the other to metaphysics—namely, mechanics and magic, respectively. Each art gives "command over nature," magic the more so because it uses the forms, the laws of nature itself, to give command over nature. Perfect knowledge, true knowledge is the power to control nature.

With Bacon, then, we can see in embryonic form the Newtonian understanding of causes, of forces acting on bodies in locomotion. This understanding of locomotion and forces would achieve fruition in Newtonian physics and would in time come to influence the physiology of the nineteenth century. Claude Bernard—eulogized as the Newton of physiological science—would also understand the human body in similar fashion.[25] What must have been magic to Bacon became for us merely what falls from efficient and formal causes, or perhaps better, what falls from the latent structures and processes of objects of inquiry. The new method in science must coerce nature in order for her to give up her secrets, the latent structures and processes of efficient and material causation. One instruments nature in order to know it, in order to have control over it. What Bacon calls forms of nature, or laws of nature, became for us the force behind the mechanisms—one thing falling on another in the latent, mechanical process. Certainly mastery over these forces must have seemed magical to Bacon. Moreover, knowledge of formal causes or laws would in time fall from the lofty metaphysical structures of Aristotle and the occult magic of Bacon's time and become mere physics and mechanics for us.[26]

So, what of Aristotle's fourth cause, final causes? In the end, Bacon does allow final causation back into the schema of knowledge after he had bracketed it. As we already noted, final causes are useless and distort our knowledge except in human action. And it is here, then, that we find the justification for the instrumentation of nature. The new science exists "to relieve the human estate."[27] It is the usefulness of information to bring effects into the world that serves to justify—morally, politically, and epistemologically—the pursuit of knowledge in Bacon's new empirical science. How do we know that we know something? We know that we know something when we can manipulate the beings of the world through the deployment of knowledge. In fact, the definition of knowledge under patent law today is precisely this; it can be patented as knowledge if we can do something with the information. True knowledge—that is, patentable knowledge—is power to bring effects into the world. True science seeks to understand the power of nature, of the laws of nature, of formal causation. Human empowerment is obtained when one has power, that is to say, knowledge of the forces of locomotion, to control nature.

I have attempted to show that it was not just Francis Bacon's method—induction—that caused a great shift in science but, instead, his understanding of the laws of nature, the metaphysics of formal causes, and power. I think that we can see as early as Bacon that more than pure observational science of inductive reasoners was at work. Instead, we see an ordering of knowledge directed at human ends, that is to say, already on the hunt for technological manipulation of nature, to relieve the human estate.[28] Even while one must bracket teleology in order to seek and to know perfectly, according to Bacon the justification for going forward on the quest for knowledge is empowerment over nature. And the justification for instrumenting nature is to coerce her to give up her secrets so that she might be coerced and ordered into human production. In other words, science is techno-logical, in much the way that Heidegger means it; we must harness the power in nature in order to control it.

POWER ONTOLOGY, POWER BIOLOGY, POWER NEUROSCIENCE

While Darwin is not known as an experimental scientist, I do believe that we can see a similar metaphysical principle of power behind an idea like natural selection and evolution. Nature puts forward new beings, which survive to procreation, perpetuating the kind of being that each one is. In other words, various new forms of life (various beings) are put forward in nature (the forms of nature are varied), and various forces in nature lead to changes in the environments. There is a power behind nature and natural selection. The hidden laws of nature, the forms of nature, and the forces of nature are at work. In other words, with Darwin, we find a kind of power ontology.[29] In order to demonstrate the relationship between a notion like power ontology or power biology and our technologies of virtue, I shall first briefly describe the history of metaphysics according to Martin Heidegger, and given the complexity of interpreting Heidegger, we would do well to take this journey with the assistance of one of the clearest interpreters of Heidegger, Iain Thomson.

Oversimplifying Heidegger's position, metaphysics determines everything. Thomson, in interpreting Heidegger, states:

> By codifying and disseminating an understanding of what things *are*, metaphysics provides each historical "epoch" of intelligibility with its ontological bedrock. And by furnishing an account of the ultimate source from which entities issue, metaphysics supplies intelligibility with a kind of foundational justification that . . . Heidegger characterizes as "theological."[30]

In short, the history of the West is a series of bifurcating understandings: the question of "what an entity is" can be understood as *what* things *are* (ontology), or it can be understood as a question about the existence of the paradigmatic entity (theology).[31] Ontology searches for *whatness*, or essence; theology searches for *thatness*, or existence.

Ontology names that branch of metaphysics that concerns itself with the being of entities. It "looks for what component element all entities share in common"; in other words, ontology looks for the being of entities "beyond which no more basic entity can be 'discovered.'"[32] Metaphysics is ontology, when it "thinks of beings with an eye for the ground that is common to all beings as such." Thus, ontology names the *ousia*, the proto-substance; yet, ontology takes on different "historical character[s]: *Phusis, Logos, Hen, Idea, Energeia,* Substantiality, Objectivity, Subjectivity, Will, Will to Power, Will to Will." Thus, ontology is named differently depending upon the historical epoch within which it held dominance.[33]

Heidegger names the other branch of metaphysics as theology, which should not be understood in a religious sense but in terms of the god of the philosophers. What an entity *is*, asks about its existence, namely, *that* it *is*. Theology understood philosophically asks two subsidiary questions about the being of things: "'What is that which is?' asks both (1) *Which* entity is in the supreme, paradigmatic, or exemplary sense? and (2) In what sense *is* it?"[34] The first question is about the highest entity (be it God or, in our time, the universe as it is), and the second is a question about the kind of being that it is. In what sense *is* it (God or, for us, the universe)? So, metaphysics thinks theologically when it "thinks of the totality of entities as such . . . with regard to the supreme, all-founding entity." Metaphysics as theology is concerned with the *causa sui*, the self-caused cause, the un-moved mover, the beingest of beings.[35]

Heidegger's interpretation of the recent history of metaphysics went something like this, according to Thomson:

> Kant thinks "theologically" when he postulates "the subject of sub-jectivity as the condition of the possibility of all objectivity," as does Hegel when he determines "the highest entity as the absolute in the sense of unconditioned subjectivity, that is, as outermost conditions on the possibility of intelligibility.[36]

Heidegger goes on to note that even Nietzsche, who is much less con-cerned with being and much more concerned with becoming, thinks theo-logically when he "thinks the *existentia* of the totality" by proclaiming the "eternal return of the same." After all, eternal recurrence is not just "the way that the totality of entities exists . . . but also their *highest* mode of existence (as the closest the endless stream of becoming comes to *being*)."[37]

Nietzsche pulls the rug out from under this drive to provide foun-dations for essence, on the one hand, and existence, on the other, but the tension between becoming and return is the same sort of tension between ontology and theology. Becoming is essence or ontology; the moment of the return of the same is the highest moment in existence. Nietzsche proclaims that there are no foundations for being, just an un-broken succession of one metaphysically grounded epoch arising from the ashes of the metaphysics that preceded it.[38] In other words, there is the eternal circulation of power, with no culmination in being, just eternal becoming.[39]

Here in Nietzsche, we see something akin to evolution, eternal be-coming. Rather than static beings or static Being about which the West seems most concerned, Nietzsche points to the Dionysian element, which has been suppressed in service of the ordering power of nature. Dionysus, as the god of Chaos, represents the creative and playful force, the force that is most free to become what it will, the power behind the organizing formal cause. Biologically speaking, that force or power is both similar to the Darwinian notion of selection and also different from it, as Nietzsche wishes to distance himself from Darwin. John Richardson calls this circulation of power Nietzsche's "power ontology" and "power biology." These powers or forces are the will to power that repeatedly brings forth new life and new possibilities; but "will" must be understood differently from agency. The will to power as creative and evolutionary force has no robust telos toward which it is aimed. "Will to power" is not conscious agency; it has only a hidden cause directed successfully to what is the case in the present. It is unpredictable in any scientific sense; its essence is becoming. In other words, "entities" are always at a stage of becoming; those entities that "exist" in the present are those that have successfully survived by virtue of the creative forces that sustain them in that momentary state. Thus, Nietzsche's will to power should be thought of as non-mentalist or non-conscious becoming—will without agency.

Our conscious ability to come up with explanations for why living entities, ourselves included, act in certain ways are false stories that cover over the non-conscious will to power.[40] In other words, our history of attributing both formal and final causes to the being of entities is in error. Thomson can help to explicate this point further: "entities *are* only concatenations of forces in the service of will-to-power, a will that strives ultimately only for its own unlimited self-aggrandizing increase" (here understood as a non-conscious will).[41] These concatenations of energy, these forces coming together and breaking apart, have "no goal beyond their own self-augmenting increase."[42] As such, "all entities, ourselves included, are thereby conceived of ultimately only as raw materials, intrinsically meaningless *resources* (*Bestand*) on standby merely to be optimally ordered and efficiently disposed of in an endless and unending spiral of constant overcoming."[43] Thus, humans are beings that just happen to be, in this momentary stage of becoming, an evolutionary achievement. This "power ontology" achieves a new stage in becoming in the evolutionary history of human becoming, a moment when a human can turn to order the creative and chaotic forces.

A central tenet of Darwinian evolutionary theory is the belief that, through selection, the creative power from whence the origin of species arises eventually succeeds—that is to say, survives—in the set of environmental circumstances within which it finds itself. However, this ontological creative force achieves, according to John Harris, a new state in human history, where evolution is no longer natural selection—with starts and stops—but, instead, deliberate selection.[44] Transitional humans have achieved the point of new possibility.

> This new phase of evolution in which Darwinian evolution, by natural selection, will be replaced by a deliberately chosen process of selection, the results of which, instead of having to wait the millions of years over which Darwinian evolutionary change has taken place, will be seen and felt almost immediately. The new process of evolutionary change will replace *natural selection* with *deliberate selection, Darwinian evolution* with *"enhancement evolution."*[45]

Never mind that Harris misses a key point, namely, that in Darwinian becoming something quite different might emerge than what human enhancement of evolution might produce. Still, the point is that rational human will directs evolutionary history. This achievement is mediated through the deployment of technology with all of its attendant powers.[46] The human will, an evolutionary achievement, turns to order the chaos of creative ontology and thereby enacts an ordering theology. The highest being turns to order its own becoming.

This new stage of becoming—a culmination in the series of non-directed creative forces—results in different creative possibilities, according to thinkers such as Harris. Earth and its fruits stand ready as a reserve of power awaiting the next iteration of these creative forces. Yet, for those like Harris, these creative forces—this will to power—turns onto itself in human becoming. Thus, the ontology of thinkers like Harris is a power ontology, where power circulates in the stops and starts of evolutionary biology. The human animal, as a moment of achievement of the natural circulation of power coming into being, harnesses these creative evolutionary forces, highlighting a different force, an ordering force that turns the chaotic forces to order. Rather than the essential force that creates, the essence of all becoming, the human will seeks to order the creative forces with a greater ordering force. The human will is a product of the creative force of becoming, which turns for the moment to master and control its own becoming; and getting to the main point of this chapter, this includes the moral and political becoming of humans.

ORDERING TECHNO-LOGIC AND POLITICAL WILL

Technology, as we today understand it, is primarily thought of as a neutral tool, an instrument grounded by inductive and experimental reasoning about nature and by which we bring desired effects into being. Humankind produces technology as a means to achieve various ends.[47] One merely has to apply the proper ethics and politics to the various means to achieve the ends. My thesis has been that, beginning with Francis Bacon, science/knowledge is already technological, in that one must instrument nature in order to know and then to deploy that knowledge instrumentally to bring good effects in the world. In other words, the facts obtained by science about nature do not themselves have *telei* or final causes; final causes are post hoc additions to the efficient mechanisms, just as Bacon describes.[48] Final causes are admitted either through the inscription of an individual will and through the addition of a political will or through a balancing of these two wills. Nowhere is this clearer than in thinkers such as Nick Bostrom, Joel Garreau, Simon Young, Ray Kurzweil, Aubrey de Grey, and Michael Rae. They suggest that we can improve upon the human condition, generally, and thinkers such as Thomas Douglas suggest that we can improve upon the moral condition of the human animal specifically.

In order to explicate how modern science itself is technological, it would be helpful to recall the argument of Heidegger's famous essay "The Question concerning Technology."[49] Reflecting on Greek thinking about *technē*, Heidegger there describes the relationship of the four traditional Aristotelian causes, showing that they cohered harmoniously in what he calls an occasioning, a kind of bringing together of causes such that entities appear in the phenomenological sense. The four Aristotelian causes let what is not yet present come into relief, and this, Heidegger concludes, is *poiēsis*. For the Greeks, *Phusis* (nature) was the highest form of *poiēsis*; *phusis* is the bursting forth or the springing forth of something present to the senses. And Heidegger goes one step further in claiming that *technē*—including the arts of handicraft, the arts of the mind, and the arts of the fine arts—is also a subset of poiēsis; they are "something poietic."

Greek *technē* then acts to bring forth, without controlling instrumentally. *Technē* is a kind of midwife that brings forth without coercion; it is the manner in which a craftsman will bring forth something through subtle and delicate work. Technology, here understood as Greek *technē*, is no mere means. It is a way of revealing. Yet, for us, Heidegger claims, technology is not a *bringing forth* so much as it is a *challenging forth*. We see this even in Bacon, where the scientist must harass nature to bring forth the formal cause, the forces at work, so that nature's power can be harnessed in order to enact the political will, to relieve the human estate. For us, technology reveals, but it reveals by challenging and coercing that which is not present to us so that it comes into being for us. For Bacon, nature must be harassed to reveal what is not present.

Thus, modern technology is manipulation and manufacturing, but it is never merely the application of physics and chemistry; for medicine, technology is never merely the application of psych neuropharmacology, or the use of deep nerve stimulators, or in the future the deployment of nanobots. Technology is instead a stance struck toward the objects of nature, and in the case of medical science/technology, a stance struck toward the human body/object. It is a way of challenging the body/object to produce what we will from it. Heidegger states:

> Man's ordering attitude and behavior display themselves first in the rise of modern physics as an exact science. Modern science's way of representing pursues and entraps nature as a calculable coherence of forces. Modern physics is not experimental physics because it applies apparatus to the questioning of nature. Rather the reverse is true. Because physics, indeed already as pure theory, sets nature up to exhibit itself as a coherence of forces calculable in advance, it therefore orders its experiments precisely for the purpose of asking whether and how nature reports itself when set up in this way.[50]

As Thomas Hibbs describes, the universal *mathesis*, the measure of all things, always already reveals itself as measurable because it is set up to reveal itself in just this way. The ordering provided by technology—literally, the ordering techno-logic—marries together the creative power of evolution with the power of technology to order this "power ontology." Nature becomes what nature is set up to become by the techniques that are applied, by the modes of harassment devised by the techno-scientist.

Heidegger claims, then, that prior to modern physics, which entraps nature as the calculable coherence of forces, there is a stance already struck toward the world, a stance that holds sway over nature. He notes that, even while technology is chronologically posterior to modern physics, technology is prior to physics in the sense that the holding sway over what presents itself for human reckoning sets nature up in just this way. Catherine Pickstock puts forth a fitting description for this mode of reckoning when she states: "There arises, therefore, an epistemological circuit whereby knowledge is based entirely on objects, whose 'being' does not exceed the extent to which they are known."[51] And they are known because they are measured. An act of the mind stabilizes those things of flux and diversity, fixes them so that they can be known and used. In fact, only those useful features of the plenum come into relief as things. What is measurable becomes the standard for what is "knowable," which in turn becomes the standard for what "is."

The challenging forth of technology—the measuring of things—delimits those things that emerge as things to those features of things that are useful. Heidegger names this challenging forth as the *Gestell*, the enframing. The enframing is what allows the objects of technology to emerge as possible objects and tools. Things are raw materials or natural resources, lacking in any inherent value or *telei*, that only attain meaning insofar as they can be put to some use by the ordering power of the human will or the political will that turns to order the chaotic concatenation of forces. They emerge as things for us only insofar as useful. Thomson states:

> For Heidegger, then, Nietzsche's legacy is our nihilistic "cybernetic" epoch of "enframing", which can only enact its own groundless metaphysical presuppositions by increasingly quantifying the qualitative—reducing all intelligibility to that which can be stockpiled as bivalent, programmable "information"—and by leveling down all attempts to justify human meaning to empty optimization imperatives like: "Get the most out of your potential!"[52]

Very little more could sum up the contemporary philosophy of medical technology than "Get the most out of your potential."

It is here that we begin to discuss the post hoc addition of purpose, *telei*, final causes. The chaotic concatenation of forces of a nature directed toward no purpose can finally attain purpose when we add back the human will or political will. In this moment, we see manifest the will to power in the raw material of the human brain. We see this power turn to order the chaos toward some human purpose: to assure proper development of technology to "get the most out of your potential." Harris articulates two principles that should serve as boundaries for research and the use of novel technologies. The first is a "do no harm" principle and the second is a Rawlsian fairness principle.[53] These two principles act as guiding principles that will both delimit and advance research on enhancement technologies. From here, Harris articulates a very powerful conclusion that, if research and the subsequent use of technology can be bounded by these governing principles, one might be able to articulate a civic obligation to participate in research. Indeed, Rawlsian fairness itself might require it.[54] After all, knowledge requires large *ns*. Indeed, "the rights and interests of research subjects are just the rights and interests of persons and must be balanced against comparable rights and interests of other persons."[55] Humans are notoriously bad at judging their own best interests and are often in need of a society (that is, the political apparatus) to do so for them.[56]

The contemporary apologists for radical technological enhancement seem to divide here along the lines of politics. Harris is more of a liberal egalitarian; those like Nick Bostrom are more libertarian individualists. For Harris, the public good of our biotechnological future might dictate that the state can incentivize participation in research, and we may in fact have good reasons to promote research in a civilized society for the good of the many. Bostrom seems to think the great tragedy of our eugenic past was that society fostered evolutionary progress by technologically and politically intervening qua government, rather than allowing particular individuals to decide for themselves. Bostrom states:

> History has shown the dangers in letting governments curtail these [morphologic and reproductive] freedoms. The last century's government-sponsored coercive eugenics programs, once favored by both the left and the right, have been thoroughly discredited. Because people are likely to differ profoundly in their attitudes towards human enhancement technologies, it is crucial that no single solution be imposed on everyone from above, but that individuals get to consult their own consciences as to what is right for themselves and their families. Information, public debate, and education are the appropriate means by which to encourage others to make wise choices, not a global ban on a broad range of potentially beneficial medical and other enhancement options.[57]

On Bostrom's account, the ethically bad features of our eugenic history are that these were government-imposed programs to enhance evolution by culling the unfit.

We have come full circle on the relationship of politics to science. As I noted at the beginning of this chapter, the great thinkers who gave us our science also gave us our political frames within which science—knowledge—is born. Every questioning of nature is already a political quest to know for the purposes of relieving the human estate—of enacting the final causes of the political apparatus—from which the question is generated. The ordering techno-logic is the political will to power over the chaotic forces of power in nature. The fight is over who—the state or the individual—enacts that will, who acts as the highest being to control its own self-aggrandizement. The birth of modernity is the birth of the twins, techno-science and political technique.

MANUFACTURING THE VIRTUOUS HUMAN, THE POST-HUMAN GOD

I have thus far not spoken of virtue. On the ontotheological view of modern science, virtue is just this, a power of doing or being good.[58] In the ancient world, virtues were excellences of practices, the goods that made other human goods possible. The virtues make possible human flourishing, and the virtues participate in that flourishing both as condition and as (at least in part) end. The virtues were to be cultivated in the arts of human practice and activity. They were brought forth in practices—brought forth under the tutelage of a midwife, a practitioner of the activity. They were contextual and required an entire community of practitioners.

Yet for us, it seems, the virtues are the powers of the brain. The social and economic context within which childhood development occurs either allows the brain to develop in such a way that a person is "moral" (that is, not having any antisocial personality disorder) or "immoral" (that is, having a propensity to antisocial behaviors or frank disorder).[59] We have theories of the brain in which we can find specific brain structures where wisdom is housed or a series of neural processes where reason occurs. For example, Thomas W. Meeks and Dilip V. Jeste distilled from various neuroscientific studies the following subcomponents of wisdom:

(1) prosocial attitudes/behaviors, (2) social decision making/pragmatic knowledge of life, (3) emotional homeostasis, (4) reflection/self-understanding, (5) value relativism/tolerance, and (6) acknowledgment of and dealing effectively with uncertainty/ambiguity.[60]

Taking just one of these subcomponents of wisdom as an example, the authors broke prosocial attitudes and behaviors into further components and found where they localized in the brain: (a) empathy, localized in the medial prefrontal cortex; (b) social cooperation, localized in the dorsolateral prefrontal cortex; and (c) altruism, localized to the ventral and dorsal striatum. They did this with each of the other five subcomponents of wisdom. The social justification for research into the neurobiology of wisdom is that it "may have considerable clinical significance," leading to development "of preventive, therapeutic, and rehabilitative interventions for enhancing wisdom."[61]

One can imagine moral enhancement developing from this research, as suggested and justified by Thomas Douglas and Mark Walker.[62] Following Douglas' justification of moral enhancement and Meeks and Jeste's Baconian project of relieving the human (political) estate and after carefully mapping the moral virtue onto the brain, one can imagine a deep brain stimulator to deliver just the right amount of stimulation to the medial prefrontal cortex so as to promote empathy. But one would have to be careful in stimulating empathy lest emotionality should cloud decision-making. One might at the same time also stimulate in proper sequence the limbic structures, the striatum, and the prefrontal cortex, all associated with pragmatic decision-making, which correlate with "forming a preference, executing an action, or evaluating an outcome," respectively.[63] Or following Walker's suggestion that, after careful mapping of moral virtue onto the genome, one might imagine genetic tests with some level of statistical certainty that might allow one to prevent the implantation of genetically vicious embryos; or one might imagine the genetic modification of such morally deficient beings. Or one might imagine the modification of one's socio-politico-economic environment, so as to reduce the number of the phenotypic expressions of genetic viciousness. This technological answer to moral virtue—this challenging forth, and harnessing the power of virtue—seems to be qualitatively different than the practical bringing forth of virtue that was entailed by the ancient Greek notion of *technē*.

Still, I am not longing for an ancient alternative, as if Aristotle might save us. Rather, I have attempted to relativize the metaphysical (ontotheological) assumptions that animate not only the techno-science and the political techniques born in modernity. Certainly, some form of an ancient alternative might keep us from a new eugenic or politically totalizing future. I do hope that the idea that virtue is cultivated and not controlled would give us pause and cause us to realize we are not gods in possession of the politico-technological truth that can be deployed to save us from viciousness. The idea that virtue is brought forth, birthed, might allow us to see that we are dependent creatures. History is strewn with the bodies of people who died at the hands of gods, those who thought themselves divine. This new divinity—the post-human, who would be the highest being toward which we are hurtling—might be prevented from coming into existence. Certainly, there is a difference between virtue that is birthed and virtue that is manufactured. Yet, even some ancient notions of virtue seem to miss the mark. Some beings aren't capable of some excellences, let alone the highest mode of being, contemplation. Some beings are capable, and they are meant to lead and to birth the great polis.

There seem to be two modern contenders for the "correct" political enactment of our post-human future: On the one hand, we have the liberal egalitarians (the do-gooders), and on the other hand, we have the liberal individualists (the morphological freedom fighters). Among the liberal egalitarians, we have people like Rosamond Rhodes, who believes people should be conscripted for scientific studies for the good of the polis, or John Harris, who believes we have a duty to do the work of human enhancement for the good of the many. We also see those like Meeks and Jeste, who strive to find the biological basis of the *universal* virtues, like altruism, emotional homeostasis, self-understanding, value relativism. Like all Baconian projects, their desire is to diagnose and treat those unfortunate, vicious souls. They would intervene to help the victims of viciousness, and they would give them a therapy such that they too become part of society. Still, in this version, one is struck by the arrogance that suggests we can relieve the human estate not by easing pain or suffering, but that we can literally relieve individual beings of human frailties by manufacturing a new being, helping to evolve the nature of the once-human. These thinkers would take the vicious and find ways of controlling the body by having us find therapeutic interventions and techniques of prevention, for the good of society. This alternative risks becoming at best totalizing and at worst totalitarian.

The other modern contender is that of those such as Nick Bostrom, the "morphological freedom" fighters. Such thinkers hold that the unit of analysis of evolutionary history is the individual. Still others seem to hold that American government—with its individual freedoms and limited government grounded in the evolutionary pinnacle of the free American—is the culmination of evolutionary history. Individuals are free to choose their own fate, take up the powers of their own body, mould and shape it, to create themselves in the likeness of their own good, their own god. But something is unsettling about this option as well. This version runs the risk of creating a very unequal society, a world where those morphological freedom fighters out-compete and out-survive those "lesser," "tribal" beings, those beings of "tribal" cultures. I am sure these freedom fighters do not intend such violent success, but it sure seems consonant with an evolutionary perspective fixed upon the individual—the human being fighting against nature and other individuals, "red in tooth and claw."[64]

Finally, we have been presented with a false dichotomy of the cosmic/transcendent morality (a chasing after false gods) or a biological/material morality (where god is the human being who describes the biological conditions for the possibility of morality). The sentiment seems to be that, by avoiding the transcendent, one also avoids metaphysics. The truth is that the transcendental (here understood in the Kantian sense) might have failed, but this does not mean that the biological is thereby correct. And it does not mean that, if one avoids the transcendental, one does not deploy a metaphysic. In fact, Darwinian biology and the various Darwinisms that it has spun off are just as metaphysical, that is to say, theological in the ontotheological sense of the word. Darwinian biology is metaphysical in the sense that there is a highest being: either (1) a general political will that should turn to order the evolutionary process of the human, or (2) each individual will that seeks to order his or her own highest good.

Techno-science, with a little help, killed god but kept him as an epistemological and moral postulate. Darwinians keep him as the ordering being, whether a body politic or a single individual. Techno-science, with a little help, destroyed the human soul and left us with the postulate of the transcendental ego with no discernible origin and hurling toward no discernible future, left alone to enact our own will to power. Techno-science, with a little help, deadened down the mystery of nature, of *Phusis*, and left us with things that can only be the reserve of power. Every day, you and I enact this condition; in the modern view (and we all share that view), we are beings captured by the immanent biological thrust of an evolutionary history, we can but attempt to produce ourselves, create ourselves, and make of ourselves our own little gods. And repeatedly, we find ourselves wanting no part of these new gods.

CONCLUSION

I look to the hills, from whence shall come our Salvation? Where wisdom shall be found? It certainly isn't with me, and I suspect it is not with those who would control our future, whether controlled by the individual will or by the political will of the state. Post-human gods are just as dangerous as those dictators who would lord it over the rest of humanity. At the birth of modernity, then, we see the birth of twin philosophies: technoscience, bent on controlling nature, and political technique, bent on producing the technological future. These twins feed off and condition one another. There are skirmishes about which form of governance might produce the best future and about the best ways to manufacture that future, but nonetheless, the overall ontotheological/metaphysical stance is the same.

There is yet another alternative, and this is one that is very uncomfortable for us all. It is a stumbling block to liberal Protestants, and folly to us philosophers. It requires humility, not magnanimity or will to power. It is the Eucharistic feast, the liturgical participation of creature and creator, the immanent and transcendent (not transcendental), where the divine transcendent Being breaks into the immanent realm of causes and effects and creates anew. The Eucharistic feast is a practice toward openness. The universal and the particular become one. It is where Spirit and Nature are married, where matter can become truly what it is. There, the signifier is one with the signified—and where the signified-signifier beckons to the sign monger, the interpreter of signs, to come unto him. It is where the self is called out of his self-constituting stupor and to a place where it is constituted by the divine Other. It is where individual bodies become not the body politic but the communal body of the incarnate One. It is where those of us who lord it over the least of these realize that we cannot transform ourselves but that we must be transformed by the Other. It is where humility—not magnanimity or even prudence—is the highest of the virtues. I cannot give a truth-proposition or a philosophical argument that convinces, once and for all, in some technoscientific and political enframing where wisdom can be found; I can only beckon you with the words of St. John the Divine, "Come and see."

NOTES

Portions of the section "Power Ontology, Power Biology, Power Neuroscience" appear in different form in Jeffrey P. Bishop, "Transhumanism, Metaphysics, and the Post-human God," *Journal of Medicine and Philosophy* 34.6 (2010): 700–720.

1. Catherine Pickstock, *After Writing: On the Liturgical Consummation of Philosophy* (Oxford: Blackwell, 1998), 58.

2. Most notably, Hibbs points to Matthew Jones, *The Good Life in the Scientific Revolution: Descartes, Pascal, Leibniz, and the Cultivation of Virtue* (Chicago: University of Chicago Press, 2006); David Lachterman, *The Ethics of Geometry: A Genealogy of Modernity* (New York: Routledge, 1989); and Amos Funkenstein, *Theology and the Scientific Imagination from the Middle Ages to the Seventeenth Century* (Princeton, NJ: Princeton University Press, 1986).

3. Thomas Hobbes, *Leviathan*, ed. Richard Tuck (New York: Cambridge University Press, 1991), 89.

4. John Locke, *Essay concerning Human Understanding*, ed. Kenneth Winkler (Indianapolis: Hackett Publishing, 1996), 95.

5. John Locke, *Second Treatise*, no. 123, in *Two Treatises of Government*, ed. Peter Laslett (New York: Cambridge University Press, 1988), 350.

6. Ibid., no. 87, 323.

7. Francis Bacon, *The New Organon*, ed. Lisa Jardine and Michael Silverthorne (New York: Cambridge University Press, 2000). For an excellent review of medicine as a Baconian project, see Gerald P. McKenny, *To Relieve the Human Condition: Bioethics, Technology, and the Body* (Albany: SUNY Press, 1997).

8. Simon Oliver, *Philosophy, God, and Motion* (Oxford: Routledge, 2005).

9. Ibid., 49.

10. Ibid., 50.

11. Ibid., 51.

12. Ibid., 51–52.

13. Ibid., 154.

14. Ibid., 168–69.

15. Bacon, *The New Organon*, 12–13.

16. Ibid., 13.

17. Ibid., 16.

18. Ibid., 17.

19. Ibid., 21.

20. Claude Bernard, the nineteenth-century physiologist and proponent of experimental science, states that the scientist must be single-minded, also ignoring men's disgust. Bernard states about vivisection: "A physiologist is not a man of fashion, he is a man of science, absorbed by the scientific idea which he pursues: he no longer hears the cry of animals, he no longer sees the blood that flows, he sees only his idea and perceives only organisms concealing problems which he intends to solve." Claude Bernard, *An Introduction to the Study of Experimental Medicine*, trans. Henry Copley Greene (New York: Dover Publications, 1957), 103. For a fuller treatment of Bernard on physiology, see Jeffrey P. Bishop, *The Anticipatory Corpse: Medicine, Power, and the Care of the Dying* (Notre Dame, IN: University of Notre Dame Press, 2011), ch. 2.

21. Bacon, *The New Organon*, II.2, p. 102. Citations to this work cite book number, aphorism number, and page.

22. Ibid., II.3, p. 103.

23. Ibid., II.6, 7, pp. 106–8.

24. Ibid., II.9, p. 109.

25. For a more thorough treatment of Claude Bernard and the rise of efficient cau-

sation in physiology and medical practice, see Bishop, *The Anticipatory Corpse*, especially ch. 2.

26. For a history of the shifting understanding of metaphysics as it relates to modern physical science, see E. A. Burtt, *The Metaphysical Foundations of Modern Physical Science* (1932; Amherst, NY: Humanity Books, 1999).

27. Bacon, *The New Organon*, I.73, II.52, pp. 20, 221.

28. Ibid.

29. I draw the terms "power ontology" and "power biology" from John Richardson, *Nietzsche's System* (New York: Oxford University Press, 1996) and *Nietzsche's New Darwinism* (New York: Oxford University Press, 2004).

30. Iain Thomson, *Heidegger on Ontotheology: Technology and the Politics of Education* (New York: Cambridge University Press, 2005), 8.

31. Ibid., 12.

32. Ibid., 14.

33. Martin Heidegger, trans. and ed. Joan Stambaugh, *Identity and Difference* (New York: Harper and Row, 1969), 70, 69.

34. Ibid., 14–15.

35. Ibid., 15. Here Thomson is providing his own interpretation of *Identität und Differenz*. Thomson translates the word *Seienden* as "entities," where Stambaugh translates it as "beings."

36. Heidegger cited in ibid., 15–16.

37. Ibid., 16.

38. Ibid., 22.

39. Much of the latter Heidegger is an attempt to avoid Nietzschean metaphysical nihilism; Heidegger's success in so doing is not the subject of this essay, however. Instead, we shall focus on Heidegger's diagnosis.

40. Thus, according to Nietzsche, genealogy is needed to dig out the non-conscious creative force from the historically constituted *telei* of conscious power.

41. Thomson, *Heidegger on Ontotheology*, 22. Thomson has here synthesized the thinking from several of Heidegger's later works.

42. Ibid.

43. Ibid.

44. John Harris, *Enhancing Evolution: The Ethical Case for Making Better People* (Princeton, NJ: Princeton University Press, 2007), 3.

45. Ibid., 3–4.

46. Ibid., 8–58.

47. Bacon, *The New Organon*, I.73, II.52, pp. 60, 221.

48. Ibid., II.2, p. 102; ibid., I.73, II.52, pp. 60, 221.

49. Martin Heidegger, trans. William Lovitt, "The Question concerning Technology" in *The Question concerning Technology and Other Essays* (New York: Harper Torchbooks, 1977), 3–35.

50. Ibid., 21.

51. Pickstock, *After Writing*, 63.

52. Thomson, *Heidegger on Ontotheology*, 22.

53. Harris, *Enhancing Evolution*, 188–91.

54. Harris, he is quick to note, is not arguing so much that we are at the point where such an obligation exists but, rather, that in principle one could justify it. While Harris is

by no means calling for a kind of conscription, others such as Rosamond Rhodes have been more bold in calling for participation in research as part of the common good bequeathed to us by politically controlled institutions like the National Institutes of Health (NIH). Rhodes makes a similar argument, but one grounded in concern for vulnerable populations. She claims that vulnerable populations are in need of research but that the entire research apparatus in its desire to protect vulnerable populations has resulted in harm to those very same populations. Rosamond Rhodes, "Rethinking Research Ethics," *American Journal of Bioethics* 5.1 (2005): 7–28.

55. Harris, *Enhancing Evolution*, 194.

56. Ibid., 191–200.

57. Nick Bostrom, "In Defense of Posthuman Dignity," *Bioethics* 19.3 (2005): 206.

58. As Alasdair MacIntyre has pointed out, virtue understood as power is quite different from virtue thought of as excellent habits. See his *After Virtue*, 2nd ed. (Notre Dame, IN: University of Notre Dame Press, 1981).

59. See Avshalom Caspi, "Role of Genotype in the Cycle of Violence in Maltreated Children," *Science* 297.5582 (2010): 851–54. See especially the elegant study of Naomi Sadeh et al., "Serotonin Transporter Gene Associations with Psychopathic Traits in Youth Vary as a Function of Socioeconomic Resources," *Journal of Abnormal Psychology* 119.3 (2010): 604–9.

60. Thomas W. Meeks and Dilip V. Jeste, "Neurobiology of Wisdom: A Literature Overview," *Archives of General Psychology* 66.4 (2009): 355–65.

61. Ibid., 357.

62. See Thomas Douglas, "Moral Enhancement," *Journal of Applied Philosophy* 25.3 (2008): 230–44; Mark Walker, "Enhancing Genetic Virtue: A Project for Twenty-First Century Humanity?" *Politics and the Life Sciences* 28.2 (2009): 27–47.

63. Meeks and Jeste, "Neurobiology of Wisdom," 358.

64. Alfred Lord Tennyson, canto 56, In Memoriam A.H.H. (1850).

10

THE MUTUAL SACRIFICE OF SCIENCE AND VIRTUE

Ralph Hancock

JEFFREY P. BISHOP INVITES US TO SEE, with Heidegger's help, that modern knowing or technological science is by no means a neutral openness to reality, to the way things are, or to the being of beings. This science, rather, is a "stance," a particular way of revealing or disclosing things. Leo Strauss would prefer to say that modern science is a "project," so as not to say a "fate." To recognize science as such a determinate stance entails practical implications for the meaning of our freedom: to imagine that we can choose freely as modern "individuals" without questioning this project or confronting this fate is a desperate wish indeed.

René Descartes has, inevitably, figured prominently in our discussions of modern science as a project. Allan Bloom was no doubt knowingly exaggerating when he wrote that all the French (unlike us less literate Americans) grow up as either Cartesians or Pascalians, but in another sense he might not have claimed enough: It seems to me that all of us moderns, at least as moderns, are left to choose between Descartes and Pascal or perhaps, rather, to oscillate between these influences or these understandings of the world and of our humanity. We are everything—all powerful—and yet nothing, nothing but matter in motion. Or, we are nothing, a worm, a speck of dust, a reed, but then we are everything or, with our God, the most important thing—a thinking reed, self-conscious and longing for another world. On the one hand, we accept the authority of science and therefore regard the world as so much material for our free transformation and consumption; on the other hand, we know that we are not simply of this world and that our freedom means something more than scientific mastery. The mysterious transcendence of this freedom is nowhere more touchingly evoked than by the very Pascalian Saint-Exupéry's *Little Prince*, so unimpressed by the serious, calculated projects of grown-ups, who learns finally to welcome the death-bearing serpent in the hope of reunion with the ordinary rose on his little star, an ordinary rose and star he has learned to embrace as unique in the universe. This oscillation between the impersonality and the personality of what is ultimate is not so evident in classical (pre-Christian) thought, but perhaps it is there, discretely contained within a narrower but very intense vibration.

Examining the relation between Science and Virtue, we are confronted with a bottomless paradox or circularity, which takes forms both ancient and modern. Socrates sacrificed a science of the whole for a virtuous conversation on virtue. But in another sense (at least, if Leo Strauss is right), he sacrificed virtue for a zetetic science of virtue. The classical loop is a tight one, because the meanings of "virtue" and "science" shade into one another: Each remains tied to the ordering of the soul and the cosmos on the model of the aristocratic city. The hierarchic rule of reason holds science and human meaning together.

The modern loop between science and virtue is somehow infinite and infinitesimal. It is as clear in Descartes as anywhere. The modern sacrifice of science to virtue could, perhaps, be set thus: The prideful ancient pretension to an elevating, soulful science must be sacrificed to the new, effective virtue; the systematic production of material benefits for all mankind, for the relief of the human condition. The modern sacrifice of virtue to science could, perhaps, be set thus: The deep, latent, purely formal/mathematical causes can only be accessed by suppressing absolutely the natural human interest in final causes, by renouncing all "anthropomorphism" (Heidegger); the question of the good (Hibbs' Descartes) can only be resolved by not allowing it to arise.

Harvey Mansfield has (in the classroom, as I recall) described Machiavelli's modern strategy thus: "We can afford anything, but we cannot afford to be moral." To receive the apparent benefit of joining together appearance and result (*Prince*, ch. 18), we have to renounce all hope that Science and Virtue both derive from Truth—that is, from a Truth above human power. This infinite negation or mutual sacrifice lies behind the fundamental paradox of modernity that has emerged in our discussions in various guises:

Bacon: To master nature we must conform to her.

Descartes: Nature sought as a ground of certitude and security reveals itself to be subject to man's will, yielding both angelism (radical dualism) and materialism. Descartes' project is somehow at once Promethean and Stoic.

Hobbes and Locke: To free men from powers of darkness requires defining freedom as material necessity.

Nietzsche: The infinite distance between pure freedom and pure necessity appears in the bond between will to power and Eternal Return. The mastery of nature and fortune thus has always come at the cost, for those who know the cost, of the most absolute resignation.

Heidegger: The dark star of our age whose ambiguous illumination we cannot escape, the author at once closest and furthest from any saving truth: technology is at once the greatest danger and the saving power. Heidegger understands the exhaustion of the science of virtue and of the virtue of science better than any man can who is not finally able to sacrifice the will to power—that "power-joy" of resolution (*Being and Time*, par. 62), that openness to the most absolute closure. Only a god can save us—the post-Christian indefinite article means that Heidegger could never quite renounce the compulsion to see himself as that god.

Heidegger's resolution, like Nietzsche's publicizing of the inhuman cost of the modern will to power, is already more than foreshadowed in Descartes' presentation of the modern project. The central practical maxim Descartes announces in *Discourse on the Method*, part 3, is as radical as can be: Lost in a forest, we must choose or will a direction and stick with it; sheer resolution is our only defense against repentance and remorse. (It is striking that two other founders of modernity, Montaigne and Luther, felt compelled similarly to recur to radical strategies to quiet the claims of repentance.)

Are we, today, not still in Descartes' forest, having pressed "forward" more or less straight ahead for some centuries, repressing any movement of remorse or repentance? We cannot deny Heidegger's sense that it is getting darker, that there is less and less livable space between our mastery and our resignation. Whether to our glory or our condemnation, the great mystery is that the extortion of nature, the reduction of being to a disposable standing reserve, somehow works both scientifically and, so far, politically. Nature submits itself to our projects, and so do people, or enough people that any dissenters have no perch upon which to stand (again, *Prince*, 18). It is as if nature were made to respond to human extortion, or to induce us ever further into the depths of Descartes' forest.

The evocation of such a darkness reminds me of another of Saint-Exupéry's stories, in *Vol de nuit* (*Night Flight*). A technological hero, Fabien, is a postal pilot serving Patagonia who gets lost in the darkness of storm clouds on his way to a station in Argentina. Running out of fuel, realizing that he has lost his way, struggling to feel his frozen hands and to command them to make a last effort to guide him and his companion to safety, he feels his will letting go.

> And at this moment there shines on his head, from a break in the storm, like a deadly bait . . . a few stars.
>
> He knew well enough that this was a trap: you see three stars in a hole, you climb towards them, and then you can no longer descend, you stay there stuck to the stars.
>
> But his thirst for light was such that he climbed. . . .
>
> . . . towards fields of light . . .
>
> He ascended little by little, in a spiral, in the well that had opened up and that closed again above him. And, as he ascended, the clouds [became] more and more pure and white. Fabien broke through.
>
> His surprise was extreme: the light dazzled him. For a few seconds he had to close his eyes. He never would have thought that, at night, one could be blinded by the stars. . . .
>
> Fabien thought he had reached some strange limbo, because everything was becoming luminous, his hands, his clothes, his wings. For the light was not coming down from the stars, but emanated from these white provisions beneath and around him.
>
> . . . "I am completely mad to smile," Fabien thought. "We are lost."
>
> And yet a thousand obscure arms had released him. One had unlocked his bonds, like those of a prisoner whom one allows to walk alone, just once, among the flowers.

"Too beautiful," Fabien thought. He was wandering among stars piled up with the density of a treasure, in a world in which no one else, absolutely no one but he and his companion, were alive. It was like those thieves in fabled cities who find themselves enclosed in a hall of treasures they cannot leave. Among shining jewels they wander, infinitely rich, but condemned.[1]

What can we do when we are lost in the forest? Press on, like good forward-looking bipeds, renewing our confidence as we progressively overcome obstacles in our path, deferring our longing for some horizon? Or find a clearing in which we can look up at the stars and, perhaps, then acknowledge the prompting to bow, and thus to see personality in infinity, a unique rose in a unique star? From such a posture we might consider that the very treasures we have been extorting from nature and that seem to dissolve in our grasping hands can only be truly received as a gift.

The modern science of virtue has always been right, but in a way it could not receive through mastery. We must be willing to sacrifice science to virtue—and virtue to science—but not because we renounce both of them in view of their forced synthesis, a synthesis that is always receding, that we are always deferring in the name of our compulsively honored Progress. We must be willing rather to sacrifice each to the other out of love of both, to love wisdom so much that it rules us like a virtue and to love virtue enough to refuse its separation from wisdom, and thus to discover love at the heart of both wisdom and virtue. This—if I may paraphrase the great John Rawls in a rare lapse into eloquence[2]—this would be true purity of heart, if we could attain it.

NOTES

1. Antoine de Saint-Exupéry, *Vol de nuit* (Paris: Gallimard, 1931). My translation.
2. The very end of *A Theory of Justice.*

11

THE SCIENTIFIC LIFE AS A MORAL LIFE?

VIRTUE AND THE CARTESIAN SCIENTIST

Tobin L. Craig

IN JANUARY 1939 LEO SZILARD, a chemist turned physicist who hap-
pened also to be a Hungarian Jew, wrote to his friend Lewis Strauss, a
former physicist turned wealthy businessman and philanthropist, about
the recent publication in the premiere German-language science journal
Naturwissenschaften of Otto Hahn's and Fritz Strassmann's discovery of
fission. Quoting Szilard:

> Apart from the purely scientific interest there may be another aspect of
> this discovery which so far *does not seem to have caught the attention of
> those to whom I spoke* [physicists at Princeton]. First of all it is obvious
> that the energy released in this new reaction must be very much higher
> than in all previously known cases. It may be 200 million electron volts
> instead of the usual 3–10 million volts. This in itself might make it pos-
> sible to produce power by means of nuclear energy, but I do not think
> that this possibility is very exciting, for if the energy output is only two
> or three times the energy input, the cost of the investment would prob-
> ably be too high to make the process worthwhile. . . .

I see, however, in connection with this new discovery potential possibilities in another direction. *These might lead to a large-scale production of energy and radioactive elements, unfortunately perhaps to atomic bombs.* This new discovery revives all the hopes and fears I had in 1934 and 1935, and which I have as good as abandoned in the course of the last two years.[1]

Later, in August 1939, Szilard drafted a letter to President Roosevelt, which he arranged to have passed on to Einstein to sign and then entrusted to Alexander Sachs to deliver, evidently concerned that a letter from someone less prominent and delivered by someone outside of Roosevelt's inner circle might not be read with sufficient attention.

Sir:

Some recent work by E. Fermi and L. Szilard, which has been communicated to me in a manuscript, leads me to expect that the element uranium may be turned into a new and important source of energy in the immediate future. Certain aspects of the situation which has arisen seem to call for watchfulness and, if necessary, quick action on the part of the Administration. I believe therefore that it is my duty to bring to your attention the following facts and recommendations.

In the course of the last four months it has been made probable—through the work of Joliot in France as well as Fermi and Szilard in America—that it may become possible to set up a nuclear chain reaction in a large mass of uranium, by which vast amounts of power and large quantities of new radium-like elements would be generated. Now it appears almost certain that this could be achieved in the immediate future.

This new phenomenon would also lead to the construction of bombs, and it is conceivable—though much less certain—that extremely powerful bombs of a new type, may thus be constructed. A single bomb of this type, carried by boat and exploded in a port, might very well destroy the whole port together with some of the surrounding territory. However, such bombs might very well prove to be too heavy for transportation by air.

The United States has only very poor areas of uranium in moderate quantities. There is some good ore in Canada and the former Czechoslovakia, while the most important source of uranium is the Belgian Congo.

In view of this situation you may think it desirable to have some permanent contact maintained between the Administration and the group of physicists working on chain reactions in America. One possible way of achieving this might be for you to entrust with this task a person who has your confidence and who could perhaps serve in an unofficial capacity. His task might comprise the following:

a) to approach Government Departments, keep them informed of the further development, and put forward recommendations for Government action, giving particular attention to the problem of securing a supply of uranium ore for the United States.

b) to speed up the experimental work, which is at present being carried on within the limits of the budgets of University laboratories, by providing funds, if such funds be required, through his contacts with private persons who are willing to make contributions for this cause, and perhaps also by obtaining the co-operation of industrial laboratories which have the necessary equipment.

I understand that Germany has actually stopped the sale of uranium from the Czechoslovakian mines which she has taken over. That she should have taken such hasty action might perhaps be understood on the ground that the son of the German Under-Secretary of State, von Weiznacker, is attached to the Kaiser-Wilhelm Institute in Berlin where some of the American work on uranium is now being repeated.

Yours very truly,

Albert Einstein[2]

It would seem that Szilard was virtually alone in recognizing what was now possible—and so, given the political situation, all but inevitable—and thus the urgency with which action needed to be taken.[3] So far as I am aware, Roosevelt received no letters from other physicists; none of those Princeton physicists, whom Szilard tells us were all abuzz about Hahn's findings, thought that perhaps the government ought to be informed. The one other exception is Fermi, who approached the Navy in spring 1939. Virtually nothing came of it.[4] In retrospect, it seems but a stroke of good fortune that the possibility of a nuclear chain reaction had been a pet idea of Szilard's at least since the time he read of a talk by Ernest Rutherford dismissing it, and probably since he read H. G. Wells' speculations about atomic weapons. Szilard refrained from publishing on the subject, recognizing the irresponsibility of doing so, a fortiori in a situation when the leading scientific nation in the world was in the grips of an anti-Semitic tyrant bent on war.[5] He even took the further step of ensuring his English patent on the nuclear chain reaction was taken out of the public domain and placed safely in the hands of the British Admiralty. Moreover, it was probably only Szilard's close relationship with Einstein that made it possible for Einstein to sign Szilard's letter in his own name, an act Einstein would later profess to regret but which doubtless impressed Roosevelt, who is recorded as replying to Sachs' presentation of the letter:

> "Alex," said Roosevelt, "what you are after is to see that the Nazis don't blow us up."
> "Precisely," Sachs said.
> Roosevelt called in his aide, General Edwin ("Pa") M. Watson: "Pa! This requires action!"[6]

By the end of the month, Roosevelt approved the creation of the Uranium Committee, the embryo of the Manhattan Project. We now know that, in Germany, similar letters were sent to Hitler and that Hitler, too, acted swiftly to constitute his own Uranium club. Szilard's fears were well-founded, and his caution amply justified.

The story is perhaps familiar, but its importance—both historical and, more importantly, for the purposes of clarifying our relationship to the enterprise we call 'science,' and to the peculiar type we know as the professional scientist—merit retelling it here complete with dramatic emphasis. Reviewing this episode and the events it set in motion leading up to the successful creation of an atomic bomb, one can scarcely help but shudder at the realization of how utterly dependent the fate of the Allied cause was—and so, if not Western civilization itself, then at least freedom in Europe—on the judgments, choices, actions (and thus virtues) of a mere handful of individuals. To be sure, this is to some extent always true, in times of crisis and war especially, but we are somewhat more accustomed to, and so perhaps comfortable with, acknowledging that we are "stuck with virtue" in our warriors and our statesmen. Direct election of the president (that is, of the commander in chief of the armed forces) is an acknowledgment of this fact; whereas, needless to say, we do not elect our nuclear physicists. Indeed, we 'the people' have no idea what they are doing, let alone whether they are doing it ably; we are essentially incapable of judging the matter.

We thus find ourselves in a position of utter dependence on our scientists' virtues, intellectual and moral, common and rare.

Now, perhaps it might be objected that I have selected an extreme, even a singular example.[7] Permit me, then, to make the essential point again from an altogether different angle, that of our everyday experience. It almost goes without saying that, for those of us in parts of the world we tellingly describe as 'developed,' the natural whole has been basically rendered tame—not, I hasten to add, that we are invulnerable to natural catastrophe but that the wildness of what was once called the wilderness is gone. In referring to nature, or even better, 'the environment' (by which we can only mean *our* environment), we accept in advance that there is nothing really to be afraid of out there; nothing can appear to us that cannot be explained in the terms of our science of nature or, if not explained, then received by us as an as-yet-unexplained-but-soon-to-be-explained phenomenon, a future research project. Even that strangest of strange experiences, a sickness in one's own body, is quickly made normal by being diagnosed; it loses its uncanniness by becoming identified as of a type familiar to those who make it their business to be familiar with illnesses. What makes this so curious is that we ourselves, as individuals, don't know in even a loose sense the 'science' behind the explanation or the diagnosis. We are comforted (not completely, I concede) by knowing that someone somewhere is at work studying the phenomenon and seeking to explain it—that is, to identify its proximate causes—and that this person is a scientist, a methodical truth seeker, part of a vast army of truth seekers working together to discover the truth about the whole. He or she knows, so I don't have to know. We say, 'we know' as if such a formulation is meaningful. In effect, we have delegated the task of understanding to someone else. We accept their authority as knowers and truth tellers about our world. But we don't know these people, and most of us aren't even in a position to read and understand them when they tell the truth about our world—that is, in the publication of their findings. We take on trust that they are doing good work, and that they haven't encountered anything major that they can't explain and that might give us pause about delegating to them this important task. And even the manifest conflict of interest here—Would they actually tell us if they found something that suggested the scientific project was fundamentally misguided? Could they ever even encounter such a counter instance?—doesn't seriously trouble us, as we go about our day-to-day business. Thus, in both our inmost lives (our personal experience of the world, even when we are altogether alone) and at our most political (in a life-or-death struggle in defense of our way of life), we democratic, freedom-loving individuals find ourselves all but utterly dependent on this strange figure we call 'the scientist.'

Who is this 'scientist'? How does he understand his activity? How did we come to find ourselves in such a situation of dependence on, let's say it, such a curious sort? What is the basis of our confidence in him? What makes such a situation intelligible and tolerable? To the extent that we late-moderns or post-moderns are moved to understand our situation and see it for what it is (that is, to see its distinctiveness and peculiarity), we cannot but ask these questions.

Fortunately, we are not alone. These are the questions, or more accurately, these are the concerns that inform Steven Shapin's recent book, *The Scientific Life: A Moral History of a Late Modern Vocation*. The story he tells and documents is a remarkable one, and it deserves the attention of all those seriously interested in understanding the peculiar features of our contemporary world. Shapin has set himself the task of showing us the scientist today, emphasizing the inescapably personal element in the scientist's authority—the inevitable impact of the individual scientist's virtues.[8]

He begins, however, by calling attention to the strangeness of such an undertaking, given the currently prevailing understanding of the scientist as a professional (who, as such, is in principle interchangeable) and of Science, as paradigmatically impersonal. "[Quoting physicist Claude Bernard] 'Art is I, Science is We,' and so the impersonality of the means of scientific production and the absence of a personal mark on the product were reliable and visible signs of its authenticity. No one man's opinion represents scientific truth."[9] This is the achievement of the redefinition of science as method and the corollary introduction of division of labor into science. For we believe that it is adherence to the scientific method—or adherence to the method supplemented by institutionalized implications of method (i.e., peer review, professional organization, open publication not only of findings but of experimental protocols, and so on)—that vouchsafes the accuracy, and therefore makes authoritative, the claims of our scientists.

As Shapin further observes, this conception of science as radically impersonal and of the individual scientist as in principle interchangeable is reinforced by the advent of the so-called naturalistic fallacy or the "is/ought" distinction. The findings of the scientist (his work) are supposed to have no moral bearing whatsoever. Precisely in declaring the utter amorality of science and thus of a life of science, the is/ought distinction becomes itself a particularly stern morality, which actually underwrites public confidence. We trust our scientists precisely because they stick to 'the facts.' They live lives oriented entirely to 'the facts.' Through extraordinary discipline and self-mastery, they have given up on ordinary human concerns, and so they see clearly. As Shapin observes, in reference to Einstein, "the most publically moralistic of modern scientists—and the one whose moral stature was most publically recognized—insisted upon the natural scientist's *lack* of moral authority."[10]

The full democratic implications of this demoralization and depersonalization of the scientific life only became clear in the world's foremost democracy: the United States. Shapin's analysis relies heavily on Robert Merton's pathbreaking work in the sociology of science. Merton's institutional approach to science downplayed to the point of irrelevancy the personal passions and qualities of the individual scientist. The success of science could be attributed entirely to institutional, a-personal factors, and there was no evidence, Merton held, that special motives or peculiar virtues mattered in the least. It is difficult with the tools of a sociologist to find or to show a necessary connection between quality of soul or motive and outcome. But Karl Popper himself famously held that even 'objectivity' is "not the product of the individual scientist's impartiality, but a product of the social or public character of scientific method."[11]

Despite his own adherence to sociological value neutrality, which precludes making explicit any evaluative conclusions, Shapin must wish his reader to see that our situation is thus doubly strange: at the very moment that the political importance of science and thus our dependence on the excellence of our scientists is manifest, the prevailing conception of the scientist is that of "moral equivalence," that is, that there are no special virtues required of a good scientist. Having shown this transformation in the public's understanding of the scientist—from 'scientist as hero' to 'scientist as professional' (and thus in the basis of the scientist's public authority), Shapin proceeds to show that, in fact, the scientific life still requires particular personal virtues and encourages certain virtues. His analysis is thus a welcome correction to a misconception that has actually become part of the American scientist's self-understanding, and not merely his public presentation. The personal qualities, the virtues, of particular scientists still matter, as they always have. And like any institutionalized activity, certain qualities or virtues are still favored and cultivated over others. But what are these virtues?

On Shapin's telling, by and large, they are thoroughly unexceptional bourgeois virtues of sociality and entrepreneurial acumen, perhaps enlivened with a dash of creativity and countercultural independence. The heroes of late twentieth-century techno-science are James Watson, Richard Feynman, Craig Ventner, and Kary Mullins. There are still grumpy, old-fashioned academic scientists who make a boast of not being industry shills and self-indulgent hedonists, but few of them seem happy as scientists, in part because the centrality of grant-seeking and patent-securing to their professional lives means they do very little actual science. The scientist today, whether in academia or in a research start-up, is in the first place an entrepreneur, seeking funding, and in the second place, a manager, organizing a lab or business venture. Only then, if at all, is he a scientist in the precise sense.

Shapin cannot comment on such a situation. But we can, and given our profound dependence on the scientist, we must. What are we to think of this situation? In light of what standard ought we to evaluate it? If we citizens of the scientific civilization have somehow lost our capacity to judge the reliable from the unreliable, the well-formed from the ill-made scientist, perhaps one of the original inventors of the type 'scientist' will help us remember what we ought to be looking for. This thought leads us back to the writings of René Descartes, with a view to recovering what he had in mind for those who would actually carry out his grand project for a new practical natural philosophy. What we find, I suggest, is that certain puzzling features of our current situation, even certain of our confusions, were anticipated by Descartes. Even more surprising, even paradoxical, is that they are crucial to his original vision.

That Descartes had in mind a grand—even civilizational—project, built around a new science of nature is manifest from even a cursory reading of part 6 of his *Discourse on the Method of Conducting One's Reason Well and Seeking the Truth in the Sciences* (hereafter *Discourse*).[12] There, in addition to positing a new technological-humanitarian aim for natural philosophy, we see Descartes arranging the partners whose marriage will give birth to this new scientific civilization—a needy public and their leaders, and a new kind of natural philosopher, whom we have since come to call 'the scientist.'

The problem in question comes to sight in part 6 of the *Discourse* as the problem of ensuring the successful execution of Descartes' grand project for a practical philosophy. On the one hand, ensuring the success of this project would seem to demand that Descartes himself do all the work, see to all the experiments, and connect all the dots. On the other hand, he is going to die. So he needs help. But help in anything important is unreliable, a fortiori in this novel project. He could pay people (Descartes seems to believe that pecuniary interest is sufficiently reliable), but Descartes is not himself wealthy. In any case, even the resources of a king may not suffice. Volunteers might offer help out of curiosity or desire to learn, but such high-minded souls, "promise more than they do, and only make beautiful promises that never amount to anything, they would infallibly want to be paid by the explanation of certain difficulties, or at least by useless compliments and conversations," which could only be a waste of time.[13] As for soliciting submissions from others, most inquirers are unwilling to communicate and share their findings openly because they are jealous of their work. And in any case, Descartes would be left with the task of sifting out the good from the bad, which would entail repeating the work himself.

After spelling out these difficulties, Descartes tells us that he nevertheless judged he had no choice but to try and get some help, and so he published the *Discourse*. Stripped bare, this is essentially his argument for publication. But how is the enumeration of these difficulties an argument *for* publication? From part 6 we learn that the *Discourse* is published as a call for help in a grand project to make man master and conqueror of nature, and this, so that we might improve our this-worldly condition. We are led to conclude that it is thus a work intended to entice a certain type or types to enlist and volunteer their services for such a project. However, because of the deficiencies of the likely candidates, it must simultaneously also be intended to educate such types, to reshape them into *useful* volunteers. In this sense, the *Discourse* is a work intended to create a new type, the type we know today as the scientist. And recalling that Descartes seemed to suggest that the only really reliable helpers are those who are actuated at least in part, if not primarily, by their pecuniary interest, it is also a call for the establishment of institutions that will provide such material support.

That Descartes, as architect of the project, is not himself an example of this new type should be clear from this fact alone. But if not, it becomes unmistakably clear upon re-reading the *Discourse* with our question in mind. Part 2—the heart of which is his simplified presentation of his method, and one could say, judging from the title, that this is the showpiece of the work as a whole—is introduced with yet another statement

of the problem of a project: "One of the first [thoughts] that I was drawn
to consider was that often there is less perfection in works composed of
several pieces and made by the hand of diverse masters than in those in
which one alone has worked."[14] Thus, buildings designed by a single architect are more beautiful whereas cities that gradually grew great are usually
poorly arranged. This is so, Descartes emphasizes, even when there are
public officials whose task is to ensure unity of style and purpose. Thus, the
superiority of the work of a single legislator to the gradual and haphazard
accumulation of experience and laws.

Having noted this, however, Descartes professes a conservative approach, apparently abjuring any and all projects for comprehensive reform.
We don't tear down whole towns simply to rebuild them according to a
more beautiful plan, but, he observes with studied casualness, sometimes
individual homeowners do renovate, especially if they lose confidence in
the security of the foundations of their homes. This, he seems to say, was
his situation with respect to "all the opinions I had hitherto accepted as
credible."[15] Anyhow, reforming opinions is altogether different from reforming even the most insignificant public institution. Thus Descartes has
nothing to do with those turbulent types who are always calling for reform. His chosen mode of conduct, as related to us in this autobiography,
is his own, he repeatedly asserts, and he offers it to his readers without any
suggestion that it should be imitated. After all:

> The world is almost entirely composed of two kinds of minds for
> whom [the imitation of Descartes] is unsuitable: namely, those who,
> believing themselves more competent than they are, cannot help
> making precipitate judgments, and lack enough patience to conduct
> all their thoughts in an orderly way, so that once they had taken the
> liberty to doubt received opinions and to depart from the common
> path, they would never be able to keep to the road that would take
> them more directly, and would remain lost all their lives; and those
> who, having enough reason or modesty to judge that they are less
> capable of distinguishing the true from the false than some others by
> whom they can be instructed, must be content to follow the opinions
> of these others, rather than seek better ones themselves.[16]

But Descartes has already identified his work as a history or a fable.[17] He
further observes that fables and histories tend to encourage in their readers

exaggerated beliefs about what is possible and, in particular, an overestimation of their own abilities.[18] Moreover, his presentation of the case for doubt of the received opinions seems designed precisely to encourage in his reader a sense of unease about the solidity of the foundations of his house, so to speak.

There can therefore be no doubt but that Descartes wishes to encourage imitation of what he describes in this fabulous autobiography and that he has calculated its effect on these two defective—that is, non-Descartes—types of which the world is *almost* entirely composed. The first type requires moderation, restraint, patience, and direction. The second type needs a model to follow and some encouragement, which the fabulous character of the *Discourse* provides. The rules of method are, for this type, a kind of assurance. For the more problematic first sort, the rules of method are the crucial discipline; and the language of the rules suggests that they target in particular the defects of this type (the repetition of "precipitation" as a danger in the first rule, and the demand of "order" in the third).[19]

Here, then, are our would-be 'Cartesian scientists': a humble and modest sort, aware of his limitations, and so of his need of a model to follow; and a brash and disorganized speculator with exaggerated confidence in his abilities. Ideally, Descartes leads us to suspect both together, checking one another with their contrasting humors, each supplying the virtues that his fellow lacks. In any case, both types stand in need of method—indeed, both would flounder without method. Their virtue as scientists, then, is adherence to method. But this virtue must be primarily self-imposed; it must rule their conduct even in the seclusion of the laboratory. How else will Descartes be able to rely upon their contributions to the project? Adherence to method must become not merely automatic but their boast, their chief source of self-respect. How does this happen?

Upon concluding his presentation of the four rules of method, Descartes turns in part 3 to his "three or four" maxims of a "provisional morality." As Kennington points out, the table of contents tells us that the rules of morality are drawn from the method, but since this is not true in the obvious sense, it can only mean that the morality is somehow necessary for one who embraces the method.[20] The first rule demands that one conform to the laws of one's country and the religion in which one is reared, or to the most moderate opinions wherever one is, or to the most moderate opinions as they disclose themselves in the actions of one's neighbors, and even then only insofar as they leave one with the flexibility required for perfecting one's judgments. The second rule demands that one be resolute in action, even as one is doubtful in thought, and act as though the most probable is certain so as to free oneself from regret and wavering. The third maxim is to accommodate to the world rather than busy oneself attempting to remake the world or be tormented by longings that cannot be fulfilled. Fourth, one must always remember or remind oneself that the life of inquiry is the best life.

There is much to say about this "provisional morality," and much that is curious. But for our purposes the crucial point to notice is how it works to attach potential volunteers to Descartes' method. For it reestablishes all other claims on the would-be scientist's devotion on a new foundation, namely, as ministerial to his fundamental devotion to science-as-method. By adopting the provisional morality, the would-be scientist becomes a scientist *first of all*. Notice that in his thumbnail defense of the scientific life that is the fourth maxim of the provisional morality, the humanitarian aim of the science is nowhere to be seen. Here the scientist is the lone inquirer, the purest manifestation of the Cartesian cogito. (I say purest, not that he is in fact simply a thinking thing, though he may misunderstand himself as such.)

Let me summarize this discovery of the scientist in the *Discourse*. The scientist is someone attracted by the philanthropic project of mastering nature with a view to relieving man's estate. Behind this, however, there is a soul quickened by the prospect of doubting all received authorities and making its way on its own. Such souls are not as uncommon as one might think, as Tocqueville indicates by attributing this desire for radical independence to Americans generally—though, as Tocqueville also tells us, most of us aren't up to it.[21] But they can be made useful contributors to the project (that is to say, good scientists) only to the extent that they become radically devoted to method. All other claims on their allegiance must become subordinate to the attachment to method. Descartes' scientist must come to love method the way Montesquieu's monk loves his order, precisely because it deprives him of everything else.[22]

This, then, is how the scientist can be entrusted to police himself and so be made a reliable contributor to the larger project. Now, there are other external and institutional checks on the scientist—peer review, publication of findings and protocols with a view to repeatability, fear of disgrace and loss of employment—and these, doubtless, have an important effect. But, as the statistics on scientific fraud make clear, these are manifestly insufficient in and of themselves, and for a variety of familiar reasons. Moreover, if we return to the phenomenon of our own strange deference to the scientist, it seems to me that one important ground of it is the picture of the scientist as the fearless and uncompromising tester of hypotheses, he who puts adherence to method above all—even, it would seem, above his own interests. Furthermore such an image is crucial to the appeal of the scientific life to the young would-be scientist.[23]

No sooner do we see this than we recognize the problem of the scientist's attachment to a particular political community. The provisional morality, which (as we have seen) is key in remaking a citizen into a scientist, therefore also remakes the political responsibility of the scientist into a matter of the scientist's prudence and self-awareness. The scientist is attached to a particular political community and so politically responsible, because—and thus, only to the extent that—he sees his dependence and the dependence of science itself on that community, and thus appreciates the necessity of accommodating himself to that community, taking care that he not jeopardize his way of life by jeopardizing the community. This is not 'patriotism' in the ordinary sense of the word, though in most circumstances it might prove to be reliable. In my conclusion I will return to this problem, but for now let me leave it at noting that, according to Descartes' teaching, this is one price one has to pay for a methodical, organized, and productive science and the goods that only it can secure.

But now consider the problem of the scientist from the other side of the equation, so to speak; that is, from the vantage of us non-scientists. What is our role in Descartes' project? Here it is useful, I believe, to supplement our reading of the *Discourse* with a quick glance at the fragmentary and posthumous dialogue entitled "La recherche de la vérité par la lumière naturelle" or "The Search for Truth by Means of the Light of Nature" (hereafter *Recherche*).[24] According to its preface, this little dialogue will "determine the opinions which *un honête homme* [a good man/an honest man] should hold touching all the things that could occupy his thoughts, and which penetrate into the secrets of the most curious of the sciences."[25] Descartes repeatedly declares or boasts of the accessibility of the argument to "*chacun*" (everyone), that it is intended to be "equally useful to all men."[26] Here, then, we encounter a work for the ordinary decent man, which somehow provides the key to real progress in all the sciences. It makes possible liberation from corrupting and misleading education and prejudice and, in so doing, opens the road to the whole knowledge a man needs for the proper conduct of his life. And should he be so inclined, it prepares him for the study of whatever he wishes to know in the sciences. I wish to underscore, however, that in the *Recherche* the life of science is but one possibility. Unlike the *Discourse*, which clearly seems crafted to encourage the pursuit of science in its reader, the *Recherche* merely opens up the possibility of a life of science; it is not an advertisement for that life.

It is with this general audience in view, Descartes tells us, that he has opted for the dialogue form. The work presents the visit of Polyander ('many men,' thus 'everyman') and Epistemon ('knower') to the house of Eudoxus ('good opinion'), and the attempted demonstration by Eudoxus of his happy discovery of an argument that has brought him peace of mind and apparently complete mental satisfaction. Epistemon knows Eudoxus to be someone free of vanity, and who has hitherto consecrated his time to "journeying, and visiting learned men, and examining everything that has been discovered that is most difficult in each science."[27] Unlike Epistemon, who despite his learning remains vexed by an insatiable desire to learn more and more, however, Eudoxus is unperturbed by what he does not know (he tells us), because he has at his disposal a surefire test whereby, were he so inclined, he could learn whatever he wished about anything, and whereby he could test the claims to knowledge of any and all.

What follows is a presentation of Eudoxus leading Polyander through the first steps of the Cartesian skeptical argument, familiar from the *Meditations* and part 4 of the *Discourse*. The first is doubt of the senses, and thus of everything built upon the authority of the senses, which is to say the whole of the external world. The two then agree that they have reached bedrock on the impossibility of the doubter's doubting his own doubt and, therefore, his own existence. "You are, then, and you know that you are, and you know it because you doubt." To this Polyander agrees, but then when asked what he is, he commits the gaff of replying that he is "a man." A man? We can almost hear Eudoxus smacking his forehead: "You pay no attention to what I ask, and the reply that you make, simple as it may appear to you, will throw you into very difficult and perplexing questions."[28] Eudoxus leads Polyander to see his mistake or, rather, the danger into which it leads him, namely, of getting caught up in a web of metaphysical jargon, with each term more obscure than the previous. In other words, Polyander learns to avoid the language of kinds and essences not because they are not first for him but because they put him in a position subordinate to and dependent on Epistemon.

Now if we take the dialogic character of this work seriously, we are led to ask what Descartes intends it to reveal. Obviously, we are meant to be impressed with Eudoxus, and in particular to prefer him to Epistemon—though the names ought to caution us against concluding that Descartes simply shares this evaluation. But the contest between Eudoxus and Epistemon is for Polyander. We are to see the appeal of Eudoxus' argument to the likes of Polyander, and the ease and readiness with which Polyander takes to it.

One audience, then, for Descartes' famous skeptical argument is 'l'homme honête,' the ordinary decent man. What Descartes offers him is freedom from the presumed authority of the knowers. The drama of this little dialogue is its presentation of Polyander's discovery of this freedom. Eudoxus' method frees Polyander from the need to simply defer to Epistemon as he does at the beginning of the work: "[Polyander to Epistemon] I consider you so happy in having seen all these wonderful things in the Greek and Latin books, that it seems to me that if I had studied as much as you, I should be as different from what I now am as angels from you. And I cannot excuse the error of my parents [for sending me to court and camp] that regret for being ignorant will remain with me my whole life."[29] By the end of the fragment, however, simply by being led through the initial steps of Descartes' famous skeptical argument, Polyander is emboldened to demand that he be shown reasons and grounds and, therefore, to trust his own understanding. This becomes clear when Epistemon calls into question the self-evidence and fundamental character of the experience of doubt by way of challenging Eudoxus and Polyander's conclusion that nothing is indubitable except that 'I' am a doubting—that is, a thinking—thing. Polyander stands firm in the face of Epistemon's challenge and declares that experience of doubt is firm and indubitable.

We are thus shown Polyander discovering confidence in his own capacity to judge, through learning Eudoxus' skeptical argument, or Cartesian doubt. On this basis I think we can say that Descartes' project for the ordinary decent man/citizen is to teach him skepticism, that is, to doubt first, and to demand of those who claim to know that they adduce their reasons. We might call this the creation of the 'show-me' type.[30] Such, Descartes teaches, should be the citizens of the scientific society. Like Machiavelli, whose *Prince* encourages skepticism toward all rulers in anyone who reads it and thereby makes it all the harder for any tyrant to tyrannize, so Descartes, while clearly envisioning a new scientific elite, nonetheless provides one part of a check on this elite by encouraging a general skepticism and doubt of all claims to knowledge.

Returning to the *Discourse* (as we must, for the *Recherche* was never published, hence Descartes must have concluded that the *Discourse* sufficed to achieve this aim), we are prepared now to notice the ways in which this work also encourages skepticism and doubt in all its readers, emboldening even the most ordinary reader to have confidence in his or her own judgment. Must we not presume this to be part of the intention behind the charming argument for equality with which the work begins? And of Descartes' self-deprecation, whereby it was only the felicitous discovery of method that separates him from all predecessors and contemporaries, an accident of his peculiar biography? Notice, furthermore, that from this vantage point method looks like mere rule following, and because the rules of method are available to any and all, the scientist, the method-man par excellence, is nothing special and is not owed any special reverence. He is merely a curious type who has decided to pursue a particular interest to the exclusion of most others.

We can now summarize Descartes' vision for an institutionalized science as it concerns the puzzle or problem of our dependence on the scientist. On the one hand, Descartes wishes to generalize skepticism of any and all claims of knowledge and of any authority based on that knowledge. He wishes to embolden even the ordinary citizen to demand reasons and evidence from even the most exalted knowers. Crucial to such an effort is, first, the popularization of doubt and a habit of skepticism and, then, the equipping of the citizen with a simplified method, a ready-to-hand test. Here, at the beginning, we already glimpse something of what Shapin calls the "moral equivalence" argument: the view that the scientist is just like any other professional, in principle interchangeable, and that the specific and peculiar qualities of the individual scientist are irrelevant. From this vantage, that of the ordinary citizen, science is an instrument, and the scientist is a public servant (a very strange kind of public servant), who should be regarded as such—that is, with a bemused contempt moderated by a grudging gratitude. In Descartes' vision, public deference to the authority of the scientist is thus ultimately founded on public skepticism, that is, on the confidence of the ordinary person in his own judgment or on the creation of the 'show-me' type. Descartes says to us non-scientists that we must maintain our habit of skepticism, always demanding that scientists justify their claims to intellectual authority. This background pressure from the public serves as a crucial check on scientific hubris, while also keeping the scientist from lapsing into complacency and losing focus and rigor.

And this then points us to the other hand, for we have also seen that Descartes is an originator of the idea of the scientist as a new kind of hero: he who makes adherence to method his virtue and the foundation of his self-regard. Only thus can this new model knower be entrusted to undertake his work, contributing to the Cartesian project, with unwavering fidelity and rigor. Only thus can he be entrusted as our authority on the natural whole or, rather, the small part of it that is his focus. The Cartesian scientist is necessarily a high-minded soul, with a lofty self-understanding. We need and so should expect our scientists to mistake themselves for philosophers. Recognizing this helps us abide their haughtiness.

Both of these two contrasting images of the scientist are necessary for an institutionalized science; both could be said to be the by-product of science as method. For, on the one hand, method, like a recipe, equalizes and obviates virtue. On the other hand, method provides ready-to-hand criteria whereby to judge excellence and, thereby, to distinguish and rank. In thus coming to see more clearly certain of the paradoxes of science as method, however, we also come to see certain dangers or signs of danger in our current situation. Let me conclude by pointing out five:

1. Particularly on issues that, for various reasons, have generated significant public controversy, I think one can discern today a growing impatience among scientists with the 'show-me' type's doubts and demands, to the point where their impatience risks compromising their adherence to method. This manifests itself most frequently in a loud and often impotent call on the part of scientists to 'shut up and listen.' On other issues, we have seen attempts to orchestrate the public presentation of evidence in an attempt to avoid certain anticipated lines of question; we have seen highly questionable overselling of the promise of certain lines of research as a way to preempt debate; we have seen incredible, because utterly immoderate, claims about the 'truth-status' and explanatory power of certain cherished if publicly misunderstood and mistreated theories. On behalf of the scientists, it might be replied that the extraordinary specialization and mathematization of science has created a situation that makes impossible a step-by-step path from the non- or pre-scientific account to the scientific account, and that leading someone or everyone on such an ascent is not worth their time. But this was never Descartes' intention. He was not

a proponent of full scientific enlightenment. He did not demand that the scientist turn the 'show-me' type into a scientist, only that he welcome—perhaps even delight in—being challenged to adduce his proofs and show off his supreme dedication to method. To a skeptical public, such a posture will always be more commanding than that of the frustrated dogmatist.

2. The flip side of this last danger is a version of the Tocquevillian danger of soft despotism: a too quick deference to our experts on the part of *l'homme honête*. On a host of questions and issues, our vigilance as 'show-me' citizens seems in decline. We are or may be becoming too lazy or too comfortable to demand of our scientists that they adduce their reasons and evidence and so too quick to give up freedoms and treasures. Indeed, this may partly explain the surprise and disappointment of our scientists on those issues where their claims are met with hostility and skepticism.

3. Turning back to our scientists, and drawing upon Shapin's study, we also seem to be witnessing the erosion of the stern and high-minded self-understanding of the scientist by democratic and bourgeois easy-going-ness. This, in all likelihood, is a graver danger and much harder to address. The great value of Shapin's study is in showing us this transformation over the course of the twentieth century. Simplifying, we watch as first the scientist learns to cooperate, not in the broad sense implied by method, but in his own lab and in his own work, which spells the end of the lone inquirer. Then the scientist becomes managed or a manager, which spells the end of his radical independence to pursue his inquiry wherever it leads. Finally the scientist becomes an entrepreneur, a money-maker, and a hedonist. Descartes, recall, insisted on a stern stoicism as the proper outlook of the scientist. Thus, while we still see and welcome the occasional virtuoso scientist-inventor—the Ventners and the Mullinses—insofar as they become the model for the typical scientist in the lab, this signals his corruption. His pride has become his productivity in patents or his grant-getting acumen, and not his adherence to method.

4. As we have seen, Descartes' creation of the scientist requires his corruption as a citizen. Perhaps in many circumstances, even most, a scientist who loves science above all can be relied upon to look to the well-being of the community that makes his life possible. But what about a situation where the scientist can leave one community for another? What about the possibility of the scientist making bad political judgments? After all, there is little in the typical scientist's education or political circumstances to encourage the development of prudence or wakefulness about and concern

for the impact of his work on the broader political community. Mandatory ethics courses and institutional review boards can hardly be relied upon to stand in for the scientist's own judgment.

5. Finally, I wish to call attention to a danger stemming from a forgetting of the project-character of Descartes' argument. We might call this 'Enlightenment as forgetfulness.' At a certain point, institutionalized and technological science came to be thought to effect progress more or less automatically. Insert coin and let the good times roll, so to speak. The primacy and necessity of politics and thus of the political supervision of science—the character of science as instrument—got forgotten. Descartes' near silence on politics doubtless is in part to blame for this, but in coming to see our way clear of this illusion, political science now has to take more seriously than it has done the task of regulating and guiding this stupendously powerful instrument.

NOTES

1. *The American Atom: A Documentary History of Nuclear Policies from the Discovery of Fission to the Present*, 2nd ed., ed. Philip L. Cantelon et al. (Philadelphia: University of Pennsylvania Press, 1991), 8–9.

2. Ibid., 9–11.

3. On Szilard as the exception, see Lawrence Badash, *Scientists and the Development of Nuclear Weapons: From Fission to the Limited Test Ban Treaty, 1939–1963* (New Jersey: Humanities Press International, 1995), 21, 25, and Szilard's letter to Hirst in *The American Atom*, 7–8.

4. Badash, *Scientists*, 27.

5. Irène and Frédéric Joliot-Curie ignored a general agreement among scientists from the Allied nations and continued to publish until October 1939.

6. Quoted in William Lanouette, "Bumbling toward the bomb," *Bulletin of Atomic Scientists*, 45.7 (September 1989): 10. For a particularly insightful and provocative reflection on this case from a very different perspective, consider Michael Frayn's play *Copenhagen*.

7. As this chapter was being prepared for publication, a controversy erupted over the proposed publication of research findings on the possibility of an airborne variant of the extremely deadly H5N1 'bird flu' virus. See Denise Grady and William Broad, "Seeing Terror Risk, U.S. Asks Journals to Cut Flu Study Facts," *New York Times*, December 20, 2011; Denise Grady and Douglas G. McNeil, Jr., "Debate Persists on Deadly Flu Made Airborne," *New York Times*, December 26, 2011. Consider further in this connection the debate (or, rather, the surprising lack of debate) about the earlier decision to publish the full genome of the 1918 flu virus in 2005, that is, against the background of global terrorism. See Ray Kurzweil and Bill Joy, "Recipe for Destruction," *New York Times*, October 17, 2005. It would seem that the fission case was but an early and particularly clear instance of a phenomenon likely to become more common.

8. Steven Shapin, *The Scientific Life: A Moral History of a Late Modern Vocation* (Chicago: University of Chicago Press, 2009), 19–20.

9. Ibid., 6–7.

10. Ibid., 12.

11. Ibid., 23; quoted from *The Open Society and Its Enemies*, vol. 2, *The High Tide of Prophecy: Hegel, Marx, and the Aftermath* (Princeton, NJ: Princeton University Press, 1966), 217.

12. Descartes, *Discourse on Method*, trans. Richard Kennington, ed. Pamela Kraus and Frank Hunt (Newburyport, MA: Focus, 2007). I will reference this edition by page number.

13. Ibid., 55.

14. Ibid., 21. Note the echo of Machiavelli, *Discourses on Livy*, I.9. We later learn, however, that Descartes "almost never trusts the first thoughts that come to [him]." Kennington, ed., Descartes, *Discourse on Method*, 52.

15. Ibid., 22.

16. Ibid., 23.

17. Ibid., 17.

18. Ibid., 18.

19. Ibid., 25.

20. Ibid., 70.

21. Tocqueville, *Democracy in America*, part 2, book 1, chs. i–ii.

22. Montesquieu, *The Spirit of the Laws*, book 5, ch. 2.

23. For a particularly vivid presentation of the allure of 'the scientist' to a certain kind of proud young soul, see Sinclair Lewis' *Arrowsmith*, and in particular the young Martin Arrowsmith's encounter with Max Gottlieb.

24. *Descartes: Oeuvres et lettres*, ed. André Bridoux (Paris: Gallimard, 1953). Translations are my own. References will be by page number.

25. Ibid., 879.

26. Ibid., 881.

27. Ibid., 883.

28. Ibid., 892.

29. Ibid., 881.

30. Consider again Tocqueville's characterization of American skepticism, or for a more amusing presentation of the peculiarity of American skepticism, consider Mark Twain's *A Connecticut Yankee in King Arthur's Court*. Hank Morgan is astonished by the credulity of the nobles, and in particular the credulity that greets Sandy, and those like Sandy, who arrive at Camelot with extraordinary tales of ogres and fair maidens in distress. He can scarcely believe that it never occurs to any of the nobles to ask for proofs or evidence or even character references in support of these claims.

12

THE DARWINIAN SCIENCE OF ARISTOTELIAN VIRTUE

Larry Arnhart

ARISTOTELIANS NEED CHARLES DARWIN. They need him because Darwin's evolutionary science of virtue supports the moral biology of Aristotle's *Nicomachean Ethics*. Aristotle was a biologist, and his biological science shapes his empirical science of ethics in the *Nicomachean Ethics*. In contrast to Plato's attempt to ground ethics in a moral cosmology, Aristotle grounds ethics in a moral biology. Darwinian science deepens this Aristotelian project by showing how a natural moral sense arises from evolutionary history.

In explaining my Darwinian understanding of Aristotelian virtue, I am dividing this chapter into five parts. In the first part, I identify the moral biology of Darwinian ethics as belonging to an empirical tradition of ethics rooted in the human sources of moral order (human desires, human cultures, and human judgments) rather than the transcendental tradition of ethics that looks to cosmic sources of moral order (cosmic God, cosmic Nature, or cosmic Reason). In the second part, I survey some of the debates between moral cosmology and moral biology—between Plato and Aristotle, between Kant and Darwin, and in the crisis faced by Friedrich Nietzsche who had to choose between Darwinian science and Dionysian religion. In the third part, I show how Aristotle's moral psychology is rooted in a biological psychology of animal minds that has been largely confirmed by Darwinian science. In the fourth part, I show how Aristotle's moral biology supports his study of the virtues—particularly, courage, friendship, and contemplation. In each case, I indicate how Darwinian science sustains the Aristotelian understanding of these virtues. In the final part, I reply to the following four objections to my Darwinian defense of Aristotelian virtue: (1) that I ignore the importance of Aristotle's theology in supporting his ethics; (2) that I ignore the importance of religion generally as the indispensable ground of all morality; (3) that Darwinian biology cannot adequately explain ethics, because Darwinism assumes the Cartesian reductionism that pervades all of modern science; and (4) that my Darwinian and Aristotelian view of ethics cannot properly understand the deepest human desires manifest in the yearning for love and the fear of death.

SIX SOURCES OF MORAL ORDER

A Darwinian evolutionary understanding of ethics supports an empiricist tradition of ethics that runs from Aristotle to David Hume and Adam Smith. This empiricist tradition of thought sees ethics as rooted in human experience—in human nature, human tradition, and human judgment. By contrast the transcendentalist tradition of ethics, from Plato to Immanuel Kant, looks to a transcendent conception of the Good as somehow woven into the order of the cosmos. A Darwinian science of ethics shows that the moral order of human life arises as a joint product of natural desires, cultural traditions, and prudential judgments. The natural desires of our evolved human nature constrain but do not determine our cultural traditions. Our natural desires and cultural traditions constrain but do not determine our prudential judgments.

There are at least twenty natural desires that are universal to all human societies throughout history, because they are rooted in our biological nature. Human beings generally desire the following goods: (1) a complete life, (2) parental care, (3) sexual identity, (4) sexual mating, (5) familial bonding, (6) friendship, (7) social status, (8) justice as reciprocity, (9) political rule, (10) courage in war, (11) health, (12) beauty, (13) property, (14) speech, (15) practical habituation, (16) practical reasoning, (17) practical arts, (18) aesthetic pleasure, (19) religious understanding, and (20) intellectual understanding.

In some of my other writings, I have elaborated what I mean by each of these desires, and I have offered some anthropological, psychological, and biological evidence for their universality.[1]

We recognize the generic goods of life as truly desirable because they satisfy those natural desires that are either useful or agreeable to ourselves or to others. Hume saw this when he observed that personal merit "consists altogether in the possession of mental qualities, useful or agreeable to the person himself or to others."[2] Hume saw that virtues are mental qualities that produce pleasure in impartial observers, and this pleasure produces social esteem for those mental qualities. Qualities of mind that are useful or agreeable—either to those with those qualities or to others—induce a pleasure that leads to those qualities' being esteemed as virtues. Hume could then catalogue the virtues according to four categories: qualities useful to others (such as friendliness and justice), qualities useful to ourselves (such as prudence and temperance), qualities immediately agreeable to others (such as wit and affability), and qualities immediately agreeable to ourselves (such as pride and greatness of mind). All of these qualities esteemed as virtues are related to the twenty natural desires on my list.

I agree with Aristotle and Thomas Aquinas that "something is good insofar as it is desirable."[3] If the good is the desirable, then the harmonious satisfaction of these desires over a complete life constitutes a universal standard for judging social practice as either fulfilling or frustrating our human nature. And yet different cultural traditions and different individuals will rank or organize these desires in different ways. Therefore, prudential judgment is required to judge what is best for particular individuals in particular cultural circumstances. Here I take the side of Aristotelian and Humean empiricism in opposition to Platonic and Kantian transcendentalism.

If we are laying out a typology of fundamental sources of moral knowledge invoked in moral and political philosophy, we should consider six possible sources: (1) cosmic God, (2) cosmic Nature, (3) cosmic Reason, (4) human nature, (5) human culture, (6) human individuals. The transcendentalists look to the first three—the *cosmic* sources of moral order—because they believe that morality cannot have "moral clout" (in Richard Joyce's phrase) unless it is believed to be part of the cosmic order of things as dictated by God, by the nature of the universe, or by universal rational order.[4] So just as we discover mathematical principles as somehow woven

...to the constitution of the world, we should be able to discover moral principles as part of the "wisdom of the world" (in Rémi Brague's phrase).[5]

The empiricists, however, look to the second three sources—the *human sources* of moral order. Human nature gives us the generic goods of life as rooted in the natural desires of the human species—the twenty natural desires that I have sketched. But within the constraints of human nature, human culture specifies the moral traditions of human morality as shaped by cultural history. Then, within the constraints of both human nature and human culture, human individuals make choices in their ranking and organization of their desires that reflect the uniqueness of their individual temperaments, abilities, and circumstances as shaped by their individual life history.

Darwinian science sustains the empirical understanding of ethics by explaining how natural desires, cultural traditions, and individual judgments arise from evolved human nature. This supports the move from moral cosmology to moral biology that was begun by Aristotle.

From Moral Cosmology to Moral Biology

The drama of the debate between the moral cosmologists and the moral biologists has moved through three acts. In the first act, Plato's moral cosmology was challenged by Aristotle's moral biology. In the second act, Kant's transcendentalist ethics was challenged by Darwin's evolutionary ethics. In the third act, which continues into the present day, we face Friedrich Nietzsche's struggle to choose between the moral cosmology of a Dionysian religion and the moral biology of a Darwinian science.

From Plato to Aristotle

In the *Stanza della Segnatura* in the Vatican Palace, Plato and Aristotle are the central figures in Raphael's painting of the Greek philosophers in the *School of Athens*. They stride forward toward the viewer. Plato points upward toward the sky with his right arm and extended index finger, while carrying in his left arm a copy of his *Timaeus*, which he holds vertically. Aristotle gestures forward and downward with his right arm and his open palm extended horizontally, while carrying in his left arm a copy of his *Nicomachean Ethics*, which he holds horizontally. It's as though Plato is saying, "Read my *Timaeus*, and you'll see that it's all up there in the heavens."

To which Aristotle responds, "No, read my *Nicomachean Ethics*, and you see that it's all right down here amongst us." The painting is balanced symmetrically, so as to indicate that Raphael was persuaded by Pico della Mirandola and other Renaissance thinkers who tried to reconcile Plato and Aristotle as teaching complementary aspects of the same reality.[6]

The possibility of such reconciliation is hard to see when one considers the contrast between Plato's *Timaeus* and Aristotle's *Nicomachean Ethics*. The *Timaeus* is perhaps the single most influential book of philosophy in history, because it shaped the prevalent cosmological model of the Western world for almost two thousand years.[7] Plato's *Timaeus* argued that Socrates' best city in speech in the *Republic* needed to be supported by the best cosmos in speech—a rational theology of cosmic order, in which the intelligible order of the cosmos manifested the intelligent design of the divine cosmic craftsman guided by the eternal Ideas. The moral and political order of human life could then be judged by how well it imitated this cosmic order of the Divine Intellect. The best political order needs to be set within the best cosmic order.

The dubious character of Timaeus's mythic presentation of his cosmology and the absence of any Socratic questioning of his claims has led some Straussian scholars, such as Joseph Cropsey and Catherine Zuckert, to conclude that Timaeus does not speak for Plato or Plato's Socrates.[8] According to Cropsey and Zuckert, Plato really teaches that the cosmos is morally neutral, because morality and politics depend upon an anthropology of human caring for ourselves in an uncaring universe. If so, this would coincide with what I am defending here as the immanent teleology of human nature, which does not require a moral cosmology. But if Plato did not intend to endorse Timaeus's cosmological myth, we must wonder why he wrote it in such a way that it would be taken seriously by many, if not most, readers, and even become the most influential of all of Plato's writings for almost two millennia.

One might also wonder about whether Timaeus's myth satisfies a Socratic yearning for moral cosmology. In the *Phaedo*, Socrates describes his youthful excitement in reading Anaxagoras's claim that "Mind" (*nous*) rules over the whole order of the cosmos and thus designs everything for the best.[9] Socrates was disappointed, however, when he discovered that Anaxagoras was ultimately a materialist, explaining things as governed by purely material causes rather than intelligent causes. This disappointment with natural philosophy set Socrates off on a "second sailing," where he decided to look for the truth of Being in the speeches or accounts (*logoi*) of things, by examining how people talk about their experience and particularly their moral and political experience. If this was a turn away from natural philosophy toward moral and political philosophy, with the understanding that the moral life is disconnected from cosmic nature, then Timaeus's moral cosmology would be contrary to this Socratic turn. But then we might notice that Socrates praises Timaeus for reaching "the very peak of all philosophy."[10] So, perhaps Socrates saw Timaeus as doing what Anaxagoras failed to do successfully—construct a moral cosmology in which the cosmos is intelligently designed by a cosmic Mind as the best of all possible worlds—and therefore Timaeus gave Socrates what he had always wanted: an intelligent-design cosmology that would explain the reason that it is best for things to be as they are.

By contrast to Plato and Plato's Socrates, Aristotle's *Nicomachean Ethics* almost never invokes any cosmic standards in laying out the view of ethics as directed to human happiness, understood as the flourishing of human nature. Turning away from Plato's cosmology of eternal and unchanging perfection that can be known with rational certainty, Aristotle studied biology as the realm of mortal life and flux that lends itself only to probable knowledge. There is at least one place in the *Nicomachean Ethics* where Aristotle refers to the divine order of the cosmos:

> It is absurd for anyone to believe that politics or prudence is the most serious kind of knowledge, if a human being is not the highest thing in the cosmos.... And if it is the case that a human being is the best in comparison to the other animals, that makes no difference, for there are other things that are much more divine in their nature than a human being, such as most visibly the things out of which the cosmos is composed.[11]

Apparently, Aristotle is referring to the heavenly bodies—the Sun, the planets, and the stars. In his *On the Heavens*, he lays out his theological astronomy. But he repeatedly reminds his reader that astronomical phenomena are too far away to be studied directly, and so most of the fundamental ideas in astronomy are "hypotheses" that must be taken on "faith" or "trust" (*pistis*), as having been passed down as ancestral myths.[12]

In justifying his biological studies, Aristotle argues that, while studying the eternally unchanging phenomena in the heavens might be honorable

and divine, such study is hard to carry out because there is so little observational evidence. By comparison, the perishable phenomena of plants
and animals are easier to study because "we live among them." Moreover,
there is intense pleasure in studying biological phenomena, because "they
are nearer to us and more akin to our nature." This goes against the disposition of Plato and the Platonists, because, believing with Heraclitus that
"all sensible things are always in a state of flux and that no science of them
exists," they turned to the abstract realm of eternal Ideas or Forms in the
search for perfect intelligibility.[13]

In Aristotle's *Ethics*, he assumes a biological teleology of living bodies
that does not depend upon any cosmic teleology of the heavenly bodies.
He rejects Plato's Idea of the Good, because the good is the desirable, and
what is desirable varies according to the desires of each species of life. "The
good is not single for all animals, but is different in the case of each."[14] Thus
does Aristotle move from moral cosmology to moral biology.

From Kant to Darwin

Darwin made a similar move in turning away from the transcendentalist ethics of Kant to the empiricist ethics of an evolved moral sense. In *The
Descent of Man*, Darwin recognizes the uniqueness of human morality. "Of
all the differences between man and the lower animals, the moral sense or
conscience is by far the most important." This moral sense is "summed up
in that short but imperious word *ought*," which is "the most noble of all the
attributes of man, leading him without a moment's hesitation to risk his
life for that of a fellow-creature; or after due deliberation, impelled simply
by the deep feeling of right or duty, to sacrifice it in some great cause."[15]

Darwin then quotes a remark by Kant: "Duty! Wondrous thought, that
workest neither by fond insinuation, flattery, nor by any threat, but merely
by holding up thy naked law in the soul, and so extorting for thyself always
reverence, if not always obedience; before whom all appetites are dumb,
however secretly they rebel; whence thy original?" This comes from a passage in Kant's *Critique of Practical Reason*, which is immediately followed by
a passage in which Kant writes about the sense of duty or "ought" as showing
us "man as belonging to two worlds"—the empirical (phenomenal) world of
natural causes and the transcendental (noumenal) world of moral freedom.[16]

By contrast, Darwin indicates that his explanation of morality will be
"exclusively from the side of natural history." So we see a fundamental dif-

ference between the Kantian approach that sees morality as belonging to a transcendent world beyond the natural world and the Darwinian approach that sees morality as belonging completely to "natural history."[17]

Darwin's first readers saw this, and many were disturbed by it. Frances Cobbe wrote a review of *The Descent of Man* in which she warned that Darwin's rejection of the Kantian view of morality as transcending natural human experience would destroy all morality. A few years earlier, Cobbe had persuaded Darwin to read some of Kant's writings on ethics, and Darwin had told her that he was interested to see "how differently two men may look at the same points . . . the one man a great philosopher looking exclusively into his own mind, the other a degraded wretch looking from the outside thro' apes & savages at the moral sense of mankind."[18]

In her review, Cobbe explained this as a fundamental conflict between two views of morality. "Independent or Intuitive Morality has always taught that there is a supreme and necessary moral law common to all free agents in the universe, and known to man by means of a transcendental reason or divine voice of conscience. Dependent or Utilitarian Morality has equally steadily rejected the idea of a law other than the law of utility." Darwin clearly took the second position. She observed:

> The Kantian doctrine of Pure Reason, giving us transcendental knowledge of necessary truths, is not entertained by the school of thinkers to which he belongs; and that as for the notion of all the old teachers of the world, the voice of Conscience is the voice of God— the doctrine of Job and Zoroaster, Menu and Pythagoras, Plato and Antonius, Chrysotom and Gregory, Fenelon and Jeremy Taylor—it can have no place in their science. As Comte would say, we have passed the theologic stage, and must not think of running to a First Cause to explain phenomena. After all (they seem to say), cannot we easily suggest how man might acquire a conscience from causes at work around him?[19]

Darwin maintained that although the moral sense was unique to human beings, it would be possible for evolutionary history to produce another species of animal with a different kind of moral sense. "Any animal whatever, endowed with well-marked social instincts, the parental and filial affections being here included, would inevitably acquire a moral sense or conscience, as soon as its intellectual powers had become as well, or nearly as well developed, as in man." But the content of the moral sense in such an animal would depend upon the desires and needs of the animal. Darwin explained:

> If, for instance, to take an extreme case, men were reared under precisely the same conditions as hive-bees, there can hardly be a doubt that our unmarried females would, like the worker-bees, think it a sacred duty to kill their brothers, and mothers would strive to kill their fertile daughters; and no one would think of interfering. Nevertheless, the bee, or any other social animal, would gain in our supposed case, as it appears to me, some feeling of right and wrong, or a conscience. For each individual would have an inward sense of possessing certain stronger or more enduring instincts, and others less strong or enduring; so that there would often be a struggle as to which impulse should be followed; and satisfaction, dissatisfaction, or even misery would be felt, as past impressions were compared during their incessant passage through the mind. In this case, an inward monitor would tell the animal that it would have been better to have followed the one impulse rather than the other. The one course ought to have been followed, and the other ought not; the one would have been right and the other wrong.[20]

It seems, then, that the moral sense or conscience—the sense of moral "ought"—is a "feeling of right or wrong" that varies according to the instinctive desires of the species. So far, the human moral sense is the only moral sense, because human beings are the only animals with the evolved intellectual capacities for moral judgment. But if any other animals were to evolve such intellectual capacities, their moral sense would differ from the human moral sense depending upon the differences in their instinctive desires.

Cobbe was appalled by the claim that, if bees had a moral sense, it would prescribe a sacred duty for sisters to murder their brothers. She saw this as

> affirming that, not only has our moral sense come to us from a source commanding no special respect, but that it answers to no external or durable, not to say universal or eternal, reality, and is merely tentative and provisional, the provincial prejudice, as we may describe it, of this little world and its temporary inhabitants, which would be looked

on with a smile of derision by better-informed people now residing on Mars, or hereafter to be developed on earth, and who in their turn may be considered as walking in a vain shadow by other races. . . . Our moral sense, however acquired, does not, it is asserted, correspond to anything real outside of itself, to any law which must be the same for all intelligences, mundane or supernal.[21]

Against what she perceived as Darwin's moral nihilism, Cobbe asserted that ethics was a normative science just like geometry, in that both ethics and geometry were based on axiomatic principles that all intelligent beings could recognize as necessary truths. "Love your neighbor" is such a necessary truth of morality, and therefore any intelligent being should eventually understand that moral duty dictates universal love, which would be as true for bees as for human beings.

The reasoning for the worry one sees in Cobbe's review that evolutionary ethics promotes moral nihilism has been elaborated recently by philosopher Richard Joyce in his book *The Evolution of Morality*. Joyce agrees with Cobbe (and Kant) that by definition moral judgments presuppose belief in a transcendent world of moral facts beyond the empirical world of natural facts. But unlike Cobbe, Joyce denies the truth of that belief, because he thinks there really are no such moral facts, and so he concludes that we cannot know that moral rightness and wrongness *really* exist. Moreover, he argues that evolutionary ethics necessarily leads us to this conclusion that morality is fictional because an evolutionary account of morality explains it as arising from the natural facts of human desires and capacities without any reference to any distinctively moral facts. Joyce is an example of how a frustrated Platonist becomes a nihilist: he affirms the necessity for a transcendent Idea of the Good, while simultaneously denying its existence.

Joyce believes that Darwin's evolutionary ethics explains the ultimate causes of ethics in a way that confirms Hume's insight that the human moral sense depends on the human tendency to project emotions onto the world. Hume spoke of the mind's "great propensity to spread itself on objects," because "taste" (as opposed to reason) "has a productive faculty, and gilding and staining all natural objects with the colors, borrowed from internal sentiment, raises in a manner a new creation." So it is that "vice and virtue may be compared to sounds, colors, heat and cold, which, according to modern philosophy, are not qualities in objects but perceptions in the mind." And yet our human moral principles can be enduring, if not universal, insofar as our moral emotions manifest the "universal constitution of human nature."[22]

For Hume, the explanation of the origins of human morality ended with some final appeal to human nature as ultimate cause, because he could not go any further to explain the original causes of human nature itself. Here is where Darwin could adopt Hume's account of the natural moral sense but then go further in developing an evolutionary explanation for how human nature as endowed with a moral sense could have arisen.

While Joyce accepts this Humean/Darwinian account of morality as an evolved propensity of human nature to project human moral emotions onto the world, he cannot believe that this is a full explanation of morality, because Joyce agrees with Kant that moral concepts necessarily presuppose belief in a transcendent world of moral facts. Like many moral philosophers from Plato to Kant, Joyce embraces a transcendental view of morality in contrast to the empirical view of morality taken by those like Hume and Darwin. Joyce believes that morality requires a moral cosmology, so that morality can be understood as having an eternal truth as corresponding to some cosmic order of God, Reason, or Nature. But since Joyce believes that modern science has refuted any moral cosmology, he cannot believe in the reality of any cosmic moral facts, and therefore he must conclude that all morality is a fictional creation of human beings who deceive themselves into thinking that this morality conforms to some cosmic reality. Thus it is that Joyce, like many modern moral philosophers, must face Nietzsche's challenge: Does the death of God—the death of all cosmic support for morality—mean the death of morality?

Nietzsche's Dilemma—Darwin or Dionysus?

It is remarkable that religious believers who fear Darwinian science as a threat to religious morality can quote Nietzsche as supporting their position. I have noticed that whenever I defend a Darwinian conception of morality, some religious believers will often remind me of what Nietzsche said about David Strauss and George Eliot. Nietzsche's long essay on "David Strauss, the Confessor and the Writer" (1873) was published as the first of four essays collected under the title *Untimely Meditations*. It is a scornful attack on Strauss's book *The Old Faith and the New*.[23]

In 1835, Strauss's book *The Life of Jesus* provoked intense criticism and even violence against him because he denied the historical reality of Jesus and argued that he was a purely mythical creation of the early Christian community. (This book was translated from the German into English by George Eliot in 1846.) Nietzsche's reading of the book as a theology student in 1864–1865 helped to convince him to reject his Christian faith and to refuse to take communion at Easter in 1865. *The Old Faith and the New* extends Strauss's reasoning by rejecting any conception of a personal God and by arguing that the moral teaching of Christianity can be preserved as part of the "new faith" in Darwinian science.

Nietzsche dismisses Strauss as a foolish philistine who does not understand that, in rejecting Christianity, he has rejected the foundation for a Christian morality of universal love that cannot be sustained by Darwinian science. According to Nietzsche, Strauss does not realize that a truly Darwinian ethic would be based on a Hobbesian "war of all against all" with the rule of the stronger over the weaker. Instead, Strauss declares: "Do not ever forget that you are a man and not a mere creature of nature: do not ever forget that all others are likewise men, that is to say, with all their individual differences the same as you, with the same needs and demands as you—that is the epitome of all morality." But, Nietzsche complains, this ignores the fact that, according to Darwin, man is "precisely a creature of nature and nothing else."[24]

Moreover, Nietzsche notes, Strauss fails to see that Darwinian science does not support his metaphysical belief in the moral character of the cosmos, his belief "that everything proceeds according to eternal laws out of the one primeval source of all life, all reason and all goodness—that is the epitome of religion." "Modern natural science and study of history have nothing whatever to do with the Straussian faith in the cosmos."[25]

In *Twilight of the Idols*, Nietzsche makes the same point, this time ridiculing George Eliot:

> G. Eliot. They are rid of the Christian God and now believe all the more firmly that they must cling to Christian morality. That is an English consistency; we do not wish to hold it against little moralistic females a la Eliot. In England one must rehabilitate oneself after every little emancipation from theology by showing in a veritably awe-inspiring manner what a moral fanatic one is. That is the penance they pay there.

We others hold otherwise. When one gives up the Christian faith, one pulls the right to Christian morality out from under one's feet. This morality is by no means self-evident: this point has to be exhibited again and again, despite the English flatheads. Christianity is a system, a whole view of things thought out together. By breaking one main concept out of it, the faith in God, one breaks the whole: nothing necessary remains in one's hands. Christianity presupposes that man does not know, cannot know, what is good for him, what evil: he believes in God, who alone knows it. Christian morality is a command; its origin is transcendent; it is beyond all criticism, all right to criticism; it has truth only if God is the truth—it stands or falls with faith in God.

When the English actually believe that they know "intuitively" what is good and evil, when they therefore suppose that they no longer require Christianity as the guarantee of morality, we merely witness the effects of the dominion of the Christian value judgment and an expression of the strength and depth of this dominion: such that the origin of English morality has been forgotten, such that the very conditional character of its right to existence is no longer felt. For the English, morality is not yet a problem.[26]

But notice the crucial assumption here in Nietzsche's reasoning—his agreement with those Christians who claim that human beings cannot know what is good for them unless they receive Christian morality as a command from God. I reject this assumption, because I believe that human beings can know what is good for them from their natural moral experience. In rejecting Nietzsche's assumption, I also reject his conclusion—that morality cannot rightly be sustained if one no longer believes in the Christian God.

In *The Descent of Man*, Darwin says that "to do good unto others—to do unto others as ye would they should do unto you—is the foundation-stone of morality," and he claims that even primitive human beings might act according to this principle as impelled by "the love of praise and the dread of blame," because they care about how they appear to others: "The moral sense perhaps affords the best and highest distinction between man and the lower animals; but I need not say anything on this head, as I have so lately endeavoured to show that the social instincts—the prime principle of man's moral constitution—with the aid of active intellectual powers and the effects of habit, naturally lead to the golden rule. 'As ye would that men should do to you, do ye to them likewise;' and this lies at the foundation of morality."[27]

That Darwin here quotes the statement of the Golden Rule from Jesus' Sermon on the Mount (Matthew 7:12) might be taken by Nietzsche as evidence for his assertion that Christian morality depends on Christian faith. But notice that Darwin presents this rule as flowing "naturally" from human experience and as combining social instincts, social habits, and intellectual activity.[28] In referring to the social instincts as "the prime principle of man's moral constitution," Darwin has a footnote citing Marcus Aurelius, which suggests that the recognition of this moral sociality does not depend on Christian theology. Elsewhere in the *Descent*, Darwin explains the Golden Rule as a conclusion from the human experience of reciprocity—the natural tendency of human beings to respond in kind, rewarding those they trust and punishing those they don't. Consequently, when Jesus states the Golden Rule, he is not commanding something human beings could not have figured out for themselves. Rather, he is reinforcing a lesson of human practical experience. Given our evolved human nature as social animals, our socially evolved habituation, and our intellectual powers for reflecting on our natural inclinations and social habits, we can understand the wisdom of the Golden Rule as "the foundation of morality."

Religious belief can reinforce our recognition of moral principles such as the Golden Rule, and that's why, as Darwin indicates, religion is important for moral history as contributing to our moral habituation. Nevertheless, that morality can stand on its own natural ground even without any specific religious doctrines. This is why I disagree with those of my critics like C. Stephen Evans, John Hare, and Carson Holloway who agree with Nietzsche that there is no natural ground for moral principles like the Golden Rule.[29]

Despite his loudly proclaimed atheism, Nietzsche felt the need for a redemptive religion that would sustain a moral cosmology. As Nietzsche fell into madness at the beginning of January in 1889, he wrote and mailed a series of letters. A letter to Peter Gast was only one sentence: "Sing me a new song: the world is transfigured and all the heavens are full of joy." It was signed "The Crucified." Other letters were signed "Dionysus."[30] To many readers, it seems odd that Nietzsche—the self-proclaimed "Antichrist" who announced the death of God—would use such religious imagery and identify himself with Jesus and the god Dionysus. We might dismiss this as only a manifestation of his madness. Yet the signs of religiosity appear throughout Nietzsche's early and late writings. For example, in *Twilight of the Idols*, Nietzsche professes his "faith" in the belief "that all is redeemed and affirmed in the whole." He declares: "Such a faith is the highest of all possible faiths: I have baptized it with the name of Dionysus."[31]

One doesn't see this religiosity in the writings of Nietzsche's "middle period" (1877–1881). In *Human, All Too Human* and *Dawn*, he strives for a Darwinian philosophy based on a scientific history of evolution. Rejecting all metaphysical and religious philosophy grounded on the idea of a cosmic teleology of eternal moral order, Nietzsche works from the thought that "everything has evolved: there are no eternal facts, just as there are no absolute truths."[32] Even though there are no eternal truths, a properly historical science can discover the "humble truths" of historical development.

Nietzsche believes that modern science continues the skeptical spirit of the Socratic tradition. He acknowledges, however, that most human beings cannot live the skeptical life of a Socratic "free spirit," because they yearn for transcendent truths and transcendent values that are absolute and eternal. Religions such as Christianity satisfy the transcendental longings of human beings to be redeemed from ordinary earthly existence so they can feel an ecstatic rapture in the prospect of entering an eternal realm of perfect bliss. In *Human, All Too Human*, he speaks of this need for redemption as an "artificial" or "acquired" need that was cultivated by the Christian church in the Middle Ages, and he suggests that a future society might eliminate this need while serving "the common true needs of all men."[33]

Yet Nietzsche also indicates that this need for redemption has become so strong that even those who believe themselves to be atheists are moved by the religious desire to find some transcendent satisfaction through art. Those who might otherwise be considered atheistic free spirits enjoy music (as in Wagner's operas) that stirs religious feelings without requiring belief in religious doctrines. Indeed, romantic art in general shows "the magic of religious feeling" as the modern artist appeals to those who have given up religious beliefs but who still yearn for religious ecstasy through art.[34]

But then, as Nietzsche began writing *Thus Spoke Zarathustra* in 1883, he seemed himself to fall under "the magic of religious feeling." In *Human, All Too Human*, he had warned against the "cult of the genius," based on the "religious or semi-religious superstition that these spirits are of superhuman [*ubermenschlichen*] origin," and that they have some deep insight into reality.[35] But then Zarathustra proclaims the "superhuman" or "overman" as the redeemer. In the *Genealogy of Morals*, Nietzsche looks to "the redeeming human of the great love and contempt," to "this human of the future who will redeem us from the previous ideal," and he foresees: "this bell-stroke of noon and of the great decision, that makes the will free again, that gives back to the earth its goal and to man his hope; this Anti-Christ and anti-nihilist; this conqueror of God and of nothingness—he must someday come."[36]

In his middle writings, Nietzsche came under the influence of Darwinian science, which overturned the romantic metaphysics and religiosity of *The Birth of Tragedy* and the *Untimely Meditations*. But, then, beginning in 1883, he returned to the religious and metaphysical propensities of those early writings. In *On the Uses and Disadvantages of History for Life*, he had warned that scientific history—and particularly, Darwinian evolutionary history—was dangerous to life, because this "science of universal becoming" denied the eternal meaning of life as supported by belief in a cosmic teleology:

> If the doctrines of sovereign becoming, of the fluidity of all concepts, types and species, of the lack of any cardinal distinction between man and animal—doctrines that I consider true but deadly—are thrust upon the people for another generation with the rage for instruction that has now become normal, no one should be surprised if the people perishes of petty egoism, ossification and greed and ceases to be a people; in its place systems of individualist egoism, brotherhoods for the rapacious exploitation of the non-brothers, and similar creations of utilitarian vulgarity may perhaps appear in the arena of the future.[37]

Thus, the deadliness of the Darwinian truth is metaphysical ("sovereign becoming"), epistemological ("the fluidity of all concepts, types, and species"), and anthropological ("the lack of any cardinal distinction between man and animal").

Nietzsche indicated that there were only two possible antidotes to this intellectual poison. The "unhistorical" antidote would require forgetting history and enclosing one's cultural life within a bounded horizon. The "suprahistorical" antidote would depend on "the powers that lead the eye away from becoming towards that which bestows upon existence the character of the eternal and recurring, towards art and religion." The problem is that science "sees everywhere things that have been, things historical, and nowhere things that are, things eternal. . . . Contemplation of history has never flown so far, not even in dreams; for now the history of mankind is only the continuation of the history of animals and plants; even in the profoundest depths of the sea the universal historian still finds traces of himself as living slime." And thus the Darwinian science of history "robs man of the foundation of all his rest and security, his belief in the enduring and eternal."[38] After going through his middle period devoted to historical or evolutionary science, Nietzsche in his later writings returned to his earlier fear of science as subversive of life as he looked to "the eternalizing powers of art and religion" as the only way to restore meaning to life.

Lou Salomé was Nietzsche's friend and lover, the woman who reputedly turned down his proposal of marriage. In her book on Nietzsche (the first book on his writings), Salomé explained the history of his writing as showing his struggle with a "religious drive" he could never shake off. On the one hand, he denied the God in whom he had devotedly believed in his Lutheran household. On the other hand, he needed to replace that orthodox religion with a new religion of Dionysus and the Overman. She thought that only in his middle writings—during the time of his deep friendships with Paul Rée and herself—did Nietzsche achieve a position of scientific skepticism free of religious ideas, during the time when he was influenced by the Darwinian view of morality that Salomé and Rée had adopted. This friendship between Nietzsche, Salomé, and Rée, with their shared interest in the new Darwinian science, was captured vividly in the famous photograph of "The Holy Trinity"—Nietzsche and Rée pulling a cart, with Salomé in the cart, holding a whip.[39]

In Bruce Benson's recent book on the "pious Nietzsche," Salomé's reading of Nietzsche as tormented by the conflict between his religious longings and his denial of God is deepened and made more precise. Benson shows how Nietzsche moved from the Christian Pietism of his youth to the Dionysian Pietism of his philosophic works. Far from being godless, he moved from one god to another.[40]

As a child, Nietzsche was shaped by Lutheran Pietism, in which Christian faith is understood as a matter of the heart rather than the head, because to have a right relationship with God one must have a childlike trust in God that does not depend upon doctrinal propositions. As an adult, Nietzsche rejected Christian Pietism because he denied the Christian God. But his Dionysian religion was a kind of Pietism in that it required a childlike trust in life, a joyful acceptance of life that allowed him to say "yes and amen" to life. In *Twilight of the Idols*, Nietzsche affirms: "Eternal life, the eternal recurrence of life; the future promised and made sacred by the past; the triumphant yes to life beyond death and change; true life as collective survival through reproduction, through the mysteries of sexuality. ... All this is signified by the name Dionysus: I know no higher symbolism than this Greek symbolism, the symbolism of the Dionysian rites. In them, the deepest instinct of life, the instinct for the future of life, for the eternity of life, is experienced religiously—the very way to life, reproduction, as the holy way."[41] Nietzsche's Dionysian religion is pietistic in the sense that it requires a change of heart—perhaps through music and dance—that will allow him to say "yes and amen" to everything in life, which would be "an ecstatic affirmation of the total character of life."[42]

Benson succeeds in laying out the character of Nietzsche's Dionysian Pietism. But one major weakness in Benson's book is that he fails to contrast this religious longing as it appears in Nietzsche's early and later writings with his Darwinian evolutionary science as it appears in his middle writings. Salomé sees this contrast, as Benson does not. Salomé shows how Nietzsche might have freed himself from religious mysticism if he had adhered to the scientific stance of *Human, All Too Human*; *Dawn*; and the first four books of the *Gay Science*.

Did Nietzsche really become a faithful follower of Dionysus? In *The Birth of Tragedy*, Nietzsche describes Dionysian rapture: "Singing and dancing, man expresses his sense of belonging to a higher community; he has forgotten how to walk and talk and is on the brink of flying and dancing, up and away into the air above. His gestures speak of his enchantment ... he feels himself to be a god, he himself now moves in such ecstasy and sublimity as once he saw the gods move in his dreams."[43] Franz Overbeck reports that in the early days of Nietzsche's insanity, he danced and improvised music at his piano, telling his friends that he could only express his feelings in music. Perhaps Nietzsche did finally achieve ecstatic union with his god Dionysus by giving up his reason and being swallowed up in a frenzy of religious madness.

Nietzsche's dilemma—his sense that Darwinian science is "true but deadly," and that the only antidote to its deadly poison is a redemptive religious cosmology—continues as a dilemma for many Nietzscheans today. One can see this, for example in the work of Leo Strauss and the Straussians. Like Nietzsche, Strauss was an atheist who could never shake off his religious longings for a moral cosmology. His friend Hans Jonas saw this.[44] Like Nietzsche, Strauss feared Darwinian natural history as "true but deadly," and as an antidote to this poisonous truth of science, he was attracted to an "atheistic religiosity" or religious Platonism, in which a few intellectually superior human beings could live a philosophic life of contemplation that could be eternalized as an expression of "the eternal basic text of *homo natura*."[45]

The Straussian fear of Darwinism is evident in Harvey Mansfield's warning: "Darwin was not a nihilist, but he prepared his generation and later generations for nihilism. His theory of evolution not only denied the eternity of the species but also undermined all eternities, all permanence of meaning." Mansfield presents the "manly nihilism" of Nietzsche and Theodore Roosevelt as a rebellion against the Darwinian teaching that there is no purposeful and eternal cosmic order of nature to provide standards for human excellence and importance.[46]

While Nietzsche looked to the manliness of the Overman (*Übermensch*), Roosevelt looked to the manliness of the "leader" (*Führer*). During the presidency of George W. Bush, Mansfield praised Bush for his attempts at "one-man rule" as showing manly leadership in the tradition of Roosevelt's manly nihilism. Isn't there a dangerous extremism in this vision of redemptive leadership? Far more healthy, I suggest, is the moderation of Nietzsche's Darwinian science in *Human, All Too Human*.

For Nietzsche, Darwin's science was a radical break from the moral cosmology of Platonism and Christianity that had dominated Western culture for thousands of years. And yet, Darwin's moral biology could be seen as reviving and deepening an empiricist tradition of thought that was begun by Aristotle. To see human morality as rooted in human biology, and in psychological traits shared with other animals, was originally an insight of Aristotle's biology that was confirmed by Darwin's biology.

The Animal Psychology of Social Intelligence

Darwin argues that human beings differ from other animals in degree but not in kind. This is often thought to be a refutation of Aristotelian biology. But while Aristotle had no theory of the evolution of species from ancestral species, a fundamental principle of his biology is the continuity between human beings and other animals, not only in their bodies but also in their mental powers, which enters his moral and political writing in those many passages where he explains human psychological nature by comparison with other animals.

Aristotle saw that the intelligence of animals tends to be proportional to their sociality, because the more social animals are generally the more intelligent. Animals living in complex societies need greater intelligence to navigate their way through the intricacies of social life. Darwin also saw this connection between intelligence and sociality, so that the evolution of animal intelligence could be explained as an adaptation to ever more complex forms of social life. Recently, some evolutionary psychologists have adopted a "social brain" hypothesis, which explains the evolution of cognition as adaptive for social animals who need complex cognitive abilities in order to solve the problems of social life. Thus, Darwinian psychologists have rediscovered one of the fundamental insights of Aristotle's biology. The continuity of animal psychology for Aristotle is evident in the following passage from the *History of Animals*:

> In most of the other animals, there are traces of the qualities of soul that are more evidently differentiated in human beings. For there are both gentleness and savagery, mildness and harshness, courage and timidity, fear and confidence, spiritedness and trickery, and, with respect to intelligence [*dianoia*], something like judgment [*sunēsis*], similar in many ways, just as we have spoken of the parts of the body. For some of these qualities differ only more or less with reference to human beings, and so is man in reference to many things of animals. Some of these qualities are greater in man, others are greater in other animals, but in others they differ by analogy. For instance, in many there is art, wisdom, and judgment, so there is some other natural capacity. This is most evident if one considers the condition at the age of infancy. For in infants it is possible to see traces and germs of their future dispositions, since there is no difference, so to speak, between the soul of a beast and the soul of an infant. So it is not unreasonable if some psychic qualities are the same, others resemble one another, and others are analogous. For nature passes little by little from the inanimate to animals, so that this continuity prevents one from seeing a border or perceiving on which side an intermediate form lies.
>
> The same holds for the actions of life. For of plants the function appears to be nothing other than producing another similar to themselves, which arises through seeds, and similarly of some animals

there is no function other than reproduction. Therefore, the actions of this sort are common to all. But if sensation is added, then their lives with respect to sexual intercourse will differ through the pleasure of this activity, and with respect to parturition and the nurturing of the young. Some animals, therefore, just like plants, complete the reproduction of their progeny according to the seasons. Others trouble themselves about the feeding of the young, but whenever this is completed, they separate themselves and have nothing more in common with them. Still others who are more intelligent and share in memory live a longer time and in a more political manner with their offspring.

One part of the life of animals, therefore, is devoted to the actions concerning reproduction, another part to the actions concerning food. For on these two all their serious pursuits and their life happen to concentrate. Their food differs mostly according to the matter of which they are constituted. For the growth of each will happen according to nature from this. Further, whatever is according to nature is pleasurable; and all animals according to nature pursue pleasure.[47]

Notice the eight points that Aristotle makes in this passage: (1) Human psychic powers are more clearly differentiated forms of powers found in other animals. Thus, there is an unbroken continuity between all species of life. (2) These common powers include both traits of moral temperament (such as courage, for example) and cognitive capacities for reasoning and judging. (3) In comparing human beings and other animals, Aristotle sees that their powers are either the same or different in degree or similar by analogy. In the case of analogy, different powers serve similar functions. (4) These comparisons are clearest if one considers human infants, because in some sense there is no difference between a young child and a non-human animal. (5) Animals are naturally adapted for survival and reproduction, and therefore the practical structure of their lives varies according to how each species feeds and propagates. (6) Unlike plants, some animals must care for their young, and how they do this shapes the life of each species. Some animals only feed the young at the beginning of life, but those who are more intelligent develop more lasting bonds with their young. Thus, higher levels of animal intelligence are connected to more extended parental care. (7) Such long-term nurturance of the young is the natural ground from which political life grows. (8) Animals act to satisfy their natural desires because by nature this gives them pleasure.

All of these points enter into Aristotle's moral and political science. Consider, for example, the importance of pleasure. "Whatever is according to nature is pleasurable; and all animals according to nature pursue pleasure." Having developed this thought in his biological works, Aristotle incorporates it into the *Nicomachean Ethics*. All human action is governed by pleasure and pain, as is true for all animals. A good man is one who feels pleasure and pain in the right manner. To deny the goodness of pleasure would be an implausible denial of the testimony of all animals. Since all creatures, the mindless as well as those with some rational judgment, pursue pleasure as good, it must be good in some sense. A man could not endure even Plato's Idea of the Good if it were painful to him.[48] While pleasure is not always the direct object of desire, it accompanies the satisfaction of every desire, which supports the observation that the good is the desirable.[49]

Each animal has a species-specific pleasure corresponding to its species-specific function, for pleasure accompanies the activity of fulfilling whatever inclinations constitute the nature of a species. Therefore, "the pleasures of a horse, of a dog, and of a human being are different."[50] But although the pleasures of each species tend to be the same, what human beings find pleasurable varies to some extent. In extreme cases, human beings can be impaired or ruined so that what is pleasurable for them is not truly pleasurable in the sense of perfecting human nature. Such people don't understand what they truly desire.[51]

The pleasures of the good and the bad differ just as the pleasures of children and adults differ, and we can properly judge the pleasures of the good person to be superior just as we do those of the adult.[52] Some pleasures are natural to human beings (or to other species), while others are unnatural. The unnatural pleasures are natural in the weak sense that they have natural causes; but they are unnatural in the strong sense that they disrupt the normal balance or order in an animal's life. Among human beings, unnatural pleasures arise either through injury or through habit or through evil natures. So, for example, a person might be driven by a mental disease to kill and eat his mother. Or a person abused from childhood might take pleasure in sexual perversion. Or a person born with some mental disorder might take perverse pleasure in eating human flesh or abusing his children.[53]

Those who would guide the education of the young and the general formation of human character must understand the motivational power of pleasure and pain. Consequently, "theorizing about pleasure and pain belongs to the political philosopher; for he is the architect of the end, to which we look in calling one thing good and another bad in an absolute sense." Furthermore, as a philosopher, he understands that the intellectual life is the most pleasurable insofar as a human being in the highest sense is his intellect.[54]

Darwin also concluded that human beings found their natural pleasures in satisfying their instincts for conjugal, parental, and social bonding generally. As refined by habit and reason, these instinctive pleasures shape the moral sense of human beings. Any person without such instincts would be an "unnatural monster." Moreover, Darwin thought that in some savage circumstances, bad habits and insufficient reasoning would lead people to commit "unnatural crimes."[55] But with the progress of civilization a few people, he believed, would discover the intense pleasures of the intellect as the source of the greatest human happiness.[56]

For both Aristotle and Darwin, therefore, morality rests on a natural union of instinctive feelings and rational judgments. They would agree neither with Hume's exaggerated claim that reason is the slave of the desires nor with Kant's exaggerated claim that reason discovers the moral law in complete abstraction from natural human desires. For Aristotle and Darwin, reason complements the natural desires by arbitrating conflicts between them to conform to a coherent plan of life, in which each natural desire finds its fullest and most appropriate expression.

Although perhaps never fully attainable, the goal of rationally ordering all the natural desires into a coherent whole can at least be more or less approximated. Success will depend not only on the individual's temperament and thought but also on his physical circumstances and on the way of life of his political community.

Political Intelligence

Human beings are superior to other animals, Aristotle believed, *not* in being the *only* intelligent animals but in being the *most* intelligent animals.[57] The more intelligent animals tend to be the more social or political animals, and human beings are the most intelligent because they are the most political.[58]

Aristotle saw the intelligence of animals such as elephants and dolphins. But he also saw that many animals that are obscure and short-lived have some capacities for learning and teaching through signs.[59] He spoke of wisdom (*sophia*), judgment (*sunēsis*), prudence (*phronēsis*), and art (*technē*) as human cognitive powers corresponding to similar cognitive powers in other animals. He repeatedly referred to the prudence of other animals.[60]

Prudence, unlike science (*epistēmē*) or wisdom, concerns things that vary. Since what is good differs for different species, what is prudent will vary across species. A prudent animal, therefore, is one that exercises foresight with respect to the way of life that is best for the species.[61] Aristotle often refers to bees and other social insects, such as ants and wasps, as outstanding examples of the more prudent animals.[62] Birds also show their prudence in building nests, in cooperating in rearing and teaching their young, and in deceiving predators and prey.[63] He identifies cranes as political animals, and he sees their prudence in their migration over long distances, during which a leader guides their flight and acts as a guard when they stop.[64]

Beginning with Darwin, many modern biologists have confirmed Aristotle's conclusions about animal intelligence. If intelligence is drawing inferences from experience to adapt means to ends, then many animals are intelligent.[65] Studies of animal behavior and cognition support Aristotle's understanding of the "if-then" reasoning in animal movement.[66]

There is also growing evidence to sustain Aristotle's insight as to higher intelligence as an adaptation for complex social life. Aristotle distinguishes solitary animals (*monadika*) and gregarious animals (*angelaia*).[67] Among the gregarious animals, he distinguishes those who are political (*politika*) from those who are not. Political animals are those who live together for some "common work" (*koinon ergon*) or collective action. Examples of political animals are human beings, bees, wasps, ants, and cranes. Some of these such as bees, cranes, and human beings have a leader (*hegemon*), while others do not.

Aristotle seems to adopt what we might call a "cybernetic definition" of politics.[68] Politics is a "steering" process for setting collective goals, organizing collective behavior to pursue those goals, and then altering both the goals and the behavior in response to experience. This requires organizational systems for social communication, social coordination, and social control.

With this understanding of politics, it is not surprising that Aristotle was impressed by the politics of the social insects, and particularly honeybees.[69] Confused by the social complexity of bees, especially in their reproduction, Aristotle confessed that there was a need for more factual observations. He mistakenly concluded that the leaders of bees were males, and that most hives required more than one leader. But he understood the intricate division of labor within a hive that is necessary for its social life, and he could see the flexibility of bees in responding to changing circumstances in order to maintain the good social order of the hive. He described the beehive as a well-ordered political community.

Darwin was also fascinated by the complex social instincts of the social insects.[70] Today, entomologists distinguish various levels of sociality among insects from the solitary to the eusocial, depending upon whether they display one or more of three traits—cooperative care of the young, reproductive division of labor, and overlap between generations so that offspring assist parents.[71] The eusocial insects who possess all three traits include ants, termites, and some bees and wasps. In identifying ants, bees, and wasps as political animals, Aristotle recognized insects with the highest level of social organization. There is hardly any form of socially intelligent behavior that cannot be found among the social insects: child care, eugenics, class structures, social division of labor, fighting over social dominance, group hunting, warfare, slavery, agriculture, animal husbandry, and the second most complex language in the animal world.

While Aristotle does not identify apes as political animals, he does see that they are an intermediate species because they "share in the nature of both man and the quadrupeds."[72] In their feet, legs, hands, face, teeth, and internal parts, the apes are humanlike. He dissected apes and monkeys to discover how their internal parts and structures might resemble those of human beings.[73]

While human beings are distinctive in their upright stance and gait, Aristotle observed that apes show the features of a potentially bipedal animal, although they spend most of their time on all fours. Human bipedalism permits the development of hands instead of forefeet, and the hands can be designed as versatile instruments for acquiring technology guided by human intelligence. The adaptability of the hands for many uses, particularly for many different kinds of weapons, displays human beings as the most versatile animal.[74]

Darwin developed the same thought: human ancestors became bipedal, which freed their hands for uses other than support and locomotion.[75] The use of the arms and hands for fighting, using weapons, and carrying food freed the jaws, mouth, and teeth to adapt for other purposes distinctive to human beings—such as language. The widening of the pelvis, the curving of the spine, and the positioning of the head that characterize human beings all depend on the bipedal stance and gait. Just as Aristotle suggested, apes show a move toward being bipedal. Observations of bonobos—possibly the apes most closely related to human beings—show a remarkably agile bipedal gait.[76]

Modern ethology also gives us some appreciation for Aristotle's comments about the faces of apes. Although he believed that only human beings can properly be said to have a face (*prosopon*), he did speak of apes as having a face that resembled the human face.[77] Aristotle's thought seems to be confirmed by Adolf Portmann's observations of how the faces of the higher animals become ever more expressive of their inner lives.[78] One can also see this in the books of Frans de Waal, Jane Goodall, and other ethologists, in which the photographs of their chimpanzees' faces testify to their mental individuality and personality.[79] One of the important factors in primate evolution was reliance on the face for personal recognition.[80] Darwin saw the universality of some patterns of facial expression as suggesting that they are innate products of evolution, and later research on facial expression supports this conclusion.[81] From research in neuroscience we now know that large portions of the motor and sensory areas of the cerebral cortex are devoted to the face. We also know that damage to the visual system of the brain can produce a syndrome (prosopagnosia) such that a person cannot recognize faces.[82]

The facial expressiveness of chimpanzees is only one of many signs of the diversity in their individual personalities that contributes to the complexity of their political life. As is the case for human beings the political instincts of chimpanzees are flexible, because they are instincts for learning what is appropriate for particular social contexts, so that there is endless variability both within and among chimpanzee communities. Comparing diverse communities reveals different behavioral patterns in communication, diet, and tool use, which represent cultural traditions passed from one generation to another by social learning, traditions apparently originated by inventive individuals and imitated by others.[83]

The intricacy of chimpanzee politics reflects—and explains the evolution of—the sharpness of chimpanzee intelligence. There is much evidence to suggest that primate intelligence, including human intelligence, originally evolved to solve the challenges of social interaction within complex communities.[84] If so, then Aristotle was right: the more political animals are also the more rational animals. But politics demands intelligence not only in the social maneuvering *within* a community but also in the social competition *between* communities. Of the activities that test the mental agility of political animals, none is more urgent or more severe than war.

Military Intelligence

Aristotle regarded human warfare as one form of animal warfare. "Among wild animals, some are always at war with one another; others, as is so for human beings, whenever this happens to occur."[85] Whether animals are friendly or at war with one another depends on the nature of their life and their food. Between predators and prey, and between those competing for the same food, there will be war. But if food is plentiful, or if they live on different kinds of food, they can live in peace.[86]

When Aristotle comments on the usefulness of superior intelligence for human beings, he emphasizes that technology can provide food and weapons.[87] From his biological perspective, the most immediate advantage for human beings in their rationality, their bipedal stance and gait, and in their versatile hand as the "tool of tools," is their flexibility in devising and using weapons. The first requirement for human security is military defense.[88]

But if human beings went to war only to secure the material resources necessary for life or to defend their communities against attack, human warfare would be far less disruptive than it is. What drives the warfare of those political communities best organized for it is the lust for tyrannical domination over other communities. And unlike wars for food or defense, the motivation behind wars for imperial expansion is insatiable.[89]

If primate intelligence evolved to solve the complex problems of social life, to secure the benefits of social cooperation, and to manage the threats of social conflict, this would provide the Darwinian explanation for Aristotle's biological observation that the more political animals are also the more intelligent. And if the most complex challenges of primate life arise in war, where individuals must cooperate with other members of their group in violent, even lethal, competition with those outside their group, then we would expect the evolution of heroic conduct in war. This would explain the evolution in human beings of the virtue of courage.

Courage

In book 3 of the *Nicomachean Ethics*, Aristotle takes up the virtue of courage. He defines it as a mean with regard to fear—and particularly, with regard to the fear of death. Death is the most fearful thing, "for it is the end of one's life, and for the dead nothing is thought to be either good or bad." Courage in the face of death is noblest in war. The cowardly person fears death too much. The rash person fears death too little. The courageous person faces death in the right way, at the right time, in the right circumstances, as dictated by reason. The courageous person fears death in war, but he also fears the bad reputation that would come from being a coward.[90] Aristotle then goes through five ways in which the term "courage" is used. The courage of citizen-soldiers in war is first, and it most resembles true courage, because like Homer's heroes, the citizen-soldiers face death in war because they are afraid of being punished and being dishonored.

Aristotle later goes on to say that the truly courageous people are those who have complete virtue, and therefore happiness, and so life is most worth living for them. Consequently, they will be courageous in war, because they will want to be noble. But these truly courageous people might not make the best soldiers. The best soldiers might be those with less to lose, who might risk their lives for little gain.[91]

In *The Descent of Man*, Darwin explains how the virtue of courage contributed to moral progress through evolutionary group selection:

> It must not be forgotten that although a high standard of morality gives but a slight or no advantage to each individual man and his children over the other men of the same tribe, yet that an increase in the number of well-endowed men and an advancement in the standard of morality will certainly give an immense advantage to one tribe over another. A tribe including many members who, from possessing in a high degree the spirit of patriotism, fidelity, obedience, courage, and sympathy, were always ready to aid one another, and to sacrifice themselves for the common good, would be victorious over most other tribes; and this would be natural selection. At all times throughout the world tribes have supplanted other tribes; and as morality is one important element in their success, the standard of morality and the number of well-endowed men will thus everywhere tend to rise and increase.[92]

In *Darwinian Natural Right*, I quote this passage and compare it with Aristotle's account of courage as manliness in the face of death in war. Carson Holloway has criticized me, however, for not seeing that, while Aristotle recognizes the courage of citizen-soldiers, he does not think this is true courage. The courage of soldiers in war typically comes from a social concern for the good of one's group and a desire to be praised by one's fellow citizens and to avoid being blamed. But this desire for honor, Aristotle suggests, falls short of the desire for nobility, which moves the truly courageous. Holloway argues that, according to Aristotle, the love of nobility or moral beauty transcends the sociable concern for being praised or honored and points to a transcendent or religious conception of perfection that goes beyond the mediocre morality of social praise and blame. Holloway argues that Darwinian ethics reduces morality to "mere sociability or decency" and thus ignores what Aristotle recognizes as the transcendent longing for "nobility or beauty of character," which expresses a "natural religious longing" that requires a "publicly sanctioned revealed religion." Thus, "virtue as Aristotle understands it requires that we transcend virtue as Darwinism understands it."[93]

My response to this criticism turns on two points—one about Aristotle and another about Darwin. First, I would note that what is commonly translated as "noble" in Aristotle's text is the Greek word *kalon*—the "beautiful." Occasionally, Holloway acknowledges this when he speaks of nobility as "moral beauty." The concern for nobility, Aristotle suggests, is a concern for appearing beautiful in the eyes of one's fellow human beings. In our common speech today, we sometimes convey this when we tell someone who has done a noble deed, "That was a beautiful thing you did." Aristotle says that doing what is "beautiful" is "the end of virtue." Moreover, he repeatedly speaks of virtue as what is praised, and of vice as what is blamed.[94] Praise and blame are the common tests of virtue and vice. And thus our morality grows out of our sociality because we are naturally concerned with winning social approbation and avoiding social disapprobation.

As Aristotle suggests in his account of magnanimity (in book 4 of the *Ethics*), those with the greatest virtues are so confident in their knowledge of their virtue that they don't depend on the praise or honor coming from others. The truly virtuous are concerned not so much with being praised as with being praiseworthy. This might explain what Aristotle means by true courage as distinguished from the courage of citizen-soldiers.

A similar thought can be found in Darwin's *Descent*:

The moral nature of man has reached its present standard, partly through the advancement of his reasoning powers and consequently of a just public opinion, but especially from his sympathies having been rendered more tender and widely diffused through the effects of habit, example, instruction, and reflection. It is not improbable that after long practice virtuous tendencies may be inherited. With the more civilized races, the conviction of the existence of an all-seeing Deity has had a potent influence on the advance of morality. Ultimately man does not accept the praise or blame of his fellows as his sole guide, though few escape this influence, but his habitual convictions, controlled by reason, afford him the safest rule. His conscience then becomes the supreme judge and monitor. Nevertheless the first foundation or origin of the moral sense lies in the social instincts, including sympathy; and these instincts no doubt were primarily gained, as in the case of the lower animals, through natural selection.[95]

So while the "first foundation or origin of the moral sense" was in the "social instincts," including the sensitivity to social praise or blame, human reasoning and experience has led to moral progress so that for some human beings, individual conscience has become "the supreme judge and monitor."

Darwin is pointing here to what Adam Smith identified as the "impartial spectator." We begin with a concern for how we appear to others—we want to look good in their eyes. But eventually, we can imaginatively conceive of how we would appear to a well-informed audience of spectators, and this becomes our "conscience" or "inward monitor." We might then act in whatever way seems praiseworthy to us, even when our behavior is blamed by those around us.[96]

Now, Holloway might point to Darwin's appeal to "the conviction of the existence of an all-seeing Deity" as supporting moral conduct that transcends ordinary praise and blame. This does show Darwin's recognition that religious belief can promote moral progress. But for Darwin, this conception of an "all-seeing Deity" can be understood as a product of human cultural evolution. "The idea of a universal and beneficent Creator does not seem to arise in the mind of man, until he has been elevated by long-continued culture."[97]

Aristotle shows the same respect for religious belief that supports morality. But there is no suggestion from either Aristotle or Darwin of any divine command theory of morality, which assumes that morality is impossible without some knowledge of God as the only source of moral norms. Instead, Aristotle and Darwin see religious morality as sanctioning the natural morality that arises from ordinary human experience and cultural evolution.

How do we explain human heroism in war? Why are we willing to sacrifice our lives in war in order to advance our group against its enemies? And why do we honor those who die fighting in war as displaying the virtues of courage and patriotism? We can't presume to understand human beings if we can't explain this universal human propensity to warrior virtues.

Many people who agree with much of what I have to say about "Darwinian natural right" object to my including the desire for war as one of the twenty natural desires. They like the idea of a natural biological basis for love, morality, and cooperation. They don't like the idea that such moral concern might be inseparable from the human disposition to war, because we have evolved to cooperate with members of our group in order to compete with those outside our group. For many of my critics, this shows that my Darwinian view of morality cannot recognize the perfection of morality in universal love, which requires a religious belief in the equal dignity of all human beings as created in the image of God. These critics assume a religious pacifism that I reject as utopian in its denial of human nature and the tragic conflicts of interest that are always part of the human condition.

Some anthropologists have rejected Darwin's scenario of morality evolving through warfare, because they have assumed that the earliest human ancestors who lived in small foraging groups were largely peaceful, and therefore warfare is mostly a product of the cultural history of the agrarian states that arose first about five thousand years ago in large agricultural societies. But now, the anthropological and archaeological evidence surveyed by Lawrence Keeley, Samuel Bowles, and others suggests that warfare was common enough among foraging human ancestors for it to be a factor in human evolution. In fact, some estimates indicate that the rate of mortality in war among primitive human ancestors might have been higher than it was for the human community in the twentieth century, which we recognize as one of the bloodiest centuries in human history.[98]

The virtue of courage displays the natural social instincts of human beings. These social instincts bind us to our community. They move us to risk our lives in fighting against the enemies of our community. They also move us to honor those who manifest the virtue of courage. But to explain these social instincts fully, we need to understand the evolutionary biology of what Aristotle called "friendship" or what Darwin called "sympathy."

Friendship

The longest section of Aristotle's *Nicomachean Ethics* is devoted to "friendship" (*philia*) (books 8–9). For Aristotle, "friendship" becomes a general term for all kinds of social bonding in which human beings show some mutual care for one another. In this way, Aristotle's "friendship" coincides with what David Hume and Adam Smith called "sympathy"—any kind of "fellow feeling" among human beings. Darwin adopted this idea and made "sympathy" one of the fundamental themes in his evolutionary account of moral and political order. More recently, biologists and psychologists have used the word "empathy" in a way that largely corresponds to what Hume, Smith, and Darwin would call "sympathy," or what Aristotle would call "friendship."[99] Running through all of this research is the idea that "friendship," "sympathy," or "empathy"—the psychic propensity for social bonding—arises originally, in evolutionary history and in the life history of individuals, from the biological bond between parent and child, and particularly, mother and child.

The Origins of Social Bonding in Parental Care: Aristotle observes that human beings are by nature not only political animals but also household animals. Indeed, the human coupling instinct is in some sense more natural than the political instinct, because human beings could exist in families even without living in political communities, as was the case throughout early human history when human beings lived in foraging groups of families. Moreover, the various forms of friendly feeling that unite human beings as individuals, fellow citizens, and members of the same species radiate out from the natural affection between parents and offspring that human beings share with birds and other animals.[100] "Consequently," Aristotle asserts, "in the household are first found the origins and springs of friendship, of polity, and of justice."[101]

Darwinian biologists have noticed that animals with the greatest cognitive capacities are often those with the longest periods of childhood dependence on adults. Aristotle agrees:

It would seem that nature wishes to provide for a sensation of attentive care for the offspring. In the lower animals, nature implants this
only until birth; in others, there is care for the complete development of the offspring; and among the more prudent animals [*phro-
nimotera*], there is care for its upbringing. Among those who share
in the greatest intelligence, there arises intimacy and friendship even
towards the completely grown offspring, as among human beings and
some quadrupeds.[102]

Through their love for their children as extensions of themselves, Aristotle observes, husbands and wives strengthen their marital bond because
children are a common good, which is the reason childless marriages are
more easily dissolved. The parental affection of mothers is greater, however, than that of fathers, both because mothers must invest more effort
in pregnancy and childbirth and because they are more certain of their
maternity than fathers are of their paternity.[103]

Beyond the bonds of kinship, unrelated individuals can develop friendly
affection based on a reciprocal exchange of benefits. Rejecting any cosmological explanation of friendship as a force of attraction in physical nature,
Aristotle argues that friendship must be a psychic relation among animals,
"for there is friendship when like-mindedness [*eunoia*] is reciprocal." In
the noblest friendships, people benefit others without expecting anything
in return. But all or most people choose what is beneficial to themselves.
In most cases, therefore, the recipient of a benefit is expected to return
the equivalent of what he has received. Social conflict arises when people
think this reciprocity has not been maintained.[104]

Not only personal friendships but also political communities are held
together by a reciprocal proportionality of benefits. People unrelated to
one another can form associations based on calculations of mutual benefit.
The political community arises from lesser associations to secure the common advantage of citizens for the whole of life. Every community rests on
some sense of friendship founded on the common advantage of its members. Although the strongest feeling of common advantage is among those
who are biologically related, other bonds can arise when there is any reciprocal sense of shared needs.[105]

As a consequence of his biological understanding of animal bonding,
Aristotle sees the moral and political obligations of human beings as a series of concentric circles around the individual. Insofar as justice coincides

with friendship, the claims of justice vary in proportion to the nearness of attachments. One's obligations are stronger to closer relatives than to more distant ones, and stronger to close friends and fellow citizens than to strangers, although there is some friendly attachment to all members of one's species based on shared humanity (*philanthropia*).[106]

As a biologist Aristotle affirms the unity of humankind as one species, "simple and having no differentiation." He believes there can be a kind of sympathy among animals of the same species, and this is especially true for human beings, so that "we praise those who love their fellow human beings."[107] But the humanitarianism of human beings will always be difficult to cultivate and almost always weaker than their egoism, nepotism, and patriotism. This explains the mistake of Plato's Socrates in proposing the community of wives and children and the communal ownership of property for the guardians in the *Republic*: it is unreasonable to ignore the natural love of oneself and one's own that makes it difficult for people to live together if they must share everything.[108] In fact, Socrates concedes that even in the best political community, the warriors would have to be taught that justice is doing good to friends and harm to enemies.[109]

Aristotle's biological claim that parental care for the young is the root from which all other social bonds grow finds support in Darwinian biology. "The feeling of pleasure from society," Darwin believed, "is probably an extension of the parental or filial affections, since the social instinct seems to be developed by the young remaining for a long time with the parents."[110]

This personal bonding between parents and their offspring distinguishes the vertebrates from the insects. Despite the functional similarities between insect and vertebrate societies, the crucial difference is that, in contrast to the impersonal character of insect societies, the vertebrates depend on personal recognition among members of a group. The efficiency of insect divisions of labor among castes was made possible by the evolutionary novelty of sterile castes, which means that the colony becomes the unit of natural selection. But vertebrates depend on individual reproduction. The cooperating castes among social insects are generally sterile, which lessens the genetic competition between cooperating individuals and makes possible the evolution of self-sacrificial altruism. Among the social vertebrates, by contrast, genetic competition between cooperating individuals impedes the evolution of self-sacrificial altruism. As Edward Wilson has noted, the evolutionary path taken by the social vertebrates involves a trade-off, because it "enhances freedom on the part of the individual at the expense of efficiency on the part of society."[111] This explains why the city described in Plato's *Republic* looks in some respects more like a beehive than a community of human beings.

Modern ethologists have shown the importance of the mother-infant bond, especially for primates, as the root of all social bonding. One distinctive trait of primates is the long period of offspring dependence on parental care, which allows for the remarkable growth of the primate brain and extended social learning for the young. Psychologists have noted the harmful, and sometimes fatal, effects of maternal deprivation on infants. We have learned much about the neural and hormonal changes during pregnancy, childbirth, and lactation that promote maternal behavior. Evolutionary psychologists have gathered evidence for the idea that, since females generally invest more in their offspring than do males, females tend to be more devoted to the raising of the young.[112] Here, as on many points of their research, Darwinian biologists and psychologists are rediscovering what was originally discovered by Aristotle in his biological studies.

Sympathy, Empathy, and Mirror Neurons

To see how Aristotle's understanding of "friendship" coincides with the modern understanding of "sympathy" that began with David Hume, consider the following passage in Hume's *Treatise of Human Nature* on the importance of sympathy for social life:

> We observe the force of sympathy thro' the whole animal creation, and the easy communication of sentiments from one thinking being to another. In all creatures, that prey not upon others, and are not agitated with violent passions, there appears a remarkable desire of company, which associates them together, without any advantages they can ever propose to reap from their union. This is still more conspicuous in man, as being the creature of the universe, who has the most ardent desire of society, and is fitted for it by the most advantages. We can form no wish, which has not a reference to society. A perfect solitude is, perhaps, the greatest punishment we can suffer. Every pleasure languishes when enjoyed apart from company, and every pain becomes more cruel and intolerable. Whatever other passions we may be actuated by; pride, ambition, avarice, curiosity, re-

venge or lust; the soul or animating principle of them all is sympathy; nor would they have any force, were we to abstract entirely from the thoughts and sentiments of others. Let all the powers and elements of nature conspire to serve and obey one man: Let the sun rise and set at his command: The sea and rivers roll as he pleases, and the earth furnish spontaneously whatever may be useful or agreeable to him: He will still be miserable, till you give him some one person at least, with whom he may share his happiness, and whose esteem and friendship he may enjoy.[113]

A few paragraphs later, Hume remarks that "the minds of men are mirrors to one another, not only because they reflect each other's emotions, but also because those rays of passions, sentiments, and opinions may be often reverberated, and may decay away by insensible degrees."[114]

In associating "sympathy," broadly understood as fellow-feeling, with "friendship," Hume suggests that this corresponds to Aristotle's use of "friendship" (*philia*) as a broad term for all social bonds. Unlike Thomas Hobbes, therefore, Hume does not think that rationality alone (Hobbes's "laws of nature") can make society possible. Rather, society requires the natural animal tendency to the affective bonding of sympathy. (Hobbes's "natural lust" for the "government of small families" in the state of nature is a confined version of Hume's sympathy.)[115]

Adam Smith elaborated this Humean conception in using sympathy as the social glue for all social bonding and moral life. Darwin then adopted this Humean and Smithian conception of sympathy in explaining the natural social instincts and moral sense. Darwin was impressed by Hume's insistence that sympathy was not uniquely human because it was found in other social animals. "'Tis evident, that sympathy, or the communication of passions, takes place among animals, no less than among men."[116]

Neuroscience is now showing how this sympathy by which the minds of social animals are "mirrors to one another" could be rooted in "mirror neurons." In the early 1990s, Giacomo Rizzolatti and his colleagues at the University of Parma in Italy reported that their neurophysiologial studies of monkeys had uncovered some neurons with remarkable properties. These neurons were activated not only when a monkey performed a certain action—like reaching to pick up a raisin—but also when the monkey observed another monkey or a human being performing the same action.

These "mirror neurons" seemed to show how primates understand the intentional actions of others by simulating those actions within their own brains.[117]

This research on mirror neurons has stirred a lot of popular interest, because if there are mirror neurons in human beings as well as monkeys, this would show how our brain allows us to understand the actions and emotions of other individuals by sharing their experiences in our own minds. The director and playwright Peter Brook observed that mirror neurons would explain the experience of great actors who become as one with their spectators. That we can share the experiences of even fictional characters is a powerful manifestation of our sympathy.

As Rizzolatti indicates, prior to the discovery of mirror neurons, it was common for neurophysiologists to assume that the motor areas of the cerebral cortex were clearly separated from those areas devoted to perception and cognition, and that the moral areas merely executed the orders coming from perceptive and cognitive processes: we perceive what is happening within and around us, we decide by cognition how to respond to these circumstances, and then we command the motor areas of our brain to execute appropriate movements. With the understanding of mirror neuron systems, we have to change the traditional view of our mental processes. The sharp division between perception, cognition, and movement is too artificial, because how we perceive or understand our surroundings is embedded in action. We cannot fully understand the movements of other people through a purely sensory or pictorial representation of those movements. We need mirror neurons through which our brains match the movements we see in others to the movements we ourselves perform. We must translate thought and sensation into movement so that we understand the movements of others by resonating with those movements in our own minds.

In the Platonic tradition of rationalist psychology, the highest activity of the mind is purely contemplative reasoning, which strives to execute its practical decisions by forcing the body to obey the orders of pure reason. In the *Timaeus*, the Divine Craftsman first creates the human mind as the immortal principle of humanity, but then he is forced to create the mortal human body as a chariot for moving the mind around the earth.[118] By contrast to this Platonic understanding of contemplative mind as separated from the moving body, the existence of mirror neurons suggests the pragmatic constitution of human thought as embodied cognition, by which we understand our world not through passive contemplation but through active movement.

In the context of evolution, it makes sense for the brain to be an instrument for active, bodily engagement with the world, because its evolutionary purpose is to organize movements to defend against threats and seek out opportunities. For social animals, the greatest threats and opportunities often come from other animals, and so the brains of social animals are adapted for understanding the thoughts and emotions of other animals so that they can navigate their way through social life to ensure their survival and well-being. Mirror neurons help primates to do this.

Even without the activity of a neural mirror mechanism, we can probably understand the actions and emotions of others through a purely reflexive processing of sensory information. But this purely intellectual understanding would be a colorless perception with no emotional depth. This is probably how psychopaths understand the moral emotions of other people but without actually feeling those emotions themselves. The impaired social understanding of autistic people probably comes from deficits in their mirror neuron systems.

Although neuroscientists have not yet observed mirror neuron activity in human beings at the level of single neurons because of the ethical limits on neural research with living human beings, there is research with human patients suffering selective neural damage and research through neuroimaging that confirms the existence of mirror neuron systems, which function in understanding both actions and emotions. For example, the emotion of disgust is a response to the undesirable taste or smelling of food, and it's associated with distinctive movements around the mouth, the wrinkling of the nose, and feelings of nausea. This experience of disgust requires the activation of the insular cortex of the brain. Our insular cortex is also activated when we observe other people showing the facial expressions of disgust. So the same neural activity necessary for triggering the sensations and expressions of disgust in ourselves is necessary for perceiving this emotion in the faces of other people. It seems that to understand someone else's disgust fully, we need a mirror neuron system that allows us to simulate the experience of disgust in ourselves.

Similarly, Rizzolatti concludes, there is evidence for such mirror neuron processes for all of the primary human emotions—anger, sadness, surprise, enjoyment, contempt, disgust, shame, and fear—that are universal to the human species. Rizzolatti infers that the emotional neuron system is a necessary condition for empathy. To empathize with others, we must share their emotions. But while this is necessary, it is not sufficient for active empathy expressed as caring for others. Understanding someone else's pain is not the same as feeling compassion for that person. (After all, a sadist understands his victim's pain and enjoys it.) Rizzolatti notes:

> Compassion depends on many factors other than the recognition of pain; just to name a few: who the other person is, what our relationship with him is, whether or not we are able to imagine ourselves in his position, whether we want to assume responsibility for his emotive state, wishes and expectations, and so on. If it is someone we know and love, the emotive mirroring caused by the sight of their plight may provoke our pity or compassion; if on the other hand, the person is an enemy or is doing something that constitutes a threat for us, or if we are declared sadists, then the situation changes radically. In all these cases, we understand the other's pain, but we do not necessarily experience empathy.[119]

So here we see the moral ambiguity of our capacity for empathy or sympathy as rooted in neural processes like mirror neurons. On the one hand, having evolved as social animals, we can extend our empathy to our fellow human beings because our minds are "mirrors to one another." On the other hand, having evolved a tribal sociality based on in-group/out-group distinctions, our empathy tends to favor those we identify as friends over those we identify as enemies.

This goes far to explain both the power and the weakness of a cosmopolitan morality of human rights. We can understand the modern history of human rights as the extension of sympathy or empathy to ever-wider groups of human beings. This extension of concern depends upon the neural capacities of human beings for sympathetic understanding and upon the cultural history of moral arguments (sometimes conveyed through literary works) that elicit this sympathetic understanding.

Historian Lynn Hunt has shown how the history of human rights manifests the complex interaction of genetic nature, neural structures, and cultural history. The emotional resonance of empathy expressed in the disgust with cruelty confirms the natural grounding of human rights in human moral emotions. Moreover, Hunt argues, this grounding of human rights in the natural biological propensity for empathy provides a purely human foundation for human rights, without any need to make any religious claims about the moral cosmology of human life as conforming to some sacred order of the cosmos.[120]

Existential Friendship

For Aristotle, a friend is "another self," and thus one's own self-conscious awareness is deepened by seeing oneself reflected in one's friend as a mirror. The most profound form of friendship might be called "existential friendship." This is suggested in those passages of the *Nicomachean Ethics*, where Aristotle uses the term *to einai* for "existence." "Existence is desirable and lovable for all."[121] We love existing, and consequently we love those activities through which we exist, and we love other human beings in whom we can see our existence at work. Love of others is an extension of one's self-loving existence. Mothers love their children as extensions of their own self-loving existence, and this mother-child bond is at the origin of all social bonding. The experience of existential friendship is most fully depicted in the following passage, where the term "existence" (*to einai*) appears four times:

> It appears then that life in the ruling sense is sensation or thought. Now if living itself is good and pleasant (and it seems to be so from the fact that all desire it, and those who are decent and blessed most of all, since the life they lead is most choiceworthy and their living is most blessed), and if one who sees is aware that he sees, and one who hears is aware that he hears, and one who walks is aware that he walks, and similarly in the other cases, there is something in us that is aware that we are at work, so that whenever we perceive, we are aware that we perceive, and whenever we think, we are aware that we think, and if being aware that we are perceiving or thinking is being aware that we are (since our existence is a good thing by nature, and it is pleasant to be aware of the good that is present in oneself), and if being alive is choiceworthy, and especially so for good people, because their existence is good and pleasant for them (since people are pleased by being additionally aware of something that is good in itself), and if a serious person is the same way toward a friend as he is toward himself (since the friend is another self), then just as one's own existence is choiceworthy for each person, so too, or very nearly so, is that of a friend.
>
> But one's existence is choiceworthy on account of the awareness of oneself as being good, and such awareness is pleasant in itself. Therefore, one also ought to share in a friend's awareness that he is, and this would come about through living together and sharing conversation and thinking; for this would seem to be what living together means

in the case of human beings, not feeding in the same place like fat-ted cattle. So if existence is choiceworthy in itself to a blessed person, since it is good and pleasant by nature, and that of one's friend is very nearly the same, then a friend would also be something choiceworthy. But that which is choiceworthy for him ought to be present to him, or he will be deficient in that respect. Therefore, for someone who is going to be happy, there will be a need for friends of serious worth.[122]

Thus, as Aristotle says in the *Eudemian Ethics*: "To perceive and to know one's friend is somehow necessarily to perceive and somehow know one's self."[123]

This full self-awareness of one's personal existence through activities of sensing and thinking shared with one's friends is said to be a "blessed" (*makarios*) state, the Greek term for the "blessed ones"—the gods—or for human beings enjoying a fully happy life of unimpeded pleasure in existence. This existential friendship is for Aristotle what the beatific vision of God in Heaven is for Christians.[124] In Thomas Aquinas's commentary on this passage, he feels compelled to add a qualification that is not found in Aristotle's text: "Here he is discussing the kind of happiness that is possible in this life."[125] Obviously, Aquinas is worried that Aristotle's readers might conclude that this existential friendship brings the deepest happiness simply, and so they might fail to see the need for the happiness of Heaven. Repeatedly, Aquinas has to tell his readers that Aristotle's account of happiness is restricted to earthly happiness and is therefore inferior to the transcendent happiness of Heaven.[126] Aristotle never says this. On the contrary, Aristotle suggests that existential friendship achieves the deepest happiness of which human beings are capable, which comes through the full and unimpeded human activity of sensing, thinking, and desiring in a life shared with one's friends.

The happiness of existential friendship does not come from a solitary life of contemplation, which casts doubt on the claim in book 10 of the *Nicomachean Ethics* that the life of solitary contemplation is the highest. This also denies the famous teaching of Descartes—derived from Augustine—that becoming fully aware of our existence requires a withdrawal from social life into a purely inward experience of one's existence as pure thought thinking itself. For Aristotle, each person's self-conscious existence is a social activity. *I think with my friends, therefore I am.*

As I have already indicated, the natural sociality of human intellectual existence is confirmed by the modern Darwinian idea of the "social brain" in neuroscience and evolutionary psychology. The evolution of the primate brain was probably driven not so much by the need to understand the complexity of the physical world but more by the need to navigate through the intricacies of the social world, which required the ability to read the minds of one's fellow primates in negotiating the terms of social cooperation. The discovery of "mirror neurons" indicates that the primate brain has been designed so that a primate individual can enter the minds of other primates by mentally simulating their conscious experiences. The need of primate offspring for prolonged parental care, which included many years of social learning, created evolutionary pressures for the evolution of primate brains capable of what Aristotle describes as existential friendship.

Contemplation

For Augustine and other early Christian philosophers, Plato's teaching about the immortality of the soul and the supreme happiness of the contemplative life was fulfilled in the Christian understanding of the beatific vision in Heaven as the eternal happiness that all human beings long for, but which only the elect will attain, while the damned go to eternal punishment in Hell.[127] Nietzsche pointed to this when he said that Christianity was Platonism for the common people. But for Plato, immortality was attained only by disembodied spirits, which denied the orthodox Christian teaching that at the Last Judgment all human bodies will be resurrected to eternal salvation or eternal damnation. In the gap between death and the Last Judgment, human souls would exist in some disembodied existence, as Plato believed, but eventually those souls would be reunited with their resurrected bodies, which Plato seemed to deny.

By contrast to Plato, Aristotle defended a biological understanding of the soul as the vital activity of the body, so that mind and body were bound together in an organic unity. Consequently, Christian theologians like Thomas Aquinas looked to Aristotle as the philosopher who could provide the philosophical psychology to justify the Christian doctrine of the resurrection of bodies to eternal life. In his commentary on Aristotle's *Nicomachean Ethics*, Aquinas explains:

> Some philosophers [Plato] held that the intellect is something imperishable and separate; and in their system the intellect would be a

divine thing, for we call those beings divine that are imperishable and separate. Others, like Aristotle, considered the intellect a part of the soul; and in this view the intellect is not something divine by itself but the most divine of all the things in us. This is so because of its greater agreement with the separate substances, inasmuch as its activity exists without a bodily organ.[128]

This comment leads into Aquinas's reading of book 10 (chapters 7–8) of the *Ethics* where Aristotle argues for the superiority of the contemplative life as the best and happiest life. Aquinas can then interpret this as Aristotle's opening to the Christian doctrine of heavenly happiness as the fulfillment of all human desires.

Straussians interpret this part of the *Nicomachean Ethics* as showing Aristotle's agreement with Plato on the philosophic life as the best life for human beings, attainable only by those few human beings who are capable of philosophy, in contrast to the merely moral life of the multitude of human beings. So while most of the *Ethics* presents the moral virtues and practical reasoning as necessary for human happiness and excellence, the Straussians suggest, Aristotle shows in book 10 that the only truly happy life is not a moral life that is available to most human beings, but a purely theoretical life of philosophic contemplation available only to a few. Although most of the Straussians are atheists, they agree with Aquinas's Christian interpretation of Aristotle's *Ethics* as pointing to contemplation as the highest human good.

The difficulties with this interpretation become clear as soon as one looks carefully at Aristotle's arguments in book 10 (chapters 7–8) of the *Ethics*. He presents eight arguments for why a life of theoretical contemplation is superior to a life of moral or political activity. Each of those arguments is remarkably weak, particularly when considered in the context of the whole of the *Ethics*. One must wonder, then, whether Aristotle is being ironical in stating arguments that assume an implausible Platonism.[129]

Consider, for example, the second and third arguments for why theoretical contemplation provides the only true happiness for human beings. Aristotle says that contemplation is the "most continuous" activity of a human being, and that this activity brings pleasures "which are wonderful in purity as well as in permanence."[130] This resembles the Platonic Idea of the Good that Aristotle criticizes in book 1 of the *Ethics*, and there he criticizes the Platonic identification of goodness with permanence. "If indeed a white thing that exists for a long time is not necessarily whiter than a white thing that exists for a day, neither will the Idea of the Good by being eternal be more good than a particular good."[131] And even if "we are able to contemplate continuously more easily than to perform any kind of action," it is still true that human beings cannot engage in any activity continuously because of their compound nature. As Aristotle says elsewhere in book 10 of the *Ethics*, "the same thing is not continuously pleasurable to us because our nature is not simple."[132] A life of continuous pleasure without pain is not possible for human beings.

The fourth argument for the supreme happiness of contemplation is that it is the most self-sufficient of the activities available to human beings.[133] "A wise person is able to theorize even if he is alone, and the wiser he is, the more he can do so by himself." And although it might be better for him to have "co-workers," the wise person is never said here to have friends. But this conception of self-sufficiency as solitariness contradicts what Aristotle says elsewhere about true self-sufficiency as encompassing all those social relationships—children, parents, friends, and fellow citizens—necessary for human beings as social and political animals.[134] Moreover, as we have seen, the longest section of the *Ethics* is the two books devoted to all the various kinds of friendship.

After laying out some of his arguments, Aristotle suggests that they are not sufficient. "We should examine the statements which we have already made by referring them to the deeds and the lives of men, and we should accept them as true if they harmonize with the deeds or facts [*ta erga*] but should regard them merely as arguments if they clash with those facts."[135] So what are the relevant "facts"? Aristotle explains:

> Now he who proceeds in his activities according to his intellect and cultivates his intellect seems to be best disposed and most dear to the gods; for if the gods had any care for human matters, as they are thought to have, it would be also reasonable that they should take joy in what is best and most akin to themselves (this would be man's intellect) and should reward those who love and honor this most, as if they cared for their friends and were acting rightly and nobly. Clearly, all these attributes belong to the wise man most of all; so it is he who would be most dear to the gods, and it is also reasonable that he would be the most happy of men. Thus if we view the matter in this manner, it is again the wise man who would be the most happy of men.[136]

But notice how conditional or hypothetical this argument is, as indicated by the repetition of "if." In Aquinas's commentary on this passage, he removes the conditional mode of expression: "For, supposing—as is really true—that God exercises solicitude and providence over human affairs, it is reasonable for him to delight in that which is best in men and most akin or similar to himself."[137]

Aquinas is confident of God's providential care of and love for human beings. But Aristotle is not. Shortly before this passage suggesting that the gods love philosophers, Aristotle ridicules the idea that the gods have any moral concerns at all.[138] The purest divine activity is completely self-contained because it is "thought thinking itself" (*nous noesis*).[139] If the happiness of the gods comes from purely self-contained contemplative activity, then why would they care for human beings or love philosophers?

The weakness and strangeness of Aristotle's arguments for the supremacy of the philosophic life at the end of the *Ethics* suggest that Aristotle's true teaching is that conveyed in the rest of the *Ethics*—that the human good is attained not just in one dominant good, philosophy, but in the whole range of moral and intellectual goods. Moreover, the intellectual life of the philosopher cannot be a continuous, self-contained activity because the philosopher, like all human beings, needs the right material, bodily, and social conditions for a good human life. Human self-sufficiency must include living with family, friends, and fellow citizens. And even when human beings are fortunate enough to secure all of these conditions for a good life, their life must come to an end, because (as Aristotle says explicitly) immortality is impossible for human beings, and death is the end of life.[140]

To the careful reader of the *Ethics*, Aristotle's Platonic arguments for the supremacy of theoretical contemplation in book 10 (chapters 7–8) actually mock the appeal of Platonic philosophy as catering to the desires for a self-contained, continuous, and invulnerable human pleasure that is free from the contingency and mortality of ordinary human life. Even as he does this, Aristotle reminds us of the fragility and impermanence of all human happiness—the real but fleeting happiness that we can know as embodied animal minds that must decay and die.

Like Aristotle, Darwin recognized man's "god-like intellect" as the supreme attribute of humanity, which allowed men like himself to probe the mysteries of the universe with concern only for "the truth as far as our reason permits us to discover it."[141] Moreover, he recognized that for scientists like himself the intellectual life was the most pleasurable life attainable by human beings.[142] The joy from the noetic contemplation of nature's beautiful order is still a part, perhaps even the primary motivation, of biology and the other sciences. Niko Tinbergen, for example, one of the founders of modern ethology, observed: "Scientific research is one of the finest occupations of our mind. It is, with art and religion, one of the uniquely human ways of meeting nature, in fact, the most active way."[143]

If biological intelligence is identified as the capacity to construct perceptual models of the world, including the social world, and if the extraordinary expansion of the brain in primates, and especially hominids, is a sign of growing intelligence, then we must infer that human intelligence emerged as primates invaded niches in which there were selective pressures to create better models in thought of their physical and social world. The adaptation of animals to their niches requires that they somehow internalize those enduring regularities of the world that are most important to their survival and reproduction. The spatial activities of animals, for example, must conform to the basic geometrical properties of three-dimensional Euclidean space. The navigational abilities of bees illustrate this wonderfully. Niches differ in the degree to which those occupying them must internalize the regularities of the world. Over the course of evolution, we can expect that new and ever more complex forms of life would display increasing degrees of internalization of external regularities. One could argue that human beings have entered the broadest niche—the "cognitive niche."[144]

Most important for social animals like human beings, who live in complex social worlds, would be the cognitive ability to read the minds of other human beings as conscious agents. Insofar as human beings can potentially internalize in thought the most general and abstract principles of the physical and social world—and the success of the natural sciences testifies to this—the human mind can become a microcosm of the whole. As Aristotle says, "The soul is in a way all things, for all existing things are either sensible or knowable."[145]

But then, if the contemplative life is so pleasurable as to provide the fullest happiness for human beings, should we wish for an immortal life of contemplation as the final satisfaction of our deepest desires? Christians long for this as the eternal bliss of the beatific vision of God in Heaven, which can be achieved only by those few human beings who are saved. But Aristotle dismisses the wish for immortality as a wish for the impossible. He also warns that anyone who wishes that he or his friends could become divine and thus immortal is mistaken, because he does not realize that, even if this were possible, it would not be desirable, because it would mean the extinction of oneself and one's friends.

Aristotle's thought seems to be that my personal existence is the activity of my embodied mind interacting with the embodied minds of my friends. My body and their bodies are ageing, and so they must die. Consequently, it would be foolish for me to wish to be immortal. If my embodied mind were somehow transformed so as to be ageless and deathless, it would no longer be *me*. One can see this in Aquinas's claim that when we are resurrected, we will all be at exactly the same age—thirty years old. So those who died in childhood will be pushed ahead to age thirty, and those who died in old age will be pushed back to age thirty. Then we will be frozen in time.[146] Is this what I really want? Or should I see that to wish for my immortality is mistaken, because it's a wish for the extinction of my personal existence. If I were to become immortal, I would be dead.

Aristotle's God

My Darwinian interpretation of Aristotelian morality as founded on a moral biology has provoked many objections. The most common objections assume that morality—including Aristotelian morality—requires religious belief in a cosmic moral order. Many of my critics, including Carson Holloway, John West, C. Stephen Evans, Richard Sherlock, and John Hare, take this position.

John Hare accuses me of ignoring the importance of religious belief in Aristotle's moral philosophy. In his book *God and Morality: A Philosophical History*, Hare tries to show the fundamental influence of theistic religion in the history of Western ethical philosophy.[147] He concentrates on four philosophers—Aristotle, Duns Scotus, Immanuel Kant, and R. M. Hare. These four thinkers represent four periods—ancient, medieval, modern, and contemporary. They represent four kinds of ethical theory as concentrating on virtue, will, duty, and consequences, respectively. And they represent four conceptions of God—God as magnet, God as lover, God as sovereign, and God as model. He pairs each of the four philosophers with successors who abandoned the theological premises of their forerunner. I am paired with Aristotle, Jean-Paul Sartre is paired with Scotus, Christine Korsgaard is paired with Kant, and Peter Singer is paired with R. M. Hare.

For his chapter on Aristotle, Hare begins with a photograph and a description of Raphael's *The School of Athens*. Hare recognizes the obvious suggestion in the painting that Plato is a more "vertical" thinker, in pointing upward to the heavens or the divine, while Aristotle is a more "horizontal" thinker, gesturing downward toward the human beings around them. Hare suggests, however, that this difference between the vertical Plato and the horizontal Aristotle is only a matter of emphasis, and that in fact Aristotle incorporates into his thought the vertical dimension of Platonic religion. He supports this with the claim that Raphael was probably influenced by Renaissance thinkers like Marsilio Ficino and Egidio da Viterbo who had sought to reconcile Plato and Aristotle. Some scholars of Renaissance art believe that Raphael was guided by a program laid down by Egidio, who argued that Plato and Aristotle agreed that humanity combined two natures—the sensual nature that is embedded in matter and the rational nature that is free from matter. While Aristotle stressed the material side of human experience more than did Plato, Aristotle showed his agreement with Plato in the tenth book of the *Ethics* by affirming that the highest part of humanity is pure intellect, which grasps what is divine and eternal by imitating the Divine Intellect.

This introduces Hare's argument that Aristotle agrees with Plato's religion—God as Cosmic Intellect toward which all human beings are drawn by their intellectual love of the Ideas. This is what Hare calls "God as magnet," the magnetic force of the divine radiating out through the Great Chain of Being. Hare offers textual evidence for this conclusion. For example, in the *Timaeus*, it is said that God has given human beings Intellect as a divinity that looks up to heaven, while struggling against the mortal desires of the body:

> When a man devotes himself to the love of learning and to true prudence, and has exercised himself in these things above all others, then there is every necessity, I suppose, that he think thoughts that are immortal and divine (if in fact he touches on truth); and again, to the extent that human nature admits to a share in immortality, he does not fall short of this; and since he's always caring for his divine part and keeping well-arrayed the divinity that dwells within him, he is supremely happy.[148]

This sounds a lot like what Aristotle says about the contemplative life in book 10 of the *Nicomachean Ethics*:

> We should not follow the recommendation of thinkers who say that those who are men should think only of human things and that mortals should think only of mortal things, but we should try as far as possible to partake of immortality and to make every effort to live according to the best part of the soul in us; for even if this part be of small measure, it surpasses all the others by far in power and worth. It would seem, too, that each man is this part, if indeed this is the dominant part and is better than the other parts; so it would be strange if a man did not choose the life proper to himself but that proper to another. And what was stated earlier is appropriate here also; that which is by nature proper to each thing is the best and most pleasant for that thing. So for a man, too, the life according to his intellect is the best and most pleasant, if indeed a man in the highest sense is his intellect. Hence this life, too, is the happiest.[149]

But as I have already noted, the reasoning offered by Plato and Aristotle for this divinization of the human intellect and the elevation of the contemplative life as divine is remarkably dubious. So the careful reader must wonder how seriously to take this.

Hare is ambiguous about this. On the one hand, he clearly thinks we are intended by Aristotle to take his theological language seriously. On the other hand, Hare admits that this theology of the contemplative life is "in tension" with much of what is taught in the *Nicomachean Ethics*. "Unfortunately," Hare admits, "Aristotle gets tentative when he starts talking about God."[150] At least initially, Aristotle is drawing from traditional religious opinions—as in Homer's depictions of the gods. But it's not clear whether Aristotle is sincere about this. Sometimes he speaks of gods in the plural, but then he shifts to speaking of God in the singular. He says that God or the gods are so self-sufficient in their lives that they don't care about human beings. But then he says they love philosophers. Sometimes he suggests divinity is inside us, but at other times he suggests divinity is outside of us. Aristotle indicates that traditionally the gods were originally human beings who were divinized for their heroic deeds by their fellow human beings, which suggests that talk of divinity is just one way of talking of heroic human virtue. Aristotle quotes Homer as having Priam recognize the exceptional goodness of Hector by saying he was a god, and thus "people are turned from humans into gods by a surpassing degree of virtue."[151]

Moreover, Hare is never clear as to what difference this confusing theological language makes for Aristotle's ethical teaching. His general argument is that the case of Aristotle illustrates how morality is impossible without God. But Hare never explains exactly how Aristotle's conclusions about morality depend on his theology. The only clear case of this is that Aristotle apparently thinks that elevating the philosophic life over all other lives requires religious language, but the confusing character of his reasoning makes the reader wonder if he is completely serious about this.

Hare tries to argue that my Darwinian Aristotelianism is not really Aristotelian, because it ignores the theological foundation—the "vertical" dimension—of Aristotle's ethics. But, then, he concedes that I and Aristotle are in agreement on the fundamental principle—that the good is the desirable, and the human good is the harmonious satisfaction of our natural desires over a complete life, which is happiness.[152] And yet Hare also insists that, since I don't accept Aristotle's theistic religion, I can't resolve the tragic conflicts in human desires: "Arnhart is stuck in a difficulty that Aristotle is not."[153]

I argue that sometimes the natural human desires create tragic conflicts between human beings that can only be resolved by force or fraud. For example, in the conflict over slavery in the United States—in which the master's desire for mastery came into conflict with the slave's desire for freedom from exploitation—the only final resolution came with the American Civil War.

Generally, Hare argues that a religiously grounded morality is free of tragedy, because the theistic teaching of universal love allows theists to overcome tragic conflicts of interest. But Hare is never clear about how this works. Does universal love require absolute pacifism and socialism in which all human beings would love one another impartially without any bias toward themselves or those close to them? Consider the famous case of the Dutch householder hiding a Jew in her attic during the Nazi occupation of her country. When the Nazis come to her to ask if there are any Jews in her house, is it immoral for her to lie? Here, Hare admits, is a tragic situation where the woman must lie, but then she must confess that she has violated the moral law against lying. Hare explains: "Putting the difficulty theologically, the person who lies is breaking God's command, but perhaps (given the situation) in the hope of mercy."[154] Hare continues: "In a similar example, some bishops in the early Christian centuries required soldiers who had killed, even in a just war, to abstain for a while from Communion on their return."[155] So does this mean that, although just killing in a just war is against God's commands, God will forgive us for our sin of not loving our enemies? Hare explains: "The position we imagine as ideal is one in which all the people involved, including ourselves, are loved the same. But that is not a position we in fact occupy. It is the position God occupies, if there is a God."[156] It is hard for me to see how this provides any reliable guidance for our moral conduct.

Even with all of his insistence that morality without God is impossible, Hare actually concedes that there is a natural moral sense that allows atheists and believers to understand one another's moral language. Some people might understand the chemical properties of water, while others might not. But they could all talk about "water" with mutual understanding, without having to talk about its chemical properties. Similarly, Hare suggests, theists and atheists can talk about what is "right" or "good" with mutual understanding, even though the atheists will not share the belief of the theists that what is "right" and "good" ultimately arises from God's commands.[157] If this were Hare's position, then he would be agreeing with me that, while religious belief can reinforce our moral judgments, our morality can stand on its own natural ground as part of our evolved human nature—even without religious belief.

God and Morality

While Christian philosophers like Hare assert that Aristotle's ethics depends on his belief in God as the cosmic source of the good, others argue, on the contrary, that Aristotle's lack of religious belief blinds him to the truth that morality can arise only from the command of God. For example, J. Budziszewski complains that Aristotle does not see that moral standards of the good are "given or sustained by a sovereign God," and consequently, Aristotle "misses the specific moral *point* of the moral virtues, seeing them not as qualities that men ought to have, but only as qualities that happy and noble men actually do have."[158]

A divine command theory of morality drives much of the criticism of my Darwinian defense of Aristotelian virtue. The assumption of divine command reasoning is that moral obligation must be grounded in the commands of a good and loving God. If God did not exist, there could be no moral obligations.

One of the best statements of this divine command theory of morality is C. Stephen Evans's book *Kierkegaard's Ethic of Love: Divine Commands and Moral Obligations*.[159] Evans has a chapter criticizing my reasoning in *Darwinian Natural Right* as an example of "evolutionary naturalism." Evans endorses what he takes to be Kierkegaard's divine command morality as founded on the command of Jesus to love our neighbors, understood as a universal and disinterested love of all human beings equally. Evans then criticizes my reasoning as flawed insofar as I don't acknowledge that all morality must be rooted in such a divine command of universal love.

As I have already indicated, Darwin sees a natural tribalism in human morality. We are inclined to be more cooperative with those close to us—relatives, friends, and fellow citizens—than to those far away. Human beings are naturally inclined to cooperate within groups so as to compete successfully with other groups. Darwin thinks a universal sympathy for humanity is possible, but only as an extension of social emotions cultivated first in small groups. He assumes that, as we expand our social sympathies to embrace all of humanity, these sympathies become weaker as we move farther away from our inner circle of family, friends, and fellow citizens. And yet this extension of sympathy to embrace all of humanity is strong enough to support the Golden Rule as the foundation of morality. Still, the tribalism of morality can never be eliminated. Charity starts at home. And in war, we properly celebrate the virtuous courage of soldiers in killing the enemy.

Although Evans does not draw out the full implications of his view of universal love as a divine command, he suggests that this requires absolutely disinterested love for all human beings equally, which would require absolute pacifism.[160] Favoring our friends, relatives, and fellow citizens over strangers violates this universal love commandment. Using violence against evil individuals violates it. And fighting in war certainly violates it, even if the war seems to be just. Universal love might even require the abolition of private property and family life. Pacifist socialism would seem to be required. It is hard to see that many human beings could embrace this as morally acceptable.

Evans finds God's commands in the Bible. But it is not clear that the Bible provides the clear moral teaching of universal love that Evans wants. God commanded Abraham to kill his son Isaac. Evans says that while God might have commanded human sacrifice in the past, we know that God cannot command that "today."[161] He seems to assume that the love command of Jesus in the New Testament overrides the bloody commands of the God of the Old Testament. The brutal commands of the Old Testament God include orders to slaughter innocent women and children as part of God's conquest of Canaan, as whole cities are put under the "curse of destruction."[162] But even the New Testament concludes with the bloodiest book of the Bible—the Book of Revelation, with its vision of the apocalyptic battle of the saints against Satan at the end of history.

Evans criticizes my Darwinian arguments for the abolition of slavery and insists that the immorality of slavery arises only from its violating God's love command.[163] But Evans says nothing about the fact that all the passages in the Bible on slavery endorse it, and thus the antebellum Christians in the American South were justified in believing that slavery was biblically sanctioned.[164]

The Bible lacks the authority, clarity, and reliability necessary for being a source of moral guidance. If the Bible reinforces morality, it is only because we pass it through our natural moral sense. We know that the biblical account of God ordering Abraham to kill his son must be somehow mistaken, because we know by natural moral experience that this is wrong. We know that the Bible's endorsement of slavery is mistaken, because again our natural moral sense condemns it. If we elevate the Golden Rule over other teachings in the Bible, it's because we have arrived at the rule through natural experience. That experience also teaches us, however, that disinterested, universal love cannot be absolutely observed because we rightly favor family, friends, and fellow citizens over strangers. The Christian tradition of "just war" reasoning shows how our natural moral sense corrects the dangerous utopianism of a universal love ethic.

THE FEAR OF CARTESIAN SCIENCE

A common objection to my Darwinian interpretation of Aristotelian virtue comes from a fear of Darwinian science as advancing the crude reductionism of modern Cartesian science. This fear of Cartesian reductionism is evident in much of the writing in this book, which shows the influence of Leon Kass and Peter Lawler.

Kass and Descartes

My relationship to Kass's writing is complicated and ambivalent. As a young man, I decided that what Leo Strauss called the "fundamental di-

lemma" of modernity explained the loss of liberal education as a comprehensive study of the whole. The natural sciences assume a materialist
reductionism that cannot account for the human mind or spirit. The humanities assume a radical dualism that treats human conscious experience as autonomous in its separation from the causal order of the natural
sciences. The social sciences are then torn between these two contradictory positions. We might overcome this dilemma, I thought, if we could
see Darwinian biology as a comprehensive science that would unify all
the intellectual disciplines by studying human experience as part of the
natural whole. This would continue the Aristotelian tradition of biology
because, as Strauss observed, Aristotle believed that biology could provide
"a mediation between knowledge of the inanimate and knowledge of
man."[165] But I found that many of those influenced by Strauss assumed
that Darwinian biology must deny the fundamental premises of Aristotelian natural right in denying the uniqueness of human beings as set
apart from the rest of animal nature and in denying the cosmic teleology
that sustains human purposefulness.

Reading Kass's *Toward a More Natural Science* helped me to see how
I might answer these Straussian objections. Kass suggested that Darwinian biology could recognize human uniqueness as a product of emergent
evolution, and it could recognize the internal teleology of living beings
as goal-directed. Darwin failed to see how his own biology allowed "that
certain differences of degree—produced naturally, accumulated gradually
(even incrementally), and inherited in an unbroken line of descent—might
lead to a difference in kind (or at least its equivalent), say, in mental capacity or inner life." So it seemed that Darwinian biology could support an
emergent naturalism in which novel traits arise in evolutionary development at each higher level of organization in an "unbroken line of descent"
leading to differences in kind. Differences in degree passing over a critical
threshold of evolution could produce differences in kind.[166]

On the question of teleology, I was impressed by Kass's distinction between "external teleology" and "immanent teleology." External teleology
is the conception of all of nature as an organic whole in which all beings
serve a cosmic purpose set by an intelligent designer or creator. By contrast to such cosmic teleology, Kass suggested that "the primary home of
teleological thought is the internal and immanent purposiveness of individual organisms, in their generation, their structure, their activities." This
immanent teleology of living things was what Aristotle had in mind, Kass

observed, when he spoke of natural teleology. And while Kass recognizes that Darwinism was generally regarded as rejecting cosmic teleology, he notes that Darwinian biology implicitly assumed the immanent teleological nature of organisms. Even if evolution by natural selection is not purposeful, it produces organic beings that are purposeful. Plants and animals grow to maturity, and once grown they act for ends set by the functional nature of the species.[167]

I was inspired by Kass's striving for "a more natural science" that would require the kind of biological understanding of nature that could account for the ethical and intellectual purposefulness of human life as an expression of nature. Like Kass, I sought a biological science that recognizes "the tacit ethical dimension of animal life," and thus the "natural, animal bases for the content of an ethical life." Like Kass, I believed that a science of living nature would reject both reductionist monism, which reduces life to homogeneous matter, and transcendentalist dualism, which sees human mental and moral experience as radically separated from the rest of nature. Like Kass, I decided that such a science could bring together Aristotle and Darwin.[168]

In recent years, however, Kass has moved away from his Aristotelian/ Darwinian naturalism, because he doubts the sufficiency of human reason unaided by the biblical revelation of God as nature's Creator.[169] Now he argues that modern science assumes a materialism that reduces all knowledge to quantifiable objectification that denies the qualitative subjectivity of "lived experience" and the "inwardness of life." As transformed into "scientism," which assumes that such scientific objectification is the only true form of knowledge, this modern scientific project threatens human freedom and dignity. Kass then wonders whether philosophy or religion can provide an adequate philosophy of nature to challenge the false claims of modern scientism.

Kass's mistake is that in his recent writing he fails to recognize (as he did in his earlier writing) that Darwinian biology refutes the Cartesian vision of science. Kass's fundamental presupposition is that René Descartes' writing is paradigmatic for all of modern science. Again and again, Kass quotes from or refers to Descartes as the authoritative spokesman for modern science. He thus implicitly takes for granted a view of the history and philosophy of early modern science that came out of the German phenomenological tradition, which was transmitted to the curriculum of St. John's College by Jacob Klein, and which has influenced Kass in his years at St. John's and the University of Chicago.

Unlike Kass, I am not convinced that Descartes' philosophical writing is canonical for all of modern science. Kass often cites Hans Jonas's *The Phenomenon of Life*, but he ignores Jonas's argument in that book that Darwinism refuted Descartes' dualistic separation of objective matter and subjective mind. "Evolutionism undid Descartes' work," Jonas explains, because "the continuity of descent now established between man and the animal world made it impossible any longer to regard his mind, and mental phenomena as such, as the abrupt ingression of an ontologically foreign principle at just this point of the total flow," and so "with the last citadel of dualism there also fell the isolation of man, and his own evidence became available again for the interpretation of that to which he belongs."[170] In fact, many Darwinian scientists now recognize that Darwinism affirms the continuity of animal minds as products of emergent evolution. For example, Steven Pinker shows how Darwinian science refutes Descartes' dualism.[171]

In following the St. John's/phenomenological tradition, Kass assumes that "mathematical physics is the jewel and foundation" of all science, and biology is reducible to mathematical physics.[172] But this ignores the autonomy of biology and biological phenomena as an emergent realm of study that must be consistent with but cannot be fully reducible to physics and chemistry. Ernst Mayr and other modern biologists have argued this position very well.[173]

Kass says that genetics cannot tell us "how the life of a cockroach differs from that of a chimpanzee."[174] But this ignores the biological study of animal behavior and cognitive ethology. For example, primatologists like Jane Goodall and Frans de Waal observe the natural lives of primates either in the wild or in captivity, and in explaining the primates' behavior they infer the emotional and cognitive experiences that constitute their subjective lives. Much of the debate in primatology today is about how far we can properly go in inferring "animal minds" from our own subjective experiences as self-conscious animals. To say, as Kass does, that all biologists assume that man is "a freakish speck of mind in a mindless universe" restates Descartes' view, but this is contradicted by those many biologists who reject Cartesian dualism and recognize the necessity to explain animal behavior as shaped by subjective consciousness.

What does religion contribute to this discussion? Kass is evasive about this. In his interpretation of Genesis 1, he rejects both "creation science" and "intelligent design," because he assumes that the Creation story in the

Bible is not really a literal description of how the universe came into being. Rather, the Creation story teaches "self-evident truths" about the "existential condition" of human beings that "do not rest on biblical authority."[175]

It is not clear whether Kass thinks he is learning something from biblical revelation that he could not know by philosophic reason alone, or whether the Bible offers an account of the human condition that confirms what we might already know by reason and common experience. In fact, when Kass refers to "the mysterious source of being itself," he seems to be following Martin Heidegger's existential philosophy of how human *Dasein* faces the mystery of Being.[176]

Kass's reading of Genesis 1—like all of his readings of the Bible—is thoughtful, imaginative, and elegant.[177] But it is not clear to me that this is the way biblical believers read the Bible. Clearly, Kass is reading the Bible under the influence of philosophical commentators like Kant and Strauss. There is surely much to ponder in such a reading. But this seems to be more philosophic than it is religious. If Kass were to return to his original project for a "more natural science" that would be both Aristotelian and Darwinian, he could argue for a Darwinian naturalism that would recognize the importance of religion insofar as it reinforces our natural moral sense and expresses our natural desire for religious understanding.

So, I am not persuaded by Kass's assumption that we can look to René Descartes—and particularly, his materialist reductionism—as determining the whole history of modern science. Descartes' dualistic separation of matter and mind and his physicalist reductionism deny the emergent complexity of living phenomena as studied by Darwinian biology. To illustrate his claim about Descartes as the founder of all modern science, Kass says that "in a revolution-making passage in the *Rules for the Direction of the Mind*, Descartes sets the program of all modern science by transforming how we should approach the study of color."[178] Descartes says that we can study colors by arbitrarily identifying them as corresponding to various geometrical figures. Kass notes: "Descartes's geometrical figures, standing for the differences among the colors white, blue, and red may be passé, but the principle he proposes is not: today we still treat color in terms of 'wave lengths,' purely mathematical representations from which all the color is sucked out. This tells the whole story: the objective is purely quantitative. All quality disappears."[179]

Is this really "the whole story" of the scientific study of color? Certainly, part of the story is that scientists explain visible light as a continuously varying wavelength. But this is not the whole story, because wavelengths of light have no color intrinsic to them. Color arises only for animals that have neural systems of vision that translate the variations in wavelength into color perceptions. Different species perceive different colors or none at all.

Many anthropologists used to say that human color perception was an arbitrary creation of culture depending on the variable color vocabularies of different human languages. But in the 1960s, a famous experiment conducted by Brent Berlin and Paul Kay showed that this variation in color vocabularies followed a regular pattern indicating a universal of human nature.[180] Native speakers of twenty languages from around the world were asked to look at a Munsell array showing the full spectrum of colors and then apply the color terms from their languages. Although there was great variation, the variation followed a universal pattern moving from two to eleven basic color terms. The reason for this is that the human sensory system for vision tends to break down the continuing varying wavelengths of visible light into discrete units.

Notice that Berlin and Kay had to ask their subjects to report their subjective experience of color in the terms of their color vocabularies. Color as a perceptual quality is known to us only by our subjective experience. But we can testify to that qualitative experience through language that can then be the basis for scientific study. It is not true, then, that for modern science, "all quality disappears."

Edward O. Wilson offers the Berlin and Kay study of color vocabularies as an example of "gene-culture coevolution" guided by "epigenetic rules." He states:

> The brain constantly searches for meaning, for connections between objects and qualities that cross-cut the senses and provide information about external existence. We penetrate that world through the constraining portals of the epigenetic rules. As shown in the elementary cases of paralanguage and color vocabulary, culture has risen from the genes and forever bears their stamp. With the invention of metaphor and new meaning, it has at the same time acquired a life of its own. In order to grasp the human condition, both the genes and culture must be understood, not separately in the traditional manner of science and the humanities, but together, in recognition of the realities of human evolution.[181]

In my chapter on "emergence" in *Darwinian Conservatism*, I indicated that although Wilson sometimes identifies "consilience"—the unity of all knowledge—as based on a strong form of reductionism, he has to recognize the emergent complexity of life that cannot be explained through strong reductionism.[182] So, for example, the epigenetic rules of human biology shape the broad patterns in color vocabularies that are universal propensities across all human societies. But within those broad patterns, the specific content of color vocabularies will be determined by linguistic practices, social customs, and deliberate choices that are peculiar to some particular group. Our scientific studies of color perception must combine quantitative methods of objectified science with the qualitative experience of human subjects expressed in language. Such scientific study of the emergent complexity of life is lost in Kass's assumption that Descartes' reductionism "sets the program of all modern science."

Lawler's Gnostic Existentialism

Much of the opposition to Darwinian explanations of human nature is rooted in the claim that modern science cannot properly account for the "transcendental self." This is the idea that human beings have some psychic or spiritual capacity that sets them apart from and above the rest of nature. Against this idea, Darwinian science explains human beings as fully within the order of nature and thus at home in the universe.

The transcendentalist rejection of Darwinism can be either religious or secular. Religious transcendentalism affirms the uniqueness of human beings as created in God's image and thus set above the rest of creation. Secular transcendentalism affirms the uniqueness of human beings as having the capacity through reason or culture to create themselves as belonging to a realm of freedom beyond the realm of natural causality. Religious conservatives often adopt the first form of transcendentalism. Secular liberals often adopt the second.

The transcendentalism that denies Darwinian naturalism assumes a radical dualism of mind and matter that follows not from orthodox Christianity but from the Christian heresy of Gnosticism. The Gnostics believed that the natural world was a prison into which the human soul was thrown by the evil god of the Old Testament. The escape from this worldly prison required Gnostic enlightenment by which the redeemed could leave the natural world for their true home beyond the cosmos. Matter is evil. Only spirit is good. Therefore, the Gnostics believed, Jesus as divine was pure spirit without body (contrary to the orthodox Christian doctrine of incarnation).

Hans Jonas wrote one of the classic books on Gnosticism.[183] His studies of Gnosticism allowed him to recognize that the modern existentialist tradition—from Pascal to Nietzsche to Heidegger—rested on the Gnostic idea of human beings as aliens in the universe, transcendental selves seeking to escape their imprisonment in nature. He saw this modern existentialist version of Gnosticism as a reaction against the modern Cartesian conception of the universe as a material mechanism without mind or spirit. The existentialist attack on modern natural science as a materialistic reductionism that denies human dignity and freedom was a modern restatement of the Gnostic image of human beings as aliens in a world of dead matter. This Gnostic idea was originally stated by Plato, who depicted the birth of human beings in the *Timaeus* as a burial and imprisonment of the divine nature in the mortal flesh of earthly life.[184]

The Gnostic attack on modern science and appeal to the transcendental self is evident in the writing of Walker Percy—particularly, his book *Lost in the Cosmos*.[185] Percy rightly argues that symbolic thought and conceptual speech are uniquely human. But to suggest that natural science cannot explain this—because it is some kind of mysterious miracle that shows a transcendental self beyond nature—ignores the possibility that the human capacity for symbolic thought evolved from the non-symbolic thought of apes.

Percy's existentialist Gnosticism has been the basis for Peter Lawler's existentialist conservatism. According to Lawler, all human beings are "aliens" in the universe, because their true selves transcend the natural order of the universe, and thus natural science can never truly account for the alienated spirit of humanity.[186] Darwinian science, in particular, denies this reality of the transcendent self. Lawler has been an influential voice among conservatives who reject Darwinian science as a reductive materialism.

These existentialist conservatives fail to see how Darwinian science actually refutes any Cartesian reductionism that separates matter and mind. Although it initially looked like the final triumph of materialism, the Darwinian concept of evolution actually rejected the terms of modern materialism by denying the absolute separation of objective matter and subjective mind. By showing how the human mind could emerge out of nature and by affirming the continuity of human beings and other animals as conscious beings, Darwinian science denied the radical transcendence of human beings as set apart from nature. But it also thereby elevated the whole living world by presenting it as the meeting place of matter and mind, and thus it overcame the Cartesian conception of human beings as isolated and alienated thinking beings in an unthinking world. Darwinian science exposed the absurdity of Cartesian dualism as denying organic reality and our psychophysical experience as bodies in which mind emerges naturally.

I reject the existentialist conservatism of Lawler and others who follow the Gnostic tradition of radical dualism in which human beings are seen as transcendent selves who wander the earth as aliens thrown into a cosmic prison. The secular transcendentalism of the Left shows the same Gnostic dualism in which matter and mind must be forever separated, and any Darwinian explanation of human nature arouses abhorrence as a degrading denial of human freedom and dignity. Against this Gnostic transcendentalist assumption that human worth requires that we set human beings apart from nature as if they were aliens from another world, the Darwinian Aristotelian would say that we have not been thrown into nature from some place far away. We come from nature. It is our home.

Love and Death

Lawler has criticized my Aristotelian Darwinism with the objection that, even if it conveys a partial truth about human life, it overlooks what human beings most care about—love and death. I don't understand Lawler's claim that "Arnhart denies that love and death are essential to our being," and that I cannot account for "the fact of our deep loneliness or of our deep longing to be known and loved by other persons."[187] I find it odd that he says this, considering that I stress the natural desires for friendship, conjugal love, parental care, and familial bonding as manifestations of our evolved nature as social animals, and that I also speak about the natural human longings for religious understanding and intellectual understanding in the face of the mysteries of life and death.

I disagree with Lawler's assertion that Darwin advanced an "impersonal theory of evolution" denying the personal reality of love and death.[188] Anyone who examines Darwin's life and writings can see how his scientific thinking was embedded in his personal life, and particularly in his experience with love and death in his family and his circle of friends. Darwin's home in Down, in southern England, has been wonderfully restored to its condition when Darwin was living there. When I spent a day there, a few years ago, I was impressed by the poignant way in which the home and the surrounding buildings and grounds evoke Darwin's life in science surrounded by family and friends who shared in his thinking. So, for example, when Darwin was studying the mental abilities of earthworms, he had his children play their musical instruments around a worm, while he took notes on the worm's movements to see if there was any evidence that worms could hear music.

One of the best studies of how Darwin's science arose from his personal struggles with love and death is Randal Keynes's book *Annie's Box: Charles Darwin, His Daughter and Human Evolution*.[189] Keynes is a great-great-grandson of Darwin and a great-nephew of John Maynard Keynes. Some years ago, he came across a child's writing case that had belonged to Annie Darwin, the first daughter of Charles and Emma who died when she was ten. The writing case was filled with personal items that Emma had saved to remember her daughter. Charles had written a note recording how Annie felt every day during her last months, and then after her death, he wrote a memorial to record his memories of her character and life. As Keynes collected this and related material, he began writing his book as a study of how Annie's death in 1851 shaped her father's understanding of love and death in ways that guided his scientific thinking about the natural world.

A few days before his wedding, Charles told Emma that, during his five years traveling on the *Beagle*, "the whole of my pleasure was derived from what passed in my mind," but he now looked to marriage to take him out of himself. "I think you will humanize me, and soon teach me there is greater happiness, than building theories and accumulating facts in silence and solitude."[190] After a short time living in London, he spent the rest of his life doing his scientific work surrounded by his family in his home in Down. The family included ten children, of whom seven lived to adulthood. Mary died in 1842, within three weeks of her birth. Annie died in 1851. Charles Waring died in 1858, at age four. Annie's death, after six months of severe illness, was especially traumatic for Charles and his family.

Charles responded to his children with both the warm feelings of a father and the methodical observations of a scientist. He kept careful records of how his children developed in infancy to support his "natural history of babies," which would help him understand the earliest psychological development of human emotions and thoughts as compared with other animals. In one of his scientific papers—"A Biographical Sketch of an Infant"—he wrote about the first evidence of a "moral sense" in one of his children:

The first sign of moral sense was noticed at the age of nearly 13 months. I said "Doddy [his nickname] won't give poor papa a kiss— naughty Doddy." These words, without doubt, made him feel slightly uncomfortable; and at last when I had returned to my chair, he protruded his lips as a sign that he was ready to kiss me; and he then shook his hand in an angry manner until I came and received his kiss. Nearly the same little scene recurred in a few days, and the reconciliation seemed to give him so much satisfaction, that several times afterwards he pretended to be angry and slapped me, and then insisted on giving me a kiss. So that here we have a touch of the dramatic art, which is so strongly pronounced in most young children.[191]

He also learned from his own paternal feelings and from Emma's maternal care the importance of parental love in nurturing the individual development of each child. Charles's mother had died when he was eight. He regretted later in life that he could not recall many clear memories of her. When Annie died, he was careful to preserve a summary of his memories of her, written one week after her death. In about fifteen hundred words, he sketched her character, her appearance, and her behavior. He wrote:

Our poor child, Annie, was born in Gower St on March 2nd 1841 and expired at Malvern at Midday on the 23rd of April 1851. I write these few pages as I think in after years, if we live, the impression now put down will recall more vividly her chief characteristics. From whatever point I look back at her, the main feature in her disposition which at once rises before me is her buoyant joyousness, tempered by two other characteristics, namely her sensitiveness, which might easily have been overlooked by a stranger, and her strong affection. Her joyousness and animal spirits radiated from her whole countenance and rendered every movement elastic and full of life and vigour. It was delightful and cheerful to behold her. Her dear face now rises before me, as she used sometimes to come running down stairs with a stolen pinch of snuff for me, her whole form radiant with the pleasure of giving pleasure. . . .

Her figure and appearance were clearly influenced by her character: her eyes sparkled brightly; she often smiled; her step was elastic and firm; she held herself upright, and often threw her head a little backwards, as if she defied the world in her joyousness. . . .

Her health failed in a slight degree‍ for about nine months before her last illness; but it only occasionally gave her a day of discomfort: at such times, she was never in the least degree cross, peevish or impatient; and it was wonderful to see, as the discomfort passed, how quickly her elastic spirits brought back her joyousness and happiness. . . . When so exhausted that she could hardly speak, she praised everything that was given her, and said some tea "was beautifully good." When I gave her some water, she said "I quite thank you"; and these, I believe were the last precious words ever addressed by her dear lips to me.

But looking back, always the spirit of joyousness rises before me as her emblem and characteristic: she seemed formed to live a life of happiness: her spirits were always held in check by her sensitiveness lest she should displease those she loved, and her tender love was never weary of displaying itself by fondling and all the other little acts of affection.

We have lost the joy of the household, and the solace of our old age: she must have known how we loved her; oh that she could now know how deeply, how tenderly we do still and shall ever love her dear joyous face. Blessings on her.[192]

At the time, no one really understood the cause of Annie's death except that she suffered from a "bilious fever." She probably died of tuberculosis, which was known at the time as "consumption," for which there was no cure. It was not until 1882 that the German bacteriologist Dr. Robert Koch identified the cause of the disease as bacterial—*Mycobacterium tuberculosis*.

So how should loving parents understand and cope with the death of a child? In Victorian England, there were a variety of beliefs about how to handle such a loss. Orthodox Christians consoled themselves that their dead children would go to Heaven, and that parents would eventually be reunited with their children in Heaven. Christians could believe that such death was designed by God to teach the need for faith in undergoing suffering. For many religious believers, death was God's punishment for the Original Sin of Adam and Eve, and even innocent children had to pay the price for the sin of Adam. Or such believers might see the death as the punishment for some personal sin of the parents.

For some people, however, such beliefs were dubious. Despite the common view that the Bible teaches eternal life after death, the biblical account of the afterlife is vague, and the character of Heaven and Hell is not clearly explained. Moreover, why should we be consoled by belief in eternal life if we can't be sure about whether we (or our children) will go to Heaven or Hell? It is hardly consoling to believe that most human beings will suffer eternal punishment in Hell. Some people decided that everyone goes to Heaven, which began the modern tendency of Christians to believe in Heaven but not Hell.

And why should we rely on scriptural authority for knowledge of an afterlife, if this is not supported by evidence from natural human experience and reasoning? In any case, it's not clear that even those who profess to believe in an afterlife really believe it strongly enough for this to overcome their natural feeling that death is the end. Some people wondered why a God who is both all-powerful and all-good would allow the innocent to suffer and die. They also wondered about the fairness of God in condemning most people to eternal punishment in Hell. Some Victorians thought that we should accept death as a consequence of natural causes that we cannot alter. This seemed to be Alfred Tennyson's response when his first child was stillborn (three days before Annie Darwin's death):

> Little bosom not yet cold,
> Noble forehead made for thought,
> Little hands of mighty mould
> Clenched as in the fight which they had fought.
> He had done battle to be born,
> But some brute force of Nature had prevailed
> And the little warrior failed.[193]

"Some brute force of Nature had prevailed." What more should be said about the death of a child—or of any human being?

How did Emma and Charles Darwin respond to the death of Annie? As a Unitarian who believed in the eternal afterlife, Emma tried to console herself with the thought that she would be reunited after death with her family in Heaven. She was troubled that Charles did not find the evidence for such beliefs convincing. Over her life, as she and Charles talked about this and read books on the debate over the evidence for personal immortality with eternal rewards and punishments, she became less confident about her beliefs, although she was always more openly pious than Charles.

In his early life, Charles Darwin was an orthodox Christian believer. By the middle of his life, he had concluded that there was insufficient evidence for the divine authority of the Bible and traditional Christian doctrines. By the end of his life, he identified himself as an agnostic. Some people assumed he was a complete atheist. But he always insisted that he was open to the possibility of God as First Cause of the natural laws governing the universe. Yet he worried that searching for the ultimate causes of all things was beyond the natural limits of the human mind. "The mystery of the beginning of all things is insoluble by us," he observed.[194]

He was clear, however, in rejecting the traditional doctrines of God as having separately created every form of life and as providentially intervening to control every event in natural and human history. He laid out the evidence and arguments for species as originating from ancestral species through natural laws of evolution, although he indicated that this was consistent with believing in God as the Creator of those natural laws. Persuaded by the evidence of experience and science that nature was governed by general laws, Darwin could not believe in any miracles, except possibly the original miracle by which the laws of nature themselves were created. He rejected the traditional teaching that God would condemn all unbelievers to everlasting punishment as a "damnable doctrine."[195]

Darwin also rejected the traditional belief in God's particular providence, because he could not see how a just God could be responsible for "the clumsy, wasteful, blundering low and horridly cruel works of nature." It would be a more sublime notion of God, he thought, to say that God was not responsible for the cruelty of nature as governed by the "universal struggle for life." He believed it was "more satisfactory to attribute pain and suffering to the natural sequence of events." So at the end of *The Origin of Species*, he leaves his reader with the image of how "endless forms most beautiful" evolved "from the war of nature, from famine and death."[196]

Darwin learned this from his personal experience of love and death. He could love Annie as his beautiful child. He could understand her death as coming from her losing struggle for life in the war of nature. He could cherish his memories of her vibrant personality, as preserved in his memorial essay, but without any expectation of being reunited with her in an afterlife. He could also engage in scientific research on the natural causes of suffering and death with the hope that such knowledge could provide some relief.

Although Darwin did not understand how Annie's disease was caused by microorganisms, he did develop an evolutionary theory of how parasites and hosts co-evolve in the struggle for life. In 1877, a scientific friend of his sent him an article by Dr. Robert Koch, who would later discover the bacillus that causes tuberculosis. The article contained the first photographs of bacteria, along with Koch's argument that such microorganisms could cause diseases. Darwin replied: "I well remember saying to myself between twenty and thirty years ago [about the time of Annie's death], that if ever the origin of any infectious disease could be proved, it would be the greatest triumph to Science; and now I rejoice to have seen the triumph."[197]

So now Darwin's science can explain why his daughter died. She died because she lost her struggle for life in the war of nature with tubercular bacteria. She was defeated by a "brute force of Nature." Without a scientific understanding of her disease, he could not save her life. But he could save his memories of her in all her beautiful exuberance. "She held herself upright, and often threw her head a little backwards, as if she defied the world in her joyousness." There is dignity in this Darwinian view of human life, as it offers us the joy of love, the pain of death, and the feeling of wonder as we try to understand it all.

CONCLUSION

After Darwin returned from his voyage on the H.M.S. *Beagle* in 1836, he began writing out his thoughts in a series of notebooks. In one of those notes, he wrote: "Read Aristotle to see whether any of my views very ancient?"[198]

In 1882, William Ogle wrote a translation of Aristotle's *Parts of Animals*, and he sent a copy to Darwin. After reading it, Darwin wrote back: "From quotations which I had seen, I had a high notion of Aristotle's merits, but I had not the most remote notion what a wonderful man he was. Linnaeus and Cuvier have been my two gods, though in very different ways, but they were mere schoolboys to old Aristotle."[199]

My argument has been that, indeed, Darwin's views—and particularly his views of the biological nature of morality—coincide with Aristotle's moral biology, and thus Darwin's science of morality supports Aristotle's empiricist morality in contrast to the moral cosmology of Plato and the transcendentalist tradition of moral thought that began with Plato. This is the argument that has led Frans de Waal to observe that, in my writings, "Darwin and Aristotle have begun to blend into a single person, perhaps to be called Darwistotle."[200]

A Darwistotelian science of virtue invites us to make ourselves at home in nature. It does that by providing an evolutionary ground for Aristotle's moral biology. That's why Aristotelians need Charles Darwin.

NOTES

When I presented this essay at Berry College, Paul Seaton responded with some comic remarks. Later, he wrote the essay that appears in this book, but I did not see his essay until this book was going to the publisher. So I had no opportunity to reply to it. Instead of replying to it here, I leave the reader to decide whether he engages my arguments.

1. Larry Arnhart, *Darwinian Natural Right: The Biological Ethics of Human Nature* (Albany: SUNY Press, 1998), 29–36; Larry Arnhart, *Darwinian Conservatism: A Disputed Question*, ed. Kenneth Blanchard (Exeter, UK: Imprint Academic, 2009), 26–34.

2. David Hume, *Enquiry concerning the Principles of Morals*, ed. Tom Beauchamp (New York: Oxford University Press, 1999), 91.

3. Thomas Aquinas, *Summa Theologica*, I.Q.5, A.6.

4. Richard Joyce, *The Evolution of Morality* (Cambridge: MIT Press, 2006).

5. Rémi Brague, *The Wisdom of the World: The Human Experience of the Universe in Western Thought* (Chicago: University of Chicago Press, 2004).

6. Marcia Hall, ed., *Raphael's "School of Athens"* (Cambridge: Cambridge University Press, 1997); Christiane L. Joost-Gaugier, *Raphael's Stanza della Segnatura* (Cambridge: Cambridge University Press, 2002).

7. See Brague, *Wisdom of the World*; Arthur O. Lovejoy, *The Great Chain of Being* (Cambridge: Harvard University Press, 1936); C. S. Lewis, *The Discarded Image: An Introduction to Medieval and Renaissance Literature* (Cambridge: Cambridge University Press, 1964).

8. Joseph Cropsey, *Plato's World: Man's Place in the Cosmos* (Chicago: University of Chicago Press, 1997); Catherine Zuckert, *Plato's Philosophers: The Coherence of the Dialogues* (Chicago: University of Chicago Press, 2009).

9. Plato, *Phaedo*, 97c–100b.

10. Plato, *Timaeus*, 20a.

11. *NE*, 1141a21–b2. In references to Aristotle's works, I use the following abbreviations: *Eudemian Ethics (EE), Generation of Animals (GA), History of Animals (HA), Metaphysics (Meta), Nicomachean Ethics (NE), Parts of Animals (PA), Politics (Pol)*. My translations of the *Nicomachean Ethics* have been much influenced by the translations of Hippocrates G. Apostle and Joe Sachs. I have used the Greek texts in the Loeb Classical Library series of Harvard University Press.

12. *On the Heavens*, 270b1–25, 279a5–32, 284a1–25, 291b24–92a20, 298b7–99a2; *Meta*, 1074a31–b14.

13. *PA*, 644b22–45a5; *Meta*, 987a30–b15.

14. *NE*, 1141a31–32.

15. Charles Darwin, *The Descent of Man, and Selection in Relation to Sex*, 2nd edition, ed. James Moore and Adrian Desmond (New York: Penguin Books, 2004), 120.

16. Immanuel Kant, *Critique of Practical Reason*, trans. Lewis White Beck (Indianapolis: Bobbs-Merrill, 1956), 89–90 (Prussian Academy edition, 86–87).

17. Darwin, *Descent*, 120.

18. Frances Power Cobbe, *Darwinism in Morals, and Other Essays* (London: Williams and Norgate, 1872), 5–8; Darwin quoted from Janet Browne, *Charles Darwin: The Power of Place* (New York: Alfred A. Knopf, 2002), 297; Cobbe, *Darwinism*, 5.

19. Cobbe, *Darwinism*, 5–8 (8).

20. Darwin, *Descent*, 122–23.

21. Cobbe, *Darwinism*, 10–11.

22. Joyce, *Evolution*, 125–27.

23. Friedrich Nietzsche, *Untimely Meditations*, trans. R. J. Hollingdale (Cambridge: Cambridge University Press, 1983).

24. Nietzsche, *Meditations*, 29–32 (29, 30, 32).

25. Ibid., 29, 30.

26. Friedrich Nietzsche, *The Portable Nietzsche*, trans. Walter Kaufmann (New York: Viking Press, 1968), 515–16.

27. Darwin, *Descent*, 137, 151.

28. Darwin, *Descent*, 151.

29. See C. Stephen Evans, *Kierkegaard's Ethic of Love: Divine Commands and Moral Obligations* (New York: Oxford University Press, 2004); John E. Hare, *God and Morality: A Philosophical History* (Cambridge, MA: Wiley-Blackwell, 2007); Carson Holloway, *The Right Darwin?* (Dallas: Spence Publishing, 2006).

30. Nietzsche, *Portable*, 685.

31. Ibid., 554.

32. Friedrich Nietzsche, *Human, All Too Human*, trans. R. J. Hollingdale (Cambridge: Cambridge University Press, 1986), sec. 2.

33. Nietzsche, *Human*, secs. 27, 476.

34. Ibid., sec. 153.

35. Ibid., sec. 164.

36. Friedrich Nietzsche, *Basic Writings of Nietzsche*, trans. Walter Kaufmann (New York: Random House, Modern Library, 1968), 532.

37. Nietzsche, *Meditations*, 112–13.

38. Ibid., 77, 78, 107, 110, 121.

39. Lou Salomé, *Nietzsche*, trans. Siegfried Mandel (Urbana: University of Illinois Press, 2001); Robin Small, *Nietzsche and Rée: A Star Friendship* (Oxford: Oxford University Press, 2005); Paul Rée, *Basic Writings*, trans. Robin Small (Urbana: University of Illinois Press, 2003); Gregory Moore, *Nietzsche, Biology and Metaphor* (Cambridge: Cambridge University Press, 2002); John Richardson, *Nietzsche's New Darwinism* (New York: Oxford University Press, 2004).

40. Bruce Benson, *Pious Nietzsche: Decadence and Dionysian Faith* (Bloomington: Indiana University Press, 2008).

41. Nietzsche, *Portable*, 561.

42. Friedrich Nietzsche, *The Will to Power*, ed. Walter Kaufmann (New York: Random House, 1967), 539.

43. Nietzsche, *Basic Works*, 37.

44. Hans Jonas, *Memoirs*, ed. Christian Wiese, trans. Krishna Winston (Waltham, MA: Brandeis University Press, 2008), 48–50.

45. Leo Strauss, "Note on the Plan of Nietzsche's *Beyond Good and Evil*," in *Studies in Platonic Political Philosophy* (Chicago: University of Chicago Press, 1983), 174–91 (191).

That this essay on Nietzsche is the central chapter in this book on "Platonic political philosophy" is significant for Straussians—indicating that Nietzsche's atheistic religiosity is the peak expression of Strauss's Platonism.

46. Harvey Mansfield, *Manliness* (New Haven, CT: Yale University Press, 2007), 83, 86.

47. *HA*, 588a15–89a10.

48. *NE*, 1152b1–8.

49. *NE*, 1174b15–76a29.

50. *NE*, 1176a6.

51. *NE*, 1153b25–36, 1176a3–22.

52. *NE*, 1174a1–3, 1176b23–25.

53. *NE*, 1148b15–49a20.

54. *NE*, 1152b1–8.

55. Darwin, *Descent*, 136, 140. See also Charles Darwin, *Charles Darwin's Notebooks, 1836–1844*, ed. Paul H. Barrett et al. (Ithaca, NY: Cornell University Press, 1987), 619–22.

56. Darwin, *Notebooks*, 548–49.

57. *PA*, 686a24–87a23.

58. *Pol*, 1253a7–18.

59. *HA*, 608a10–17, 630b–31b2.

60. *HA*, 588a29–31, 611a15, 612a2, 614b19, 618a24.

61. *NE*, 1141a22–33.

62. *PA*, 648a6–8, 650b24–26.

63. *HA*, 612b18–20b9.

64. *HA*, 614b19–26.

65. Charles Darwin, *The Formation of Vegetable Mould, through the Action of Worms* (London: John Murray, 1881), 34–35, 64–98, 312–13; J. T. Bonner, *The Evolution of Culture in Animals* (Princeton, NJ: Princeton University Press, 1980); Donald Griffin, *Animal Thinking* (Cambridge: Harvard University Press, 1984); Sue Savage-Rumbaugh, Stuart G. Shanker, and Talbot J. Taylor, *Apes, Language, and the Human Mind* (New York: Oxford University Press, 1998).

66. Martha Nussbaum, *Aristotle's "De Motu Animalium"* (Princeton, NJ: Princeton University Press, 1978).

67. *HA*, 488a1–14.

68. Peter Corning, *The Synergism Hypothesis* (New York: McGraw-Hill, 1983), 6–7, 209–11, 313–18.

69. *HA*, 553a17–54b21, 623b5–29b4; *GA*, 759a8–61a12.

70. Charles Darwin, *The Origin of Species and The Descent of Man* (New York: Random House, The Modern Library, 1936), 59, 186, 193–202, 473, 639.

71. Edward Wilson, *The Insect Societies* (Cambridge: Harvard University Press, 1971).

72. *HA*, 502a16.

73. *HA*, 502a17–27, 502b25–26; *PA*, 689b1–35.

74. *PA*, 656a3–14, 686a24–88a11, 689b2–90b8, 694b26–95a14.

75. Darwin, *Origin*, 433–36, 439–40.

76. Frans de Waal and Frans Lanting, *Bonobo: The Forgotten Ape* (Berkeley and Los Angeles: University of California Press, 1997).

77. *HA*, 491b9–11, 502a20–21; *PA*, 662b19–23.

78. Adolf Portmann, *Animal Forms and Patterns* (New York: Schocken Books, 1967).

79. Frans de Waal, *Chimpanzee Politics: Power and Sex among Apes* (Baltimore: Johns Hopkins University Press, 1997); Jane Goodall, *The Chimpanzees of Gombe* (Cambridge: Harvard University Press, 1986).

80. Edward O. Wilson, *Sociobiology: The New Synthesis* (Cambridge: Harvard University Press, 1975), 516–17.

81. Charles Darwin, *The Expression of the Emotions in Man and Animals*, 3rd edition, ed. with introduction, afterword, and commentaries by Paul Ekman (New York: Oxford University Press, 1998); Paul Ekman, ed., *Darwin and Facial Expression: A Century of Research in Review* (Cambridge, MA: Malor Books, 2006).

82. Oliver Sacks, *The Man Who Mistook His Wife for a Hat* (New York: Summit Books, 1985); Dale Purves et al., eds. *Neuroscience*, 4th ed. (Sunderland, MA: Sinauer Associates, 2008), 671–73.

83. Goodall, *Gombe*, 143–45, 265, 560–64; A. Whiten, J. Goodall, W. C. McGrew, T. Nishida, V. Reynolds, Y. Sugiyama, C. E. G. Tutin, R. W. Wrangham, and C. Boesch, "Cultures in Chimpanzees," *Nature* 399 (1999): 682–85; Kevin N. Laland and Bennett G. Galef, eds., *The Question of Animal Culture* (Cambridge: Harvard University Press, 2009).

84. Robin Dunbar, Louise Barrett, and John Lycett, *Evolutionary Psychology* (Oxford: Oneworld, 2007), 110–27.

85. *HA*, 610a3–4.

86. *HA*, 608b20–10a33.

87. *PA*, 686a24–88a11.

88. *NE*, 1177b1–27; *Pol*, 1265a19–39, 1267a18–37, 1323a14–25b32.

89. *Pol*, 1271b1–11, 1324b1–12.

90. *NE*, 1115a10.

91. *NE*, 1117b1–20.

92. Darwin, *Descent*, 157–58.

93. Holloway, *The Right Darwin?*, 45–46, 51, 58.

94. *NE*, 1101b32, 1103a10, 1109b30–35, 1115b13, 1155a17–21.

95. Darwin, *Descent*, 682.

96. Adam Smith, *The Theory of Moral Sentiments* (Indianapolis: Liberty Classics, 1982), 129.

97. Darwin, *Descent*, 682.

98. Samuel Bowles, "Did Warfare among Ancestral Hunter-Gatherers Affect the Evolution of Human Social Behavior?" *Science* 324 (June 5, 2009): 1293–98; Jung-Kyoo Choi and Samuel Bowles, "The Coevolution of Parochial Altruism and War," *Science* 318 (October 26, 2007): 636–40; Carsten K. W. De Dreu et al., "The Neuropeptide Oxytocin Regulates Parochial Altruism in Intergroup Conflict among Humans," *Science* 328 (June 11, 2010): 1408–11; Azar Gat, *War in Human Civilization* (Oxford: Oxford University Press, 2006); Lawrence Keeley, *War before Civilization* (New York: Oxford University Press, 1996).

99. Jean Decety and William Ickes, eds., *The Social Neuroscience of Empathy* (Cambridge, MA: MIT Press, 2009); Jean Decety and Philip L. Jackson, "The Functional Architecture of Human Empathy," *Behavioral and Cognitive Neuroscience Reviews* 3 (2004): 71–100; Gustav Jahoda, "Theodor Lipps and the Shift from 'Sympathy' to 'Empathy,'" *Journal of the History of the Behavioral Sciences* 41 (2005): 151–63; Stephanie Preston and Frans de Waal, "Empathy: Its Ultimate and Proximate Bases," *Behavioral and Brain Sciences* 25 (2002): 1–72; Frans de Waal, *The Age of Empathy: Nature's Lessons for a Kinder Society* (New York: Harmony Books, 2009).

100. *NE*, 1155a1–33, 1159a27–37, 1160b23–62a29.

101. *EE*, 1242b1–2.

102. *GA*, 753a8–14.

103. *NE*, 1161b16–29, 1162a16–28, 1166a1–9, 1168a20–27.

104. *NE*, 1155b34.

105. *NE*, 1132b33–33a5, 1159b25–62a34.

106. *NE*, 1155a16–29, 1159b25–60a8, 1165a14–36.

107. *HA*, 490b18; *NE*, 1155a20–21.

108. *Pol*, 1262b22–25, 1263a31–b31.

109. Plato, *Republic*, 332a–c, 375a–e, 469b–d; *Cleitophon*, 410b.

110. Darwin, *Descent*, 129.

111. Wilson, *Insect Societies*, 460.

112. Sarah Blaffer Hrdy, *Mothers and Others: The Evolutionary Origins of Mutual Understanding* (Cambridge: Harvard University Press, 2009); Melvin Konner, *The Evolution of Childhood* (Cambridge: Harvard University Press, 2010).

113. David Hume, *Treatise of Human Nature*, ed. David Fate Norton (New York: Oxford University Press, 2000), 2.2.5.15. Citations to this work refer to book, part, section, and paragraph.

114. Ibid., 21.

115. Thomas Hobbes, *The Leviathan*, ed. Richard Tuck (Cambridge: Cambridge University Press, 1991), ch. 13, p. 89.

116. Hume, *Treatise*, 2.2.12.1. See also Darwin, *Notebooks*, 591, 627; Darwin, *Descent*, 132.

117. Giacomo Rizzolatti, *Mirrors in the Brain* (Cambridge: MIT Press, 2008); Giacomo Rizzolatti, Leonardo Fogassi, and Vittorio Gallese, "The Mirror Neuron System: A Motor-Based Mechanism for Action and Intention Understanding," in Michael Gazzaniga, ed., *The Cognitive Neurosciences*, 4th ed. (Cambridge: MIT Press, 2009), 625–40.

118. Plato, *Timaeus*, 69b–c.

119. Rizzolatti, *Mirrors*, 191.

120. Lynn Hunt, *Inventing Human Rights: A History* (New York: Norton, 2007).

121. *NE*, 1168a1–10.

122. *NE*, 1170a25–b19.

123. *EE*, 1245a35–38.

124. Augustine, *City of God*, xxii, 27–30.

125. Thomas Aquinas, *Commentary on Aristotle's "Nicomachean Ethics,"* trans. C. I. Litzinger (Notre Dame, IN: Dumb Ox Books, 1993), sec. 1911.

126. Ibid., secs. 113, 129.

127. Augustine, *City of God*, viii, 4; xxii, 25–29.

128. Aquinas, *Commentary*, sec. 2084.

129. For this interpretation, see Germaine Paulo Walsh, "The Problematic Relation between Practical and Theoretical Virtue in Aristotle's *Nicomachean Ethics*," in Kenneth Grasso and Robert Hunt, eds., *A Moral Enterprise: Politics, Reason, and the Human Good* (Wilmington, DE: ISI Books, 2002), 59–81, 354–60.

130. *NE*, 1177a21–28.

131. *NE*, 1096b4–5.

132. *NE*, 1154b21–23, 1177a21–23.

133. *NE*, 1177a28–34.

134. *NE*, 1177a 28–34.

135. *NE*, 1179a20–22.

136. *NE*, 1179a23–34.

137. Aquinas, *Commentary*, sec. 2133.

138. *NE*, 1178b8–18.

139. *Meta*, 1074b15–75a11.

140. *NE*, 1111b19–23, 1115a25–29.

141. Darwin, *Descent*, 689.

142. Darwin, *Notebooks*, 549.

143. Niko Tinbergen, "On War and Peace in Animals and Man," *Science* 160 (1968): 1411–18 (1411).

144. R. N. Shepard, "Evolution of a Mesh between Principles of the Mind and Regularities of the World," in J. Dupré, ed., *The Latest on the Best: Essays on Evolution and Optimality* (Cambridge, MA: MIT Press, 1987), 251–75.

145. *De Anima*, 431b19.

146. Aquinas, *Summa Theologica*, Suppl., Q.81, A.1.

147. Hare, *God and Morality*.

148. Plato, *Timaeus*, 90b–c.

149. *NE*, 1177b31–78a8.

150. Hare, *God and Morality*, 17, 19.

151. *NE*, 1145a20–24.

152. Hare, *God and Morality*, 55, 69, 71, 254, 271, 278.

153. Ibid., 72.

154. Ibid., 282.

155. Ibid., 282–83.

156. Ibid., 285.

157. Ibid., 272.

158. J. Budziszewski, *Written on the Heart: The Case for Natural Law* (Downers Grove, IL: InterVarsity Press, 1997), 187–88.

159. Evans, *Kierkegaard's Ethic of Love*.

160. Ibid., 319, 328.

161. Ibid., 307.

162. Numbers 31; Deuteronomy 20.

163. Evans, *Kierkegaard's Ethic*, 239–44.

164. Mark Noll, *The Civil War as a Theological Crisis* (Chapel Hill: University of North Carolina Press, 2006).

165. Strauss, Letter to Alexandre Kojeve, May 28, 1957, in Leo Strauss, *On Tyranny*, revised and expanded edition, ed. Victor Gourevitch and Michael S. Roth (New York: Free Press, 1991), 279.

166. Leon Kass, *Toward a More Natural Science: Biology and Human Affairs* (New York: Free Press, 1985), 12, 14 (also 39, 59–63, 76–79).

167. Ibid., 253–64 (253, 254).

168. Ibid., 277, 284, 295, 347; Leon Kass, *The Hungry Soul: Eating and the Perfecting of Our Nature* (Chicago: University of Chicago Press, 1999), 62.

169. Leon Kass, *Life, Liberty and the Defense of Dignity: The Challenge for Bioethics* (San Francisco: Encounter Books, 2002), 277–97; Leon Kass, *The Beginning of Wisdom: Reading Genesis* (New York: Free Press, 2003), xiv–xv, 1–4, 15, 68.

170. Hans Jonas, *The Phenomenon of Life: Toward a Philosophy of Biology* (New York: Dell, 1966), 57.

171. Steven Pinker, *The Blank Slate: The Modern Denial of Human Nature* (New York: Viking, 2002), 8–10.

172. Leon Kass, "Science, Religion, and the Human Future," *Commentary* (April 2007): 37.

173. Ernst Mayr, *What Makes Biology Unique? Considerations on the Autonomy of a Scientific Discipline* (Cambridge: Cambridge University Press, 2004).

174. Kass, "The Human Future," 39.

175. Ibid., 39, 45–46.

176. Ibid., 46.

177. Ibid., 44–46; Kass, *Wisdom*, 1–122.

178. Kass, "The Human Future," 47–48 (47); also Kass, *Defense of Dignity*, 277–97.

179. Kass, "The Human Future," 48.

180. Brent Berlin and Paul Kay, *Basic Color Terms: Their Universality and Evolution* (Berkeley and Los Angeles: University of California Press, 1970).

181. Edward O. Wilson, *Consilience: The Unity of Knowledge* (New York: Knopf, 1998), 163.

182. Arnhart, *Darwinian Conservatism*, 106–8.

183. Hans Jonas, *The Gnostic Religion: The Message of the Alien God and the Beginnings of Christianity*, 2nd ed. (Boston: Beacon Press, 1958).

184. Plato, *Timaeus*, 74a–d.

185. Walker Percy, *Lost in the Cosmos: The Last Self-Help Book* (New York: Farrar, Straus and Giroux, 1983).

186. Peter Augustine Lawler, *Aliens in America: The Strange Truth about Our Souls* (Wilmington, DE: ISI Press, 1999).

187. Peter Augustine Lawler, "All Larry Needs Is Love (and Death)," in Blanchard, *Darwinian Conservatism*, 180.

188. Ibid.

189. Randal Keynes, *Annie's Box: Charles Darwin, His Daughter and Human Evolution* (London: Fourth Estate, 2001).

190. Ibid., 188.

191. Charles Darwin, "A Biographical Sketch of an Infant," in *The Collected Papers of Charles Darwin*, ed. Paul H. Barrett, 2 vols. (Chicago: University of Chicago Press, 1977), 2:197–98.

192. Keynes, *Annie's Box*, 200.

193. Ibid., 300.

194. Darwin, *Descent*, 200.

195. Ibid., 201.

196. Darwin, *Origin*, 440.

197. Keynes, *Annie's Box*, 300.

198. Darwin, *Notebooks*, 325.

199. Darwin, Letter to William Ogle, February 22, 1882.

200. Frans de Waal, *The Ape and the Sushi Master: Cultural Reflections of a Primatologist* (New York: Basic Books, 2001), 81.

13

LOGON DIDONAI THE CASE OF THE DARWINIAN CONSERVATIVE

Paul Seaton

WITH DR. LARRY ARNHART, A NEW FORM OF THOUGHT and, perhaps, of life has emerged among us. As such, it elicits wonder and calls for consideration. As thoughtful life, it possesses more interest for me, a Socratic, than the appearance of a new star. Moreover, as a form of thoughtful life, it is self-aware and it can talk. It has even named itself. It is a hybrid, it is "Darwinian Conservatism."

Moreover, it is a form of life and thought on a mission; it is animated by missionary zeal. For example, within the past year or so it traveled to China, where it instructed and exhorted adherents of Confucianism to become Darwinian Confucians. After that it repaired to Georgia, where it attempted to do the same with Aristotelians. As this globe trotting indicates, it is convinced of its truth and of its goodness for humanity. Therefore, while in Darwinian terms this new form of thought wants to propagate itself, in more standard religious terms, it wants to announce its glad tidings of reconciliation, teach sound doctrine, and form human beings and communities more or less after its image and likeness. As such, it bears comparison with other forms of missionary life going back to St. Paul. Therefore it is of interest to me as a Catholic.

It is at this juncture, though, that I must note another feature of this way of life and draw a self-protective inference. To state matters directly: this form of life and thought is dangerous to be around; it is a lightning rod, regularly attracting bolts of criticism from various quarters and throwing its own bolts in return. One runs the risk of being struck, singed, scorched, or even fried by being in its vicinity. My inference from this, put in the language of my religious communion, is *Caveat proximus, caveat specialiter criticus*. Let those in the vicinity beware, especially the critic.

This danger is near-nigh unavoidable, though. This apparently militant form of thought is enlisted in a great struggle; it is a participant in our culture wars. Its self-designation, Darwinian Conservatism, indicates as much. On one hand (the conservative hand), it does battle with those Darwinians—and with others whom Arnhart calls "the Left"—who think that Darwinism has progressive entailments, that man can make and remake himself and society as he desires or sees fit. Not so, retorts the Darwinian Conservative. We have evolved as humans and we are hardwired a certain way, so that certain progressive hopes and projects are *contra naturam*. Darwin himself, for example, was quite pro-traditional family, he laid great stress upon the mother-child bond and its all-important role in human socialization and in humanization *tout court*.

Darwinism rightly understood also recognizes and legitimates politics and even war as essential features of the human scene; it resists any pacific transpolitical hopes we, or progressives, might entertain. And, rightly understood, Darwinism also recognizes the human need, desire, or instinct for religious faith and practice (although, truth be told, it also places certain strictures on these). In these ways and others, the Darwinian Conservative maintains that Darwinism is the friend and (here the pun is irresistible, but also meaningful) the *natural* ally of conservative moral commitments and public policy options. (The pun is significant because Arnhart takes his view of Nature and the natural as normative, as the chief evaluative yardstick for morality as well as religious belief and practice, not to mention political and economic life.)[1]

Therefore, conservatives, says the Darwinian Conservative, should get over their animosity toward Darwinism and see it properly, for what it is. While not a member of the believing fold (an important segment of the sometimes fractious conservative coalition), Darwinism is an ally in contemporary battles. It is particularly valuable because it has the credibility of science behind it, one of the modern world's few acknowledged authorities. As a Darwinian conservative, you can be credible, contempo, and conservative at the same time. A nice trifecta.

Here, too, however (that is, among conservatives), the Darwinian Conservative's ambition has been regularly frustrated. Rather than gratefully receiving his benevolent offer, all too many conservatives, especially religiously minded ones, have refused it and have turned on him in critique and in real or apparent hostility. Hence, the reciprocation of lightning bolts, as he practices his own Darwinian-based-and-tinged understanding of the Golden Rule, which is not the same as Jesus'.

After reading and reflecting on Arnhart's lengthy essay, I put my observations, thoughts, comments, and criticisms into two broad categories: those that are extrinsic to and those that are intrinsic to Arnhart's text and argument. He talks about Plato and, especially, Aristotle, for example, so I could work within his text and ask about this or that feature of what he says about the two, not to mention other authors he engages (St. Thomas, David Hume, Adam Smith, Leon Kass, etc.). On the other hand, he never mentions an author whom I read regularly, Joseph Ratzinger, formerly Benedict XVI, but the two do share common interests in nature, morality, science, culture, and religion, so I could bring them into dialogue with one another.

Many reasons, however, led me to the conclusion and conviction that genuine philosophical dialogue was unlikely with Arnhart. This was a disconcerting conclusion. I will have to present the evidence and reflections that led to it. But even in the face of this conclusion, I was duty-bound to say something about the author and his text. And truth be told, I did find his mind, his form of reading and thinking, his worldview and his ethics, genuinely worth considering as well as critically engaging. But, as I said, I had strong reasons for thinking he and I would not be able even to "achieve disagreement," as the phrase goes. So, as a sort of apologia for my doubts, I decided to lay out two strands of my reasoning to this conclusion (parts 1 and 2) and then turn, in a sort of second sailing, to Socrates for help in engaging Arnhart (part 3).[2] Let me dilate a bit on this structure and these decisions, as I am acutely aware of their oddity as a critical response to Arnhart's lengthy essay.

I.

For the record, I do think that the human phenomenon is more complex, puzzling, and even mysterious than Darwinism of any sort can acknowledge, much less account for. But this remains to be determined—determined in the first instance, though, by the phenomena themselves, what in a fancy way we could call the *explinanda* (the things to be explained), in contradistinction from the *explinantes* (explanatory factors and frameworks). Arnhart's chief and characteristic adjective in his scientific lexicon is the past participle "evolved," and his characteristic intellectual move is to look back in evolutionary history and "down-and-around," that is, to seek for pre-human prototypes-and-sources of distinctively human characteristics. It would take a special effort on his part to consider anything human in its own right and terms, apart from its genetic origins. Throughout, there was, it seemed to me, a decided *parti pris*, a strong and generally unresisted backward "gravitational" pull, to his thinking. For example, he articulates and advocates for "evolutionary psychology," so human psychological traits need to be connected with and more *and less* construed in terms of various other animals' (and in terms of contemporary brain science).[3]

I, however, believe that before one does evolutionary psychology (or evolutionary anthropology, or cultural evolution), one should do psychology (et cetera), that is, closely observe, faithfully and adequately describe, and try to put into a coherent picture, the recognizably human traits of thought and emotion and volition and character and aspiration and. . . . To be sure, this is a massive field to survey, it is a huge intellectual task in its own right, and no one individual is up to it. But it is only on such a basis that what calls out for explanation—*all* that calls out for explanation— stands forth. To speak colloquially, if one doesn't get one's ducks lined up in order initially, one might fail to see that there's a particular duck that needs to be accounted for, or one might let one's preferred explanatory factor or framework predetermine what duck-things have to be. That would be a falsifying of data in a very special way.

Nor am I particularly daunted by the oft-made claim that there are no facts apart from theory. I believe (and practice and observation have confirmed this belief) that one can exercise *haute naiveté*, what Paul Ricoeur called "a second naiveté," and become critically self-aware in one's looking, observing, and describing of the relevant facts.[4] Plus, theories themselves can become the objects of philosophical examination and assessment (more on this in a moment).

Hence, I characteristically turn to thinkers in the phenomenological tradition, especially in controverted areas, to serve as honest brokers, as respectable middlemen. Inaugurated by Edmund Husserl, phenomenology is a form of thinking that wants to look freshly at phenomena and to describe them faithfully and not prejudge them, much less immediately place them in this or that purportedly explanatory framework (including that of "evolved"). Otherwise, as I said, one runs the risk of ignoring relevant data, of obscuring them, of reducing them to something else.

Then, and only then, does it make sense (to my mind at least) to turn to and consider the purportedly explanatory factors of the phenomena. Now, Darwinism is not the only explanatory framework and account of the human phenomenon in its manifold features and traits. As but one of the players in the distinctively human game of self-consciously giving accounts, Darwinian Conservatism should be willing to enter into a critical dialogue with other proffered explanations. Arnhart himself is both aware of this intellectual desideratum—he develops his naturalistic account by contrast with something he calls "moral cosmology," with its human centerpiece the transcendentalist self—*and he eschews* this engagement, precisely by the constricted binary alternatives he posits.

To cite the classical formula of this logical fallacy, *tertium non datur*—many *tertia* or intellectual options, in fact. Given the starkly dichotomous cast of the options presented by the Darwinian Conservative, I could not but feel that the dealer had stacked the deck. But in fact there are more than two cards to play in this high-stakes game concerning the nature of nature and of morality, of immanence and transcendence, of intelligibility and of mystery, of reason and faith, and I most certainly do not agree with the cards Arnhart allots to non-Darwinians.

In my view, to engage the issues connected with explanatory frameworks and factors one has to engage in a meta-scientific—that is, a philosophical—discussion of what explanation and causation (among other things) are, presuppose, and entail. To take the example of a thinker with whom Arnhart appears to have little agreement, Immanuel Kant knew that in the context of modern science there was an urgent need for a philosophical exploration of the very concept of "experience" (not to mention causality and freedom). One does not have to agree with the direction he took in this investigation or with his findings to recognize the legitimacy of the issues he raised.

This meta-scientific discussion, I would venture, would sooner or later lead to thorny questions concerning the possibility and nature of *metaphysical* causes and realities. They certainly did for Arnhart's hero, Aristotle, and in another way for Kant. These sorts of issues and discussions concerning the relationship between the natural and the metaphysical (*latu senso*) would be challenging to both the proponents of scientific natural-ism *and* the advocates of points of view (including faith-based ones) going beyond Nature, or naturalism. Science and faith would have to give accounts of their ways of giving accounts, and philosophy would serve as the com-mon ground, or arbiter of sorts, between the parties. Moreover, as my two examples above—one ancient, the other modern—indicate, philosophy itself is not something that speaks with a sole voice. Complexities abound. They, however, have the advantage of ruling out complacency and dogmatism.[5]

Arnhart in his lengthy text indicated to me no evidence of having grap-pled with these sorts of bracing—and rationally legitimate, even rationally imperative—issues. His use of the phrase "natural causes," for example, does not, as he may think, decide matters. To my mind it *raises* a host of issues and questions. It is the beginning of a discussion, not its end, or its unquestionable arbiter. Be all that as it may, there was no indication in the lengthy essay with which I dealt that his binary structure, which I found intellectually quite constricting, was merely rhetorical, or perhaps heuris-tic. It seemed cast in bronze.[6] It augured not well for intellectual openness.

Let me make one more point in this vein, then I will move in the next section to a discussion of how Arnhart considers those special phenom-ena, the *texts* of other minds and thinkers. This second point concerns a fundamental stratum, or category, of his binary thought, one I have al-ready mentioned: "experience." As a professor of philosophy I was struck by the empirical tradition of thought that Arnhart posited, one involv-ing Aristotle, Hume, Smith, Darwin, and himself. As a teacher I spend a certain amount of time indicating to my students that Aristotle's "empiri-cism" (a word he did not use, hence my employment of scare-quotes) is not Hume's. In fact, I would argue that Hume's notion of experience was designed to counter Aristotelian views of *aisthêsis* (sense perception), *em-pereïa* (often translated as "experience," but with a distinctive meaning),[7] and *epistēmē* (science, but in a non-modern sense).

To give an indication of what I mean, let me cite the Aristotle transla-tor and scholar Joe Sachs (whom Arnhart acknowledges as an authority). Sachs rightly observes that Aristotle's notion of *aisthêsis* (sense perception) is "always the reception of organized wholes. Never sensation as meant by Hume or Kant, as the reception of isolated sense-data."[8] One of the dividing lines between Aristotle and early modern thought in general, both of the rationalist (Cartesian) and empiricist (Locke, Hume) sorts, is the status of natural substances (*ousiai*), of "organized wholes," as well as the nature of perception: Aristotle maintains that we naturally perceive organized instances of natural kinds, while the latter thinkers, with their reworkings of human cognition (usually in terms of "consciousness") deny this. They replace integral wholes of distinctive kinds with "ideas" and/or "impressions" and "ideas."[9] In short, Hume's doctrines of experience and of reason are not Aristotle's, far from it.[10] Any effort to construct an empirical tradition joining them must acknowledge these chasms, something Arnhart does not do.[11] This is not the only place in the essay where Aristotle's distinctiveness is glossed over by Arnhart's schemata and categories.

Because of these (and similar)[12] considerations, I found myself at an impasse: How to raise philosophical questions with someone who shows little to no sign of being philosophical? As I indicated above, my first thought was: bring in a middleman, bring in Husserl. Let's at least try to agree on the phenomena that need to be accounted for. In a gesture of intellectual friendship (tempered by some critical reservations), I would have enlisted two thinkers whom Arnhart knows, Erwin Straus and Hans Jonas, and one he may not know, Robert Sokolowski.[13]

Following their leads, we would start with man's distinctive "upright posture," our unique blend of "physique" (including "physiology") and "psychology," as Straus termed our essential dimensions as psychosomatic beings.[14] An entire way of "being-in-the-world" is inscribed in our posture, and Straus's long, incisive essay lays out both practical and theoretical developments and dimensions for our attentive consideration and regular wonderment. Getting up, standing, walking, shaking hands, and pointing to near objects or far horizons are seen as the marvels they are when highlighted by this once-famous phenomenological psychologist. After this survey of the human *gestalt*, which ends with the human head and face as they bring to a culmination our erect posture, we would turn to Jonas's phenomenological analysis of "the nobility of sight" in an essay by that title.[15] In it he deftly displays the sorts of *freedom* that sight bestows upon the human animal, as well as the predicates it lays for our intellectual life—ideas of objectivity, theory, and infinity, among others. Here, too, phenomenology helps us detect and appreciate the extraordinary powers and achievements present in what we all too often take for granted, in this case, the deliverances of human sight.

Finally, in a kind of completion to this trajectory, we would turn to Sokolowski's descriptive analysis of the distinctive type of minding the world that constitutes human rationality, what he calls "categorial intentionality." Being able to articulate explicitly that "S is P," to recognize expressly and propose to others the syntax linking "whole and parts" in the objects we encounter, is at once an ordinary human achievement and a defining mark of our humanity. As Sokolowski unpacks this achievement, he carefully lays out the deeper levels of human being and being-in-the-world at work therein. Employing phenomenology's technical vocabulary, he brings to light a "transcendental ego" that neither naturalism nor psychologism can recognize or account for, but which is presupposed by the very truth-claiming activities of their proponents.

As my seven-league boots synopses indicate, in all the foregoing I would have been keen to highlight aspects of being-human that I found lacking or underdeveloped in Arnhart's essay, especially (but not solely) in the cognitive area. However, as I thought about what would be the likely outcome of this procedure, given the evidence before me of how Arnhart receives alternative points of view, I had overriding doubts. Therefore, I decided to turn to Socrates instead of Husserl.

As presented by Plato in the *Theatetus*, Socrates claimed to possess a distinctive maieutic art, intellectual midwifery, one that involved interrogation and, sometimes, *elenchus* of another person.[16] The maieutic exchange always involved giving an account.[17] When done under Socrates' tutelage, giving such an account often revealed more than one's views or opinions and their coherence or incoherence, it revealed one's character (*êthos*), including one's dominant (sometimes conflicting) passions (*pathē*). In brief, giving an account brought to light one's state-of-soul. I thought it worth the while to bring Arnhart into the Socratic orbit.

For example, in his text he employs the term "wonder" from time to time. He wonders at features of an Aristotelian text and he wonders at the plausibility of an interpretation of a Platonic text, he marvels at the coherence between "the navigational abilities of bees" and geometric space, and he practically ends his essay by waxing eloquent about "the feeling of wonder as we try to understand it all." It is well known that classical philosophers, including Aristotle, maintained that philosophizing begins in wonder. It would be instructive, I thought, to see Arnhart pull these wonderments together, perhaps expand upon them (as I suspect there are other objects and, perhaps, forms of wonderment that he acknowledges), and then essay a Darwinian-inspired account of wonder. Then we readers could wonder at his experiences and account of wondering.

Along these lines, therefore, and in an effort to elicit more self-revelation on Arnhart's part and to prompt him to think outside his beaten tracks, I decided to pose, in a final section, two sets of questions to him. They are an effort to enter into a mode of discussion that both of us could find intellectually congenial and productive. But first, I have to address the evidence at hand concerning how he characteristically conducts his mind.

II.

I have been rather candid about my reservations, apprehensions, and a few of my disagreements. I, however, did not start with such suspicions but, rather, came to them. In the first instance, I came to them via a recognition and assessment of *how Arnhart reads texts*. Here, he touches on what for me is quasi-sacred ground, ground that all participants in intellectual discussion should take with the utmost seriousness and scrupulosity. I certainly take reading seriously. Among other things, it is a great way to learn. But it has certain inherent criteria, I firmly believe. I take authorial intention very seriously; I take the integrity of a text and its argument very seriously. I consider myself duty-bound in many ways when engaging with another person's considered views and textual compositions. Conversely, I believe that a person's reading habits imply and exhibit *how he treats other minds and human beings* as a matter of deliberate policy.

As I read, then read again, through Arnhart's pages, I asked myself, How does he read? What are the intellectual and moral dispositions that the Darwinian Conservative practices as he reads others? I assumed that a "Darwinian science of Aristotelian virtue" was not just a doctrine but a virtuous way of life, one not merely articulated and defended by its chief adherent but also practiced by him. I wanted to see what attitudes and dispositions were present and operative as the Darwinian Conservative engaged with other minds in the privileged form that is reading their texts.

The results accumulated and in the aggregate were revealing. In the candid language of the Declaration of Independence, they revealed a long train of abuses that displayed a settled mind-set, one rather narrowly fixed and all too often distorting, a reading-and-thinking mind that in the main could not get outside of itself and which systematically tailored others' thinking to its own way of thinking. It was the antithesis of philosophically open-minded, much less interpersonally sympathetic.

This form of mind, however, is what I have to display at some length if my negative conclusion is to have any merit. To be sure, it is an unseemly business in more ways than one. I do so therefore without particular pleasure, wishing the case were otherwise. Nonetheless, one must follow the Arnhartian *logos* where it leads.

Let me begin with two apparently small instances of Arnhartian misreading, what I would call *miscitation*, mistaken or misleading citation. Then I will proceed to larger matters, starting with his reading of Plato and the attitude he exhibits toward that great Greek thinker. After that, we will spend a certain amount of time canvassing his way of reading Aristotle. Again, I beg the reader's indulgence, since this rehearsal may appear at times to be tedious and/or overkill and/or beside the point. I am firmly convinced, however, that how a person reads is revealing of his intellectual and moral character. As I have made such harsh characterizations, it would be irresponsible of me not to lay out ample evidence.

Two passages to begin with, therefore, one from Arnhart, the other from Aristotle: "In book 3 of the *Nicomachean Ethics*, Aristotle takes up the virtue of courage. He defines it as a mean with regard to fear—and particularly, with regard to the fear of death" (Arnhart). "First let us speak of courage. That it is a mean condition concerned with fear and confidence has already become evident" (*Nicomachean Ethics*, 3.6.1115a6–7).[18] The reader, no doubt, detected a discrepancy. Arnhart omitted the pathos of confidence found in Aristotle's statement. According to Aristotle courage is more—it is more complex—than simply dealing with fear. This is a small thing, a slight omission, one might think,[19] and even Homer nods; but still it is a noticeable nod from someone claiming to be presenting a defense (admittedly a Darwinian-inspired defense) of Aristotelian virtue ethics. Hindsight will give it rather emblematic value.[20]

Now, a second Arnhartian citation and utterance—this time concerning two traditional authorities, Aristotle and his famous medieval commentator, Thomas Aquinas. In his essay Arnhart declares: "I agree with Aristotle and Thomas Aquinas that 'something is good insofar as it is desirable.'" He cites Aristotle and Thomas as agreeing on an important proposition concerning the good and desire, one with which he concurs. In this connection he refers to Thomas's "*Summa Theologica* [*sic*], I.Q.5, A.6," which references a phrase from the opening lines of the *Nicomachean Ethics*: "in which the Philosopher . . . says that the good is what all things desire (*appetunt*)."[21]

Now, while I am not exactly a Thomist, I am a longtime reader of St. Thomas. Arnhart's enlisting of Thomas to support his particular naturalistic understanding of the good (and, thereby, of a morality "rooted in" evolved human nature's desires or instincts) immediately struck me as problematic.[22] Thomas's ethics of the good and the right are grounded in a theistic—or better put, creationist—metaphysics of the sort that Arnhart eschews. Thomas's creationist view of Nature and the natural in general and his view of natural law and morality in particular are, one might say, as far from Darwin's as the heavens are from the earth. The common employment of the terms 'nature,' 'the good,' and even 'appetite' must reckon with the fact that two very different intellectual and spiritual frameworks are being invoked.

Among the elements of Thomas's metaphysics are the transcendentals— features of being (*ens*) found wherever and whenever being is instantiated or realized. The transcendentals include being itself, unity, truth, beauty, and (relevant to the foregoing citation) the good.[23] Everything that is, whether God, created substance, a quality, or another category, is one, true, beautiful, and good insofar as it is or exists. (To be sure, there are categorical differences between uncreated being, God, and created substances. The former is uniquely called *Ipsum Esse Subsistens*, the latter are limited, albeit real compositions of *essentia* and *esse*.)[24] Thomas's basic doctrine of the good is thus metaphysical: the good has an ontological density and a priority in being to appetite or desire that the quotation "good is what all things desire" fails to convey. These were my initial thoughts.

Nonetheless, I dutifully looked up the reference. It was correctly cited, but it was taken out of context and thus rendered misleading. The reader only needs to read Question 5 in its entirety, not to mention its proximate context (from Question 2 to Question 26), to see this. Thomas was not arguing, as Arnhart glosses, that "the good is the desirable." Here is what Thomas says on the above-cited Aristotelian passage in his commentary on Aristotle's *Nicomachean Ethics* (a text that Arnhart refers to later in his argument when arguing *against* Thomas's reading of Aristotle on happiness). I cite it here, in lieu of reproducing several passages from the *Summa theologiae*, simply because of space limitations but with the same intent, which is to bring Thomas's own meaning of the good and its connection to desire more fully to light. Here is Thomas commenting on Aristotle's words at the beginning of the *Ethics*:

Then [2], at "For this reason," he manifests his intention by *the effect of the good*. In regard to this we should bear in mind that good is enumerated among the primary entities to such a degree—according to the Platonists—that good is prior to being. But, in reality, *good is convertible with being*. Now *primary things cannot be understood by anything anterior to them, but by something consequent*, as causes are understood through their proper effects. But *since good properly is the moving principle of the appetite*, good is described as movement of the appetite, just as motive power is usually manifested through motion. *For this reason* he says that the philosophers have rightly declared that good is what all desire [italics added].[25]

According to Thomas, the phrase "the good is what all things desire" is a *faute de mieux* characterization; it attempts to get at something fundamental and primary (the good as a transcendental, as "convertible with being") via its effects or consequences—in this case, appetite or desire. In reality, the good is not strictly or properly speaking defined by its desirability (much less, as a consequence or effect of desire itself). As the interested reader can discover for himself or herself, Question 5 introduces further concepts such as "perfection" and "final cause" ("that for the sake of which . . .") in Thomas's fuller effort to elucidate the nature (*ratio*) of the good. Of special importance is the famous dictum, which Thomas borrowed from Pseudo-Dionysius, *bonum est diffusivum sui* (the good overflows and communicates itself). In general, one needs to attend to the way that Thomas weaves together Aristotelian, Augustinian, and Pseudo-Dionysian elements as he articulates "the good." Of note, too, should be the distinction and connections Thomas makes between the good as such, as a transcendental, and the *human* good with its threefold distinction into *honestum*, *delectabile*, and *utile*, as noble or honorable, as pleasant, and as useful.

The reader should understand that in the foregoing I have not intended to give a full account of Thomas on the good but, rather, to put in relief an aspect of Arnhart's relationship to Thomas's text and thought. The rather loose way that Arnhart invoked Thomas as an ally for his quite different moral view struck me, both as a Catholic and a professor of philosophy, rather forcefully. Upon reflection, I wondered whether he was genuinely interested in understanding or coming to grips with Thomas's actual thinking on the good and morality.

Two possibilities came to mind.[26] One was that Arnhart was more interested in enlisting a highly respected pre-modern Christian thinker for a decidedly modern, non- (even perhaps anti-) Christian position, even though he knew that the alliance was spurious. Or, more benignly, that he had found a passage in Thomas that resonated in a verbal way with his own thought and he judged it too good a coincidence to pass by. In neither scenario, though, would he be genuinely interested in Thomas's real thinking on the matter of the good (and desire and nature). This, however, I consider irresponsible, in the strict sense of the term, in that it fails to respond appropriately to the thought and thinker it invokes.[27] It is use rather than engagement.

That Arnhart has a decidedly ambivalent, sometimes hostile, attitude toward Thomas was made clear by subsequent discussions of Thomas's exegetical and theological thought. These much harsher engagements made the earlier alliance stand out and seem to me more tactical than genuine. Again, what initially seemed a small thing implied greater ones: in this case, whether Arnhart respects Thomas enough to accurately represent—and genuinely engage—his thought rather than lift a passage out of its context.

It was in connection with Arnhart's treatment of Plato, however, that I really began to see the bias at work in his reading of others. Let's therefore turn to Plato—and to those Arnhart calls "the Straussians," or at least two Strauss-inspired scholars whom he discusses.[28] Arnhart wants to use the Platonic dialogue, the *Timaeus*, in his classificatory category of "moral cosmology." The French scholar Rémi Brague lends scholarly credibility to this effort, as do C. S. Lewis and Arthur Lovejoy. Arnhart knows, however, that there is an issue here, one that scholars influenced by Strauss (among others) are aware of, which is, How should one read Plato? He wrote dialogues, not treatises. They need to be interpreted. How to do so? Can we simply, or easily, identify Plato with any of his characters and their (oftentimes contradictory) opinions? In addition we read, in the Seventh Letter, that Plato stated he would never write down his deepest thoughts or philosophy. This puts the status of the dialogues in a further perplexing light. To declare that "Plato thought [or, in Arnhart's term, 'endorsed'] X or Y" are words that must be dearly earned and should be uttered *en pleine connaissance de cause*, with full awareness of how difficult it is to make such a claim.

Arnhart references Joseph Cropsey and Catherine Zuckert as having non-moral cosmological readings of Plato's *Timaeus*. He brings in this fact, briefly indicates two reasons for their views, then provides an alternative rendering of the status and meaning of the *Timaeus*.[29] The moral cosmology offered in it by Timaeus, he suggests, satisfies a desire the young Socrates once had, as reported by the soon-to-be-executed Socrates in the *Phaedo* (99cff).[30] Arnhart then somewhat abruptly breaks off the discussion. Important issues of interpretation are raised but left unresolved between the parties, and in the sequel he simply persists with his own reading. I could not but notice this willfulness on his part.[31] On his own terms ("perhaps"), he has not really earned or justified his view since he did not adequately dispose of the alternatives. Why does he persist in taking it as Platonic teaching? Why does he need it to be so? What, in the final analysis, is Plato to him?

The matter of reading Plato is connected by Arnhart himself to the matter of engaging with his Straussian commentators. The reader who has read Cropsey and Zuckert is in a position to notice other features of Arnhart's treatment of them—and of Plato. Arnhart *does not report the massive facts* about the Platonic corpus, and not just the *Timaeus*, that Cropsey's and Zuckert's interpretations address. To note these facts would be to be fairer to them and would make their interpretations more intelligible and arguably more plausible. In any event, they would bring forward matters that *any adequate interpretation would have to deal with and which Arnhart does not.*

In addition to the aforementioned fact of the dialogic form, the *dramatic sequence and coherence of the dialogues* is recognized and raised as an interpretive issue by both commentators. Cropsey reads the seven dramatically linked dialogues that deal with Socrates' last days, while Zuckert, in a Herculean way, reads the entirety of the Platonic corpus. Zuckert also is keen to understand the salient, and obviously significant, facts that (1) the Platonic corpus presents a variety of philosophic voices, not just Socrates', and that (2) the Platonic oeuvre presents a variety of accounts of what many have called "the Socratic turn," that is, important junctures in his thinking dramatically reported by the character Socrates (*Phaedo*, *Apology*, and *Symposium*; to which Zuckert adds the *Parmenides*). In these dialogues, we have a Socrates before Socrates, in Michael Davis's felicitous phrase, a "pre-Socratic Socrates."[32] Plato clearly (even emphatically, I would say) wants his reader to attend to distinct philosophical voices, as well as "the Socratic turn(s)." These are "Plato intends" that the reader of any proffered interpretation can take seriously. Shortly, we will see that Arnhart ignores the Socratic turn and its implications for "moral and political philosophy" in Aristotle and not just in Plato. His "Darwinian science of Aristotelian virtue" is anything but dialogical and dialectical, hence it is anything but classical.[33]

Given the above, I did not see that Arnhart indicates a genuine desire to understand Plato's dialogues in their distinctive characteristics and (possible) coherence and meaning. Even Plato (the great Plato!) must be bent to Darwinian ends and frameworks, even though he knows there are plausible grounds for alternative readings.

I would hope that the importance of reading Plato well—of facing up to the entirety of the Platonic phenomenon—would bear its importance on its face. Let me, however, say a word or two concerning my view. I take Plato to be one of the most intelligent human beings who ever lived. He is a blessing to Western civilization and to humankind. When we read him, it is safer to assume that he is challenging us, taking our measure, not the other way around. To use a Socratic image, one wrestles with him in coming to grips with a dialogue, always in danger of being tossed and pinned. The exercise, however, develops muscles of mind and heart that are essential to our intellectual development and humanization. Hence, to see Arnhart deliberately turn away from the Platonic puzzle—that is, the Platonic facts to be accounted for, as well as interpretative options that Cropsey and Zuckert reasonably put forth—again indicated to me that he is far from open to philosophical alternatives and challenges but rather places things (in this special case, Plato himself) in his own categories and boxes.

Arnhart's less than satisfactory engagement with the Platonic dialogic form and oeuvre (as well as the two commentators he reports on) thus raised for me a number of connected issues: How, in general, does he read? How does he read commentators? How does he read critics, or those with whom he has disagreements? As we will see, all these come into play when it comes to his way of dealing with Aristotle.

In general, in the essay he reads Darwin and evolutionary theorists with care and sympathy (and almost never critically),[34] whereas he reads others with less care (e.g., Hume and Smith) and some with much less sympathy (e.g., Leon Kass and Harvey C. Mansfield, Jr.). Some critics, Jay Budziszewski for example, he reports inadequately.[35] With some authors and critics, his antipathy comes to the fore and leads him to the commission of injustice. Leon Kass, caricatured as an existentialist/Heideggerian, is one example. If using the term "existence" in a text qualifies one as an existentialist, then on Arnhart's own criterion Aristotle would be one. And if acknowledging that God (*ex hypothesi* the non-worldly, transcendent "source of being") would be "mysterious" is enough to make one a Heideggerian, then every orthodox Christian is a Heideggerian—and I would have to acknowledge that Arnhart has the sovereign freedom to name things that the book of Genesis ascribed to Adam.[36] In truth, calling Leon Kass a Heideggerian existentialist is evidence indicating that Arnhart's binary categories cannot begin to grasp philosophical and religious worldviews that transcend his immanent naturalism.

In a connected vein, as Peter Augustine Lawler can attest, one either accepts Arnhart's immanent or naturalistic articulation of the person—or at least "personality" (one that ascribes it to lower animals as well)—or one runs the risk of being called a Gnostic. These two categories, Gnostic or immanent-and-at-home-in Nature, are far from exhausting the biblical, theological, or even philosophical conceptions of the person, however. As I indicated above, phenomenology's well-known critique of naturalism and its attendant positive articulation of personal being avoids these forced alternatives. Robert Sokolowski's *Phenomenology of the Human Person* would be a good place to begin to consider it.

Sometimes Arnhart implicates others in his misreadings. One case in point is Thomas Hobbes. "Unlike Thomas Hobbes, therefore, Hume does not think that rationality alone (Hobbes's 'laws of nature') can make society possible. Rather, society requires the natural animal tendency to the affective bonding of sympathy."[37] Hobbes would be surprised to hear he believes that rationality alone makes society possible. At the end of the famous chapter 13 of the *Leviathan* ("Of the Natural Condition of Mankind, as concerning their Felicity, and Misery"), he declares: "The Passions that encline men to Peace, are Feare of Death; Desire of such things as are necessary to commodious living; and a Hope by their Industry to obtain them. And Reason suggesteth convenient Articles of Peace, upon which men may be drawn to agreement." In Hobbes, passion and reason collaborate to move and guide men into society under a sovereign. Arnhart thus makes a double mistake, one in omitting the Hobbesian passions that incline men to peace and into society and another in ignoring Hobbes's decidedly human passions, replacing them with an animal tendency to affective bonding.

He, perhaps, may be somewhat aware of this injustice to Hobbes's thought because he immediately adds a parenthetical remark: "(Hobbes's 'natural lust' for the 'government of small families' in the state of nature is a confined version of Hume's sympathy.)" But even this amendment fails to report Hobbes's own thought accurately (as we saw above), and it continues to frame or read Hobbes through a purportedly Humean lense. Once again, Arnhart appeared to have a difficult time letting others speak their own minds.

Hobbes was a great anti-Aristotelian. Arnhart, on the other hand, presents himself as very pro-Aristotle. It is now time to consider Arnhart's treatment of the Stagirite. This is especially revealing of Arnhart's bent of mind because of his declared pro-Aristotle stance, his intention to "support" the Stagirite and his "insights." We, however, will see that in truth he provides a tailored and skewed "Darwinian understanding of Aristotelian virtue," which is not to be confused with an Aristotelian understanding. As with Thomas and Plato, Aristotle must be brought within a Darwinian framework, he must be made to orbit around Darwin's sun, he cannot be allowed to lead Arnhart beyond his elsewhere-derived commitments.

In general, I would characterize Arnhart's employment of Aristotle as (1) eccentric (i.e., shaped and guided by external sources and considerations); (2) highly selective; and (3) very uneven, but with a clear bias and trajectory. He claims he is going to connect Aristotle, especially the *Nicomachean Ethics*, the classical statement of Aristotle's ethical thinking, with Darwin. Arnhart, however, does not give a reading of the *Ethics* in any comprehensive or adequate way. He selects passages from it; he does not read it as an integral whole. He does not report and attend to Aristotle's own statements of purpose in the *Nicomachean Ethics*. In no way does he respect or read the text as a whole with parts, as a continuous argument. (This selectiveness, moreover, extends to the other Aristotelian texts he cites.) Arnhart's "Aristotle" is very much tailored to his own purposes, needs, and agenda; it is not Aristotle as Aristotle presented himself or his thought. This leads Arnhart, inter alia, to miss the dialectical character of Aristotle's ethical thinking.[38] In general, he misses the opportunity to reflect upon what Aristotle understood by ethical reflection and discourse. In particular, his manner of reading fails to acknowledge that, in a highly complex way, moral life and ethical reflection for Aristotle can and should be connected with wider-ranging thinking, including metaphysical and theological reflection.

To his credit, Arnhart is up front about the framework within which he puts Aristotle's ethical texts and thinking. According to him, "Aristotle *grounds* ethics in a moral biology" and "his biological science *shapes* his empirical science of ethics in the *Nicomachean Ethics*" (italics added). As such it can be "support[ed]" by "Darwin's evolutionary science of virtue"—

and not merely supported: "Darwinian science deepens this Aristotelian project." With these pronouncements, one has reason to suspect that the Darwinian dog is wagging the Aristotelian tail, casting Aristotle in a secondary or supporting role to Darwin and Aristotle's *Ethics* to "moral biology." In other words, they indicate the hegemonic character of Arnhart's Darwinian-based, -oriented, and -tethered thinking.

The meaning of my first adjective, "eccentric," thus becomes clearer. Arnhart reads Aristotle's *Ethics* eccentrically, seeing it rooted in and shaped by Aristotle's biological thinking and locating both within Darwin's evolutionary account of nature, morality, and ethics. To shed light on this approach's distinctiveness, let me cite a few of Aristotle's own statements of investigative purpose in the *Nicomachean Ethics*. Here is book 1, chapter 2, *ad initium*:

> If, then, there is some end of the things we do that we want on account of itself, and the rest on account of this one, and we do not choose everything on account of something else (for in that way the choices would go beyond all bounds, so that desire would be empty and pointless), it is clear that this would be the good, and in fact the highest good. Then would not an awareness of it have great weight in one's life, so that, like archers who have a target, we would be more apt to hit on what is needed? But if this is so, one ought to try to get a grasp, at least in outline, of what it is and to what kind of knowledge or capacity it belongs. (1094a18–20)

And *ad medium*:

> And it would seem to belong to the one that is most governing and most a master art, and *politikē* appears to be of this sort, . . . So, our pursuit aims at this, and is in a certain way political [*politikē*]. (1094a28–29)[39]

And one last opening passage (chapter 3, *ad medium*):

> The things that are beautiful and just, about which *politikē* investigates, . . . and the things that are good also. (1094b15–16)

I would sum up the foregoing as follows: the announced *topoi* of the investigation are *the* end (*telos*), *the* good (or "the highest good"), of human choice and action (*prohairesis kai praxis*), together with the beautiful or noble things (*ta kala*), the just ones (*ta dikaia*), and goods (in the plural, *t'agatha*; Aristotle instances wealth and courage). It is far from clear, though, how they go together or, from the cited passages, how Aristotle will investigate them and what the results of his investigation will be. Nonetheless, even from this initial survey, one is aware that Aristotle's stated agenda in the *Ethics* is not Arnhart's.

Now, it is true that seeing Aristotelian biological teachings (or aspects thereof) in the *Ethics* is not simply far-fetched or imposed.[40] When Arnhart announced his agenda I immediately thought of the famous *ergon* argument in book 1, chapter 7, which discusses the human "work" or "function" (*ergon*) in comparison and contrast with plants and animals, that is, in terms of the distinctive capacities of the human soul and of human nature.[41] But this famous discussion, in addition to bringing to light Aristotle's intention to distinguish the human from the animal, involves more than the differences between human and animal nature, it also intimates conundra, it announces *cogitanda* ("what needs to be thought about").

Among the conundra, I would put what I call the problem of completeness. To see it, we need to continue a bit further in chapter 7. Having pursued his *ergon*-discussion, Aristotle concludes: "if this is so, the human good comes to be disclosed as a being-at-work [*energeia*][42] of the soul [*psuchē*] in accordance with virtue [*aretē*], and if the virtues are more than one, in accordance with the best and most complete virtue [*kata ten ariston kai teleiotaten*]" (1098a16–18).[43] The human good, rightly said to be happiness (*eudaimonia*), is activity of the soul in accordance with virtue or excellence, but if there is more than one virtue of the human soul, then the one that is the best and most complete will have to fit the bill.

Now, one should see this criterion—the best and most complete virtue—as a central thread in the subsequent investigation which is the *Ethics*. Aristotle subsequently pursues human virtue-wholeness, and after an important distinction-making discussion in book 1, chapter 13, he considers various candidates for the excellent active state (*hexis*) that would complete and perfect the soul. Four virtues appear in the sequel as candidates: *megalopsychia* or magnanimity, complete or legal justice, *sophia* or wisdom, and *phronēsis* or practical wisdom. At no point, though, does he declare one—or the sum—to be what he has been looking for. Then, after having surveyed the so-called moral or ethical virtues, then the dianoetic ones in book 6, at the beginning of book 7 he says he must undertake "a new beginning." I do not need to rehearse either the reasons, explicit and implicit, for his dissatisfaction with the two moral and two intellectual virtues, nor provide an overview of books 7 through 10, to propose that any purported understanding of Aristotle's *Nicomachean Ethics*, of his ethical science, that fails to acknowledge these claims and features of the argument cannot plausibly be characterized as authentically Aristotelian. It is more like saying "I agree with Thomas that 'the good is the desirable'" than any open-minded engagement with Aristotle's thought in its own manner and matter, in its distinctive development and accumulating results.

It is passing strange that, in a long essay devoted to supporting Aristotelian virtue, Arnhart never quotes the canonical definition that Aristotle proposes of *aretē ethikē*. This leads to various lacunary consequences, including treating friendship in Aristotle's *Ethics* without noting that it is not a virtue and without raising any questions about the placement of Aristotle's longish discussion of *philia* at a particular juncture of the *Ethics*' argument. To what problems brought to light by the argument to that point does the long and complex discussion of friendship respond? Instead, in Arnhart's treatment Aristotelian *philia* becomes an ingredient in what I must style a smorgasbord of animal characteristics, Hume's and Smith's thought, and neurological postulates that is concocted by the Darwinian Conservative. In his treatment, one moves from a most generic understanding of sentimental connection, through civic friendship, to the friendship of the noble in the noble that involves intense conversation and delicate deference, without much wondering at significant differences in kind among the *philiai* or exploring possible or even likely differences in psychic sources (*archai*) for them. Being pressed into Darwinian service tends to flatten such differences and mute such queries.[44]

But let us return to the definition of virtue found in book 2, considered in its context in book 2 of the *Ethics*, one can see issues that Arnhart's preferred biological grounding of the *Ethics* ignores or obscures. "The virtue we are seeking is *human* virtue," declared Aristotle.[45] As such, it implicates what is distinctive to human nature, features that Aristotle's book 2 discussion engages. Here is the famous definition (as rendered by Sachs): "Therefore, virtue [*hē aretē*] is an active condition that makes one apt at choosing [*hexis prohairetikē*], consisting in a mean condition in relation to us [*en mesotēti ousa tē pros hemas*], which is determined by a proportion [*hōrismenē logō*] and by the means by which a person with practical judgment would determine it [*kai hōs an ho phronimos horiseien*]" (1107a1–3).

As one follows Aristotle's discussion leading up to this definition and flowing from it in book 2, one sees that leaving it out allows Arnhart to avoid confronting Aristotle's confronting the marvelously complex character of human nature, in which phrases such as "second nature" are appropriate, in which "choosing" mysteriously combines thinking and desiring, and in which the agent has to navigate between the beautiful, the pleasant, the useful (and their opposites) as general objects of choice, but always following the lodestar of the beautiful—if, that is, he is to fulfill his distinctively human nature by rightly discerning and appropriately responding to the morally inflected realities and possibilities around him. Human nature and second nature; the soul as first *energeia* and moral virtue as its liberating, perfecting complement; and beauty in character and deed, fittingly ordered to situations and others—these are the themes of Aristotle's virtue ethics as discussed in book 2, as brought to a focus in the definition of ethical virtue.[46] Moreover, in recalling them I have said nothing concerning the exquisite finesse—at once theoretical and rhetorical or pedagogical—with which Aristotle discusses these matters. Making appropriate distinctions *and* striking the right pedagogical note combine harmoniously in his practice of ethical science. Neither, however, is conspicuous in Arnhart's "Darwistotelian" construction.

"Very uneven but with a clear bent" therefore was my third characterization. According to Aristotle, however, even those who are fundamentally mistaken from time to time are compelled by the truth to recognize things that go beyond their express positions and doctrines. It comes as no great Aristotelian surprise, then, that even Arnhart cannot simply stay on the "moral biology–biological ethics" plane that he first establishes for reading the *Ethics*. About two-thirds into his engagement with the *Ethics* he introduces a new note into the text and into his discussion. Aristotle, he senses, may not be "sincere" in what he says about the contemplative life in book 10. This is as close as Arnhart comes to wondering about Aristotle's "voice," that is, his pedagogy and rhetoric in the text.

There is irony upon irony in this acknowledgment. On one hand, while Arnhart believes he is arguing against the Straussian reading of book 10 of the *Ethics*, it is thanks to a Straussian scholar that he can make his case.[47] The house of Strauss is more divided than he knows or can acknowledge. Second, he introduces at this juncture a new virtuous figure into his discussion and a new norm: "the careful reader" and "look[ing] carefully at Aristotle's arguments." On their basis (and with the assistance of the careful Straussian scholar Germaine Paulo Walsh), he judges himself entitled to declare that "each of those arguments [in 10.7 and 8] is remarkably weak, particularly when considered in the context of the whole of the *Ethics*." Would that he would consistently apply the last criterion! He would see more than one intratextual disagreement or puzzle in the *Ethics* (a well-known one recognizes that Aristotle early on declares honor to be the greatest external good, while much later he says friendship is).[48] Enough of these adding up might lead him to suspect some sort of dialectical dimension to the entire argument. At the least it would make picking and choosing passages to make a point a risky venture.

A careful reader of Arnhart cannot fail to note that this new standard and this positive appeal to another scholar are fitted into his Darwinian agenda involving his ongoing attack on Platonism, as well as removing anything in Aristotle's ethical thought that might be discordant with the naturalism Arnhart wants to advocate. This entails ignoring one of the core elements of the theoretical life according to Aristotle, *nous*. In Aristotle's thinking, however, human *nous* points to divine *Nous* and to the metaphysical and theological ordering of the cosmos.[49] Arnhart may find the arguments in book 10 to be dubious (as it happens, I myself am sympathetic to that reading), but does he also find the line of thinking connecting *de Anima* 3.4 and 5 and *Metaphysics* 12.6 and 7 "insincere" or mocking?[50] There human *nous* and divine *Nous* are expressly, if enigmatically, connected.

This topic is important because of its introducing immateriality into the discussion, into the consideration of the human soul's capacities and activities and in (or outside) the cosmos. The phenomenologist Erwin Straus has a particularly striking formulation of the reality of immateriality in man and in the world; he does so in terms I would think congenial to the Darwinian scientist: "Science obviously is not a thing among other things. Scientific propositions are statements about. . . . The so-called laws of nature are no forces in nature. Chemistry does not consist of any chemical elements; it contains no compounds, known or unknown. A scientist may leave all his property to his heirs; he cannot bequeath his knowledge to them."[51] Straus sums up by saying that "there is a striking ontological difference between things known and the human knowledge of things."[52] As these brisk formulations indicate, the *aporiai* of the theoretical life are not gotten rid of by ruling out one version, or one set of arguments, concerning it.

Therefore, finding *these* arguments about *this* version of the contemplative life dubious is far from absolving one from considering the place and

role of *nous*—human and divine—in Aristotle's thinking. In addition to
the texts I referenced above, critiquing book 10, chapters 7 and 8, is not
tantamount to dealing with book 6, chapters 3 and 6, of the *Ethics* and
their discussion of *nous*'s indispensable role in the intellectual life. And
if one recognizes the indispensability of *nous*, one is also obliged to ask
about its nature, implications, and consequences. This certainly was the
case with Aristotle himself. It led him to both metaphysical and theological reflections, to questions of being and divinity beyond the natural.

In connection with the topic of *nous*, both human and divine, I would
ask self-declared agnostics or atheists to justify their use of the phrase
"god-like intellect" when describing faculties of human beings. Perhaps
they can, but I would need an explanation. If there is no divine referent,
what legitimate meaning can the phrase have? In general, I would be curious to find out whether Arnhart's science warrants *façons de parler*. More
important, however, I would like to hear much more about Arnhart's
understanding of Aristotle's teaching about human form (*eidos*) or soul
(*psuchē*). Let me briefly explain why. Once again, my puzzlement began
with something Arnhart wrote.

"By contrast to Plato, Aristotle defended a biological understanding of
the soul as the vital activity of the body, so that mind and body were bound
together in an organic unity."[53] Here we have yet another Arnhartian affirmation about Aristotle that cannot but raise an eyebrow. The point at
issue is so important it may call into question his credentials as an Aristotelian. Why do I say this? The soul (*psuchē*), it is true, is the first *energeia*
of a natural body potentially possessing life (*De Anima*, 2.4,1215–6). But
the soul is not adequately translated as mind, nor is it equivalent to *nous*.
Nous, as I indicated, is a mysterious part and power of the human soul. It
is not, however, one of the two inherent principles (*aitiai*) of organic being
according to Aristotle. 'Soul and body' is Aristotelian, 'mind and body' is
rather more Cartesian.[54]

At the very least, therefore, with equivalences of this sort one has to wonder what Arnhart's understanding of Aristotle's central doctrine concerning
form (*eidos*) is. Here the reader will pardon a bit of pedantry. Form, according to Aristotle, is found throughout reality, in connection with artifacts and
within Nature, but especially in living nature, actively doing its formative
work in plants, animals, and man. *Eidos* is the grand genus within which one
finds *psuchē*, organic form or soul, the animating principle of living things,
itself self-distinguishing into the aforementioned genera. Form as soul or-

ganizes and animates appropriate bodies, it empowers them and enables distinctive activities and ways of life. It is typically signaled by powers (*dunameis*), secondary (but perfective) activities (*energeiai*), and works or functions (*erga*) of various kinds. It is absolutely central for any understanding of Nature and the natural, including human nature, in Aristotle.

It is striking, therefore, how infrequent is the term "soul" (or form) in Arnhart's lengthy exposition of human nature and natural virtue. Desire is emphasized to a great extent, function is noted but not developed, and the good linked to both. But their ground in Aristotle's thought in organic form and the myriad formal differences between man and beast that are recognized by Aristotle—differences connected with *logos* (articulate speech), with the *kalon* (the beautiful, the noble) and *prohairesis* (choice, deliberate desire or desiring thought), with *epithumia, eros*, and *hexis*; in general, with the rational soul's distinctive *dunameis* (powers, capacities), *praxeis* (deeds, doings), *telē* (ends), and *telos* (the end)—are visibly slighted. Some of these elements (not all) are noted and catalogued by the Darwinian Conservative, but they are far from being given adequate exegetical or philosophical treatment. Given these lacunae, one cannot but have doubts about the "Aristotelity" (Hobbes's phrase) of Arnhart's natural science of virtue. Too much is missing, too much unacknowledged, too much underdeveloped.

In contrast to Arnhart, consider another thinker who has sought to consider human nature and ethics in an Aristotelian perspective. Leon Kass has devoted significant thought to "the primacy of form" in any Aristotelian optic, as well as to the distinctiveness of the human organism's nature, powers, and the challenges of humanity's ethical life. His work shows that one can adopt Aristotle's perspective and basic categories, while freely developing them in conjuction with other philosophical and religious wisdom.[55] I invite the interested reader to pick up Arnhart's *Darwinian Natural Right* and Kass's *The Hungry Soul*, compare and contrast them, and evaluate their fidelity to Aristotle and, more importantly, their adequacy to the human phenomenon as we experience and know it.

We have seen at some length how Arnhart treats the texts of those intellectually greater than he. In closing this section, let's turn to the other end of the human spectrum and invite him to explain how he would treat the youngest, the most immature, among us. During the course of his essay he quotes, then endorses, Aristotle in the *History of Animals* saying that "in some sense there is no difference between a young child and a non-human animal." With the specter of Peter Singer hovering among us (not to mention legalized partial-birth abortion), I ask how Darwinian Conservative ethics views infants and young children? What is their moral status? What is their ontological status? What duties are owed them and by whom, what sentiments and attitudes are appropriate and even morally obligatory in their regard? For example, does their being lovable depend upon their being actually loved by their parents, especially their mother? What if both parents are killed? Or the mother turns out to be a moral monster? In the absence of such love, what norms ought to guide individuals and society in their treatment of infants and children?

This would seem to be a good test case for Darwinian ethics to display its inclusive humanity, its competitive advantage among other moral systems, including Christianity. It also is an opportunity to display its intellectual penetration. It would seem that Aristotelian categories of form and matter, actuality and potentiality, and entelechy would be necessary for any sort of Aristotelian to come to grips with this sort of "not-complete-yet-but-on-the-way" human being. Or perhaps Arnhart agrees with the master that exposure of infants is a viable option for individuals and societies? So, to repeat: What is the ontological character and status of infant human life and what moral worth or dignity does it possess, what moral claims can it be seen as making even when it lacks the developed capacities of speech and choice?

III.

Man's special status in the cosmos has long been affirmed in the West (although on various grounds and not without dissent). Often, it has been cast in terms of man as the microcosm, the little cosmos, the special part within the Whole that most resembles the Whole, that "sums" it up in a particularly emblematic and revealing way. In this connection, I wonder how Arnhart himself relates, both intellectually and morally, to the great object of his concern and thinking, Nature itself. As a preliminary, I note that, as far as I can see, his view of Nature does not allow the ascription of personality—of interiority, reason, designs, volition, and so forth—to It. Nonetheless, he claims to be at home in the beautiful natural order. But he also affirms that it frequently works with brutal and arbitrary cruelty to snuff out individual human lives. There is matter here for reflection one would think.

To make things somewhat manageable, I chose four themes in his essay that I would like him to develop and then to weave together in a statement of his own being-in and being-toward the natural whole. The themes are gratitude, justice (including indignation at injustice), wonder, and mystery. The first two raise the question whether moral criteria are applicable to Nature itself or only to (and among) human beings? Can one rationally be indignant toward Nature when it "prematurely" kills a vivacious young girl such as Darwin's daughter Annie? Or was Spinoza right on this score, that such sentiments are consequent upon anthropomorphic imaginings? What does it tell us about Darwinian scientific motivation that Darwin himself claimed "the greatest triumph to Science" would be discovering "the origin of any infectious disease," not, say, the mechanism of natural selection? It would seem that some sort of indignant resistance to Nature is involved in such a judgment on the master's part. On the other hand, Nature had given Darwin and his wife a few joyful years with their daughter. In some sense she was a gift and they themselves were employing procreative gifts in conceiving her. In all this there is ample matter for thought. What are the grounds and nature (and possible limits) of Darwinian gratitude toward Nature? What, if any, is the applicability of standards of justice and injustice to Nature?

As I noted earlier, the classics declared that philosophizing begins in wonder. Aristotle added that the wonder that begins in *aporia* or puzzlement eventually leads to its resolution and the end (in two senses) of wonder. Earlier, I invited Arnhart to collect, reflect upon, and give an account of the objects and types of wonder that he experiences or recognizes. I repeat the invitation. What does the complex phenomenon of wonderment tell him about the character of man and his—or our—mode of being-in-the-world? What are wonder's sources in human nature and, I would add, in Nature and being itself? What is its structure as a human mode-of-being?[56] Among other things, I wonder if it is adequate to characterize wonder as a "feeling," as he does at the end of his piece.

As I mentioned just above, wonder in Aristotle promises resolution of human puzzlement; it incites to intellectual inquiry and ends in comprehension. It is a legitimate question to pose to Aristotle, however, just how far this description is meant to range, how faithfully such promises are kept. The inconclusive character of the discussion in *de Anima* book 3, chapters 4 and 5—as well as the fact that the *Metaphysics* continues for two more books after apparently culminating in book 12 with an analysis of the ultimate *archē kai aitia*—would indicate that for Aristotle himself not all wonder ends in conclusive comprehension. In other words, it remains true for him that the questions concerning being and human knowing will always reassert themselves in the face of any given answer.

As for Arnhart himself, he is clear that perfect comprehension of Nature is not to be. The human mind, he tells us, must recognize mystery, even "mysteries" in the plural. He acknowledges, for example, "the mysteries of life and death" and "the mysteries of the universe." I would like him to unpack and expound upon these acknowledgments. How does he define mystery? Can it be defined? Are there different types? Is there a unity to them? More broadly, what does the reality of mystery tell us about the nature of Nature or the Whole? Of being itself? What does it tell us about the nature of the human mind? Is "mystery" simply a way of describing the inadequacies of human cognition, or is it both inherent in reality and required by the distinctive character of human intelligence? In other words, what does it tell us about the world and about man that the former poses and the second raises unanswerable conundra concerning the origins of the Whole, the meaning of life and of death, and whatever else Arnhart may care to designate as mystery?

After venturing answers to these questions, I would think that Arnhart and I would have more to talk about than how (or how not) to read books, or the virtues of phenomenology, or the vices of the genetic fallacy. If so, then Socrates would once again have worked his magic; he would have shown yet again why he is one of the indispensable pillars of Western civilization. Then and now, Socrates constantly prods people of science, philosophy, and faith to go beyond their comfort zones, to give accounts of themselves as well as of "the beings" and "the human things," so that both truth and self-knowledge may be advanced. This, I believe, is the grand human community—one of the quintessential human *koinōniai*—into which Socrates invites all truth-claimants and all truth-seekers, including Darwinians.[57] Required for admittance, of course, is a desire for greater self-knowledge and some measure of intellectual openness and adventuresomeness. Required, too, is a willingness to field Socrates' probing queries. Without these, however, is one genuinely leading the life of the mind?

NOTES

1. To be somewhat more accurate and expansive, Arnhart also recognizes the roles

of *culture* and of *prudence* in the formation of the human world and the shaping of one's life. His view of Nature and human nature, though, is his intellectual anchor and normative lodestar.

2. The phrase "second sailing" is found in Plato's *Phaedo* (99d–100a). It is used by the character Socrates to indicate an important juncture in his intellectual development, where he took to the oars of dialogical engagement with others and their accounts of things.

3. I should make clear that I am speaking in shorthand here, simply *indicating* Arnhart's characteristic framework and causal/explanatory moves in this essay. As I stated above (note 1), culture and individual prudence also figure into his picture of the human world and of moral order. In addition, the "less" in my formulation "more *and less*" should be duly noted. He does *not* equate animal and human psychology. My point is that, before one tries to articulate human differences, samenesses, and continuities with animals, one needs to squarely address the human in its full and characteristic display.

4. One can do this in the dialogical—confirming, disconfirming, qualifying, and refining—company of others.

5. For examples of the open-minded, wide-ranging discussion I have in mind, the reader may consult *Darwinism and Philosophy*, ed. Vittorio Hösle and Christian Illies (Notre Dame, IN: University of Notre Dame Press, 2005), as well as Marjorie Grene and David Depew, *The Philosophy of Biology: An Episodic History* (New York: Cambridge University Press, 2004), to get some idea of the *philosophical* issues involved with biological reality and theories.

6. "If we are laying out a typology of fundamental sources of moral knowledge invoked in moral and political philosophy, we should consider six possible sources. . . ." From time to time, Arnhart varies his terminology but not his binary dichotomy. For a conservative publication, he cast the alternatives as "evolutionary conservatism" and "metaphysical conservatism." Larry Arnhart, "Darwinian Conservatism versus Metaphysical Conservatism," *Intercollegiate Review* 45 (Fall 2010): 22–32. In any version, however, metaphysics (like religion) is to be measured by his understandings of what science is and countenances (the rational) and of evolutionary human nature (the normative). For alternative accounts of the sources of moral knowledge, the reader may consult C. S. Lewis, *The Abolition of Man* (New York: HarperOne, 2001), and Joseph Ratzinger, *On Conscience* (San Francisco: Ignatius Press, 2007).

7. Cf. Aristotle, *Metaphysics* 1.1.980b25–26.

8. Joe Sachs, *Aristotle's "Physics": A Guided Study* (New Brunswick: Rutgers University Press, 1995), 252. For Hume's doctrine of "the perceptions of the mind," one may consult David Hume, *An Enquiry concerning Human Understanding*, ed. Eric Steinberg (Indianapolis: Hackett Publishing, 1977), section 2, "Of the Origin of Ideas," 9–11.

9. Cf. Richard Kennington, "The 'Teaching of Nature' in Descartes's Soul Doctrine," in *On Modern Origins: Essays in Early Modern Philosophy*, ed. Pamela Kraus and Frank Hunt (Lanham, MD: Lexington Books, 2004), 161–86; and Pamela Kraus, "Locke's Discovery of the Self," *Proceedings of the ACPA* (1985): 149–57.

10. For rich developments of this theme, the interested reader should consult T. H. Green's magisterial introduction to his edition (with T. H. Grose) of Hume's collected works. As a sign of the important differences between Aristotle's ethical thought and Hume's moral theory, one could note (as Arnhart in fact does) that Hume locates temperance under the category of the useful (to oneself) and that Aristotle places it additionally, then finally,

under the sign of the beautiful or noble (*to kalon*) (cf. *Nicomachean Ethics*, 3.11.1119a18ff. and 3.12.1119b13ff.). More generally, one should explore the significant differences in their accounts of moral psychology contained in the differences between the Humean "moral sense" which "projects" and Aristotelian *aisthêsis* which discriminatingly perceives the beautiful *meson* (mean) and between Humean "new creation" and Aristotle's "second nature."

11. All of the phenomenologists I mention below self-consciously base their descriptions and analyses upon human experience. For example, Erwin Straus's anthropological approach consists in "relating the basic forms of human experience to man's upright posture." Erwin Straus, "The Upright Posture," in *Phenomenological Psychology* (New York: Basic Books, 1966). For Robert Sokolowski, "Phenomenology is the study of human experience and of the ways things present themselves to us in and through such experience." Robert Sokolowski, *Introduction to Phenomenology* (New York: Cambridge University Press, 2000).

12. Similar queries could be addressed to his (largely tacit) conception of science. I am far from confident that he has adequately addressed the issues that would have to be resolved in order to connect Aristotle's complex philosophical conception of *epistēmē* with Darwin's scientific search for a *vera causa*, or *verae causae*; not to mention the conundra involved in the phrase "ethical science." For some of the issues connected with the first, see Christian Illies, "Darwin's A Priori Insight: The Structure and Status of the Principle of Natural Selection," in Hösle and Illies, *Darwinism and Philosophy*, 58–82. As for the complexities involved in the notion of ethical science, Aristotle clearly indicates his awareness of its distinctive character and status among the *epistēmai*. Cf., inter alia, *Nicomachean Ethics*, 1.3.1094b12–14 and 1.4.1095b2–4.

Arnhart mentions a youthful desire on his part for "a comprehensive study of the whole" and the possibility that we might "see Darwinian biology as a comprehensive science that would unify all the intellectual disciplines." In this connection, he reports he was inspired by Kass. He has not followed Kass in worrying about the genetic fallacy in such efforts, as well as the need for a genuinely phenomenological beginning of the science of man. For helpful discussions of both these features, see Richard F. Hassing, "Darwinian Natural Right?" *Interpretation* 27.2 (Winter 1999–2000): 129–60, esp. 130, 139–42.

13. Straus, "The Upright Posture"; Hans Jonas, "The Nobility of Sight," in *The Phenomenon of Life* (Chicago: University of Chicago Press, 1966); Sokolowski, *Introduction to Phenomenology*; and Sokolowski, *Phenomenology of the Human Person* (New York: Cambridge University Press, 2008).

14. Here is how Straus lays out his agenda in "The Upright Posture": "This writer's interest is in what man is and not in how he supposedly became what he is. Paleontology tells us what man or what his ancestors once were but not what man actually is. Even if one concedes to paleontology that it has discovered the living or extinct ancestors of man, it has little to say about how the change to modern man came about or about what its final result was. Looking from man to the hominids or the other primates, we see what man no longer is. Looking from the other primates to man, we see what the other primates are not yet. Any explanation of the causes of evolution demands a knowledge of both the old and new forms. . . .

"With all due respect for the accomplishments of those early ancestors, we should not forget to investigate our own situation. Man is not only the end of a long development; he also represents a new beginning. One may doubt if old rocks will reveal all the secrets of human existence" (140).

15. Jonas, "The Nobility of Sight." I also would have liked to consider, with Arnhart, Jonas's famous essay, "Tool, Image, and Grave: On What Is beyond the Animal in Man," in *Mortality and Morality* (Evanston, IL: Northwestern University Press, 1996), 75–86. The title indicates Jonas's interest in articulating "the human difference" by reflecting upon the phenomena of tools, pictures, and tombs, which are coterminous with the human. Jonas, for example, provocatively writes that "metaphysics arises from graves" (84).

16. Plato, *Theatetus* 149a.

17. Plato, *Apology of Socrates*, 39c–d. Cf. 1 Peter 3:15; also Romans 14:12.

18. Translations of the *Nicomachean Ethics* are taken from Joe Sachs, *Aristotle's "Nicomachean Ethics"* (Newburyport, MA: Focus Publishing, 2002). Cf. "So as was said, courage is a mean condition concerning things that are confidence-inspiring or frightening in the circumstances stated; it chooses something and endures it because it is a beautiful/noble [*to kalon*] thing, or because not to do so would be a shameful thing" (*NE*, 3.7.1116a10–11).

19. Actually, it is quite important for understanding Aristotle's ethical thought to note accurately the presence, number, and absence of *pathē* in the discussion. For a penetrating illustration of this (as well as one model of how to read the *Ethics* dialectically), see Ronna Burger, "Ethical Reflection and Righteous Indignation: *Nemesis* in the *Nicomachean Ethics*," in *Essays in Ancient Greek Philosophy*, vol. 4, ed. John P. Anton and Anthony Preuss (Albany: SUNY Press, 1991). Burger's full-length analysis of the *Ethics* is tellingly entitled *Aristotle's Dialogue with Socrates: On the "Nicomachean Ethics"* (Chicago: University of Chicago Press, 2008).

20. Here is another more revealing juxtaposition of Arnhartian paraphrase and comment and the Aristotelian original. First, Arnhart: "The more intelligent animals tend to be the more social or political animals, and human beings are the most intelligent *because* they are the most political" (italics added). The causal accent is put on man's political nature, with the degree of his intelligence its consequence. This is in keeping with Arnhart's Darwinian thesis that animals' and humans' intellectual development is consequent upon their sociality and its evolutionary development. To bolster the foregoing claim and to ascribe it to Aristotle's thought, Arnhart references "*Pol*, 1253a7–18." The passage to which he refers reads as follows: "That man is much more a political animal than any kind of bee or any herd animal is clear. For, as we assert, nature does nothing in vain; and man alone among the animals has speech [*logos*]. The voice indeed indicates the painful and the pleasant, and hence is present in other animals as well; for their nature has come this far, that they have a perception of the painful and pleasant and indicate these things to each other. But speech serves to reveal the advantageous and the harmful, and hence also the just and the unjust. For it is peculiar to man as compared to the other animals that he alone has a perception of good and bad and just and unjust and other things [of this sort]; and partnership in these things is what makes a household and a city." Aristotle, *The Politics*, trans. Carnes Lord (Chicago: University of Chicago Press, 1984). Aristotle's own accent is upon the naturally bestowed human capacity for *logos* that enables human political (and domestic) association, and in the passage human articulate speech (*logos*) is *contrasted* with animals' sub-*logos* "voice." Aristotle's own emphasis thus tends to reverse the causality. As such, it runs counter to Arnhart's Darwinian-inspired gloss.

21. The fuller passage in Thomas reads as follows: "Manifestum est autem quod unumquodque est appetibile, secundum quod est perfectum; nam omnia appetunt suam perfectionem" (It is clear that each thing is desirable insofar as it is perfect; for everything

desires its perfection). The reader will notice that "perfect" (*perfectum*) and "perfection" (*perfectio*) enter the picture, which is a dimension not discussed by Arnhart. Perfection is very much a metaphysical category in Thomas's thinking, involving act and potency, *esse* and essence, and final causality, not to mention the subtle interplay of divine and natural causality, as other passages in Question 5 indicate.

22. Central to Arnhart's moral theory is a doctrine of "desires" (or "instincts" or "instinctive desires"). Unlike Aristotle and Thomas, however, he does not philosophically analyze this important feature (these distinctive features) of organic being, of human nature, and of being. There are no distinctions in Arnhart among *orexis, epithumia,* and *erôs,* as there are in Aristotle. For Arnhart, desires are the subjects of cataloguing (and for individual arrangement or ordering), not wonder and reflection. Both Jonas and Kass, however, make "appetite" or "felt need" central to their accounts of the adventure of life, of the distinctive nature of organic being.

23. On the transcendentals, see *An Introduction to the Metaphysics of St. Thomas Aquinas,* trans. and ed. James F. Anderson with a new introduction by W. Norris Clark, S.J. (New York: Regnery Publishing/Gateway Editions, 1997), 45–98, esp. 72–87.

24. Cf. Robert Sokolowski, "The Metaphysics of the Christian Distinction," in *The God of Faith and Reason* (South Bend: University of Notre Dame Press, 2005).

25. St. Thomas Aquinas, *Commentary on Aristotle's "Nicomachean Ethics,"* trans. C. I. Litzinger, O. P., foreword by Ralph McInerny (Notre Dame, IN: Dumb Ox Books, 1993), 4.

26. In laying out these alternatives, I hope to have avoided the *tertium non datur* fallacy, i.e., proposing, as exhaustive, binary alternatives ("Have you stopped beating your wife?").

27. "Responsibility is obviously associated with freedom, but etymologically it is also related to truth, because it carries the overtone of answering to something. To be responsible is to respond in an appropriate way to something that shows up, and it also implies that we take the trouble to find out what the truth is, to find out what we must answer to. Truth seems to imply and demand responsibility and responsibility seems to demand truth." Robert Sokolowski, "Freedom, Responsibility, and Truth," in *Freedom and the Human Person,* ed. Richard Velkley (Washington, DC: Catholic University of America Press, 2007), 39 (cf. 48–49).

28. Arnhart's attitude toward Leo Strauss and toward those he generically calls "Straussians" is worth noting. Here too I found that Arnhart's Darwinian Conservative readings too often distort, rather than reveal, others' thought. For example, in a footnote, Arnhart refers to "Leo Strauss, 'Note on the Plan of Nietzsche's *Beyond Good and Evil,*' in *Studies in Platonic Political Philosophy* (Chicago: University of Chicago Press, 1983), 174–91." He then continues the note, applying what he takes to be a Straussian interpretive key to Strauss himself: "That this essay on Nietzsche is the central chapter in this book on 'Platonic political philosophy' is significant for Straussians—indicating that Nietzsche's atheistic religiosity is the peak expression of Strauss's Platonism."

Unfortunately, though, Arnhart fails to cite Joseph Cropsey's foreword to the collection, which puts matters in a different light. At the time of his death, Cropsey tell us, Strauss was working on an essay on Plato's *Gorgias* for the collection. This would have changed the number and location of texts. In the Strauss-intended collection of sixteen texts, Nietzsche would have shared middle billing with "Jerusalem and Athens." The dialectical center and central interlocutors would therefore be rather different. I leave it to the reader to ponder the sweeping claim made by Arnhart that "most of the Straussians are atheists," a claim offered without a shred of evidence.

29. Arnhart states: "The dubious character of Timaeus's mythic presentation of his cosmology and the absence of any Socratic questioning of his claims has led some Straussian scholars, such as Joseph Cropsey and Catherine Zuckert, to conclude that Timaeus does not speak for Plato or Plato's Socrates." Arnhart does not tell us in what the "dubious character" of Timaeus's presentation consists. Given that he reports Timaeus's "mythic presentation," it would have been relevant to note that Timaeus himself purports to offer "an 'iconic'/likely account [*eikôs logos*]" as well as "an 'iconic'/likely story [*eikôs muthos*]" (29d). Ambiguity is contained in the letter of the dialogue.

30. In addition he asks: "if Plato did not intend to endorse Timaeus's cosmological myth, we must wonder why he wrote it in such a way that it would be taken seriously by many, if not most, readers." I suggest he read Plutarch's *Life of Nicias* for one plausible answer to the question. See David Lowenthal, "Leo Strauss's *Studies in Platonic Political Philosophy*," *Interpretation: A Journal of Political Philosophy* 13.3 (September 1985): 297–320. I would also recommend Paul Stern's study *Socratic Rationalism and Political Philosophy* (Albany: SUNY Press, 1993) for its treatment of Plato's "Platonism." Stern plausibly argues that Plato both anticipated "Platonism" as a way some would take his thought and put it forth as an element of many dialogues for pedagogical and practical reasons. The careful reader then has the task of thinking about its function in the dialogue, as well as its intrinsic merits.

31. I say "willfulness" because it is an interpretive decision unjustified by adequate reasons *on the decider's own account*. Arnhart has been exposed to Strauss-inspired interpretations that take the question of how to read Plato with appropriate seriousness. He, in contrast, chose to locate Plato in a binary system of thought, rather than entering into the Platonic labyrinth. Rather than trying to live with an *aporia* (an intellectual puzzle or knot), he simply cut the knot and pressed Plato into his own intellectual grid.

32. Michael Davis, "Socrates' Pre-Socratism: Some Remarks on the Structure of Plato's *Phaedo*," *Review of Metaphysics* 33 (1980): 559–77.

33. A classical sense of irony (*eirôneia*) will be lacking as well (although Arnhart employs the term "irony" once). Arnhart substitutes modern categories of "sincerity" (Rousseau) and "mockery" (Voltaire) for irony, for dialogue, dialectics, pedagogy, and rhetoric—all at work in the *Nicomachean Ethics*. For a reading of the *Ethics* that is attuned to all of these, see Leon Kass, "Professor or Friend? On the Intention and Manner of Aristotle's *Nicomachean Ethics*" (lecture delivered in the Hellenic Civilization Lecture Series, the University of Chicago, February 19, 1980).

34. He does take issue with E. O. Wilson's *Consilience* flirtation with "strong" reductionism, his failure to appreciate the possibility of "emergent" organic being and properties—but only within the parameters of Darwinism itself.

35. To label Budziszewski "a divine command" theorist is as enlightening as calling Aristotle "the son of a Macedonian physician, who studied at Plato's Academy." Budziszewski's most recent critique of Arnhart can be found in J. Budziszewski, *The Line through the Heart* (Wilmington, DE: ISI Books, 2009), 88–95. The disagreement between Arnhart and Budziszewski bears upon the important issue of conscience (Budziszewski's preferred term) or the moral sense (Darwin/Arnhart's preferred term, although they also speak of conscience).

36. On the page preceding the one from which Arnhart draws the phrase "mysterious source of being," Kass wrote: "Human beings, alone among the creatures, can think about the whole, marvel at its many-splendored forms and articulated order, wonder about

its beginning, and feel awe in beholding its grandeur and in pondering the mystery of its source." Leon Kass, "Science, Religion, and the Human Future," *Commentary* (April 2007): 45. In the passage Arnhart cites, "being" is synonymous with "the whole," found in the earlier passage, which he failed to cite. Fixating on the term "being" and using it to justify the ascription of "Heideggerian existentialist" to Kass's thought reveals Arnhart's framework and categories, not Kass's.

Kass, perhaps, should not feel too badly since Arnhart even Heideggerizes Plato's Socrates. Instead of Heidegger's "truth of Being" (with a capital B—*Sein*), the Platonic Greek of the *Phaedo* refers to "the truth of the beings" (*skopein tōn ontōn tēn alētheian*; the phrase *ta onta*—the beings—is found twice more in this passage). There is a difference between Being and beings (as Heidegger himself would insist). As we will see in connection with his reading of Aristotle, Arnhart is more akin to a natural philosopher dealing with moral matters *more physico* than a Socratic who has taken to the oars and dialectically considers human speeches as well as deeds. Merely acknowledging the need to attend to verbal expressions of subjective experience, as Arnhart does in connection with brain science and color perception, is not actually to engage in dialogue or dialectics.

37. By "Hobbes's 'laws of nature'" Arnhart references chapter 13 of the *Leviathan*.

38. Commenting on a passage in book 1, chapter 6, of his translation of the *Ethics* Joe Sachs states: "The discussion here is a dialectical beginning, and one must ask how it holds up at the end of the whole ten books of inquiry, especially since a different and better threefold distinction of goods is made at 1104b 30–31" (Sachs, p. 8, #11). See also, "This picks up the question that was dismissed at 1096b 30, not with the precision that would carry it outside the inquiry about ethics, but with a definite dialectical step forward, and later observations will continue the upward motion from the evidence of human action toward a single governing meaning of the good" (ibid., p. 25, #28).

39. As the term *politikē* indicates, Aristotle's virtue ethics are connected by him with the polis. Arnhart acknowledges this in his own way when he speaks of "Aristotle's moral and political science." This "and political" needs to be acknowledged and thought through. To take one contemporary example, Alasdair MacIntyre certainly has done so. The polis-rooted, political cast of Aristotle's ethical science raises many questions: How does Arnhart's purportedly Aristotelian virtue ethics fit into contemporary liberal or pluralistic society and within the framework of the nation-state? What stance does it take up vis-à-vis liberal theory and practice? The mention of MacIntyre's name—a fierce critic of liberalism, of the nation-state, and of modern capitalism—indicates how serious and challenging these questions should be for soi-disant proponents of Aristotle. Therefore, when I use the phrase "ethical science" in connection with Aristotle's thought, the reader should supply the Greek original and this enlarged sense.

40. This type of observation, however, can cut in two directions. What is sauce for the biologistic goose (Arnhart), however, is sauce for the more philosophical, even metaphysical, gander as well. That is, someone with more open-minded curiosity concerning Aristotle's own thought and its interconnections and coherence can look toward other texts (the *Physics*, the *Metaphysics*) and topics (the nature of nature and of being, of *eidos* or form, and of being-at-work) than Arnhart's biologism does.

41. "Now this might come about readily if one were to grasp the work of a human being. . . . But then what in the world would this be? For living seems to be something shared in even by plants, but *something peculiarly human is being sought*. Therefore, one must divide off the life that consists in nutrition and growth. Following this would be some sort of life that consists in perceiving, but this seems to be shared in by a horse and a cow

and by every animal. So what remains is some sort of life that puts into action that in us that has articulate speech [*logos*]; of this capacity, one aspect is what is able to be persuaded by reason, while the other is what has reason and thinks things through. And since this is still meant in two ways, one must set it down as a life in a state of being-at-work [*energeia*], since this seems to be the more governing meaning" (chapter 7, 1097b2298a7–10). One notices that the accent is on human differences from animals, not continuities, much less samenesses.

42. "[*Energeia* is] the central notion in all of Aristotle's philosophy, the activity by which anything is what it is. To understand any of Aristotle's inquiries is to grasp the centrality in it of being-at-work. In the *Metaphysics*, everything that is derives from and depends upon the things that have their being only by constant activity. In the *Physics*, nature is not explainable by material but only by the formative activities always at-work in material. In *On the Soul*, a soul is not a detachable being but the being-at-work-staying-itself of an organized body. In the *Nicomachean Ethics*, everything depends upon the idea of an active condition (*hexis*) that can be formed by a deliberately repeated way of being-at-work, and that can in turn set free the being-at-work of all the human powers for the act of choice (Bk. II, Chaps. 2–3)." (Sachs, *Nicomachean Ethics*, p. 202.) Sachs dilates on the last thought as follows: "The characteristic human way of being-at-work is the threefold activity of seeing an end, thinking about means to it, and choosing an action. Responsible human action depends upon the combining of all the powers of the soul: perception, imagination, reasoning, and desiring. These are all things that are at work in us all the time. Good parental training does not produce them, or mold them, or alter them, but sets them free to be effective in action" (ibid., xvii). Given the centrality of *energeia* in Aristotle's thought and its ubiquity in reality, certain disciplinary distinctions show themselves to be less than hard and fast: "[*Energeia* is] the central idea in all of Aristotle's thinking. Here [1103b14–22] it ties his ethics to his whole account of nature, and to the structure of being" (ibid., xv).

43. Aristotle continues: "But also, this must be in a complete life, for one swallow does not make a Spring." Arnhart includes this criterion as number one in his list of twenty natural desires (which, as we just saw, is not where Aristotle located it).

44. For such an investigation, one attuned to the complexities of Aristotle's discussion, see John M. Cooper, "Aristotle on the Forms of Friendship," *Review of Metaphysics* 30 (1976–1977): 619–48.

45. "And it is clear that one ought to examine virtue of a human sort, since we were looking for the human good and a human happiness, and by human excellence we mean the kind that belongs not to the body but to the soul, and we assert that happiness is a being-at-work of the soul" (book 1, chapter 13, 1102a15–17).

46. In addition to the topics mentioned above, one must add the practical and theoretical *aporiai* connected with pleasures (and to a lesser extent, pains) that are contained in book 2. While Arnhart talks at some length about pleasure, he fails to register the complexities of Aristotle's treatment. For example, he never raises the issue of the distinctive kinds of pleasure available to, or at work in, the virtuous agent, starting with his experience of temperance. Is the pleasure and satisfaction the virtuous agent experiences in the temperate act merely, or even primarily, physical or sensual? If not, what does this (begin to) tell us about *hedonē* in its distinctively human form or forms? In book 2 one would find the beginnings, or elements, of what I would call Aristotle's notion of "moral pleasure."

47. Germaine Paulo Walsh, whom he cites "for this interpretation," studied with Mary P. Nichols, who studied with Joseph Cropsey, who coedited the famous Strauss-Cropsey reader, *History of Political Philosophy*.

48. This particular peripety is already contained in book 1, chapter 5, in Aristotle's critique and reformulation of the purpose of honor (*timē*). What is initially reported as held by some as the goal of political life, honor, under Aristotle's dialectical tutelage becomes an ingredient in self-knowledge, a self-knowledge that involves one's friends, who know one well and who praise one on the basis of virtue.

49. Cf. Joe Sachs, "An Outline of the Argument of Aristotle's *Metaphysics*," *St. John's Review* (Summer 1981): 38–46.

50. Cf. Joseph G. De Filippo, "The 'Thinking of Thinking' in *Metaphysics* 12.9," *Journal of the History of Philosophy* 33.4 (October 1995): 543–62.

51. Erwin Straus, "Preface," *Phenomenological Psychology*, v.

52. Ibid., vi.

53. Other passages in Arnhart's essay make the same claim. Cf. "the real but fleeting happiness that we can know *as embodied animal minds* that must decay and die" (italics added). "Aristotle's thought seems to be that my personal existence is the activity of my embodied mind interacting with the embodied minds of my friends."

54. As Arnhart himself acknowledges: "Descartes' dualistic separation of objective matter and subjective mind." Cf. K. V. Wilkes, "Psuchē versus the Mind," in *Essays on Aristotle's "De Anima,"* ed. Martha C. Nussbaum and Amélie Oksenberg Rorty (Oxford: Clarendon Press, 1995), 109–27.

55. Leon Kass, *The Hungry Soul* (New York: Free Press, 1994).

56. For Aristotle, the formal structure of aporetic wonder is when the mind recognizes two things (the moon as eclipsed, green wheat in the spring, taciturn John talking) that are seen as going together as a one, but where the mind does not (yet) see the reason why they go together.

57. I say "one of the quintessential human *koinōniai*" because I would want to acknowledge political community and religious community as essential human communities, too, and include them as indispensable participants in any discussion concerning human nature, human distinctiveness, human well-being and excellence, as well as human origins and destiny.

ACKNOWLEDGMENTS

T HIS BOOK HAS ITS ORIGINS in the first conference in "The Stuck with Virtue Lecture Series." That lecture series was made possible by a generous grant from the University of Chicago's New Science of Virtues Project. Held in November of 2010 at Berry College in Rome, Georgia, this conference focused on René Descartes', John Locke's, and Charles Darwin's teachings on the nature of science and the nature of virtue. All the contributors to this volume participated in this conference, and all but two of the volume's essays were presented there in an early form. In addition to the New Science of Virtue Project and Berry College, we wish to express our gratitude to Mallory Owens and Stacey Fronek of Berry College and to Amy Farranto of Northern Illinois University Press. Generous support for this work was provided by the Department of Government and International Studies, Berry College.

P. A. L
M. D. G.

ABOUT THE CONTRIBUTORS

Larry Arnhart is Presidential Research Professor of Political Science at Northern Illinois University. He is the author of *Darwinian Natural Right: The Biological Ethics of Human Nature* and *Darwinian Conservatism*.

Jeffrey P. Bishop, M.D., Ph.D., is the Director of the Albert Gnaegi Center for Health Care Ethics at St. Louis University. He is the author of *The Anticipatory Corpse: Medicine, Power, and the Care of the Dying*.

Tobin L. Craig is Assistant Professor of Political Theory and Science Policy at James Madison College at Michigan State University. He has published essays on Francis Bacon's *New Atlantis* and on the relationship of technology and utopianism.

Samuel Goldman is a Postdoctoral Fellow in the Religion Department at Princeton University. He is revising his dissertation on Leo Strauss and Enlightenment critiques of religion for publication.

Marc D. Guerra is Associate Professor and Chair of the Theology Department at Assumption College. He is the author of *Christians as Political Animals: Taking the Measure of Modernity and Modern Democracy* and editor of *Reason, Revelation, and Human Affairs* and of *Jerusalem, Athens, and Rome*.

Lauren K. Hall is Assistant Professor of Political Science at Rochester Institute of Technology. She has written on topics in modernity including biotechnology, as well as on the political thought of Edmund Burke.

Ralph Hancock is Professor of Political Science at Brigham Young University and President of the John Adams Center for the Study of Faith, Philosophy, and Public Affairs. He is the author of *Calvin and the Foundations of Modern Politics* and of *The Responsibility of Reason: Theory and Practice in a Liberal-Democratic Age.*

Sara M. Henary is Visiting Assistant Professor of Political Science at Wake Forest University. She is currently working on a book manuscript with the working title *Nature and Convention in Locke's Political Philosophy.*

Thomas Hibbs is Dean of the Honors College and Distinguished Professor of Ethics and Culture at Baylor University. He has published three books on Thomas Aquinas and is currently writing a book on Pascal.

Peter Augustine Lawler is Dana Professor of Government and International Studies at Berry College. Among his books are *Postmodernism Rightly Understood, Aliens in America, Stuck with Virtue, Homeless and at Home in America,* and *Modern and American Dignity.*

Daniel P. Maher is Associate Professor of Philosophy at Assumption College in Worcester, Mass. Some of his recent publications appear in *Review of Metaphysics, Hermathena, Society,* and *Nova et Vetera.*

Paul Seaton, Ph.D., is Assistant Professor of Philosophy at St. Mary's Seminary & University, Baltimore, Md. His area of expertise is political philosophy, with a special concentration on French thought.

James R. Stoner, Jr., is Professor and Chair of Political Science at Louisiana State University. He is the author of *Common Law and Liberal Theory: Coke, Hobbes, and the Origins of American Constitutionalism* and *Common-Law Liberty: Rethinking American Constitutionalism.*